Technologies and Practices for Constructing Knowledge in Online Environments: Advancements in Learning

Bernhard Ertl
Universität der Bundeswehr München, Germany

INFORMATION SCIENCE REFERENCE

Hershey · New York

Director of Editorial Content:	Kristin Klinger
Director of Book Publications:	Julia Mosemann
Acquisitions Editor:	Lindsay Johnston
Development Editor:	Beth Ardner
Typesetter:	Gregory Snader
Production Editor:	Jamie Snavely
Cover Design:	Lisa Tosheff
Printed at:	Yurchak Printing Inc.

Published in the United States of America by
Information Science Reference (an imprint of IGI Global)
701 E. Chocolate Avenue
Hershey PA 17033
Tel: 717-533-8845
Fax: 717-533-8661
E-mail: cust@igi-global.com
Web site: http://www.igi-global.com/reference

Library of Congress Cataloging-in-Publication Data

Technologies and practices for constructing knowledge in online environments :
advancements in learning / Bernhard Ertl, editor.
     p. cm.
  Includes bibliographical references and index.
  Summary: "This book details practices of and technologies for e-collaborative knowledge construction, providing insights in the issue of how technologies can bring advancements for learning"--Provided by publisher. ISBN 978-1-61520-937-8 (hardcover) -- ISBN 978-1-61520-938-5 (ebook) 1. Technological innovations--Social aspects. 2. Education--Computer network resources. I. Ertl, Bernhard, 1973-
  HM846.T433 2010
  303.48'3--dc22
                                2009046556

British Cataloguing in Publication Data
A Cataloguing in Publication record for this book is available from the British Library.

Table of Contents

Section 1
Practice Examples for E-Collaborative Knowledge Construction

Section 2
Technologies

Section 3
Outlook

Detailed Table of Contents

Section 1
Practice Examples for E-Collaborative Knowledge Construction

This first section illustrates technology application by good practice examples for e-collaborative knowledge construction. It shows how learning environments can provide advancements for learning and which particular role technology can take in these environments. It takes up good practices for different target groups like school children, university students, and senior learners. Authors provide insights into development of their learning environments and provide lessons learned during planning, implementing and running them.

Qiu focuses on content-specific knowledge construction. She describes an example in the domain of science education using a learning-by-doing approach. Students work in Qiu's environment collaboratively on a corrosion problem and execute several investigations to find a solution for it. This chapter provides particular insights in a learning environment and learners' options for actions within this environment.

Helling and Petter give insights in e-collaborative knowledge construction in the context of a multi-week course. This course was dedicated to teachers of senior citizens and aimed at familiarizing them with special needs of elderly persons for learning in the ICT context. They describe their design rationale and the implementation in Moodle, evaluation results, lessons learned, and identify particular good practices.

Chapter 3

Daniel Firpo, Claremont Graduate University, USA
Sumonta Kasemvilas, Claremont Graduate University, USA
Peter Ractham, Thammasat University, Thailand
Xuesong Zhang, California State University, USA

Firpo, Kasemvilas, Ractham and Zhang use also a community approach and describe the design and implementation process of a community for graduate students. They show which opportunities communities can offer to graduate students and also how they can stimulate collaboration. The authors deal with the issue of commitment to the community, which is essential to create a sense of community and to work productively. Concluding, the chapter reflects on implementation practices and lessons learned.

Section 2
Technologies

As the examples have shown, all of the environments rely on information and communication technologies to support communication (e.g., by chat, videoconferencing, and discussion boards) and collaboration (e.g., by shared workspaces/whiteboards or collaborative authoring tools) to empower learners engaging in e-collaborative knowledge construction. Chapters in this section describe these technologies and—more important—how they can be applied in context of ECKC. This how relates to the issue that collaboration partners need more than just a technology for ECKC, they work with this technology in a particular setting to experience beneficial collaboration and knowledge gains. Thus, the technologies have to be integrated in environments for collaboration, which can provide further support (e.g., by agents or other dedicate features).

Chapter 4

Stylianos Hatzipanagos, King's College London, UK
Anthony Basiel, Middlesex University, UK
Annette Fillery-Travis, Middlesex University, UK

Hatzipanagos, Basiel, and Fillery-Travis show the use of web video conferencing for e-collaborative knowledge construction. They focus particularly on the context of work-based learning and provide two case studies. These case studies demonstrate important issues of web video conferencing, the advisor/ candidate relationship, which deals with the provision of an appropriate setting for the videoconferencing session, and the need for clear organizational structures, which is demonstrated by a project called "Work Based Learning Wednesdays". Based on both case studies, the authors show aspects to consider when applying web video conferencing as mean for e-collaborative knowledge construction.

The chapter of Hu and Gollin describes a system for collaborative authoring. They explain how such a system can be used for collaborative case-solving and thesis work. The authors take up the issue how far the individuals contribute to group work and present functionality for evaluating the collaboration partners' contributions with respect to different dimensions. Such features allow the assessment of the amount each partner worked on the collaborative output and also how much each partner contributed to the final collaborative outcome. The issue of assessment is further explored in the chapter of Sluijsmans and Stribos in the next section.

Chapter 6

Cascera, D'Andrea, Ferri and Grifoni describe the technologies of discussion forms, whiteboards, audio/ videoconferencing, newsgroups, and blogs in a comparative way and discuss how far each of them can enable virtual communities. This chapter gives an overview on the advantages and disadvantages of different kind of technologies for their application in the context of e-collaborative knowledge construction. The chapter introduces the approach of agents to support collaboration partners in virtual learning communities and to study their interaction.

Okita deepens the agent approach and deals with the issue of technological boundary objects. Such objects may be robots, avatars or other kind of agents. They can take part in knowledge construction processes by analyzing learners' behaviour and interaction in the environment and giving feedback to the learners. Okita distinguishes different kind of such objects with respect to their functionality, their realism and their application for learning environments. She presents results of three studies which show how children perceive robotic animals and how technological boundary objects can act as learning partners.

Section 3
Outlook

The outlook section puts e-collaborative knowledge construction in a broader context and discusses critically educational, and cultural perspectives. Chapters in this section describe possible developments of e-collaborative knowledge construction in future and driving and hindering forces.

Chapter 8

Lakkala, Ilomäki, and Kosonen conclude this section by presenting a framework for the evaluation of e-collaborative knowledge construction. They consider the pedagogical design of learning environments as the building of appropriate infrastructures and propose a technical, a social, an epistemological and a cognitive dimension as dimensions for analysis. They exemplify the application of their framework by evaluating three different course designs which comprise of question-driven knowledge creation through wiki, a qualitative methods seminar, and a collaborative course design for engineering students.

Chapter 9

Olaniran, Olaniran, and Edgell take an intercultural perspective on e-collaborative knowledge construction. They show some challenges for knowledge construction and manifest them by the example of blogs. They further discuss collaboration partners' underlying cultural dispositions towards collaboration and learning and discuss how far they may have an impact on e-collaborative knowledge construction—particularly in an inter-cultural context.

Chapter 10

The chapter of Zuzeviciute and Butrime takes a socio-cultural perspective on e-collaborative knowledge construction. It identifies how far information and communication technologies penetrate society and culture and discusses the effects of this penetration with respect to e-collaboration and e-learning. It shows further how far e-learning can be considered as socio-cultural system.

Preface

Since more than a decade, technologies contribute to learning (Ertl, Winkler, & Mandl, 2007). There are different scenarios like for example computer supported collaborative learning (Koschmann, 1994; Strijbos, Kirschner, & Martens, 2005), mobile learning (e.g., Chen, Kao, & Sheu, 2003), and Web based trainings (Horton, 2000). Many of these learning scenarios apply the Internet for collaboration, information access, social networking, or just for keeping up to date. Furthermore, several learning scenarios are fully Internet based, which means that learners just use the Web for entering their learning opportunities from wherever they want. Such flexibility and adaptability of technology has led to a comprehensive application of computers for learning, going from pre-school to senior education. Technologies were further developed to become tools for learning and to facilitate specific learning styles, like e.g. inquiry learning (Quintana et al., 2004) or e-collaborative knowledge construction (Ertl, 2010).

However, it is not technology itself that provides the learning; it is also dependent on different environmental factors. Thus, a learning environment also comprises of teaching strategies, instructional methods, learning material and the technology (see also Mandl, & Reinmann-Rothmeier, 2001). Depending on the instructional design, a learning environment can provide more than just means for knowledge acquisition. DeCorte (2003) introduces the concept of powerful learning environments that relates to careful instructional design that enables learners an active knowledge construction and the development of applicable knowledge, which implies that learners are able to use the knowledge and skills acquired productively (see also Renkl, Mandl, & Gruber, 1996). One key to designing powerful learning environments is the implementation of situated learning scenarios (see Lave & Wenger, 1991) that facilitate learners' active knowledge construction. They apply authentic problems for the learners to work with—and also a social context for learning that allows multiple perspectives on the learning material. Such environments allow learners to construct their knowledge (e-) collaboratively (see Fischer, Bruhn, Gräsel, & Mandl, 2002) and to build a shared understanding of the learning material (see also Puntambekar, 2006). In general, e-collaborative knowledge construction (ECKC) can show different implementations to provide powerful learning environments (DeCorte, 2003). Theoretical foundations, insights into processes, and the issue of support mechanisms for ECKC are covered by Ertl (2010) "E-Collaborative Knowledge Construction: Learning from Computer-Supported and Virtual Environments" which complements this book. Here we focus on practices of and technologies for e-collaborative knowledge construction. The book provides particular insights in the issue of how technologies can bring advancements for learning. Thereby it offers practice examples that show how e-collaborative knowledge construction takes place in a learning environment and how technology supports learning in this environment. It further focuses on particular technologies and how they can be applied now and/or in the future for e-collaborative knowledge construction.

STRUCTURE OF THE BOOK

This book comprises three sections which take up the aspects of how technology can facilitate and provide advancements in e-collaborative knowledge construction. It starts with practice examples that give an impression about scenarios of e-collaborative knowledge construction and the technology applied in these scenarios. The middle section focuses on technologies that enable collaborative knowledge construction processes and shows how they can be framed to support ECKC. The book concludes with broader perspectives which set ECKC back in a cultural context. In the following, the sections and chapters are described more detailed.

Practice Examples for E-Collaborative Knowledge Construction

This first section illustrates technology application by good practice examples for e-collaborative knowledge construction. It shows how learning environments can provide advancements for learning and which particular role technology can take in these environments. It takes up good practices for different target groups like school children, university students, and senior learners. Authors provide insights into development of their learning environments and provide lessons learned during planning, implementing and running them.

Qiu focuses on content-specific knowledge construction. She describes an example in the domain of science education using a learning-by-doing approach. Students work in Qiu's environment collaboratively on a corrosion problem and execute several investigations to find a solution for it. This chapter provides particular insights in a learning environment and learners' options for actions within this environment.

Helling and Petter show e-collaborative knowledge construction in the context of a multi-week course. This course was dedicated to teachers of senior citizens and aimed at familiarizing them with special needs of elderly persons for learning in the ICT context. They describe their design rationale and the implementation in Moodle, evaluation results, lessons learned, and identify particular good practices.

Firpo, Kasemvilas, Ractham and Zhang use a community approach and describe the design and implementation process of a community for graduate students. They show which opportunities communities can offer to graduate students and also how they can stimulate collaboration. The authors deal with the issue of commitment to the community, which is essential to create a sense of community and to work productively. Concluding, the chapter reflects on implementation practices and lessons learned.

Technologies

As the examples have shown, all of the environments rely on information and communication technologies to support communication (e.g., by chat, videoconferencing, and discussion boards) and collaboration (e.g., by shared workspaces/whiteboards or collaborative authoring tools) to empower learners engaging in e-collaborative knowledge construction. Chapters in this section describe these technologies and—more important—how they can be applied in context of ECKC. This how relates to the issue that collaboration partners need more than just a technology for ECKC, they work with this technology in a particular setting to experience beneficial collaboration and knowledge gains. Thus, the technologies have to be integrated in environments for collaboration, which can provide further support, (e.g., by agents or other dedicate features).

Hatzipanagos, Basiel, and Fillery-Travis show the use of Web video conferencing for e-collaborative knowledge construction. They focus particularly on the context of work-based learning and provide two case studies. These case studies demonstrate important issues of Web video conferencing, the advisor/candidate relationship, which deals with the provision of an appropriate setting for the videoconferencing session, and the need for clear organizational structures, which is demonstrated by a project called "Work Based Learning Wednesdays.". Based on both case studies, the authors show aspects to consider when applying Web video conferencing as mean for e-collaborative knowledge construction.

The chapter of Hu and Gollin describes a system for collaborative authoring. They explain how such a system can be used for collaborative case-solving and thesis work. The authors take up the issue of how far the individuals contribute to group work and present functionality for evaluating the collaboration partners' contributions with respect to different dimensions. Such features allow the assessment of the amount each partner worked on the collaborative output and also how much each partner contributed to the final collaborative outcome.

Cascera, D'Andrea, Ferri and Grifoni describe the technologies of discussion forms, whiteboards, audio/videoconferencing, newsgroups, and blogs in a comparative way and discuss how far each of them can enable virtual communities. This chapter gives an overview on the advantages and disadvantages of different kind of technologies for their application in the context of e-collaborative knowledge construction. The chapter introduces the approach of agents to support collaboration partners in virtual learning communities and to study their interaction.

Okita deepens the agent approach and deals with the issue of technological boundary objects. Such objects may be robots, avatars or other kind of agents. They can take part in knowledge construction processes by analyzing learners' behaviour and interaction in the environment and giving feedback to the learners. Okita distinguishes different kind of such objects with respect to their functionality, their realism and their application for learning environments. She presents results of three studies which show how children perceive robotic animals and how technological boundary objects can act as learning partners.

Outlook

The outlook section puts e-collaborative knowledge construction in a broader context and discusses critically educational, and cultural perspectives. Chapters in this section describe possible developments of e-collaborative knowledge construction in future and driving and hindering forces.

Lakkala, Ilomäki, and Kosonen conclude begin this section by presenting a framework for the evaluation of e-collaborative knowledge construction. They consider the pedagogical design of learning environments as the building of appropriate infrastructures and propose a technical, a social, an epistemological and a cognitive dimension as dimensions for analysis. They exemplify the application of their framework by evaluating three different course designs which comprise of question-driven knowledge creation through wikiWiki, a qualitative methods seminar, and a collaborative course design for engineering students.

Olaniran, Olaniran, and Edgell take an intercultural perspective on e-collaborative knowledge construction. They show some challenges for knowledge construction and manifest them by the example of blogs. They further discuss collaboration partners' underlying cultural dispositions towards collaboration and learning and discuss how far they may have an impact on e-collaborative knowledge construction—particularly in an inter-cultural context.

The chapter of by Zuzeviciute and Butrime takes a socio-cultural perspective on e-collaborative knowledge construction. It identifies how far information and communication technologies penetrate society and culture and discusses the effects of this penetration with respect to e-collaboration and e-learning. It shows further how far e-learning can be considered as socio-cultural system.

CONCLUSION

This book provided provides different practice examples for learning environments, tools, and also for technologies. Comparing these technologies, one may ask about the best technology for a particular learning scenario, like is it better to use discussion boards or videoconferencing for a particular task. Cascera et al., for example, contrasted different technologies by analyzing their advantages and disadvantages. Such contrasts can be a starting point of considerations about instructional design to resolve the issue about what technology to take for a particular scenario. Mandl, Ertl, and Kopp (2007) made the case by contrasting a learning environment that used asynchronous communication with a learning environment that used a synchronous one. They discussed that the focus of instructional design should guide the decision about what technology to choose (see also Clark, 1994). Asynchronous discussion can encourage learners to reflect about a problem by themselves and then build a shared understanding based on their reflection, which has the advantage that learners are able to also discuss about differences within their reflections. In contrast, a synchronous discussion can facilitate learners to get to a shared solution to a problem by intense exchange and collaboration. Thus, using one technology may focus learners more on a shared reflection while using the other may focused rather on developing a shared solution (see Mandl et al. 2007). Thus, technology provides just one infrastructure for learning, which has to be complemented by other infrastructures. This aspect is elaborated by the chapter of Lakkala who raised the issue about providing different infrastructures for technology enhanced knowledge construction.

REFERENCES

Chen, Y. S., Kao, T. C. & Sheu, J. P. (2003) A mobile learning system for scaffolding bird watching learning. Journal of Computer Assisted Learning, 19, 347-359.

Clark, R. E. (1994) Media will never influence learning. Educational Technology Research and Development, 42, 21-29.

De Corte, E. (2003) Designing learning environments that foster the productive use of acquired knowledge and skills. In De Corte, E., Verschaffel, L., Entwistle, N. & Merrienboer, J. J. G. v. (Eds.) Powerful learning environments: Unravelling basic components and dimensions. Amsterdam, Pergamon.

Ertl, B. (Ed.) (2010) E-Collaborative Knowledge Construction: Learning from Computer-Supported and Virtual Environments, Hershey, PA, IGI Global.

Ertl, B., Winkler, K. & Mandl, H. (2007) E-learning - Trends and future development. In Neto, F. M. M. & Brasileiro, F. V. (Eds.) Advances in Computer-Supported Learning. Hershey, PA, Information Science Publishing.

Fischer, F., Bruhn, J., Gräsel, C., & Mandl, H. (2002). Fostering collaborative knowledge construction with visualization tools. Learning and Instruction, 12, 213-232.

Horton, W. (2000) Designing Web-Based Training: How to Teach Anyone Anything Anywhere Anytime, Oxford, Wiley.

Koschmann, T. D. (1994) Toward a theory of computer support for collaborative learning. The Journal of the Learning Sciences, 3, 219-225.

Lave, J. & Wenger, E. (1991) Situated learning: Legitimate peripheral participation, New York, NY, Cambridge University Press.

Mandl, H., Ertl, B. & Kopp, B. (2007) Computer support for collaborative learning environments. In Verschaffel, L., Dochy, F., Boekaerts, M. & Vosniadou, S. (Eds.) Instructional psychology: Past, present and future trends. Sixteen Essays in Honor of Erik De Corte. Amsterdam, Elsevier.

Mandl, H. & Reinmann-Rothmeier, G. (2001) Environments for learning. In Smelser, N. J. & Baltes, P. B. (Eds.) International Encyclopedia of the Social & Bahavioral Sciences. Oxford, Elsevier Science.

Puntambekar, S. (2006) Analyzing collaborative interactions: divergence, shared understanding & construction of knowledge. Computers & Education, 47, 332-351.

Quintana, C., Reiser, B. J., Davis, E. A., Krajcik, J., Fretz, E., Duncan, R. G., Kyza, E., Edelson, D. & Soloway, E. (2004) A scaffolding design framework for software to support science inquiry. The Journal of the Learning Sciences, 13, 337-386.

Renkl, A., Mandl, H. & Gruber, H. (1996) Inert knowledge: Analyses and remedies. Educational Psychologist, 31, 115-121.

Strijbos, J. W., Kirschner, P. A. & Martens, R. L. (2004) What we know about CSCL, Dordrecht, Kluwer.

Acknowledgment

My acknowledgements go to the authors who provided their proposals and put many efforts in the writing and revising of their chapters. Furthermore, I appreciated that there were so many colleagues who served as reviewers. By their thorough reviews they helped the authors and me to strengthen the chapters and to increase the quality of this book. My particular thank goes to Heinz Mandl, Frank Fischer, and the editorial advisory board who provided valuable advice and feedback. For supporting me in all kind of organizational and technical issues, my special acknowledgements go to Ms. Elizabeth Ardner and the staff of IGI Global who guided me through the smooth production process of this book.

Bernhard Ertl

Section 1
Practice Examples for E–Collaborative Knowledge Construction

Chapter 1
Computer Support in E-Collaborative Learning-By-Doing Environments

Lin Qiu
Nanyang Technological University, Singapore

ABSTRACT

With the recent widespread use of computer and web technologies, web-based tools have been developed to mediate collaboration and facilitate knowledge construction. However, how to effectively design these tools to stimulate and maintain productive knowledge construction remains a challenge. This chapter describes a virtual learning-by-doing environment where students take the role of consultants to investigate the cause of recurring pipe corrosion in a paper processing company. We illustrate how the learning environment is designed to provide both pedagogical and technological support to collaborative knowledge construction. Our goal is to provide an example and offer guidance to professionals and educators who are interested building such virtual environments.

INTRODUCTION

The social theories of learning have demonstrated the importance of situating learning in social interactions and collaborations (e.g., Lave & Wenger, 1991; Hicks, 1996). Learning is no longer considered as a cognitive process that happens in an individual's mind, but a social process that often occurs through conversations as well as the collaborative construction of conceptual artifacts (e.g., Collins, Brown, & Newman, 1989; Graesser, Person, & Magliano,

1995; Palincsar & Brown, 1984). Meanwhile, knowledge construction, the ability to actively understand existing knowledge and create new ideas has become increasingly emphasized in education (Scardamalia, 2003). Students are often engaged in collaborative tasks where they negotiate ideas and construct knowledge based on each other's understanding (Roschelle & Teasley, 1995). Their collaboration results in continuous meaning making and learning (Stahl, Koschmann, & Suthers, 2006).

To facilitate collaborative knowledge construction, e-communication tools such as chat rooms, discussion forums, and videoconferencing have

DOI: 10.4018/978-1-61520-937-8.ch001

been used to allow geographically dispersed group members to work together. Research has found that computer-mediated collaboration can reduce production blocking in face-to-face collaboration (e.g. Gallupe, Bastianutti, & Cooper, 1991; Valacich, Dennis, & Nunamaker, 1992). Production blocking occurs when only one person can speak at one time. It causes difficulty in simultaneous idea generation and often leads to the loss of productivity (Diehl & Stroebe, 1987). Computer-mediated communication allows group members to present ideas simultaneously without the interference from peers. Multiple ideas can be generated at the same time. Furthermore, computer-mediated collaboration often allows one to view the performance of other team members and therefore causes the effect of social comparison (Festingerís, 1954). This comparison motivates one to outperform others and can result in the improvement in task performance (Munkes & Diehl, 2003). In addition, artifacts created in e-communication tools can be easily changed through redo and undo. They can be quickly duplicated through copy-and-paste and moved around through drag-and-drop. This allows learners to easily refine, reorganize, and augment their discussion. These artifacts can also serve as a permanent record and be used as the basis for future reflection. They can be adapted to provide scaffolding and representational formats appropriate to the competence of individual learners and the performance of the whole group (Stahl, Koschmann, & Suthers, 2006).

While e-communication tools have many advantages, how to effectively use them to stimulate and maintain productive knowledge construction remains a challenge. For example, while discussion forums have been found to produce more conversations with deeper thinking than face-to-face dialogues (Hawkes & Romiszowski, 2001), their structure makes them difficult for users to keep track of ideas brought up during discussion. Users tend to pay more attention to recent ideas rather than the ones discussed earlier (Hewitt, 2003). In addition, it is difficult for users to reference

materials or representations outside the discussion forum. Users have to repeatedly go back and forth between their communication medium and the object under discussion. In addition, most of the communication tools lack the flexibility of providing multiple ways of representing and integrating ideas. This inevitably hinders the reorganization and connection of ideas in knowledge construction.

One way to support collaborative knowledge construction is to embed tools into a learning environment where students need to negotiate and share meaning construction through group interaction and negotiation. In this chapter, we discuss how to support collaborative knowledge construction in a learning-by-doing environment for problem-based learning. Problem-based learning has been proven as an effective pedagogy for collaborative knowledge construction (Bereiter & Scardamalia, 2003). It situates learning in the process of solving complex and ill-structured realistic problems (Hmelo & Evensen, 2000). Students work in groups to tackle problems more complex than what individuals could do alone (Hmelo, Narayanan, Newstetter & Kolodner, 1995). They are engaged in collaborative exploration, reflection, and articulation. Their problem solution represents the product of their shared meaning-making and knowledge construction (Schon, 1987; Brown & Campione, 1990; Scardamalia & Berierter, 1994).

In the following, we first describe background research related to collaborative knowledge construction. Then, we describe Corrosion investigator, a learning-by-doing environment where students can run simulated experiments, analyze data, generate hypotheses, and construct arguments. We further illustrate computational support in Corrosion Investigator specially designed to promote collaboration and knowledge construction. Our goal is to provide an example of how to support collaborative knowledge construction in learning-by-doing environments, and offer guidance and suggestions to professionals who are interested building such virtual environments.

BACKGROUND

Learn-by-doing is a pedagogical strategy that can be traced back to Dewey's educational philosophy. Dewey (1916) advocates that students should learn by actively manipulating artifacts and testing their ideas rather than passively absorbing knowledge from teachers. This idea has been supported by the situated cognition theory which shows learning as a process involved in the practical doings of things and situated in the practice of communities (Bateson 1976; Lave & Wenger, 1991). Cognition is viewed to take place through the interaction between a person and the environment rather than purely in the mind (e.g., Dewey & Bentley, 1949; Bickhard, 1992; Brown, Collins, & Duguid, 1989; Erickson & Schultz, 1982; Lave, 1988; Lave & Wenger, 1991; Schon, 1983). Kolb (1984) identifies four stages in learning: concrete experience, observation and reflection, the formation of abstract concepts, and testing in new situations. Doing is considered as the key in the first stage to initiate the learning process.

Collaborative learning (Slavin, 1990) engages students in learning-by-doing in a group setting. It is different from competitive and individual learning situations where students work against each other in order to perform better. Competitive learning generates negative interdependence that makes students either work harder than others or give up because they think there is little chance to win. Students often focus on their self-interest and consider their learning unrelated to others (Johnson & Johnson, 1989). In contrast, collaborative learning requires a team of students working together to accomplish learning goals (Artz & Newman, 1990; Slavin, 1990, 1991). Students have to share information, create ideas, and make learning progress as a team. Research has found that compared to comparative and individualistic learning, collaborative learning promotes higher learning achievement, greater social competence, and more supportive relationship (Johnson & Johnson, 1989; Stevens & Slavin, 1995). However,

simply putting students in a team does not necessarily make them collaborate. Johnson, Johnson, and Holubec (1993) identified five critical factors to ensure effective collaboration. First, team members need to work towards a common goal. Each member should have his or her unique role in achieving the learning goal and be considered as indispensable to the group success. This helps students develop positive interdependence and make them feel one cannot succeed without the others. Second, the learning task should require students to share resources, discuss ideas, and teach each other. These supportive interactions will help students develop interpersonal commitment. Furthermore, Webb (1985) found that students learn better when they teach others and receive help. Third, individual accountability should be implemented so that each group member is accountable and assessed for his or her performance. This will help groups members know who needs assistance and who deserves applauds. It will reduce the problem of only a few members complete all the tasks. Fourth, students need to learn social skills to manage teamwork issues such as leadership, decision-making, trust-building, and conflict resolution. As conflicts and cooperation often co-exist (Johnson & Johnson, 1995), social skills will help students maintain healthy and supportive group relationships. Fifth, students should continuously improve their collaboration. They need to analyze each member's work and the collaboration between them to decide how to maintain good practices and discontinue ineffective strategies. All the above five elements are key factors in establishing effective collaboration. They help to maximize group performance as well as individual achievement.

Recent research on socially shared cognition provides other insights on how people create, distribute, and use knowledge in group settings (e.g., Higgins, 1992; Hinsz, Tindale, & Vollrath, 1997; Levine, Resnick, & Higgins, 1993; Nye & Brower, 1996; Resnick, Levine, & Teasley, 1991; Thompson, 1998). Cannon-Bowers, Salas, and

Converse (1993) found that groups often share mental models to help them coordinate their tasks and improve team performance. Mental models are knowledge structures that enable people to understand the behaviors of objects or environments around them (Johnson-Laird, 1983; Wilson & Rutherford, 1989, Rouse & Morris, 1986). In team collaboration, members need to share multiple mental models to obtain common understanding of the task as well as how to work as a team. These models facilitate teams to handle difficulties in cooperation and adapt to changing conditions (Cannon-Bowers et al., 1993). They include technology models that help team members understand how to interact with the tools that they use, task models that help members understand how the task should be accomplished in terms of procedures and strategies, team interaction models that describe how members should communicate and how information should flow, and team member models that contain information about each member's knowledge, attitudes, strength, and weakness (Cannon-Bowers et al., 1993). The above models can further be categorized as task-related models (e.g., the technology models and task models) and team-related models (e.g., the team interaction model and team member models) (McIntyre & Salas, 1995; Morgan, Glickman, Woodard, Blaiwes, & Salas, 1986). These models affect communication, strategy, and interpersonal relationships in the team and consequently impact team performance (Klimoski & Mohammed, 1994; Mathieu, Goodwin, Heffner, Salas, & Cannon-Bowers, 2000). Team members develop better convergence in their mental models when they gain experience with their task and each other (Mathieu et al., 2000). When new comers enter a group, they have to learn the shared metal models in order to work effectively with the group (Moreland & Levine, 2008).

Besides shared mental models, research has been done to understand information sharing within a group. Larson (1997) found that shared information is discussed earlier than unshared information. Furthermore, shared information is discussed more often and thoroughly than unshared information (Larson & Harmon, 2007; Wittenbaum & Park, 2001). This is often caused by the person who leads the discussion of the group repeatedly directing the group's attention to previously discussed formation (Larson, Christensen, Franz, & Abbott, 1998). Research has also shown that when members have similar problem-solving styles, the group as a whole tends to perform better than its average members, but not necessarily better than its best members. However, when group members have very different problem-solving styles, the group as a whole performs better than its best members (Larson, 2007).

Social psychologists found social identities as another factor that affects group performance. Research has shown that despite shared interests and cooperative interdependence, team members tend to categorize themselves into different social categories (Tajfel & Turner, 1986; Turner, Hogg, Oakes, Reicher, & Wetherell, 1987). This causes positive affect such as trust and liking among members within the same category but also negative intergroup attitudes and discriminatory behaviors between members with different categorical identities (Brewer, 1979; Mullen, Brown, & Smith, 1992; Schopler & Insko, 1992). To solve this problem, several models have been developed to reduce intergroup conflict and prejudice. The personalization model (Brewer & Miller, 1984) proposes to have group members focus on each other's personal characteristics during interaction. It aims to replace categorical identity with personal identity. The common ingroup identity model (Gaertner, Mann, Murrell, & Dovidio, 1989; Gaertner, Mann, Dovidio, Murrell & Pomare, 1990; Gaertner, Dovidio, Anastasio, Bachman, & Rust, 1993) proposes to create new inclusive categories that include both the ingroup members and outgroup members. It aims to have team members think themselves as in one superordinate category rather than different subcategories. The above decategorization and recategorization models have been tested in experimental settings and proved to be effective in improving intergroup relations and producing more positive intergroup attitudes (Miller, Brewer, & Edwards, 1985; Bettencourt, Brewer, Croak, & Miller, 1992).

In the education domain, four learning-by-doing pedagogies have been identified as effective strategies that promote collaborative knowledge construction (Bereiter & Scardamalia, 2003). They include learning-by-design, project-based science, problem-based learning, and knowledge building. Learning-by-design engages students in the design of an artifact where students need to create their prototypes, collect performance data, and refine their designs (Holbrook & Kolodner, 2000). Project-based science situates learning in scientific inquiries where students need to answer challenging questions through the creation of authentic artifacts (Marx, Blumenfeld, Krajcik, & Soloway, 1997). Problem-based learning challenges students with complex and ill-structured problems to help them learn critical thinking and reasoning skills (Hmelo & Evensen, 2000). Knowledge building emphasizes the process of discovering new problems based on existing knowledge and develop new knowledge through solving the problem (Bereiter & Scardamalia, 2003). The above four pedagogies engage students in different learning activities, they all situate learning in a process where students need to collaboratively create an artifact, either in the form of a model, a product, or a report, and extend their knowledge by continuously elaborating on their ideas, making connections between existing knowledge, and finding opportunities for improvement and integration.

To facilitate collaborative knowledge construction, a number of software tools have been developed. For example, CoVIS (Edelson, Pea, & Gomez, 1995) and CSILE (Scardamalia & Bereiter, 1991) let students post data such as images and documents in common electronic workspaces to refute or support claims. They encourage students to bring information from various sources to generate different perspectives. Knowledge Forum (Bereiter & Scardamalia, 2003) allows students to construct notes and link them together to form concept maps. Students are encouraged to connect their own ideas with the work of their peers to present arguments and develop theories. Knowledge Forum further uses a series of prompts to encourage students to contribute ideas, organize information, and develop new understanding. It has been used by more than 250 schools, ranging from K-12 to graduate education, in a wide range of domains including biology, chemistry, philosophy, English, mathematics, and education. Studies have shown that the use of the Knowledge Forum improves students' collaborative skills and the quality of their collaborative inquiry (e.g., Bereiter, et al., 1997; Hewitt, 2002; Oshima, 1977; Scardamalia, 2002; Scardamalia, Bereiter, & Lamon, 1994).

While the overall design of the learning environment determines the learning activities, the representational tools that students use impact the focus of their collaborative discourse (Suthers, Vatrapu, Medina, Joseph, & Dwyer, 2007). For example, graphical representations such as concept maps make students pay more attention to the relationships between their ideas. Students have been found to raise more hypotheses and discuss them more often when using concept maps than text-based discussion (Suthers & Hundhausen, 2003). The constraints and salience of different visual representations direct the focus of collaborative discourse to different aspects of the representations (Suthers, Vatrapu, Medina, Joseph, & Dwyer, 2008). It is important to choose the appropriate representational tools to mediate different learning tasks.

Artificial intelligence technology has recently been employed to facilitate collaborative knowledge construction. Back in the 1970s, artificial intelligence was mainly used to support individual learning by providing corrective feedback through the use of detailed cognitive modeling (Wenger, 1987). Starting in the mid 90s, artificial intelligence has been used to guide the process of discourse in collaborative learning. It identifies problems in the discussion based on dialogical theories (Hicks, 1996) and prompts students for further elaboration. For example, Belvedere is an e-learning environment where students construct evidence maps made up of nodes that are either hypotheses or evidence points in their scientific inquiry (Suthers, Connelly, Lesgold, Paolucci, Toth, & Weiner, 2001). Belvedere analyzes the augmentation structure of the evidence map by comparing it with the one generated by subject matter experts and provides coaching on how to improve the consistency and completeness of the argument. While empirical results have shown that Belvedere can effectively assist collaborative argument construction (Suthers, Connelly, Lesgold, Paolucci, Toth, Toth, & Weiner, 2001), its technology is based on the analysis of the structure of the argument rather than its meaning. Providing accurate feedback based on true understanding of the argument still remains a challenge.

The e-learning environment, Corrosion Investigator, described in this chapter is based on goal-based scenario (GBS) (Schank, Fano, Bell, & Jona, 1993; Schank & Neaman, 2001), a framework for constructing interactive learn-by-doing environments. GBS focuses on creating realistic settings where students play real-life roles to solve challenging problems. For example, Sickle Cell Counselor (Bell, Bareiss, & Beckwith, 1994) is a GBS environment where students work as reproductive counselors advising newly married couples on their children's risk of having sickle cell disease. Volcano Investigator is a GBS environment where students play the role of geologists to investigate the likelihood of volcano eruption in a small town (Dobson, 1998). These learning environments use fictional scenarios with videos and simulations to create engaging settings, and provide video clips of expert advice and automatic critiquing to guide student learning. While GBS environments have been used to teach students problem-solving and provide on-the-job training for professionals, previous GBS environments are only for individual learners. Corrosion Investigator extends the GBS framework by providing collaboration support such as data sharing and argument construction in the learning environment. It is designed to facilitate a group of students to share and interpret the data that they collected and argue about the conclusions that they can draw from the data. In the following, we briefly introduce Corrosion Investigator and then discuss its design for collaborative knowledge construction.

SOFTWARE INTERFACE

Corrosion Investigator is a learning-by-doing environment designed for collaboratively problem-solving. Its focus is to provide a structured environment with authentic simulated data and a set of tools to direct and facilitate collaboration. It is not intended to be used as the only medium through which students collaborate. Students can use it either during classroom hours or outside of the class. They can communicate face-to-face or through existing tools such as instant messengers to discuss their problem-solving strategies and coordinate their collaboration. Corrosion Investigator is aimed to be used as a focal point for students to share data, propose and defend ideas, and receive coaching.

When students first enter Corrosion Investigator, a *challenge* screen (see Figure 1) tells them that they need to work as engineering consultants to diagnose the cause of two corrosion problems in a paper processing company. After reading the challenge, students can go to the *reference* screen. This screen contains background information about the company, including the location and condition of the corrosion and four characters that students can contact for more information: the plant foreman, the plant manager, the scientific consultant and the supervisor. Questions directed to these characters will be forwarded to the instructor and the instructor will provide answers to students' questions.

Figure 1. The challenge screen in corrosion investigator

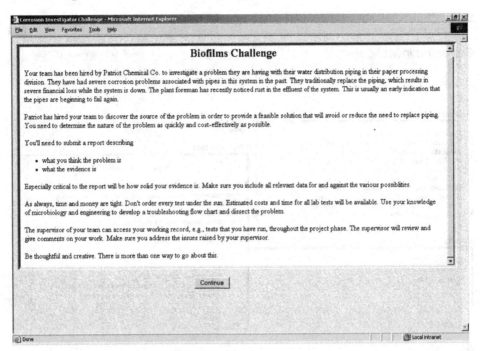

To diagnose the corrosion problem, students go to the *experiment* screen to run experiments (see Figure 2). The left-hand side of the screen has a *notebook*. It collects all the experiment results that students receive from the system and splits them into single items with labels indicating their experiment names and conditions. Items in the notebook are clickable. Students can select them to use as evidence in their report. The right-hand side of the *experiment* screen allows students to look for experiments by entering experiment names into a textbox. Experiments matching the name will be shown.

When students decide to run an experiment, they can specify the parameters for the experiment on a separate screen (see Figure 3). Experiments in Corrosion Investigator often have complex options so that students have to think hard about which experiments to run. The *cost* and *delay* field displays the simulated amount of money and the days that the experiment takes. These values are dynamically calculated and displayed based on the parameter selection. They will be added to

the value of the *project cost* and *day* field on the top of the screen, if students choose to run the experiment. These fields remind students to solve the challenge using minimum time and money. Before running an experiment, students need to enter reasons for ordering the experiment.

To receive experiment results, students need to press the *advance date* button at the top of the screen to advance the simulated project date to the time when the most recent experiment results are available. New experiment results automatically appear in the *notebook* and *result* area on the *experiment* screen.

The *report* screen allows students to construct their report using experiment results as evidence (see Figure 4). Students can select a result in the *notebook* and enter the reason for using the result. When students complete their report, they can submit it for evaluation.

While students are working in the system, their work is recorded and organized as a report for their instructor to review. The instructor can add comments to the students' work. Students can

Figure 2. The experiment screen in corrosion unvestigator

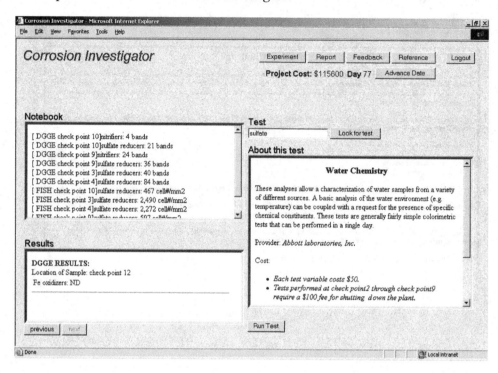

review these comments on the *feedback* screen, and provide responses (see Figure 5).

DESIGN FOR COLLABORATIVE KNOWLEDGE COSTRUCTION

In the following, we discuss computational supports in Corrosion Investigator designed for collaborative knowledge construction. These supports allow students to actively participate in collaborative problem-solving and develop artifacts that represent the product of their knowledge construction.

Shared Problem-Solving Task to Foster Collaboration

Collaborative knowledge construction requires each group member to make sense of others' understanding and advance the knowledge of the whole group through negotiation and elaboration.

It is critical to maintain a shared understanding of the problem at hand so that new ideas can be developed based on this common ground (Cannon-Bowers et al., 1993). In Corrosion Investigator, the notebook provides a common knowledge repository for students to share their findings. It automatically collects all the experiment data generated by students so that students do not need to combine their findings together. It ensures that all members in the collaboration have access to the same knowledge base.

For collaborative learning to be effective, team members need to have a common group goal (Slavin, 1996; Johnson & Johnson, 1989, 1990). In Corrosion Investigator, we develop a task setting where group members share the cost and result of each other's action. Each experiment has a time delay and cost. Whenever a student runs an experiment, the time and cost of the experiment will be automatically added to the total time and cost spent by the whole group. Different from environments where individuals bear the cost of their

Figure 3. The parameter value selection screen in corrosion investigator

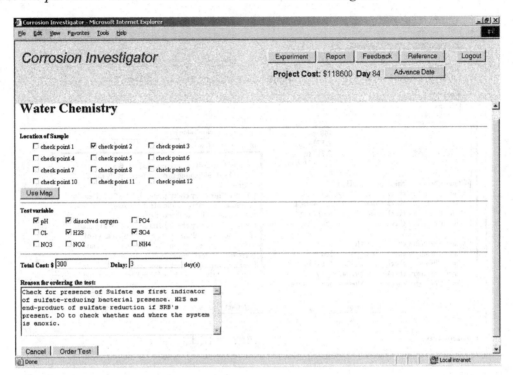

own actions, Corrosion Investigator automatically accumulates the cost of each individual's action on a group level. This makes the action of every student directly impact the performance of the whole group. Students have to coordinate their actions and formulate team strategies to minimize the cost of their investigation. The individual accountability and shared responsibility make the problem-solving task a collaborative effort rather than an individual endeavor (Johnson, Johnson, & Holubec, 1993).

In virtual environments, participants often feel isolated due to the remote nature of the communication medium (Puntambekar, 1996). In Corrosion Investigator, we provide a progress report to help students obtain an overall picture of their group activities. The report combines all the actions that individual members have performed in chronicle order. It allows students to quickly review activities performed by other team members and understand the progress of the whole group. Every student

receives the opportunity to develop a sense of being a member in a community and see how his/her activities fit into the team effort.

Structured Interface for Collaborative Argument Construction

In collaborative knowledge constructions, team members need to exchange and negotiate ideas to develop new knowledge. The argument construction tool in Corrosion Investigator allows students to argue about and reflect on each other's ideas. Students can collect evidence to support their hypotheses, or provide contradictory data to refute their hypotheses. Through this argumentation process, students will develop a better understanding of the corrosion problem, the underlying causes of the problem, and the relationship between the causes.

In addition, different user interfaces representations offer different affordances (Norman, 1999).

Figure 4. The report screen in corrosion investigator

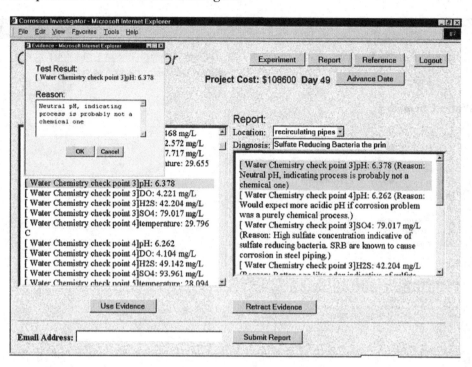

The design of user interfaces can direct students' focus to different aspects of their learning and lead them through different learning courses (e.g., Baker & Lund, 1996; Dillenbourg, 2005; Guzdial & Hmelo, 1997; Suthers & Hundhausen, 2003; Suthers et al., 2007). In Corrosion Investigator, we structure the argument construction interface to require students to always create a hypothesis first and then add evidence to argue about their hypothesis. This ensures students to follow the typical scientific inquiry process where hypotheses are generated first and then verified by experimental data. It also helps to center students' discussion around their hypotheses. The goal is to avoid the problem in standard discussion forums where participants often lose concentration and cannot generate a conclusion in the end (Hewitt, 2001).

The argument construction tool also requires students to provide experimental evidence for every argument point that they make. This ensures that students' arguments are always grounded on real data. To help students use experimen-tal evidence in their arguments, the argument construction tool is closely integrated with the data collection notebook. Students can select an experiment result from the notebook, attach a note to explain why he or she wants to use the result, and insert it into the argument. While the requirement of using experimental data for every argument point may limit the flexibility of argument construction, preliminary results show that argument reports generated using the tool have the same quality as the ones generated in face-to-face collaboration (Qiu, 2005).

Coaching for Problem-Solving and Reflection

Problem-based learning encourages students to pursue free exploration and direct their own learning. While this strategy allows students to learn in a realistic setting, students often miss key learning resources or fail to think deeply. It is essential to have teachers provide just-in-time

Figure 5. The feedback screen in corrosion investigator

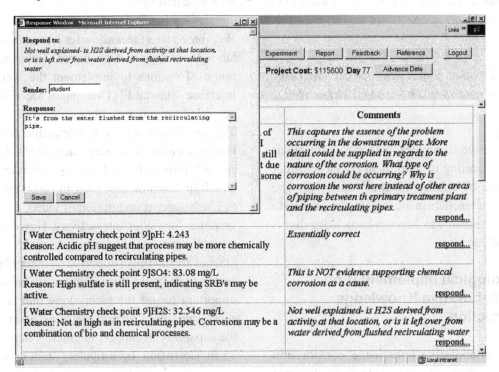

coaching to help students reach expected learning goals (Collins, Brown, & Newman, 1989).

In Corrosion Investigator, we provide an interactive report for teachers to review student activities in the learning environment. The report includes the time and money that students have spent, experiments that students have scheduled and run, reasons for running those experiments, and hypotheses and arguments that students have created. Teachers can click on items in the report and add critiques. The interactive report is automatically updated every time when students perform an action in the learning environment.

The interactive report allows teachers to work closely alongside with students to provide critiquing. Empirical results show that teacher's critiquing often provokes students to reflect on their own thinking (Qiu, 2005). We analyzed 32 critiques collected during two preliminary studies and found that these critiques can be categorized into three types. The first type confirms the correctness of the student's thinking. For example,

"That is correct- H2S a byproduct of SRB metabolism."

The second type points out that the student thinking is incorrect. For example,

"This is NOT evidence supporting chemical corrosion as a cause."

The third type asks for more explanation. For example,

"Why is corrosion the worst here instead of other areas of piping between the primary treatment plant and the recirculating pipes?"

"More detail could be supplied in regards to the nature of the corrosion."

"There are other possibilities for chemical corrosion at neutral pH's - should acknowledge this."

These critiques prompt students to correct their misunderstanding or help them develop further knowledge by confirming their reasoning. The inclusion of teachers in the learning environment facilitates students to develop knowledge that is valid and complete.

Technological Implementation for Collaborative Knowledge Construction

Online collaborative knowledge construction requires students to participate from different locations. It presents unique technical challenges for learning-by-doing environments. Up until the early 2000s, learning-by-doing environments are all built as monolithic systems. They use immersive multimedia to create engaging settings and scaffolding tools to support problem-solving. For example, Alien Rescue (Liu, Williams, & Pedersen, 2002) is a learning environment where students need to find a new home in the solar system for aliens to survive. BioWorld (Lajoie, Lavigne, Guerrera, & Munsie, 2001) is a learning environment for students to diagnose patients in a simulated hospital setting. These learning environments are installed on individual computers and cannot be accessed remotely from other machines. This makes them difficult to support collaboration. In the following, we describe the technological support in Corrosion Investigator for collaborative knowledge construction.

Accessibility

Web-based interfaces allow team members to collaborate through web browsers. There is a wide range of options to implement the web-based interface. Standard HTML pages are widely accessible from any web browser on any platform. They are, however, not very interactive. JavaScript webpages introduce more interactions, but they can only provide limited options such as textboxes and drop-down menus. Plug-in based tools such as Flash support integration of video, audio, and graphics for richer interactivity. However, they typically run on Windows, sometimes on Mac OS, but are not fully supported on other platforms such as Linux. To encourage participation, it is important to use the technology that is widely accessible from different platforms and maintain the capability to support interactive activities.

In Corrosion Investigator, student learning activities include choosing experiments, specifying parameters, receiving data, and constructing arguments. They do not require complex interactions such as drawing diagrams. Therefore, we use standard JavaScript for the user interface. The Javascript implementation allows the interface to be easily accessible from modern web-browsers such as Internet Explorer and Netscape without special software plug-ins. It provides wide deployability with the least commitment to third-party vendor support. This lowers the technical barrier for using the learning environment and allows students to participate with minimum technical requirement.

Data Consistency

Learning-by-doing environments need to make sure that information presented to every student is always consistent and up-to-date. In Corrosion Investigator, we save the learning content and student activities into a central server and loads data from the server whenever students interact with the learning environment. This ensures that every student has access to the most current experiment data generated by the team. The storage of learning content on the server also facilitates the authoring of the learning environment (Qiu & Riesbeck, 2008). With a web-based authoring tool, authors can modify the learning content anytime, anywhere through web browsers. When the learning content is modified, students can immediate see the change in their web browsers because the learning environment is constructed real-time from the server.

The storage of student activities on the server allows instructors to easily access them in a centralized location. Instructors no longer need to collect student records from individual machines. They can view these records through web-based interactive reports that we provide. The report is updated every time a student makes a move in the learning environment so that the instructor always sees the most recent student activity.

Interactivity

Learning-by-doing environments need to be highly interactive because students need to perform problem-solving activities such as exploring background information, running experiments, and comparing results. Speed is one of the key factors in determining interactivity. Users often accept delays of one to two seconds, but no more than ten to fifteen second (Olsen, 1998). Therefore, it is important to provide immediate feedback to keep the learning activity interactive and engaging.

In Corrosion Investigator, we run the program that generates complex experiment results on the server and run the program that handles user interactions in the web browser. For example, students' experiment requests are sent to the server for processing. These requests require complex algorithms and simulations with multi-parameter constraints. Running them on the server reduces the time needed and avoids the requirement to have powerful computational capability on students' machines. In contrast, the dynamic display of cost

and time of an experiment is handled by JavaScript run in the web browser. Students can immediate see the change of the cost and time when they choose different parameter values. This allows students to easily explore different experiment options without long-time delay. Students can have fast interactivity even when their network bandwidth is low.

The above describes the pedagogical and technological support in Corrosion Investigator for collaborative knowledge construction. We have conducted preliminary evaluation studies and results have been promising (Qiu, 2005). More thorough evaluative research is underway.

FUTURE RESEARCH DIRECTIONS

In Corrosion Investigator, we introduced an instructor into the learning environment to critique student learning. We plan to use natural language processing techniques such as Latent Semantic Analysis (LSA) (Foltz, 1996; Landauer & Dumais, 1997; Landauer, Foltz, & Laham, 1998) to provide automatic feedback to students' arguments. LSA has been used successfully in AutoTutor (Graesser, Wiemer-Hastings, Wiemer-Hastings, Harter, Person, & the TRG, 2000) to compare student writings against stored examples and provide suggestive comments. In Corrosion Investigator, we plan to use LSA to compare students' reasons for running an experiment with stored examples of correct and wrong reasons, and return corresponding critiques. While the potential to provide automatic feedback remains promising, it is important to note that computers can easily lose credibility if users notice inappropriate feedback (Reeves & Nass, 1996). When users have low trust of computers, they pay little attention to the feedback even when it is correct. The need for extremely accurate feedback significantly increases the difficulty of building learning systems with automatic coaching capability. For example, intelligent tutoring systems that provide individualized feedback often require two hundred hours of development for one hour of instruction (Woolf & Cunningham, 1987). Future research is needed to develop effective and inexpensive methods for automatic feedback generation.

While collaborative learning-by-doing environments change the traditional learning practice into a collaborative effort, they also change the social relationships among their users (Levin & Kareev, 1980). Several studies have found that the use of computers in the classroom reduces teacher-centered activities and weakens teachers' authority role (e.g., Gearhart, Herman, Baker, Novak, & Whitteier, 1994). When students have access to individuals or information resources more knowledgeable than their teachers, they become less dependent on their teachers (Schofield, 1995). Student-student relations also become more cooperative as students work as collaborators rather than simply classmates (Hawkins, Sheingold, Gearhart, & Berger, 1982). These social impacts of learning software should be fully aware by technology adopters.

Educational games have recently received a lot of attention. Games such as Second Life provide immersive and animated environments for anyone in the world to access. Research has shown that students are fairly comfortable of using avatar to represent themselves in games and carry out collaborative learning activities (Virvou, Katsionis, & Konstantinos, 2005). Pedagogical agents in such games can stimulate student learning and maintain high level of engagement (Conati & Zhao, 2004). With these new technologies, students can interact with their team members (including computer agents) in 3D environments that are much more natural than chat rooms or discussion forums. They can construct virtual artifacts similar to the ones in real life. With these new developments, the study of knowledge construction in immersive environments becomes an emerging topic worth further investigation.

Besides learning, virtual environments have also been employed for studying social behaviors.

Blascovich, Loomis, Beall, Swinth, Hoyt, and Bailenson (2002) found that virtual environments can reduce methodological issues in traditional experimental settings such as the lack of replication and unrepresentative sampling. Furthermore, when social behaviors happen in a virtual environment, researchers can perform "reverse engineering" by manipulating components in the virtual environment to understand the cause of particular behaviors and identify their components. This helps researchers perform more fine-grained examination of social behaviors and their elements.

CONCLUSION

In this chapter, we described Corrosion Investigator, a virtual learning-by-doing environment where students take the role of consultants to investigate the cause of recurring pipe corrosion in a paper processing company. We discussed how to provide support to e-collaborative knowledge construction by a) creating a shared task to engage students in collaboration, b) providing an argument construction tool to facilitate idea exchange and knowledge construction, c) providing instructor coaching to guide problem-solving, and d) using technological implementation to ensure data consistency, accessibility, and interactivity. The synergy of the above design provides multi-level support for collaborative knowledge construction. We believe it serves as an example of how to design learning-by-doing environments to effectively support collaborative knowledge construction.

REFERENCES

Artz, A. F., & Newman, C. M. (1990). Cooperative learning. *Mathematics Teacher*, *83*, 448–449.

Baker, M. J., & Lund, K. (1996). Flexibly Structuring the Interaction in a CSCL environment. In P. Brna, A. Paiva & J. Self (Eds.), *Proceedings of the EuroAIED Conference* (pp. 401-407). Lisbon, Portugal: Edições Colibri.

Barrows, H. S. (2000). *Problem-based learning applied to medical education*. Springfield, IL: Southern Illinois University Press.

Bateson, G. (1976). Some Components of Socialization for Trance. In Schwartz, T. (Ed.), *Socialization as Cultural Communication* (pp. 51–63). Berkeley, CA: University of California Press.

Bell, B. L., Bareiss, R., & Beckwith, R. (1994). Sickle cell counselor: a prototype goal-based scenario for instruction in a museum environment. *Journal of the Learning Sciences*, *3*, 347–386. doi:10.1207/s15327809jls0304_3

Bereiter, C., & Scardamalia, M. (2003). Learning to Work Creatively With Knowledge. In De Corte, E., Verschaffel, L., Entwistle, N., & Van Merriënboer, J. (Eds.), *Unravelling basic components and dimensions of powerful learning environments*. EARLI Advances in Learning and Instruction Series.

Bereiter, C., Scardamalia, M., Cassells, C., & Hewitt, J. (1997). Postmodernism, knowledge building, and elementary science. *The Elementary School Journal*, *97*, 329–340. doi:10.1086/461869

Bettencourt, B. A., Brewer, M. B., Croak, M. R., & Miller, N. (1992). Cooperation and reduction of intergroup bias: The role of reward structure and social orientation. *Journal of Experimental Social Psychology*, *28*, 301–319. doi:10.1016/0022-1031(92)90048-O

Bickhard, M. H. (1992). How Does the Environment Affect the Person? In Winegar, L. T., & Valsiner, J. (Eds.), *Children's Development in Social Context*. Hillsdale, NJ: Lawrence Erlbaum Assoc.

Blascovich, J., Loomis, J., Beall, A. C., Swinth, K. R., Hoyt, C. L., & Bailenson, J. N. (2002). Immersive virtual environment technology as a methodological tool for social psychology. *Psychological Inquiry*, *13*, 103–124. doi:10.1207/S15327965PLI1302_01

Bransford, J. D., Brown, A. L., & Cocking, R. R. (Eds.). (1999). *How people learn: Brain, Mind, Experience, and School*. Washington, DC: National Academy Press.

Brewer, M. B. (1979). In-group bias in the minimal intergroup situation: A cognitive-motivational analysis. *Psychological Bulletin*, *86*, 307–324. doi:10.1037/0033-2909.86.2.307

Brewer, M. B., & Miller, N. (1984). Beyond the contact hypothesis: Theoretical perspectives on desegregation. In Miller, N., & Brewer, M. (Eds.), *Groups in contact: The psychology of desegregation* (pp. 281–302). New York: Academic Press.

Brown, A. L., & Campione, J. C. (1990). Communities of learning and thinking, or a context by any other name. In D. Kuhn (Ed.), Contributions to Human Development, 21, 108-125.

Brown, J. S., Collins, A., & Duguid, P. (1989). Situated cognition and the culture of learning. *Educational Researcher*, *18*(1), 32–42.

Cannon-Bowers, J. A., Salas, E., & Converse, S. A. (1993). Shared mental models in expert team decision making. In Castellan, N. J. Jr., (Ed.), *Current issues in individual and group decision making* (pp. 221–246). Hillsdale, NJ: Erlbaum.

Chicago: Open Court.

cognitive theory and classroom practice (pp. 201-228). Cambridge, MA: MIT Press.

Collins, A., & Brown, J. (1988). The computer as a tool for learning through reflection. In Mandl, H., & Lesgold, A. (Eds.), *Learning issues for intelligent tutoring systems*. New York: Springer Verlag.

Collins, A., Brown, J. S., & Newman, S. E. (1989). Cognitive Apprenticeship: Teaching the crafts of reading, writing and mathematics. In Resnick, L. (Ed.), *Knowing, Learning and Instruction*. Hillsdale, NJ: Erlbaum.

Collins, E., & Green, J. L. (1992). Learning in classroom settings: making or breaking a culture. In Marshall, H. H. (Ed.), *Redefining student learning: roots of educational change*. Norwood, NJ: Ablex.

Conati, C., & Zhao, X. (2004). Building and Evaluating an Intelligent Pedagogical Agent to Improve the Effectiveness of an Educational Game. In *Proceedings of International Conference on Intelligent User Interfaces 2004*.

Derry, S. J., Hmelo-Silver, C. E., Nagarajan, A., Chernobilsky, E., & Beitzel, B. (2006). Cognitive transfer revisited: Can we exploit new media to solve old problems on a large scale? *Journal of Educational Computing Research*, *35*, 145–162. doi:10.2190/0576-R724-T149-5432

Dewey, J. (1916). *Democracy and Education*. New York: MacMillan.

Dewey, J., & Bentley, A. (1949). *Knowing and the Known*. Boston, MA: Beacon Press.

Diehl, M., & Stroebe, W. (1987). Productivity loss in brainstorming groups: Toward the solution of a riddle. *Journal of Personality and Social Psychology*, *53*, 497–509. doi:10.1037/0022-3514.53.3.497

Dillenbourg, P. (2005). Designing biases that augment socio-cognitive interactions. In Bromme, R., Hesse, F. W., & Spada, H. (Eds.), *Barriers and Biases in Computer-Mediated Knowledge Communication-and How They May Be Overcome*. Dordrecht, The Netherlands: Kluwer. doi:10.1007/0-387-24319-4_11

Dobson, W. D. (1998). *Authoring tools for investigate and decide learning environments*. Unpublished doctoral dissertation, Northwestern University, Evanston.

Dochy, F., Segers, M., Van den Bossche, P., & Gijbels, D. (2003). Effects of problem-based learning: A meta-analysis. *Learning and Instruction*, *13*, 533–568. doi:10.1016/S0959-4752(02)00025-7

Edelson, D. C., Pea, R. D., & Gomez, L. (1995). Constructivism in the collaboratory. In Wilson, B. G. (Ed.), *Constructivist learning environments: Case studies in instructional design* (pp. 151–164). Englewood Cliffs, NJ: Educational Technology Publications.

Erickson, F., & Schultz, J. (1982). *The Counselor as Gatekeeper: Social Interaction in Interviews*. New York: Academic Press.

Festinger, L. (1954). A theory of social comparison processes. *Human Relations*, *7*, 117–140. doi:10.1177/001872675400700202

Foltz, P. W. (1996). Latent semantic analysis for text-based research. *Behavior Research Methods, Instruments, & Computers*, *28*(2), 197–202.

Gaertner, S. L., Dovidio, J. F., Anastasio, P., Bachman, B. A., & Rust, M. (1993). The Common Ingroup Identity Model: Recategorization and the reduction of intergroup bias. In Stroebe, W., & Hewstone, M. (Eds.), *European review of social psychology* (*Vol. 4*, p. 1-26). Chichester, UK: Wiley.

Gaertner, S. L., Mann, J., Dovidio, J. F., Murrel, A., & Pomare, M. (1990). How does cooperation reduce intergroup bias? *Journal of Personality and Social Psychology*, *59*, 692–704. doi:10.1037/0022-3514.59.4.692

Gaertner, S. L., Mann, J., Murrel, A., & Dovidio, J. F. (1989). Reducing intergroup bias: The benefits of recategorization. *Journal of Personality and Social Psychology*, *57*, 239–249. doi:10.1037/0022-3514.57.2.239

Gallupe, R. B., Bastianutti, L. M., & Cooper, W. H. (1991). Unblocking brainstorms. *The Journal of Applied Psychology*, *76*(1), 137–142. doi:10.1037/0021-9010.76.1.137

Graesser, A. C., Person, N. K., & Magliano, J. P. (1995). Collaborative dialogue patterns in naturalistic one-on-one tutoring. *Applied Cognitive Psychology, 9*, 495–522. doi:10.1002/acp.2350090604

Graesser, A. C., Wiemer-Hastings, P., Wiemer-Hastings, K., Harter, D., & Person, N.TRG. (2000). Using Latent Semantic Analysis to Evaluate the Contributions of Students in AutoTutor. *Interactive Learning Environments, 8*, 128–148. doi:10.1076/1049-4820(200008)8:2;1-B;FT129

Guzdial, M., & Hmelo, C. (1997). Integrating and guiding collaboration: Lessons learned in computer-supported collaborative learning research at Georgia Tech. In Proceedings of Computer Supported Collaborative Learning '97, Toronto, Ontario (pp. 91-100).

Hawkes, M., & Romiszowski, A. (2001). Examining the reflective outcomes of asynchronous computer-mediated communication on in service teacher development. *Journal of Technology and Teacher Education, 9*(2), 285–308.

Hawkins, J., Sheingold, K., Gearhart, M., & Berger, C. (1982). Microcomputers in schools: Impact on the social life of elementary classrooms. *Journal of Applied Developmental Psychology, 3*, 361–373. doi:10.1016/0193-3973(82)90008-9

Hewitt, J. (2001). Beyond Threaded Discourse. *International Journal of Educational Telecommunications, 7*(3), 207–221.

Hewitt, J. (2002). From a focus on tasks to a focus on understanding: The cultural transformation of a Toronto classroom. In T. Koschmann, R. Hall, & N. Miyake (Eds.) Computer Supported Cooperative Learning Volume 2: Carrying forward the conversation, (pp. 11-41). Mahwah, New Jersey: Lawrence Erlbaum Associates.

Hewitt, J. (2003). How habitual online practices affect the development of asynchronous discussion threads. *Journal of Educational Computing Research, 28*(1), 31–45. doi:10.2190/PMG8-A05J-CUH1-DK14

Hicks, D. (1996). Contextual inquiries: A discourse-oriented study of classroom learning. In Hicks, D. (Ed.), *Discourse, learning and schooling* (pp. 104–141). New York: Cambridge University Press.

Higgins, E. T. (1992). Achieving "shared reality" in the communication game: A social action that creates meaning. *Journal of Language and Social Psychology, 11*, 107–131. doi:10.1177/0261927X92113001

Hinsz, V. B., Tindale, R. S., & Vollrath, D. A. (1997). The emerging conceptualization of groups as information processors. *Psychological Bulletin, 121*, 43–64. doi:10.1037/0033-2909.121.1.43

Hmelo, C., Narayanan, N. H., Newstetter, W. C., & Kolodner, J. L. (1995). *A multiple-case-based approach to generative environments for learning.* Paper presented at the Second Annual Symposium on Cognition and Education.

Hmelo, C. E., & Evensen, D. H. (2000). Introduction. In Evensen, D. H., & Hmelo, C. E. (Eds.), *Problem-Based Learning, A Research Perspective on Learning Interactions* (pp. 185–195). Mahwah, NJ: Lawrence Erlbaum Associates.

Hmelo-Silver, C. E., & Barrows, H. S. (2006). Goals and strategies of a problem-based learning facilitator. *Interdisciplinary Journal of Problem-based Learning, 1*, 21–39.

Hmelo-Silver, C. E., Duncan, R. G., & Chinn, C. A. (2007). Scaffolding and achievement in problem-based and inquiry learning: A response to Kirschner, Sweller, and Clark (2006). *Educational Psychologist, 42*, 99–107.

Holbrook, J., & Kolodner, J. L. (2000). Scaffolding the development of an inquiry-based (science) classroom. In B. Fishman & S. O'Connor-Divelbiss (Eds.), *Fourth International Conference of the Learning Sciences* (pp. 221-227). Mahwah, NJ: Lawrence Erlbaum Associates.

Johnson, D. W., & Johnson, R. T. (1989). *Cooperation and competition: Theory and research.* Edina, MN: Interaction Book Company.

Johnson, D. W., & Johnson, R. T. (1995). *Teaching students to be peacemakers* (3rd ed.). Edina, MN: Interaction Book Company.

Johnson, D. W., Johnson, R. T., & Holubec, E. J. (1993). *Cooperation in the Classroom* (6th ed.). Edina, MN: Interaction Book Company.

Johnson-Laird, P. (1983). *Mental models.* Cambridge, MA: Harvard University Press.

Klimoski, R., & Mohammed, S. (1994). Team mental model: Construct or metaphor? *Journal of Management, 20,* 403–437. doi:10.1016/0149-2063(94)90021-3

Koh, G. C., Khoo, H. E., Wong, M. L., & Koh, D. (2008). The Effects of Problem-based Learning During Medical School on Physician Competency: A Systematic Review. [CMAJ]. *Canadian Medical Association Journal, 178*(1). doi:10.1503/cmaj.070565

Lajoie, S. P., Lavigne, N. C., Guerrera, C., & Munsie, S. (2001). Constructing Knowledge in the Context of BioWorld. *Instructional Science, 29*(2), 155–186. doi:10.1023/A:1003996000775

Landauer, T. K., & Dumais, S. T. (1997). A Solution to Plato's Problem: The Latent Semantic Analysis Theory of Acquisition, Induction, and Representation of Knowledge. *Psychological Review, 104*(2), 211–240. doi:10.1037/0033-295X.104.2.211

Landauer, T. K., Foltz, P. W., & Laham, D. (1998). An Introduction to Latent Semantic Analysis. *Discourse Processes, 25,* 259–284. doi:10.1080/01638539809545028

Larson, J. R. Jr. (1997). Modeling the entry of shared and unshared information into group discussion: A review and BASIC language computer program. *Small Group Research, 28,* 454–479. doi:10.1177/1046496497283007

Larson, J. R. Jr. (2007). Deep diversity and strong synergy: Modeling the impact of variability in members' problem-solving strategies on group problem-solving performance. *Small Group Research, 38,* 413–436. doi:10.1177/1046496407301972

Larson, J. R. Jr, Christensen, C., Franz, T. M., & Abbott, A. S. (1998). Diagnosing groups: The pooling, management, and impact of shared and unshared case information in team-based medical decision making. *Journal of Personality and Social Psychology, 75,* 93–108. doi:10.1037/0022-3514.75.1.93

Larson, J. R. Jr, & Harmon, V. M. (2007). Recalling shared vs. unshared information mentioned during group discussion: Toward understanding differential repetition rates. *Group Processes & Intergroup Relations, 10,* 311–322. doi:10.1177/1368430207078692

Lave, J. (1988). *Cognition in Practice.* Cambridge, UK: Cambridge University Press. doi:10.1017/CBO9780511609268

Lave, J., & Wenger, E. (1991). *Situated learning: Legitimate peripheral participation.* Cambridge, UK: Cambridge University Press.

Lave, J., & Wenger, E. (1991). *Situated Learning: Legitimate Peripheral Participation.* Cambridge, UK: Cambridge University Press.

Levin, J. A., & Kareev, Y. (1980). *Personal computers and education: The challenge to schools. Technical report no. CHIP 98.* La Jolla, CA: Center for Human Information Processing, University of California at San Diego.

Levine, J. M., Resnick, L. B., & Higgins, E. T. (1993). Social foundations of cognition. *Annual Review of Psychology, 44,* 585–612. doi:10.1146/annurev.ps.44.020193.003101

Liu, M., Williams, D., & Pedersen, S. (2002). Alien Rescue: A Problem-Based Hypermedia Learning Environment for Middle School Science. *Journal of Educational Technology Systems, 30*(3). doi:10.2190/X531-D6KE-NXVY-N6RE

Marx, R. W., Blumenfeld, P. C., Krajcik, J. S., & Soloway, E. (1997). Enacting project-based science. *The Elementary School Journal, 97,* 341–358. doi:10.1086/461870

Mathieu, J., Goodwin, G. F., Heffner, T. S., Salas, E., & Cannon-Bowers, J. A. (2000). The influence of shared mental models on team process and performance. *The Journal of Applied Psychology, 85*(2), 273–283. doi:10.1037/0021-9010.85.2.273

Mcintyre, R. M., & Salas, E. (1995). Measuring and managing for team performance: Emerging principles from complex environments. In Guzzo, R., & Salas, E. (Eds.), *Team effectiveness and decision making in organizations* (pp. 149–203). San Francisco: Jossey-Bass.

Mergendoller, J. R., Maxwell, N. L., & Bellisimo, Y. (2006). The effectiveness of problem-based instruction: a comparative Study of instructional method and student characteristics. *Interdisciplinary Journal of Problem-based Learning, 1,* 49–69.

Miller, N., Brewer, M. B., & Edwards, K. (1985). Cooperative interaction in desegregated settings: A laboratory analogue. *The Journal of Social Issues, 41,* 63–79.

Moreland, R. L., & Levine, J. M. (2008). Building bridges to improve theory and research on small groups. In Salas, E., Burke, C. S., & Goodwin, G. F. (Eds.), *Team effectiveness in complex organizations and systems: Cross-disciplinary perspectives and approaches* (pp. 17–38). San Francisco: Jossey-Bass.

Morgan, B. B., Jr., Glickman, A. S., Woodard, E. A., Blaiwes, A. S., & Salas, E. (1986). *Measurement of team behaviors in a Navy environment* (NTSC Tech. Rep. No. 86-014). Orlando, FL: Naval Training Systems Center.

Mullen, B., Brown, R., & Smith, C. (1992). Ingroup bias as a function of salience, relevance, and status: An integration. *European Journal of Social Psychology, 22,* 103–122. doi:10.1002/ejsp.2420220202

Munkes, J., & Diehl, M. (2003). Matching or Competition? Performance Comparison Processes in an Idea Generation Task. *Group Processes & Intergroup Relations, 6*(3), 305–320. doi:10.1177/13684302030063006

Norman, D. A. (1999). Affordance, Conventions, and Design. *Interactions (New York, N.Y.), 6,* 38–42. doi:10.1145/301153.301168

Nye, J. L., & Brower, A. M. (Eds.). (1996). *What's social about social cognition? Research on Socially Shared Cognition in Small Groups.* Thousand Oaks, CA: Sage.

Olsen, D. R. (1998). *Developing User Interfaces* (1st ed.). San Francisco: Morgan Kaufmann.

Oshima, J. (1997). Students' construction of scientific explanations in a collaborative hypermedia learning environment. In Hall, N. M. R., & Enyedy, N. (Eds.), *Computer Support for Collaborative Learning '97.* Toronto.

Palincsar, A. S., & Brown, A. L. (1984). Reciprocal teaching of comprehension-fostering and comprehension-monitoring activities. *Cognition and Instruction, 2*, 117–175.

Perkins, A. (1986). *Knowledge as design*. Hillsdale, NJ: Erlbaum.

Piaget, J. (1954). *The construction of reality in the child*. New York: Basic books. doi:10.1037/11168-000

Puntambekar, S. (1996) *Investigating the effect of a computer tool on students' metacognitive processes*. Unpublished doctoral dissertation, School of Cognitive and computing sciences, University of Sussex, UK.

Qiu, L. (2005). *A web-based architecture and incremental authoring model for interactive learning environments for diagnostic reasoning*. Unpublished doctoral dissertation, Northwestern University, Evanston.

Qiu, L., & Riesbeck, C. K. (2008). Human-in-the-loop: A Feedback-driven Model for Authoring Knowledge-based Interactive Learning Environments. *Journal of Educational Computing Research, 38*(4), 469–509. doi:10.2190/EC.38.4.e

Reeves, B., & Nass, C. (1996). *The media equation*. Cambridge, MA: SLI Publications, Cambridge University Press.

Resnick, L., Levine, J., & Teasley, S. (Eds.). (1991). *Perspectives on socially shared cognition*. Washington, DC: American Psychological Association. doi:10.1037/10096-000

Resnick, L. B. (1987). *Education and learning to think*. Washington, DC: National Academy Press.

Roschelle, J., & Teasley, S. (1995). The construction of shared knowledge in collaborative problem solving. In O'Malley, C. (Ed.), *Computer-supported collaborative learning* (pp. 69–197). Berlin, Germany: Springer Verlag.

Rouse, W. B., & Morris, N. M. (1986). On looking into the black box: Prospects and limits in the search for mental models. *Psychological Bulletin, 100*, 349–363. doi:10.1037/0033-2909.100.3.349

Scardamalia, M. (2002). Collective cognitive responsibility for the advancement of knowledge. In Smith, B. (Ed.), *Liberal education in a knowledge society* (pp. 76–98).

Scardamalia, M. (2003). Knowledge building. *Journal of Distance Education, 17*(S3), 10–14.

Scardamalia, M., & Bereiter, C. (1991). Higher Levels of Agency for Children in Knowledge Building: A Challenge for the Design of New Knowledge Media. *Journal of the Learning Sciences, 1*(1), 37–68. doi:10.1207/s15327809jls0101_3

Scardamalia, M., & Bereiter, C. (1994). Computer support for knowledge building communities. *Journal of the Learning Sciences, 3*(3), 265–283. doi:10.1207/s15327809jls0303_3

Scardamalia, M., Bereiter, C., & Lamon, M. (1994). The CSILE project: Trying to bring

Schank, R., Fano, A., Bell, B., & Jona, M. (1993). The design of goal-based scenarios. *Journal of the Learning Sciences, 3*, 305–345. doi:10.1207/s15327809jls0304_2

Schank, R., & Neaman, A. (2001). Motivation and Failure in Educational Simulation Design. In Forbus, K. D., & Feltovich, P. J. (Eds.), *Smart Machines in Education* (pp. 99–144). Menlo Park, CA: AAAI Press/MIT Press.

Schofield, J. W. (1995). *Computers and classroom culture*. New York: Cambridge University Press.

Schon, D. A. (1983). *The Reflective Practitioner: How Professionals Think in Action*. NY: Basic Books.

Schon, D. A. (1987). *Educating the Reflective Practitioner*. San Francisco, CA: Jossey-Bass.

Schopler, J., & Insko, C. A. (1992). The discontinuity effect in interpersonal and intergroup relations: Generality and mediation. In Stroebe, W., & Hewstone, M. (Eds.), *European review of social psychology* (pp. 121–151). Chichester, UK: Wiley.

Slavin, R. E. (1990). *Cooperative learning: Theory, research, and practice*. Englewood Cliffs, NJ: Prentice Hall.

Slavin, R. E. (1991). *Student team learning: A practical guide to cooperative* (3rd ed.). Washington, DC: National Education Association of the United States.

Slavin, R. E. (1996). *Education for all*. Exton, PA: Swets & Zeitlinger Publishers.

Stahl, G., Koschmann, T., & Suthers, D. (2006). Computer-supported collaborative learning. In Sawyer, R. K. (Ed.), *Cambridge handbook of the learning sciences*. Cambridge, UK: Cambridge University Press.

Stevens, R. J., & Slavin, R. E. (1995). The cooperative elementary school: Effects on students' achievement, attitudes, and social relations. *American Educational Research Journal, 32,* 321–351.

Suthers, D., Connelly, J., Lesgold, A., Paolucci, M., Toth, E., Toth, J., & Weiner, A. (2001). Representational and Advisory Guidance for Students Learning Scientific Inquiry. In *Forbus, K. D., and Feltovich, P. J. (2001). Smart machines in education: The coming revolution in educational technology* (pp. 7–35). Menlo Park, CA: AAAI/Mit Press.

Suthers, D., Connelly, J., Lesgold, A., Paolucci, M., Toth, E., Toth, J., & Weiner, A. (2001). Representational and Advisory Guidance for Students Learning Scientific Inquiry. In Forbus, K. D., & Feltovich, P. J. (Eds.), *Smart machines in education: The coming revolution in educational technology* (pp. 7–35). Menlo Park, CA: AAAI/MIT Press.

Suthers, D. D., & Hundhausen, C. (2003). An experimental study of the effects of representational guidance on collaborative learning. *Journal of the Learning Sciences, 12*(2), 183–219. doi:10.1207/S15327809JLS1202_2

Suthers, D. D., Vatrapu, R., Medina, R., Joseph, S., & Dwyer, N. (2007). Conceptual representations enhance knowledge construction in asynchronous collaboration. In C. Chinn, G. Erkens & S. Puntambekar (Eds.), *The Computer Supported Collaborative Learning (CSCL) Conference 2007* (pp. 704-713). New Brunswick: International Society of the Learning Sciences.

Suthers, D. D., Vatrapu, R., Medina, R., Joseph, S., & Dwyer, N. (2008). Beyond Threaded Discussion: Representational Guidance in Asynchronous Collaborative Learning Environments. *Computers & Education, 50*(4), 1103–1127. doi:10.1016/j.compedu.2006.10.007

Tajfel, H., & Turner, J. C. (1986). The social identity theory of intergroup behavior. In Worchel, S., & Austin, W. (Eds.), *Psychology of intergroup relations* (pp. 7–24). Chicago, IL: Nelson-Hall.

the classroom into World 3. In K. McGilley (Eds.), *Classroom lessons: Integrating*

Thompson, L. (1998). *The mind and heart of the negotiator*. Upper Saddle River, NJ: Prentice Hall.

Turner, J. C., Hogg, M., Oakes, P., Reicher, S., & Wetherell, M. (1987). *Rediscovering the social group: A self-categorization theory*. Oxford, UK: Basil Blackwell.

Valacich, J. S., Dennis, A. R., & Nunamaker, J. F. (1992). Group size and anonymity effects on computer-mediated idea generation. *Small Group Research, 23*(1), 49–73. doi:10.1177/1046496492231004

Virvou, M., Katsionis, G., & Konstantinos, M. (2005). Combining software games with education and evaluation of its educational effectiveness. *Educational Technology & Society, 8*(2), 54–65.

Webb, N. (1985). Student interaction and learning in small groups: A research summary. In Slavin, R., Sharan, S., Kagan, S., Hertz-Lazarowitz, R., Webb, C., & Schmuck, R. (Eds.), *Learning to cooperate, cooperating to learn* (pp. 148–172). New York: Plenum.

Wenger, E. (1987). *Artificial Intelligence and Tutoring Systems: Computational and Cognitive Approaches to the Communication of Knowledge.* Los Altos, CA: Morgan Kaufmann Publishers, Inc.

Wilson, J. R., & Rutherford, A. (1989). Mental models: Theory and application in human factors. *Human Factors, 31,* 617–634.

Wittenbaum, G. M., & Park, E. S. (2001). The collective preference for shared information. *Current Directions in Psychological Science, 10,* 70–73. doi:10.1111/1467-8721.00118

Woolf, B. P., & Cunningham, P. A. (1987). Multiple knowledge sources in intelligent teaching systems. *IEEE Expert, 2,* 41–54. doi:10.1109/MEX.1987.4307063

ADDITIONAL READING

Bereiter, C. (2002). *Education and mind in the knowledge age.* Hillsdale, NJ: Lawrence Erlbaum Associates.

Bransford, J. D., Brown, A. L., & Cocking, R. R. (Eds.). (1999). *How people learn: Brain, Mind, Experience, and School.* Washington, DC: National Academy Press.

Bromme, R., Hesse, F. W., & Spada, H. (Eds.). (2005). Barriers and biases in computer-mediated knowledge communication, and how they may be overcome. In P. Dillenbourg (Ed.), Computer-supported collaborative learning book series. New York: Springer.

Bruffee, K. (1993). *Collaborative learning.* Baltimore, MD: Johns Hopkins University Press.

Cannon-Bowers, J. A., Salas, E., & Converse, S. A. (1993). Shared mental models in expert team decision making. In Castellan, N. J. Jr., (Ed.), *Current issues in individual and group decision making* (pp. 221–246). Hillsdale, N J: Erlbaum.

Collins, A., & Brown, J. (1988). The computer as a tool for learning through reflection. In Mandl, H., & Lesgold, A. (Eds.), *Learning issues for intelligent tutoring systems.* New York: Springer Verlag.

Gaertner, S. L., Dovidio, J. F., Anastasio, P., Bachman, B. A., & Rust, M. (1993). The Common Ingroup Identity Model: Recategorization and the reduction of intergroup bias. In Stroebe, W., & Hewstone, M. (Eds.), *European review of social psychology* (*Vol. 4,* p. l-26). Chichester, UK: Wiley.

Hmelo-Silver, C. E., & Barrows, H. S. (2006). Goals and strategies of a problem-based learning facilitator. *Interdisciplinary Journal of Problem-based Learning, 1,* 21–39.

Johnson, D. W., & Johnson, R. T. (1989). *Cooperation and competition: Theory and research.* Edina, MN: Interaction Book Company.

Lave, J., & Wenger, E. (1991). *Situated learning: Legitimate peripheral participation.* Cambridge, UK: Cambridge University Press.

Mcintyre, R. M., & Salas, E. (1995). Measuring and managing for team performance: Emerging principles from complex environments. In Guzzo, R., & Salas, E. (Eds.), *Team effectiveness and decision making in organizations* (pp. 149–203). San Francisco: Jossey-Bass.

Moreland, R. L., & Levine, J. M. (2008). Building bridges to improve theory and research on small groups. In Salas, E., Burke, C. S., & Goodwin, G. F. (Eds.), *Team effectiveness in complex organizations and systems: Cross-disciplinary perspectives and approaches* (pp. 17–38). San Francisco: Jossey-Bass.

Newman, D., Griffin, P., & Cole, M. (1989). *The construction zone: Working for cognitive change in schools.* Cambridge, UK: Cambridge University Press.

Norman, D. A. (1999). Affordance, Conventions, and Design. *Interactions (New York, N.Y.), 6,* 38–42. doi:10.1145/301153.301168

Nye, J. L., & Brower, A. M. (Eds.). (1996). *What's social about social cognition?: Research on Socially Shared Cognition in Small Groups.* Thousand Oaks, CA: Sage.

O'Malley, C. (1995). *Computer supported collaborative learning.* Berlin, Germany: Springer Verlag.

Reeves, B., & Nass, C. (1996). *The media equation.* Cambridge: SLI Publications, Cambridge University Press.

Resnick, L. B. (1987). *Education and learning to think.* Washington, DC: National Academy Press.

Roschelle, J., & Teasley, S. (1995). The construction of shared knowledge in collaborative problem solving. In O'Malley, C. (Ed.), *Computer-supported collaborative learning* (pp. 69–197). Berlin, Germany: Springer Verlag.

Schank, R., & Neaman, A. (2001). Motivation and Failure in Educational Simulation Design. In Forbus, K. D., & Feltovich, P. J. (Eds.), *Smart Machines in Education* (pp. 99–144). Menlo Park, CA: AAAI Press/MIT Press.

Schopler, J., & Insko, C. A. (1992). The discontinuity effect in interpersonal and intergroup relations: Generality and mediation. In Stroebe, W., & Hewstone, M. (Eds.), *European review of social psychology* (pp. 121–151). Chichester, UK: Wiley.

Stahl, G., Koschmann, T., & Suthers, D. (2006). Computer-supported collaborative learning. In Sawyer, R. K. (Ed.), *Cambridge handbook of the learning sciences.* Cambridge, UK: Cambridge University Press.

Thompson, L. (1998). *The mind and heart of the negotiator.* Upper Saddle River, NJ: Prentice Hall.

Webb, N. (1985). Student interaction and learning in small groups: A research summary. In Slavin, R., Sharan, S., Kagan, S., Hertz-Lazarowitz, R., Webb, C., & Schmuck, R. (Eds.), *Learning to cooperate, cooperating to learn* (pp. 148–172). New York: Plenum.

Wenger, E. (1987). *Artificial Intelligence and Tutoring Systems: Computational and Cognitive Approaches to the Communication of Knowledge.* Los Altos, CA: Morgan Kaufmann Publishers, Inc.

Wittenbaum, G. M., & Park, E. S. (2001). The collective preference for shared information. *Current Directions in Psychological Science, 10,* 70–73. doi:10.1111/1467-8721.00118

KEY TERMS AND DEFINITIONS

Collaborative Learning: A pedagogical approach that embeds learning in collaborative activities where students work in teams to accomplish a common goal.

Collaboration Technologies: Computer technologies designed to facilitate group collaboration.

Educational Technology: Technologies designed to facilitate education.

Goal-Based Learning: A pedagogical approach that embeds learning in the pursuit of a specific goal.

Learning-by-Doing: A form of learning that obtains new knowledge through the practical doing of things.

Problem-Based Learning: A pedagogical approach that situates learning in the process of solving complex and ill-structured realistic problems.

Web-Based Learning: A pedagogical approach that uses web-based tools to facilitate learning.

Chapter 2
Collaborative Knowledge Construction in Virtual Learning Environments:
A Good Practice Example of Designing Online Courses in Moodle

Kathrin Helling
Institute for Future Studies, Austria

Christian Petter
Institute for Future Studies, Austria

ABSTRACT

In this chapter, a practical example of designing and implementing a Virtual Learning Environment (VLE) building on aspects of collaborative knowledge construction is presented. Based on a theoretical section on collaborative knowledge construction in VLEs, the potential of the VLE Moodle with regards to its collaboration tools is introduced. The subsequent central section of the chapter has a focus on the actual design and implementation of an online course in Moodle, following principles of constructivist course design. The final two sections reflect on the evaluation of the course by course participants, and possible conclusions to be drawn from designing and implementing the online course.

INTRODUCTION

The relevance of collaborative learning is emphasised with regard to computer-based educational and instructional approaches. Theory and research of educational communication processes and the use of technologies for communication purpose (cf. Jonassen, 2004) is discussed widely and re-

lated challenges and possibilities for the facilitation of effective learning processes are taken into account in the current discussion (cf. Bromme, Hesse & Spada, 2005). The book at hand brings in new perspectives on the topic of computer-based collaborative knowledge construction and in this chapter the authors aim at contributing to the book by providing a practical example of designing and implementing a Virtual Learning Environment (VLE) for collaborative knowledge construction.

DOI: 10.4018/978-1-61520-937-8.ch002

In general, for the implementation of online courses a large variety of VLEs is available (e.g. Blackboard, Sakai, Moodle, ATutor, etc.) which all have different functionalities for the design of learning activities and processes. For the online course described in this chapter the VLE Moodle was chosen due to its Open Source nature and the large developer and user community behind it. It allows course designers to build on an extensive knowledge base of pedagogical and technical solutions for Moodle course implementation. Furthermore, the VLE Moodle has an explicit orientation towards learning from a social constructivist perspective (cf. Cole & Foster, 2007). This was also an important aspect for choosing Moodle, because the pedagogical approach of the online course is based on theory of collaborative knowledge construction in VLEs. In this context the authors consider three central aspects for the design and implementation of VLEs from a constructivist and situated learning perspective: *Guiding learners, feedback and support processes* and *recognising learning processes*. The theoretical outline on collaborative knowledge construction in VLES is provided in the second section of this chapter, following the introduction part. Further details on specific aspects of designing courses with Moodle are then provided in the third section with a focus on utilising collaboration tools.

The fourth section is the central part of this chapter. It describes the so called ICT4T online course. The course was designed and offered in the frame of the "ICT4T – ICT Training for Trainers – Meeting Senior Learner Needs" project, which was financially supported by the Socrates Grundtvig Programme of the European Union (http://www.ict4t.net). The participants of the ICT4T course were trainers interested in computer-based teaching for the specific target group of senior learners. The ICT4T course itself was presented as an example of designing courses based on collaborative knowledge construction with a VLE. The authors of this chapter were responsible for the pedagogical and technical implementation of the ICT4T course, and both authors implemented several other online and blended learning environments with Moodle. Furthermore, they worked as tutors in the ICT4T course offers and other Moodle courses. Therefore, the description of the course implementation process refers to practical experiences of the authors.

The evaluation results of the course are described in section five. The focus is on data which provides information on the course implementation, taking into account the aspects *guiding learners, feedback and support processes* and *recognition of learning*, which aimed at supporting collaborative knowledge construction. Finally, in the concluding section the authors discuss the design and implementation of the ICT4T course from a perspective which considers technological and pedagogical challenges of designing VLEs for collaborative knowledge construction.

COLLABORATIVE KNOWLEDGE CONSTRUCTION IN VIRTUAL LEARNING ENVIRONMENTS

From a perspective of situated cognition, learning is seen as a process of active knowledge construction by learners, situated in a specific physical, social, cultural and historical context. It is based on a constructivist understanding of learning which sets a focus on the learners and their active role in constructing knowledge (cf. Mandl, Gruber & Renkl, 2002). Collins, Brown & Duguid (1989) explain that conceptual knowledge is linked to the situation in which it is acquired through active application and interaction within situations. It is distinctive for authentic activities that their meaning is socially negotiated, taking into account the cultural frame of the domain and situation. Similarly, Lave and Wenger (1991) consider participation in social practice and social negotiation of meaning central for situated learning. In communities of practice new members perform new tasks and gain understanding through the negotiation of meaning with older members. By this they reproduce the structure of social communities of practice and become full members themselves.

Mandl et al. (2002) discuss the implementation of "situated instruction" (p.143) and refer to the use of new technologies as facilitating factors for situated learning and collaborative knowledge construction processes. In designing situated learning environments the integration of complex problems and authentic situations serves as a starting point for the construction of applied knowledge. Offers of multiple perspectives for each problem and the initiation of reflection processes support learners to transfer the knowledge in different situations and contexts. Social interaction and collaborative problem solving activities correspond with situated learning.

Considering the theory on instructional approaches to situated learning, Mandl et al. (2002; p. 143-144) describe the following requirements for designing situated Virtual Learning Environments (VLEs):

- *Complex problems*: An interesting and motivating problem to be solved by the learners should be provided as initiating element of the learning process. By this, learners acquire knowledge through problem solving activities in a concrete application situation.
- *Authentic and situated context*: The situation and problems introduced in the learning environment need to be realistic and authentic. They serve as framework for the application of acquired knowledge.
- *Multiple perspectives*: Providing problems with changing context supports the learners to identify problems from different perspectives and acquire knowledge which can be transferred flexibly to different situations.
- *Articulation and reflection*: By reflecting on problem solving processes learners should

acquire abstract knowledge which can be transferred to and applied in other situations and is not tied to a specific context.
- *Learning by social interaction*: Collaborative learning activities and group work should be a central element of the learning environment. Tutors and experts should be involved in these social and interactive processes.

Consequently to the above considerations, a constructivist and situated VLE is more than a mere collection of learning materials. Below, specific aspects for designing and implementing VLEs following this approach are described. The focus is on supporting collaborative knowledge construction processes through three complementary and interlinked aspects: *guidance of learners, feedback and support processes* and the *recognition of learning*.

Guiding Learners: Learning is determined by teachers and learners alike, e.g. by finding an agreement on learning objectives and content. The teacher does not control the learning progress; the learners are responsible for controlling and reflecting on the problem solving processes themselves guided by teachers. Teachers and learners communicate and collaborate on a partnership basis, and solutions for problems are suggested and discussed. To activate the learners and motivate self-regulated learning processes, it is important to provide learners with explicit descriptions of tasks and learning objectives, including background information and a possibility for collecting ideas on the described problem (Höbarth, 2007).

The importance of guidance in problem-based learning is also discussed by Kirschner, Sweller and Clark (2006). They define direct instructional guidance "as providing information that fully explains the concepts and procedures that students are required to learn as well as learning strategy support that is compatible with human cognitive architecture" (p. 75). The authors argue that current problem based learning approaches rather focus on minimal guidance and do not take into account the cognitive architecture, e.g. the importance of short-term memory for processing information and long-term memory for storing it. They summarise empirical evidence supporting the statement that especially for learners with low experience or prior knowledge in an area, unguided inquiry and problem solving has negative effects on learning outcomes. The increased cognitive load from searching for problem solutions is too demanding for the working memory and impedes learning. Therefore, knowledge construction should be guided e.g. by provision of worked examples instead of problems in information-rich environments and through process worksheets which provide instructions on the required phases for problem solving. Guidance can only be relaxed with increasing expertise of the learners.

Reiserer and Mandl (2001) discuss the necessity to design problem-based learning environments in a way that supports central individual competences for self-regulated and collaborative learning. They consider these competences on several levels: motivational level (e.g. related to goals, interests and self-efficacy), cognitive level (e.g. related to learning strategies, meta-cognition, and management of resources), and social level (e.g. related to communication processes and the structuring of social interaction processes for collaborative knowledge construction). In the context of computer-supported learning, structuring of social interaction for the direct facilitation of interaction and collaborative learning processes is discussed in connection with the concept of collaboration scripts (e.g. Dillenbourg 2002, Weinberger, Reiserer, Ertl, Fischer & Mandl, 2005). Based on a review of educational and psychological literature, Kollar, Fischer and Hesse (2006) identified the following conceptual components of collaboration scripts: learning objectives, type of activities, sequencing features, role distribution for collaboration, and type of representation of instructions. Weinberger et al. (2005) differentiate between epistemic scripts and social scripts.

Epistemic scripts aim at structuring a task with the intention to focus the learners' attention on issues which are central for the process of collaborative knowledge construction (e.g. by providing a graphical representation of abstract aspects). Social scripts, on the other hand, provide patterns for interaction which support the structuring of learners' discourse processes (e.g. by sequencing learning phases and learning activities, or by assigning roles to learners associated to certain learning tasks). The authors found evidence for the facilitation of collaborative learning processes and individual learning outcomes through social scripts in two studies on collaborative knowledge construction in text-based communication and a video-conferencing setting. However, epistemic scripts did not proof as effective and they even hampered the individual learning outcomes of collaborative knowledge construction. Probably, learners filled in relevant concepts as induced by the epistemic script as long as it was available; however they did not internalise the concepts and developed their own conceptual understanding. Accordingly, Dillenbourg (2002) discussed the risk of over-scripting collaborative knowledge construction. Scripts can bridge collaborative learning and traditional instructional design; however following a script will seem artificial, if there is no profound reason for collaboration.

Considering the technical context of computer-based learning, an overarching element for guiding learners is the usability design of VLEs. According to the International Standards Organization (ISO) usability is defined as "effectiveness, efficiency and satisfaction with which a specified set of users can achieve a specified set of tasks in a particular environment" (ISO 9241-11:1998). In the context of website design usability is important to prevent users from "leaving" a website which will certainly happen, if they are dissatisfied with the design and if the tasks they are required to perform on the website cannot be accomplished easily, quickly and without making too many errors (Nielsen, 2000; 2003). These aspects can be transferred to the usability of VLEs: user interfaces which meet usability requirements support users to focus on the learning contents instead of being distracted by the concentration needed for using the VLE (Ihamäki & Vilpola, 2004). Results from a study by Mackey and Ho (2008) support this view. The perceived learning outcome of undergraduate students who used web-based multimedia tutorials for learning about web page creation was influenced positively by the usability factors which supported the effective design of the tutorials (e.g. the synchronisation of audio and video or the response time of the application). Meislewitz and Sandera (2008) found in a study with university students that the assessment of learning outcomes needs to take into account usability factors of the VLE (e.g. learner control, structure and organisation) because their presence or absence can influence the outcomes positively or negatively.

Feedback and support processes: In the context of designing computer-based learning activities Salmon (2002) refers to feedback on two levels: an initial level – related to the technical and social experiences of online learning at the beginning of a course, a further level – related to the learning contents and complex activities and knowledge construction processes in later stages of a course.

Hattie and Timperley (2007) see feedback as "information provided by an agent (e.g., teacher, peer, book, parent, self, experience) regarding aspects of one's performance or understanding" (p. 81). The aim of feedback is to reduce the gap between the current understanding and performance of learners and the desired goals. Hattie and Timperley (2007) review evidence on the power and effectiveness of feedback to improve teaching and learning. In order to avoid ineffective feedback, however, circumstances of feedback provision have to be carefully considered. Feedback needs to focus on the specific goals of a learning activity, the progress in reaching the goals and any option for improving this progress. Furthermore, feedback should be directed at four levels: the level of understanding a task (e.g.

corrective feedback about faulty interpretations), the level of processes for task performance (e.g. on strategies for error detection and as a cue for effective information search), the level of self-regulation with the aim to encourage performance on a task (e.g. by supporting self-control and self-direction of learning actions), and the level of the self as a person (e.g. praise of the learner) which is considered least effective due to often lacking relation to task performance aspects.

Functions of feedback from a constructivist perspective were summarised by Mory (1995; 2006). She suggests that feedback from a constructivist perspective supports learners to construct an own internal reality, to solve complex problems set into relevant contexts, to negotiate in social settings, to guide learners in dealing with various forms of representation and insufficiently structured domains, to remind them of learning objectives, and challenge their development. Reinmann (2005) points out that in pure online learning settings as well as in blended learning scenarios support and feedback are of major importance for the learning process (e.g. in order to prevent learners to drop-out of the course and to promote reflective thinking). She suggests providing personal, constructive and explicit feedback to individuals and groups of learners instead of automatic electronically generated responses to support social interaction processes, e.g. through the provision of information on opportunities for improved task solution.

Recognising learning processes: Because of the fact that this book chapter mainly builds on the description of a course which was offered outside the formal education system, the focus of this paragraph is on the recognition and validation of learning in non-formal settings, which is widely discussed in the context of lifelong learning in Europe (cf. Bjørnåvold, 2002; Werquin, 2008). In this context, Werquin (2008) sees recognition of learning as the acknowledgement that learning has taken place. Furthermore, he suggests that recognition of learning outcomes results from summative assessment processes (e.g. using methods such as observation or written examination on the basis of agreed standards to assess the level proficiency) and formative assessment processes (e.g. self-recognition through portfolio development). In contrast to the usual definition of assessment as an activity which assesses the proficiency of learners Hattie and Timperley (2007) suggest to see assessment as the activity by which feedback is provided to learners as defined above. They criticise that "most current assessments provide minimal feedback, too often because they rely on recall and are used as external accountability thermometers rather than as feedback devices that are integral to the teaching and learning process" (p. 104).

In this context, the portfolio method is shortly presented because of its relevance for qualitative and self-reflective assessment of learning (c.f. Davis & Le Mahieu, 2003; Klenowski, 2002). A (learning) portfolio can be defined as "[…] a purposeful collection of student work, that tells the story of the students' efforts, progress and achievements in (a) given area(s). This collection must include student participation in selection of portfolio content; the guidelines for selection; the criteria for judging merit; and evidence of students' self-reflection" (Arter & Spandel, 1992, p. 36). According to Davis and Le Mahieu (2003) the advantage of portfolio use in assessing learning lies in their potential to represent development over time and to provide evidence for sustaining effort and performance. Furthermore, the choice of content provides insight into the learners' understanding and learners can use the portfolio to reflect and interact with their work. Chang (2001) points to the potential of electronic portfolios as means of storing, recording and sharing student work online and thus enhance interaction between learners and teachers. According to Attwell (2005) an electronic portfolio can function to support learners' recog-

nition of learning to record personal formal and non-formal learning processes, to reflect on these processes, plan further learning activities, and to validate learning through providing evidence for the achievements. Chang (2001) reports results from a user evaluation of a Web-Based Learning Portfolio (WBLP) and mentions positive effects of the portfolio use during a university course on "Computer and Instruction". The impact on learning was assessed positively, e.g. considering the helpfulness of the portfolio for knowing about learning outcomes of other learners and the feedback provided by the teacher and other learners. Browsing the WBLP of other learners supported the reflection on shortcomings in the own learning process, facilitated mutual understanding, and improved relationships.

Additionally, concept mapping is mentioned here as one complementary method to portfolio usage. Concept mapping can be considered appropriate for organised and visualised recognition of learning since concept maps facilitate the construction of individual knowledge, following on phases of collaborative knowledge construction (Conceição, Desnoyers & Baldor, 2008). In their study the authors found that concept maps supported students "to prioritize information, integrate concepts, confirm knowledge, and construct new knowledge" (p. 448). The reflective components of the concept mapping tasks and the iterative process of map development are seen as most valuable for rethinking concepts based on knowledge acquired during discussions with other learners. However, Cañas and Novak (2006) discussed reasons for problems that learners might have with concept maps and referred to technically imposed challenges, a lack of training of learners and teachers in using this method, or underestimation of the theoretical foundation of concept mapping.

DESIGNING COURSES WITH MOODLE UTILISING COLLABORATION TOOLS

Moodle is an Open Source Virtual Learning Environment (VLE) which is widely used to enhance educational courses with new media, either as pure online courses or as blended learning courses, in which the VLE is used to supplement face-to-face sessions. The educational philosophy behind Moodle is social constructivism, "based on the idea that people learn best when they are engaged in a social process of constructing knowledge through the act of constructing an artefact for others" (Cole, & Foster, 2007, p. 4). This is implemented in Moodle by learning tools which have a strong emphasis on providing applications for discussions and knowledge sharing, rather than a focus on the mere presentation of static content.

The four standard Moodle activities forum, wiki, chat, and glossary are especially suited to support collaboration and group work. These four activities will be looked at taking into account the three central aspects for designing constructivist online learning environments - "guiding learners", "feedback processes", "recognizing learning processes" - laid out earlier. In addition to these activities the optional integration of an ePortfolio tool into Moodle as well as general aspects of usability and accessibility are taken into consideration.

The *Moodle forum* can be best used for asynchronous discussions and knowledge exchange between participants and tutors, and can be considered as the central means for text-based communication within the VLE. It provides several technical moderation options and can be regarded as well suited for various collaborative learning activities (e.g. expert interviews, peer assessment activities, role plays, etc.) as well as a complementary tool to be used in combination with other Moodle tools. The forum tool is integrated in each Moodle course by default and can be described as a kind of online message board in which the threaded structure of discussions allows for tracking the learners' and tutors' contributions (Cole, & Foster, 2007), which in consequence supports the recognition of learning processes over time. The authors point out that due to the asynchronous nature of the tool, learners can take their time for formulating and reflecting on their contributions. In order to guide and stimulate learners' discussions Cole and Foster (2007) recommend the use of ice-breaker questions with a strong prompt (p. 80). Furthermore, to keep the discussion alive, course goals need to be pointed out clearly and contributions should be appreciated by the tutor, e.g. by referring to the online discussions during face-to-face lessons. The authors, moreover, suggest that "good moderation and intelligent deployment of discussion opportunities are more important to the success of a course than the static content" (p. 80). A study by Mazzolini and Madison (2007) about the role of instructors in discussion forums of pure online learning settings shows that the way of moderation is central to the success of a forum. In forums, where instructors made too many and long postings, and tried actively to initiate new topics, the participants reduced the amount and length of their contributions. Nevertheless, high quality instructor postings may support learning; and therefore the quality of a forum discussion cannot be measured by the overall amount of postings. Although it did not influence participation of students, they appreciated if instructors answered questions and asked follow-up questions during their postings. However, the survey revealed that only a few instructors followed this approach.

The *Moodle chat* is a communication tool that supports real-time communication between participants. According to Cole and Foster (2007), the quality of a chat is improved by good moderation and the formulation of basic rules, because it can be hard for participants to follow a discussion where everyone is chatting at the same time. This also ties in very well with the notion of guiding learners. The chat can be used for several communication activities, e.g. exchange between tutors and students during a scheduled consultation-hour or for group work which requires synchronous discussions. The tool is therefore very well suited for providing ad hoc support and feedback to learners. Since chat protocols can be made available to learners also after the actual chat session, they may also be used as artefacts for the recognition of students' work.

The *Moodle wiki* allows learners to create a joint product by working collaboratively on a shared document. Collaborative wiki tasks could be the joint note taking on a lecture or brainstorming on a certain topic. At this point it should be noted that a combination of Moodle tools seems reasonable for the completion of tasks. In the case of the wiki tool the collaborative learning process can be specifically supported by the additional use of the forum for feedback provision. With regards to guiding learners Cole and Foster (2007) consider the communication of a wiki's purpose and goals of central importance for the effective implementation of the wiki tool. Additionally, the tutor should specify an editing policy, e.g. what to do in case of inappropriate contributions.

The main purpose of the *Moodle glossary* is the structured collection of terms and expert vocabulary which can be automatically linked if used in other tools, e.g. in forum entries. Due to its integrated comment functionality it also supports collaboration as well as the possibility to support and guide learners. By default setting, the glossary allows only one author per entry. However, by giving learners extended editing rights wiki-like collaboration on the entries is possible in addition to the standard commentary functionality. To trigger entries of students Cole and Foster (2007) suggest inserting some sample entries right from the beginning and ask students to complete the glossary collaboratively by assigning the responsibility for creating definitions to students. Again, this approach allows for providing structured guidance to learners, e.g. by outlining the components of a definition that should be included for each entry.

As described earlier *ePortfolios* are specifically suited for the recognition of individual as well as social learning processes, but also often include an optional sharing of contents with peers. Moodle provides several options for implementing the portfolio method, e.g. by giving each student a wiki for individual collection of and reflection on content relevant to their learning activities, or even by setting up separate Moodle course spaces for learners, where they get overall editing rights and develop their ePortfolio with the available Moodle tools. However, there is also the possibility for a seamless integration of specific ePortfolio tools into Moodle, e.g. through installing the Exabis ePortfolio block (http://www.moodlekurse.org) or linking it to external tools like Mahara (http://mahara.org). Both tools provide extensive ePortfolio functionalities for note taking, sharing notes with peers and commenting on each other's entries. Exporting the ePortfolio data in Shareable Content Object Reference Model (SCORM)-format is also possible for continuing the recognition of learning processes in other VLEs.

A final and overarching aspect that should be considered when designing online learning offers is the aspect of *usability and accessibility*. According to McNaught (2006) Moodle meets basic web-accessibility requirements. Furthermore, the continuous development of Moodle takes accessibility aspects into account (Moodle Accessibility Specification, 2007). However, Moodle course implementation can be challenging taking into account critical usability and accessibility aspects of website design, e.g. concerning homogenous design of navigation throughout different courses and the possibilities to structure content in the topics of a course without producing lists of text and links that can be accessed only by extensive page scrolling. Therefore, course designers should critically reflect on the usability of the learning offer designed, and if possible, carry out basic usability testing to ensure that the learning offer is presented as straightforward and homogeneous as possible. Ideally, the VLE should be designed in a way that provides learners with the appropriate amount of guidance that allows learners to focus on contents and learning activities rather than being distracted by an unclear design.

ICT4T ONLINE COURSE: A GOOD PRACTICE EXAMPLE OF CONSTRUCTIVIST COURSE DESIGN

The ICT4T online course was targeted at trainers and training organisers with an interest in computer-based teaching for the specific target group of senior learners. It was offered three times free of charge to an international audience as a pure online offer without face-to-face contact between the participants. 48 people from several European countries and with different work related backgrounds and experiences participated in at least some of the 8 consecutive modules; 22 people completed all eight course modules. Two tutors guided the learners through the 8 weeks duration of each of the three course offers.

The course was designed to showcase the appropriate implementation of learning activities in Virtual Learning Environments (VLEs) taking into account the special needs of older people in the context of learning with new media and web 2.0 applications. By this approach, the trainers had the chance to get a first hand experience on learning with VLEs from a senior learner perspective. The VLE Moodle was chosen for the implementation of the ICT4T course offers due to its social constructivist learning approach basis. The focus was on problem-based learning activities, reflection processes, feedback measures, and the interaction of learners and tutors (Petter & Helling, 2008).

In the following, the course is described taking into account the three dimensions laid out in the theoretical chapter above. Examples from the first of the three course offers are provided to illustrate the learning and knowledge construction processes of the learners. The experiences of the authors of this chapter made in implementing

and tutoring the ICT4T course with Moodle are taken into account. Based on the positive results from the course evaluation (see below) this course can be considered as a good practice example for constructivist course design and collaborative knowledge construction.

Guiding Learners

The pedagogical approach of the ICT4T course focused on self-guided and collaborative learning activities from a social constructivist perspective, taking into account the facilitation of interaction between participants (Kearney, 2007). To support these processes the course was created as a consistent learning environment where learners could easily find all relevant information and focus their cognitive resources on the tasks and activities. The didactical structuring of the Moodle pages aimed at providing clear information about the learning objectives for each module and activity, and the expected individual and collaborative learning processes were described in specific task descriptions and by defining the expected outcomes. All necessary resources and learning materials were provided in the learning environment and grouped together with the respective task descriptions. By this, the learners had a common starting point for negotiating a shared understanding of the learning situation. However, learners could bring in own resources as well and select from additional offers according to their personal interests which were not obligatory for task completion. The following screenshot (figure 1) shows the information for one learning activity available to learners at first sight.

This overview provided the learners with several details which helped them to organise the completion of the activity in a self-regulated way. On first sight, the learners recognise that this activity is collaborative (instead of individual) and requires input to a forum discussion from all participants. The indicated timing suggests that it should be completed by the end of the week; however, due to its collaborative nature learners

Figure 1. Screenshot of an activity overview

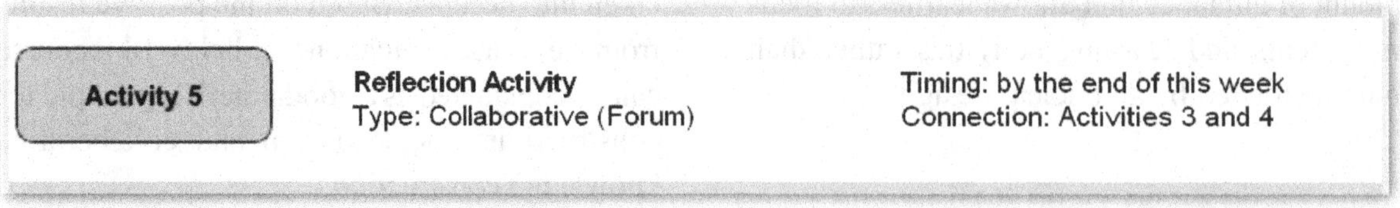

Activity 5	**Reflection Activity** Type: Collaborative (Forum)	Timing: by the end of this week Connection: Activities 3 and 4

were additionally reminded not to start working on the activity on the last day of the week because this would prevent collaborative knowledge construction through joint discussion. Furthermore, the learners were informed about a connection between this activity and the activities 3 and 4 of the same module which need to be completed first to ensure successful knowledge construction related to the specific objectives of the activity.

The learning materials prepared for each activity (e.g. videos, articles, web resources) were to be seen as background information, meant to provide the learners with a common understanding on a task-related topic and to initiate discussions and reflections on theses contents. For this reason, all learning activities were connected to different online collaboration tools provided by the VLE Moodle (e.g. forum, chat, wiki, and glossary). Several of the activities required from participants to work on tasks and related background material individually as a kind of preparation for the following collaborative interaction of participants. Such collaborative activities involved the exchange of information and the discussion of practical problems from several perspectives and based on the different experiences and knowledge of the participants. One of the interactive learning activities implemented during the course is the role play which was organised in a chat session during one of the modules. Its objective was to provoke reflection on the problem of designing an ICT-based learning offer for people with different age-related impairments, taking into account multiple perspectives such as the needs of the impaired learners and those of the course

designers. For preparation of the role play, the participants had to read information on the role they chose to represent and they were offered simulation activities in which they could collect experiences of impairment-related problems in using computers. By this, it was ensured that all learners had some knowledge – based on information material and experiences – in order to be able to actively contribute to the discussion (for more detailed information on the learning activities see "ICT4T Course Description & Materials", available at http://www.ict4t.net/materials).

Knowledge construction on the collaborative level was furthermore encouraged by explicit reflection activities. Initiating questions were provided in the task descriptions and by tutors to trigger reflective discussions (see figure 2). The learners posted their opinions to the questions, and in several cases – as intended – the discussion developed and went in a direction which focused on details, experiences and information relevant to the personal situation of each of the participants, giving the others the opportunity to learn from each others' input. The heterogeneity of the learner group proved very advantageous in the context of these reflection activities. Especially the differences in age and training experiences of the participants as well as the level of their technical competences helped to trigger reflection.

In figure 3 postings produced in the context of the above displayed reflection activity show how participants reacted on each other's comments and made contributions about new aspects not considered before. It was in the responsibility of each of the learners to further reflect on the

Figure 2. Screenshot of a reflection activity task description

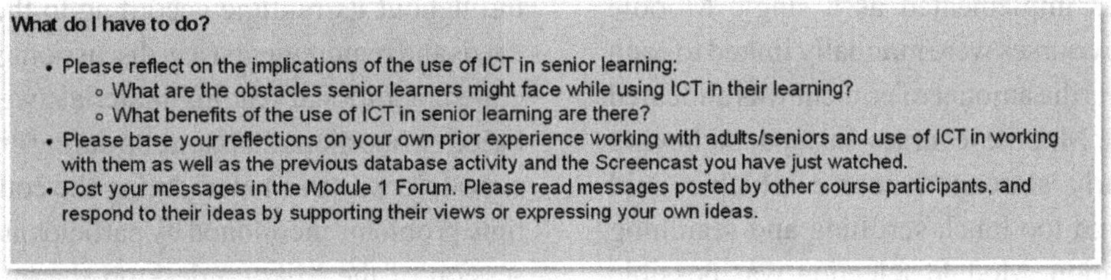

What do I have to do?
- Please reflect on the implications of the use of ICT in senior learning:
  - What are the obstacles senior learners might face while using ICT in their learning?
  - What benefits of the use of ICT in senior learning are there?
- Please base your reflections on your own prior experience working with adults/seniors and use of ICT in working with them as well as the previous database activity and the Screencast you have just watched.
- Post your messages in the Module 1 Forum. Please read messages posted by other course participants, and respond to their ideas by supporting their views or expressing your own ideas.

aspects that came up in the discussion process and deepen the knowledge on the different perspectives according to their specific interest, e.g. by continuing discussions in an extra thread, by exchange of information via eMail, by taking notes in the ePortfolio, by researching information on the internet, etc.

It has to be mentioned at this point that learning progress during the course was not the sole concern of the course participants but also included the course tutors, resulting from the input provided by participants. For example, the participants suggested the use of the Mikogo desktop sharing tool (http://www.mikogo.com) which was new to the tutors, and the experiences of using this tool brought in by two of the participants were valuable in the interactive process of testing the tool and constructing knowledge about its implementation

possibilities in training senior learners. Additionally, the fact that some of the participating trainers were seniors themselves was valuable for the learning experience; they formed an important source of knowledge and experiences for the tutors as well as for the other participants.

Similar to the consistent didactical design of the VLE the usability design of the ICT4T learning environment aimed at supporting self-guided learning processes and knowledge construction. The usability aspects aimed at directing the learners' attention to the learning activities and facilitating recognition of didactical elements by making consistent use of structures, colours and labels.

Several adaptations were made during the course implementation process such as simplifying site navigation and supporting recognition of learning activities and content by carefully

Figure 3. Postings in the Moodle forum on a reflection activity

Learner 1: I fully agree with Learner 2's comments on the obstacles, in particular I can point to my own difficulty in learning how to use this forum, very senior person, new to Moodle, etc. Learner 3's comment about learning step by step is important, as Senior learners are learning slowly to understand the jargon, technology - they are aware of the benefits of learning but have to understand it will not happen quickly.

Learner 4: The contribution of Learner 2 is indeed very interesting but in getting the seniors interested we tutors will need to patiently go step by step as Learner 3 rightly pointed out but it is also important that threaded discussions should not be lengthy in order to continue to sustain their interest. So software designer an tutor need to work a good idea on that.

Learner 5: Hmm, I think the main benefit is to open the world for new contacts, possibilities to learn from other people in other contexts, having discussions and conversations with people I could not meet otherwise, learn independent of f2f trainers, adapting the speed of learning to my own needs, etc. If learning materials are really made for the target group they could be a stimulus as well but my experience of available materials is different ...

structuring the Moodle sites. Each ICT4T course module was implemented as a single Moodle course. The courses were manually linked to each other. By this the amount of content was allocated to different Moodle courses instead of having one unclearly structured course which would have required too much scrolling and searching for information. Module selection was possible on a start page on a superior level, including an overview and description of each module's aim, objectives and assessment criteria. Figure 4 displays the structure implemented for each of the ICT4T course modules. The navigation options were stripped down and simplified as much as possible. For example, navigation blocks were located on the left of each site only, and redundant links were hidden in the breadcrumb menu. From the numerous available navigation blocks only the three blocks considered most relevant in the context of the course were chosen, e.g. People, Online Users, and ePortfolio. The People and Online Users blocks support communication processes between learners by providing an easy option for contacting other course participants. The ePortfolio block was always present to give the learners the possibility to take notes on individual reflections and ideas. Additionally, a navigation block for switching between different levels of the course (e.g. Home, Module Description and Module Activities) was inserted manually. Furthermore, each module had an activities table in the central area of the module site, including navigation buttons for direct access to the learning activities. By this the presentation of too much text and information in the centre window was avoided. The learning activities itself were again designed consistently throughout all modules of the course.

Feedback and Support Processes

Based on the constructivist learning approach, the tutors had a rather supportive role by guiding the learners through the learning environment and designing and adapting the course in advance and throughout its runtime according to the learners' needs and requirements (e.g. discussions were moderated, additional reading materials were offered based on questions that came up during discussions, a module was shortened during the course due to time problems mentioned by participants, a testing session of the Mikogo desktop sharing tool was organised as wished by participants). Feedback related to learning contents and learning activities was given in a personal and qualitative way. It was not based on results of tests and questioning but on the contributions of the participants to forum discussions, their ePortfolio, and group activities. Depending on the activity and structure of the related tasks, the tutors provided personal feedback either for individuals, for working groups or for all participants together. Especially in the discussion forums feedback was provided by summarising the contributions of participants in a structured way and, if necessary, by posting follow-up questions to guide the process of discussion and collaborative knowledge construction in the direction specified in the learning objectives of the related activity.

In addition to these structured feedback measures which addressed the learning content and processes the participants were offered several *explicit* support measures which aimed at supporting the use of the VLE from a technical perspective (cf. Salmon, 2002); and consequently to reduce distraction by problems related to technical difficulties and challenges of computer usage. These, support measures were offered right from the beginning of the course.

• Help section: From the start page of the course the participants had access to a help section with information on "how to use this learning environment". It included several screencast videos about the usage of the ICT4T learning environment, which was structured differently to a standard Moodle installation (see above, figure 4). The help section was also linked directly

Figure 4. Screenshot – ICT4T course module. (© 2009, Institute for future studies, Austria)

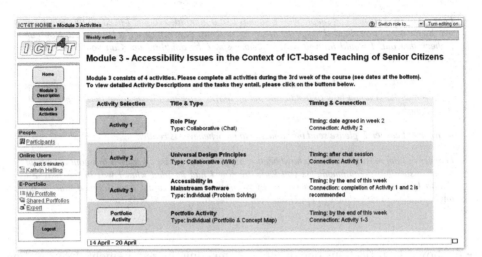

from certain critical points within the learning activities of the course modules, e.g. if the use of the Moodle wiki was suggested, a link to the relevant screencast explaining the wiki functionalities was provided.

- Personal Help: The learners had also the possibility to receive personal and individual help from the course tutors. Several communication channels were offered for this purpose, e.g. eMail, a forum with a special FAQ section, Skype-IDs (http://www.skype.com) and a mobile number. Especially in the beginning of the course, eMail was used by several participants who faced login problems or problems with certain file formats and plug-ins. Additionally, the support offered in the forum was available to all participants. They had the possibility to post questions, to react on each other's requests, and to profit from responses already provided by tutors or other participants.

Figure 5 shows an excerpt from a dialogue in one of the forums. It provides an example for the collaboration of participants on a technical support level. It is only a short insight in this kind of collaboration processes, however it represents a wide range of participant support which came up during the course, ranging from the provision of technical manuals to the offer of sending a laptop – which had served its time for one participant but was still fully operative – to another participant who had severe equipment problems due to living in Nigeria.

Recognising Learning Processes

For the recognition of individual learning processes the participants were asked at the end of each module to reflect on the module's learning activities. The integrated ePortfolio application for Moodle constituted the most important element for these reflection activities. The participants were suggested to use the ePortfolio for the individual monitoring of their learning progress as well as for collecting information relevant to their personal learning objectives. The ePortfolio allowed participants to take individual notes, upload files and collect internet addresses. Moreover, by sharing the contents of the ePortfolio with the tutors and other participants on a voluntary basis the exchange of personal ideas and perspectives was supported. The following excerpt from an ePort-

Figure 5. Postings in a Moodle forum on support issues

Learner 6: Hi, Learner 7, <simple view> sounds like a good idea to me. I need all the help I can get. By the way, I downloaded Skype the other day and now I am not sure if it is installed. How can I check that out. I would hate to waste memory space by doubling up. Can you help? Senior learner Learner 6

Learner 7: Hi, Learner 6! I will send you an e-mail message with instructions as word document (with screenshots) about how to install and set up Skype. Give me please some time to prepare it. Best regards.

Learner 4: Learner 7, please send the same file to me whenever is ready.

Learner 6: I am most grateful, you have been so supportive ever since I started this course without the necessary basic equipment. As you know by now I had no idea what I was in for. maybe I should have given up, but that is not really an option for me, and I have learned quite a bit anyhow. Maybe I can still catch up. Thank you, Learner 6

folio (figure 6) shows the reflections one of the participants made on the course, its content and the personal learning progress and contributions.

Additionally, the participants were offered the online mind mapping tool Mindmeister (http://www.mindmeister.com) as another means of reflecting on and recognising their learning progress. The tool complemented the rather text-based ePortfolio by providing a way for visual representation of contents. Figure 7 shows a part of a concept map produced by one of the course participants. Starting from a box in the middle which represents the complete ICT4T online course the concept map shows four main branches representing four course modules. For "Module 2 – Age Related Needs" personally important notes on the module content are displayed. The learners had the possibility to upload the completed concept to the ePortfolio and share it with the other course participants and tutors.

A certificate was issued after the course to confirm successful participation. The certificate was based on certain assessment criteria such as the quality of the forum discussions or the usage of the ePortfolio. The learners were informed about the specific criteria in advance of the course. In order to support them in meeting the assessment requirements, additional criteria were specified on the level of each learning activity, and the tutors continuously monitored the learners' progress in

meeting the requirements by providing personal and individual feedback throughout the duration of the course.

EVALUATION RESULTS

In the following, the evaluation results of the ICT4T course are summarised from the data and report provided by the evaluating institution IACM/FORTH (2008) and based on observations of the course tutors. The results are structured according to their relevance for the aspects of *guiding learners, feedback and support processes* and *recognition of learning*.

For the purpose of data collection an online questionnaire was made available to the participants and drop-outs of the ICT4T courses after course completion. In total all 48 learners participating in one of the three online courses were asked to fill the questionnaire. Eventually, 18 out of the 22 students who received a certificate for successful completion of one of the three ICT4T courses completed the questionnaire; 8 questionnaires were answered by course drop-outs. The questionnaire primarily contained closed questions (likert scale) on the contents, didactical and usability design and e-learning tools used during the courses. Further questions concerned tutor-student interactions as well as students'

Figure 6. Learner's reflection in the ePortfolio on two modules

Week 2

Structured prompts from the tutors are very helpful in the forum. Helps to keep focused on the main points. All information - text and videos is very clear and informative.
Very interesting to hear the comments of other members in the group especially the members who are seniors!
Learnt about two types of strategies - encouraging seniors to teach other seniors and implementing inter generational contact in learning situation.
Contribution OK.

Week 4

Learnt about new learning theory - connectivism for the Internet age! Also learnt about the emphasis on learning communities- which is now being recommended.
Hard to generalise about how seniors learn. There seem to be so many factors. Maybe it is not possible to generalize too much. Beginning to wonder if seniors really do learn any differently from younger people - or does it just depend on the individual and their own experiences and learning styles etc. Maybe more concrete examples in the following sections will clarify.
Participation - not so good this week.
Did not manage to get interview with suitable senior learner.
Summary of how seniors learn is still incomplete.
Contribution to forums was OK I think.

views about their learning. Course drop-outs were additionally asked to answer a separate set of questions on their reasons for dropping out.

Guiding Learners. The general structuring of the course and its activities was evaluated very positively by course participants. About 80% stated that the course was well structured but at the same time left enough room for students' initiatives. The clear description of module activities as well as assessment criteria was appreciated by almost 90% of the respondents. With regards to guidance, in addition to the general module and activity descriptions, 80% found templates offered to pre-structure contributions for some tasks very

helpful. These results suggest that course participants were offered the right amount of structural guidance necessary to complete the activities of the online courses.

With regards to the usability of the VLE and its tools, the majority of active course participants (between 80-90%, depending on the tool) did not face considerable difficulties in using the collaborative tools offered in the Virtual Learning Environment (VLE) and no serious technology barriers were encountered. This result probably is affected by the good prior knowledge of participants. When asked to evaluate their own competences with regards to e-Learning technologies,

Figure 7. Part of a concept map produced by a participant of one of the ICT4T courses

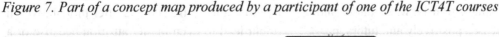
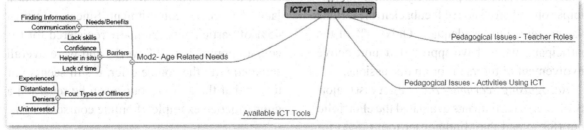

61% stated to have good knowledge, skills and understanding of e-Learning technologies and 33% good prior knowledge of e-course design. The course tutors also observed that after the first orientation phase, in which learners explored the VLE and got familiar with it through completing the first activities, the learners seemed to feel quite comfortable with the course structuring (e.g. navigation, consistence of design). Results from a usability analysis performed by the University of Linz (2008) also show that the course design met main usability criteria (e.g. with regard to site navigation, access to learning materials, page structure and graphical design).

Feedback and Support Processes. The climate during the course can be described as supportive due to the feedback provided in the VLE and the interaction of tutors and participants with regard to support issues. About 90% of the participants agreed that a climate of supportiveness between students and tutors was developed. Although some participants were undecided regarding the constructiveness of the interaction between students, 80% of the students consented that reading comments and ideas from other participants was very important for their learning, and they stated to have gained knowledge and competences relevant and valuable for their daily work. The participants (94%) reported further that they received as much individual feedback and support as needed by the course tutors. Furthermore, the tutors experienced that support was needed mainly in the beginning of the online course – especially with regard to technical problems, and with the progress of the course the participants also directly supported each other. The interaction between tutors and students was assessed positively and tutors' participation and provision of feedback in the forums was perceived to be adequate. Only 24% of the participants would have appreciated more active involvement of tutors in forum discussions.

Recognising Learning Processes. A vast majority of course participants evaluated the ePortfolio tool (88%) and the Mindmeister tool (75%) for

the development of concept maps positively. However, only 50% of the respondents agreed that the concept map activities contributed a lot to their learning, and only a few learners developed extensive maps with lots of nodes and branches. Reasons might be the learners' lack of familiarity with or a personal disliking of this reflective technique. The same learner behaviour was observed by the tutors regarding the use of the integrated ePortfolio tool. Only few learners used this opportunity to reflect regularly and in depth on their learning processes, or comment on others' ePortfolio entries. Nevertheless, the entries made by participants proved very helpful to tutors to give very specific feedback and guidance to learners, and also helped to assess individual learning progress.

All in all, the evaluation results point to the fact that the active course participants were overall satisfied with the design and implementation of the online course, and the modular course structure provided response to their learning interests which, however, were quite heterogeneous (e.g. getting a first hand experience on online learning, practice English, improve skills for the design and delivery of online courses, meeting people who share an interest in teaching senior people). Furthermore, 7 out of 8 drop outs stated that the reason for dropping out was related to unexpected personal issues and not to the course and its design. While valid data on drop-out rates for other free online course offers is scarce, figures primarily from higher education courses suggest drop-out rates as high as 80% (Flood, 2002) or between 20-50% (Diaz, 2002). The ICT4T course seems to fit that picture, being a free course offer though, which might lead to even higher attrition because of a lack of financial commitment. Since more than 45% of participants originally registered for the courses completed all 8 weeks and were overall satisfied with the course offer, it still seems fair to say that the ICT4T course can be regarded a good practice example of online course design.

CONCLUSION

The modular ICT4T online course was designed from a perspective of situated learning and instruction, based on a constructivist understanding of learning (cf. Mandl et al., 2002). It aimed at supporting collaborative knowledge construction by guiding learners through clear structuring of the learning environment and activities, by providing constructive and explicit feedback and support, and by initiating self-reflective recognition of learning processes. The evaluation results showed a general satisfaction of learners with the course and specifically with regard to the structuring of the learning environment, the supportive climate and social interaction processes. Therefore, the ICT4T online course can be considered a good practice example of constructivist course design with the Virtual Learning Environment (VLE) Moodle.

Guidance for learners was implemented from two perspectives. On the one hand, the didactical design of learning activities aimed at drawing the learners' attention to relevant aspects of a task. Collaborative knowledge construction was supported by structuring the expected learning processes (e.g. by clearly suggesting a timeframe for the production of collaborative outcomes or the processes of joint reflection and discussion on a topic) and pre-structuring learning materials (e.g. the provision of templates for wiki documents which were then jointly edited by all learners). The evaluation results show that the clear task descriptions and didactical structuring of learning activities were appreciated by learners and seen as supportive for the completion of the several learning activities.

On the other hand, the graphical and usability design aimed at focusing the learners' attention on the learning content (cf. Ihamäki & Vilpola, 2004) and supporting the easy and efficient performance of interactions with the learning environment (cf. Nielson, 2000; 2003). The usability evaluation provided positive results with regard to this respect. However, in a critical reflection of the course

design it has to be admitted that strictly tested against technical accessibility criteria (defined as the possibility for "people with disabilities [to] perceive, understand, navigate, and interact with the Web"; W3C, 2005) the VLE could only meet some requirements. In this context, course designers might find themselves confronted with the following dilemma: on the one hand – based on their pedagogical competences – they are supposed to design a VLE supportive for collaborative knowledge construction; on the other hand, including supportive usability and accessibility aspects in an online course requires technical competences (e.g. knowledge of programming languages, web design, website administration) which educational staff is often lacking. However, these competences are especially important, as the way of providing content, help structures and motivating task design further influences accessibility of a VLE (cf. McNaught, 2006)

The experiences from designing the ICT4T online course showed that finding a balance between pedagogical and usability aspects can be challenging. Therefore, the implementation of online courses in accordance with usability and accessibility should be considered in training trainers. The central concern, however, should still be to equip trainers with the necessary competences to ensure effective course design, and as a consequence support learners in their collaborative knowledge construction processes in a VLE.

The provision of feedback in the course was based on interaction among participants as well as on constructive and personal contributions from the tutors. The evaluation results proof that a climate of supportiveness was reached among trainers and course participants, and taking into account comments and ideas from other participants was important for the individual learning processes.

With regards to the separate help section provided within the VLE, the screencast videos on the ICT4T course navigation and the usage of the tools were seen to be most helpful, since they introduced learners to the course and VLE in a quick and effective way and provided help if the course participants faced problems using the VLE and its tools. Only a few learners had difficulties accessing the provided videos, and additional support channels (e.g. eMail, forum) helped to solve individual problems in a timely manner. The clear communication of support measures appears, in any case, essential for a successful implementation of an online course.

Integrating self-reflection tools such as eP-ortfolio (cf. Atwell, 2005) and concept mapping (c.f. Conceição et al., 2008) for the recognition of learning in a VLE was considered supportive for learners' knowledge construction and reflection processes. In the case of the ICT4T online course, the results of the evaluation support this expected outcome, and the tools were in general assessed positively by the majority of participants. However, the participants did not work on the reflection activities to the extent intended by the course designers, although they were introduced to learners with the same structuring and detailed description of the tasks and its objectives as the other learning activities. As Salmon (2002) puts it, the completion of reflection activities is depended on the learners' individual preferences, e.g. they might either enjoy reflection or see it as something which prevents them from moving forwards within the course. Therefore, inviting and encouraging learners' expression of personal views and experiences and questioning the views of others is vital to effectively implement the important reflection activities. Additionally, a general lack of familiarity with reflection tools might be a reason for the low engagement of learners. Although more and more projects on ePortfolio use in e.g. workplace learning and education of adults and adolescents are initiated, the experience of its use outside formal learning settings is low (Attwell, 2005) and relevant competencies for ePortfolio implementation in educational settings still need to be developed by learners and trainers alike (Attwell, Chrzaszcz, Pallister, Hornung-Prähäuser

& Hilzenhauser, 2007).

In conclusion, there are challenging aspects worth considering for future improvement of the course to better facilitate learning processes through guidance, feedback and support processes, and the recognition of the actual knowledge construction processes. Nevertheless, the ICT4T course can be seen as good practice example which provides valuable experience of and insights into designing and implementing a Virtual Learning Environment for collaborative knowledge construction.

REFERENCES

W3C Web Accessibility Initiative. (2005). *Introduction to Web Accessibility, Version: 2.0*. Retrieved January 7, 2009, from http://www.w3.org/WAI/intro/accessibility.php

Arter, J. A., & Spandel, V. (1992). Using portfolios of student work in instruction and assessment. *Educational Measurement: Issues and Practice, 11*(1), 36–44. doi:10.1111/j.1745-3992.1992.tb00230.x

Attwell, G. (2005). *Recognising Learning: Educational and pedagogic issues in e-Portfolios*. Retrieved February 9, 2008, from http://www.knownet.com/writing/weblogs/Graham_Attwell/entries/ 5565143946/7575578504/attach/graham_cambridge.pdf.

Bjørnåvold, J. (2002). Identification, assessment and recognition of non-formal learning: European tendencies. In European Centre for the Development of Vocational Training (CEDEFOP) (Ed.), AGORA V. Identification, evaluation and recognition of non-formal learning (pp. 9-32). Luxembourg: Office for Official Publications of the European Communities. Bromme, R., Hesse, F. W. & Spada, H. (Eds.), Barriers and Biases in Computer-Mediated Knowledge Communication. New York: Springer.

Cañas, A. J., & Novak, J. D. (2006). Re-examining the foundations for effective use of concept maps. In A. J. Cañas & J. D. Novak (Eds.), *Proceedings of the Second International Conference on Concept Mapping* (pp. 247-255). San Jose, Costa Rica: Universidad de Costa Rica.

Chang, C. (2001). A study on the evaluation and effectiveness analysis of web-based learning portfolio. *British Journal of Educational Technology, 32*(4), 435–458. doi:10.1111/1467-8535.00212

Cole, J., & Foster, H. (2007). Using Moodle (2nd Ed.). Sebastopol, CA: O'Reilley.

Collins, A., Brown, J. S., & Duguid, P. (1989). Situated Learning and the Culture of Learning. *Education Researcher, 18*(1), 32–42.

Conceição, C., Desnoyers, M., & Baldor, J. (2008). Individual construction of knowledge in an online community through concept maps. In A. J. Cañas, P. Reiska, M. Åhlberg, & J. D. Novak (Eds.), *Proceedings of the Third International Conference on Concept Mapping* (Vol. 2, pp. 445-452). Retrieved February 7, 2009, from http://cmc.ihmc.us/cmc2008/cmc2008Program.html

Davies, A., & Le Mahieu, P. (2003). Assessment for learning: reconsidering portfolios and research evidence. In Segers, M., Dochy, F., & Cascallar, E. (Eds.), *Innovation and Change in Professional Education: Optimising New Modes of Assessment: In Search of Qualities and Standards* (pp. 141–169). Dordrecht: Kluwer Academic Publishers. doi:10.1007/0-306-48125-1_7

Diaz, P. D. (2002). Online Drop Rates Revisited. *The Technology Source, May/June 2002*. Retrieved June 4, 2009, from http://technologysource.org/article/online_drop_rates_revisited/

Dillenbourg, P. (2002). Over-scripting CSCL: The risks of blending collaborative learning with instructional design. In Kirschner, P. A. (Ed.), *Three worlds of CSCL. Can we support CSCL* (pp. 61–91). Heerlen, The Netherlands: Open Universiteit Nederland.

Flood, J. (2002). Read all about it: online learning facing 80% attrition rates. *Turkish Online Journal of Distance Education, 2*(2). Retrieved June 4, 2009, from http://tojde.anadolu.edu.tr/tojde6/articles/ jim2.htm

Hattie, J., & Timperley, H. (2007). The power of feedback. *Review of Educational Research, 77*(1), 81-112. Retrieved May 24, 2009 from http://rer.sagepub.com/cgi/content/abstract/77/1/81

Höbarth, U. (2007). Konstruktivistisches Lernen mit Moodle. Praktische Einsatzmöglichkeiten in Bildungsinstitutionen. [Constructivist Learning with Moodle. Practical application possibilities in educational institutions]. Boizenburg, Germany: vwh Verlag.

IACM/FORTH. (2008). *ICT4T Final Evaluation Report* [Internal Project Document]. Retrieved February 14, 2009, from http://www.ict4t.net/?q=system/files/Final+Evaluation+Report.pdf

Ihamäki. H. & Vilpola, I. (2004). Usability of a Virtual Learning Environment concerning safety at work. *Electronic Journal on e-Learning, 2*(1), 103-112.

ISO 9241-11:1998. (2008). *Ergonomic requirements for office work with visual display terminals (VDTs) - Part 11: Guidance on usability* [ISO Standard]. Retrieved January 7, 2009, from http://www.iso.org/iso/iso_catalogue/catalogue_tc/catalogue_detail.htm?csnumber=16883

Jonassen, D. H. (Ed., 2. Edition), Handbook of Research on Educational Communications and Technology. Mahwah, NJ: Lawrence Erlbaum.

Kearney, N. (2007). *Pedagogical Model for the ICT4T course including a draft course structure* [Internal Project Document]. Retrieved February 7, 2009, from http://www.ict4t.net/?q=system/ files/ICT4T_WP4_Pedagogical_Model.doc

Kirschner, P. A., Sweller, J., & Clark, R. E. (2006). Why Minimal Guidance During Instruction Does Not Work: An Analysis of the Failure of Constructivist, Discovery, Problem-Based, Experiential, and Inquiry-Based Teaching. *Educational Psychologist, 41*(2), 75–86. doi:10.1207/s15326985ep4102_1

Klenowski, V. (2002). *Developing Portfolios for Learning and Assessment. Processes and Principles*. London: Routledge.

Kollar, I., Fischer, H., & Hesse, F. W. (2006). Collaboration scripts – a conceptual analysis. *Educational Psychology Review, 18*(2), 159–185. doi:10.1007/s10648-006-9007-2

Lave, J., & Wenger, E. (1991). *Situated learning. Legitimate peripheral participation*. Cambridge, UK: University Press.

Mackey, T. P., & Ho, J. (2008). Exploring the relationships between Web usability and students' perceived learning in Web-based multimedia (WBMM) tutorials. *Computers & Education, 50*(1), 386–409. doi:10.1016/j.compedu.2006.08.006

Mandl, H., Gruber, H., & Renkl, A. (2002). Situiertes Lernen in multimedialen Lernumgebungen. [Situated Learning in multi-media learning environments] In Issing, L. J., & Klimsa, P. (Eds.), *Information und Lernen mit Multimedia und Internet. Lehrbuch für Studium und Praxis* (pp. 139–148). Weinheim, Germany: Beltz, Psychologische Verlagsunion. [Information and learning with multi-media and internet. Teaching book for studies and practice]

Mazzolini, M., & Maddison, S. (2007). When to jump in: the role of the instructor in online discussion forums. *Computers & Education, 49*(2), 193–213. doi:10.1016/j.compedu.2005.06.011

McNaught, A. (2006). Is Moodle accessible? *Joint Information System Committee, TechDis*. Retrieved July 12, 2008, from http://www.techdis.ac.uk/index.php?p=3_10_6_2

Meislewitz, G., & Sandera, W. A. (2008). Investigating the Connection between Usability and Learning Outcomes in Online Learning Environments. *Journal of Online Learning and Teaching, 4*(2), 234–242.

Moodle Accessibility Specifications. (2007, June 18). *Development: Moodle Accessibility Specifiations*. Retrieved May 18, 2009, from http://docs.moodle.org/en/ Development:Moodle_Accessibility_Specification

Mory, E. H. (1995, February). *A new perspective on instructional feedback: From objectivism to constructivism*. Paper presented at the annual meeting of the Association for Educational Communications and Technology, Anaheim, CA.

Mory, E. H. (2004). Feedback Research Revisited. In Jonassen, D. H. (Ed.), *Handbook of Research on Educational Communications and Technology* (pp. 745–783). Mahwah, NJ: Lawrence Erlbaum.

Nielsen, J. (2003). Usability 101: Introduction to usability. *Jakob Nielsen's Alertbox*. Retrieved January 20, 2009, from http://www.useit.com/alertbox/20030825.html

Nielson, J. (2000). *Designing Web Usability: The Practice of Simplicity*. Indianapolis: New Riders Publishing.

Petter, C., & Helling, K. (2008). Designing ICT-based learning scenarios for special target groups. Meeting senior learners needs. In A. Lingau, A. Martens, & A. Harrer (Eds.), *Proceedings of the Workshop on Inclusive E-Learning: Special Needs and Special Solutions (IEL-2008)*, Maastricht, The Netherlands. Retrieved, June 4, 2009, from http://sunsite.informatik.rwth-aachen.de/Publications/CEUR-WS/Vol-387/

Reinmann, G. (2005). *Blended Learning in der Lehrerbildung. Grundlagen für die Konzeption innovativer Lernumgebungen* [Blended Learning in Teacher Education. Basics for the Conception of Innovative Larning Environments]. Lengerich, Germany: Pabst.

Reiserer, M., & Mandl, H. (2001). *Individuelle Bedingungen lebensbegleitenden Lernens. (Forschungsbericht Nr. 136)* [Individual Requierements for Lifelong Learning (Research Report No. 136)]. München, Germany: Ludwig-Maximilians-Universität, Lehrstuhl für Empirische Pädagogik und Pädagogische Psychologie.

Salmon, G. (2002). *E-tivities. The key to active online learning*. London: Kogan Page.

University of Linz – Institute Integriert Studieren. (2008). *ICT4T Accessibility Evaluation Report*. [Internal Project Document]. Retrieved January 20, 2009, from http://www.ict4t.net/?q=system/ files/ Accessibility+Evaluation+Report-Moodle.pdf

Weinberger, A., & Reiserer, M. B., Ertl, B., Fischer, F., & Mandl, H. (2005). Facilitating Collaborative Knowledge Construction in Computer-Mediated Learning Environments with Cooperation Scripts. In R. Bromme, F. W. Hesse, & H. Spada (Eds.), Barriers and Biases in Computer-Mediated Knowledge Communication (pp. 15-37). New York: Springer.

Werquin, P. (2008). Recognition of non-formal and informal learning in OECD countries: A very good idea in jeopardy? *Lifelong Learning in Europe, 3*, 142–149.

Chapter 3

Constructing a Sense of Community in a Graduate Educational Setting Using a Web 2.0 Environment

Daniel Firpo
Claremont Graduate University, USA

Sumonta Kasemvilas
Claremont Graduate University, USA

Peter Ractham
Thammasat University, Thailand

Xuesong Zhang
California State University, Fresno, USA

ABSTRACT

This chapter posits that information technology and "Web 2.0 technology" such as blogs and wikis can be used to expand the "Claremont Conversation" by changing the nature of scholarly communication. By using social technologies, conversations outside class among students and professors help build an intellectual community that is the hallmark of a liberal education. We describe the design and implementation of an initial project that targeted only the School of Information Systems and Technology (SISAT) at Claremont Graduate University (CGU). The artifact developed was an online community for the purpose of improving the sense-of-community amongst students, faculty, and alumni of SISAT. This chapter then proposes future steps in how to improve the intellectual community at CGU by expanding the online intellectual community established for SISAT to the entire campus.

DOI: 10.4018/978-1-61520-937-8.ch003

INTRODUCTION

Intellectual community is an idea that drives most of the initiatives at Claremont Graduate University (CGU). The core ideal of CGU, oftentimes referred to as the "Claremont Conversation" by CGU's Board of Trustees, is that the center of a great university is in great conversation, and from the everyday talk of college life springs everything else. This ideal is possible mainly due to CGU's status as a small graduate-only university. CGU's small population of motivated and mature students creates a close-knit environ where intellectual community can more easily thrive than at a larger university. Class sizes are usually small and professors oftentimes are on a first-name basis with their students, as opposed to larger universities, where students often feel like just another face in classrooms with populations over a hundred.

However, recent problems have arisen that threatens the university's close-knit atmosphere. As opposed to before, when students were required to live on campus, many students live far from campus – some with commutes of several hours to travel to and from campus. Such students oftentimes arrange their schedules so they only have to travel to campus once a week, and miss most campus events. Also, a higher proportion of students also have work or family commitments that limit their presence on campus. It has become more common for PhD students to seemingly disappear once they finish their coursework, divorcing themselves from the everyday talk of campus life. A strong sense of community, affiliation, and togetherness are prerequisites for intellectual community, positively influencing the community's social norms towards knowledge sharing (Bock, Zmud, and Lee, 2005). Social relationships, trusts, and mutual interdependencies need to be built and sustained to allow members in a group to effectively collaborate (McGrath & Hollingshead, 1994). Informal communication plays an important role in effective collabora-

tion. It provides random participants who have no arranged agenda with interactive, rich content, and an informal language (Kraut, Fish, Root, and Chalfonte, 1990). In other words, community building is a prerequisite for successful collaborative knowledge construction.

The Board of Trustees has entrusted the Social Learning Software Lab (SL^2) with finding solutions to mitigate this problem. SL^2, a research lab in CGU's School of Information Systems and Technology (SISAT), commits itself to finding innovative ways in which Web 2.0 technologies such as blogs, discussion boards, wikis, and podcasting can be used to enhance learning and bring about positive social change to the university environment. SL^2's challenge has been to see how information technology could enhance the Claremont Conversation by breaking down the barriers of communication between students. This study started as an attempt to use SISAT as a test bed to experiment ideas on how to enhance the sense of community across the other departments and the entire campus.

According to many experts, such as O'Reilly Media, we are now in the era of Web 2.0, in which web applications provide a rich environment for collaboration and creativity. Web 2.0 refers to a new generation of Web applications that enables community interactions within an open environment. Web 2.0 technologies, such as blogs and wikis, enable people to become both the author and the reader, enhancing collaboration among groups of people. There is an overall emphasis on participation that allows users or website visitors to add value to a site, and an added emphasis on social networking and generating conversation. A small example of this trend is the ability users now have on several news websites to post a comment on a news story, or to post a rebuttal or response to a previous user's comment. Many businesses employ the benefits of Web 2.0 into their business practices – an approach sometimes referred to as Enterprise 2.0 – adapting them in their organizations to support their employees' relationships, and forming work processes to attain their business strategies ("What Is Enterprise 2.0?," n.d.).

On the educational side, many educators and teachers have adopted Web 2.0 technology to assist learning and teaching. Williams and Jacobs (2004) demonstrate two examples of using blogs to serve an active role as learning spaces for students in a higher education setting. Williams and Jacobs provide a collection of methods used in Harvard Law School courses in which blogging software plays a part in learning. The Brisbane Graduate School of Business at Queensland University of Technology records the students' experiences through the use of an 'MBA blog'. Williams and Jacobs conclude that blogging has the potential to be a transformational technology for teaching and learning, because "they provide students with a high level of autonomy while simultaneously providing opportunity for greater interaction with peers" (Williams and Jacobs 2004, p. 244).

In a March 1997 interview with Forbes, CGU's own Peter Drucker predicted that the modern "university-as-a-residential-institution" will quickly become a relic, in an era when colleges are already starting to deliver lectures and classes off-campus cheaply via satellite or two-way video (Drucker, 1993). Since then, many have predicted the rise of the "New University," in which participants can engage in scholarly conversation, separated from the need for a "same-place same-time" requirement. Two-way video technologies like Skype™ and iChat™ have the potential to render the same-place requirement moot, as blogs, message boards, discussion groups, and other asynchronous online discussion tools do to the same-time requirement.

According to Preece (2000), social interaction and human-computer interaction need to be addressed before creating a healthy and vibrant online community, due to the blending of social and technological aspects in the developmental process. This is especially the case for technologies that support social relationships. Our paper aims to demonstrate the process of design and implementation of community-based social software that affects communities from a social presence perspective, to investigate the impact of technologies that influence sense of community, and to propose results from an eighteen-month case study. The key question considered is: How does the adoption of community-based software affect the sense of community in an organization?

This chapter will first describe in detail the problem that plagues the university. Next, it will provide a theoretical background by discussing prior research on sense of community, social presence, and motivation to participate in online communities. Next, the chapter will chronicle the design process through which the project team developed our community software artifact, and the phase-by-phase breakdown of how we prototyped, unveiled, and maintained the artifact, while evaluating lessons learned from each phase of the project's life cycle. Finally, the chapter will discuss possible avenues for future research and draw lessons and design principles for other researchers to guide development of similar communal software in their organization.

Problem Statement

As SL^2 saw it, there were four main problems that had a negative effect on the intellectual community at CGU:

First was an inability to attend campus events. Events, from professional workshops, guest lectures, seminars, conferences, roundtable discussions, and forums, to more casual fare such as parties and barbeques, are regularly held on campus. However, to those students who are only on campus once a week, these events often seem like the gatherings of a community they do not belong to. Since these students often pile several classes into one day a week, if an event they would like to attend just happens to be scheduled for a day they are on campus, they would have a schedule conflict and would be unable to attend anyways. Many stakeholders referred to this as the "same-place same-time" requirement for campus events. "Same-place" refers to the need for students to be physically present at an event to participate (for example, if a student wants to see a guest lecture on campus but cannot make it to campus that particular day), and "same-time" refers to the need for synchrony for students to communicate (for example, if students do not have an asynchronous channel through which to communicate).

The second problem was the lack of a true common space. The lab sees two definitions of a common space: One as a place students can gather to converse, and one as an outlet of community news. In SISAT's microcosm, there is one commons room that is sorely underused: The computers and equipment were outdated and barely functioning, thus many students opted to work and study in one of the campus's computer labs instead. As for an outlet of community news, the university had been using e-mail to distribute news of campus events and news. However, few students bothered to use this source. Students would receive mail for events not just within their department, but from all the other departments on campus, as well as for events from other universities within the Claremont Consortium. Bombarded with several irrelevant e-mails, news of events that a particular student might be interested in would be lost in the sea of e-mails he or she would receive on a daily basis.

The third problem was a limited means for students to focus the attention of their peers on their academic output. Students had to rely on methods such as personal connections or word-of-mouth to let others know of their research, their work, their publications, etc., making it difficult to find and network with others with similar research interests.

Finally, students without any official social ties were left out of the academic inner circles of their departments. Many students belonged to research labs or worked under a particular faculty

member. These students can find others of similar research interest within their labs, or perhaps a faculty member would be able to recommend to students other students he or she knew with similar interests to network and collaborate with. These benefits would be absent to any students who lacked such ties.

A computer network connects many computers together, whereas a social network connects many people (Wellman, Salaff, Dimitrova, Garton, Gulia, & Haythornthwaite, 1996; Hiltz & Wellman, 1997). Currently, there are many Web 2.0 social networking sites for users to connect with each other, such as Facebook™, MySpace™, LinkedIn™, and hi5™. However, these sites may not be a good fit with educational organizations, such as CGU, that have more specific needs. When attempting to build an online community for CGU using Web 2.0 technology, it was observed that the real problems occurring here could not be dealt with by simply using existing social networking sites alone. Thus, the project team sought to build our own social software to enhance the sense of community through action and design research. Action research is one of the more effective research approaches that allows researchers to be involved in change. Corey (1953) showed that practitioners can utilize the action research approach to analyze and find solutions for their own problems.

BACKGROUND

Sense of Community

Sarason (1974) defined a sense of community as "the perception of similarity to others, an acknowledged interdependence with others, a willingness to maintain this interdependence by giving to or doing for others what one expects from them, and the feeling that one is part of a larger dependable and stable structure" (p. 157). McMillan and Chavis (1986) identify four elements of sense of community: Membership, influence, integration and fulfillment of needs, and shared emotional connection. Membership is an element with several attributes: boundaries that are respected by themselves and others, a guaranteed level of emotional safety, a sense of belonging and identification, personal investment in the community, and familiarity a common label system. Influence is the perception of community members that they have an influence on the community, as well as the perception that they are influenced by the community (Chavis and Newbrough, 1986). Integration and fulfillment of needs refer to the degree to which members feel rewarded by their participation in the community. Finally, shared emotional connection refers to the bonds forged between community members through participation or shared history. Shared emotional connection is the most important element for a true community (McMillan and Chavis, 1986). McMillan (1996) would later update this model to replace "influence" with "trust."

To empirically measure the sense of community within a group, the Sense of Community Index (SCI) was developed (Chipuer and Pretty, 1999; Long and Perkins, 2003). Wright (2004) adapted the SCI for educational communities by developing the School Sense of Community Index (SSCI). The SSCI adds a fifth element to the four identified above – sense of purpose – which refers to the context in which participants are willing to sustain community cohesion for individual and community outcomes, and combined "influence" from McMillan and Chavis (1986) and "trust" from McMillan (1996) into one element: "influence and trust."

Social Presence

The concept of presence is both broad and multidimensional. There are many different kinds of presence (Nowak and Biocca, 2003). Presence, for example, can refer to its ability to make a user feel like he or she is in the company of others, in the case of copresence; or it can also refer to its ability to make a user feel like he or she is present in the media, in the case of telepresence (Schroeder, 2002). The kind of presence this chapter is concerned with is social presence. Short, Williams, and Christie (1976, p. 65) define social presence as the "degree of salience of the other person in a mediated communication and the consequent salience of their interpersonal interactions." In other words, social presence is the degree that one senses being with another individual – or group of individuals – in a mediated environ (Biocca, Burgoon, Harms, & Stoner, 2001). Social presence strongly affects the degree to which one's perception of an online community affects his or her level of participation in that community. It was originally thought to be an aspect of the community environment or the underlying medium, a la Daft and Lengel's (1986) Media Richness Theory. That is, it was believed that communication media varied in their degree of social presence, and that these variations determined the way participants interacted across a medium (IJsselsteijn, Baren, & Lanen, 2003). Later research has demonstrated that social presence is variable amongst members in the same community using the same medium (Swan and Shih, 2005.

When measuring social presence, there are several factors to take into account amongst the community members, the community as a whole, and the medium used, such as the community's attitude towards online communication, or each community member's personal attitudes towards privacy (Tu, 2002). If there are restrictions in communication channels, social presence will be decreased within a group. The greater the social presence, the higher the level of group interaction, connectedness, involvement, and engagement (Short, Williams, & Christie, 1976). Social presence, as applied in mediated communication, is the degree to which community members believe themselves to be useful members of the community, as well as the degree to which they can feel, interact with, and participate with others as intellectual entities within the community (Tu and McIsaac, 2002). When the other members of the community are perceived to be real entities, trust in the community is established, and the community comes to be seen as a valid outlet for social interaction. This allows individuals using computer-mediated communication to effectively collaborate and communicate with each other as real intellectual entities without the need for same-time, same-place restrictions (Sarbaugh-Thompson & Feldman, 1998).

Social presence has often been used in studies to evaluate people's ability to connect via computer mediated communication (Rice, 1993, Walther 1996). Gunawardena (1995) looked at the implications social presence theory had for computer-mediated communication and demonstrated that while online communication lacks the social context cues one finds in face-to-face conversation, social presence can be established in an online medium. Gudawardena and Zittle (1997) followed this study up by demonstrating the effectiveness of high levels of social presence in improving instructional effectiveness and building a sense of community within a scholarly online community. Previous research on computer mediated communication in educational settings has shown that establishing social presence is one of the most significant factors for fostering online interaction and a strong sense of community (Stacey, 2002).

The model of social presence presented by Biocca and Harms (2002) and Biocca, Harms, & Burgoon (2003) defines three levels of social presence. The shallowest level – the perceptual level – pertains to the detection and awareness of co-presence of another's mediated body. The next level – the subjective level – involves being able to sense the awareness of another person across the medium, and a level of accessibility to the other's emotional state. The deepest level of social presence – the intersubjective level – entails a perceived symmetry of social presence, i.e. it involves an individual being able to sense the

other's sense of social presence of them across the medium (Biocca et al. 2001; Biocca and Harms 2002; Biocca et al. 2003).

Cameron and Anderson (2006) view online social presence as having five dimensions: focus, the ability for community members to discuss subjects that interest them; ownership, the ability for community members to control their environment and communication; identity and style, the ability for community members to nurture their own personal voice, whether through the content of their online communications, adoption of a formal or informal tone when communicating, stylistic decisions, or customization and personalization of their online persona; and safety, which Putnam (2000) defines as a member's ability to feel secure when participating in his or her community.

The concept of social presence is related to the concept of connectedness and group awareness (Rettie, 2003b). Dourish and Bellotti (1992) defined group awareness as an "understanding of the activities of others, which provides a context for your own activity" (p.107). According to Tran, Raikundalia, and Yang (2006), two of the five most significant elements in supporting group awareness for collaborative writing is "Being able to comment on what other users have done," and "Knowing what actions other users are currently taking," (p. 1006). Awareness plays a vital role in supporting group collaborative work because it helps learners feel engaged, enables collaborative learning, increases effectiveness when learners work with others, and assists learners to easily interact with others (Wang & Chee, 2001).

Smith and Mackie (2000) assert that in social behavior, connectedness is a fundamental factor for supporting social relationships. Senses of belonging and connectedness, as well as awareness are vital in building and maintaining social relationships. Hallowell (1993) defines connectedness as "a sense of being a part of something larger than oneself," "a sense of belonging, or a sense of accompaniment," and "the force that urges us to ally, to affiliate, to enter into mutual relationships, to take strength and to grow through cooperative behavior." (p. 196) Succinctly, connectedness is the degree and the quality of connections (both in real life and online) that community members have with other people: The more socially connected a person is, generally the greater their sense of self-control and self-determination. Kuwabara, Watanabe., Ohguro, Itoh, & Maeda (2002) defines 'connectedness orientated communication' as exchanges that allow people to be aware of each other and contribute to maintaining social relationships. Rettie (2003a) found that the need for connectedness was the most important factor in making a choice between communication channels.

Motivation to Participate

Motivation to participate in an online community was also a cause of concern to the project team. Previous research (Andrews, Preece, and Turoff, 2001) has been done on resistance to actively participate in an online community. The Theory of Reasoned Action states that the two main factors that affect an individual's intention to engage in a certain activity are the individual's personal attitudes towards the activity, and the social norms of their community in regards to that activity (Fishbein and Ajzen, 1975). Bock, Zmud, and Kim (2005) look at the motivators that affect an individual's intention to contribute knowledge using the Theory of Reasoned Action. They found that fostering a felt need for extrinsic rewards for contribution would actually hinder the development of favorable attitudes towards contributing, and that an individual's attitude towards knowledge sharing is more influenced by social, rather than economic, exchange. They also found that a community climate with a strong sense of affiliation positively influenced a community's social norms towards contributing knowledge, as well as the community member's intention to contribute.

Wasko and Faraj (2005) found reputation to be a strong motivator to contribute knowledge. They also found centrality to be a strong motiva-

tor to contribute: those who have connections to a large portion of the community are more likely to contribute knowledge. Commitment to the community and – more surprisingly – reciprocity were not motivators to contribute knowledge. Kimmerle, Wodzicki, and Cress (2008) look at the effects social norms and social identity have on knowledge contribution. Social norms rules and standards accepted by members of a community. Social identity concerns the integration of group membership into a person's individual self concept. Factors that affect this integration include the individual's level of commitment to the community, and the situations in which social identity is affected by the community, i.e. no-threat situations, situations in which a threat to an individual's identity originates from his or her relationship with the group, and situations in which group identity is threatened (Ellemere, Spears, and Doosje, 1999; Ellemere, Spears, and Doosje, 2002). Kimmerle, Wodzicki, and Cress (2008) assert that to encourage knowledge sharing, the process of contribution should be affirmed as a valuable opportunity, and encouraged as such. They echo Wasko and Faraj's findings that reputation and recognition are motivating rewards for contributing information. Kimmerle, Wodzicki, and Cress (2008) also stress that cooperation should be a social norm within the community – that is, cooperation should be established as a nexpectation. Cress, Barquero, Schwan, & Hesse (2007) and Kimmerle and Cress (2008) found that participants within a community who receive feedback on their group's cooperativeness would contribute more than those without such feedback.

In addition to quantity of contribution, previous research has looked at increasing the quality of knowledge contribution. Cress et al. (2007) found that knowledge about the importance of one's own information influences the quality of their contributions. In their study, participants in situations where contribution costs for information was equal no matter what the importance would opt to contribute more important information.

They also determined that providing a use-related bonus – i.e. a bonus that is determined by how many times their contributions are used – would encourage participants to pay more attention to the importance of their information, when deciding to contribute.

According to Fogg 2003, Social Facilitation theory states that individuals are more likely to participate when their peers are present, participating, or observing. Also according to Fogg 2003, Social Comparison theory states that people will have more motivation to participate if they are given information on how their participation compares with that of their peers. Individuals are also more likely to participate in a community if doing so satisfies intrinsic motivators. An intrinsic motivator is a motivator that originates from an inherently rewarding activity (Malone & Lepper 1987, Fogg 2003). Recognition is an example of an intrinsic motivator – the idea behind recognition is that by offering public recognition upon an individual, one can increase the likelihood that that person, or others in the community who also hope to receive public recognition, will adopt a desired behavior or attitude.

CASE STUDY

Approach

The purpose of this chapter is to describe the community's reaction to the deployment of community-based social software in a graduate setting within an 18 month period. In this chapter, we will demonstrate how the SISAT community utilized the software, how we designed and modified the system over the course of its lifecycle, and how we furnished the artifact.

This study's approach combined design research and action research methodologies. Action Design provides a model for combining action and design research approaches (Cole, Purao, Rossi, & Sein, 2005). According to Hevner,

March, Park, and Ram (2004, p. 79), "design science addresses research through the building and evaluation of artifacts designed to meet the identified business need." As opposed to natural science, which is concerned with understanding reality, design research emphases science of the artificial, which is concerned with the ways things ought to be, and in order to achieve a certain goal, the design research practitioner builds an artifact to solve a specific and concrete problem (Simon, 1996). Natural science research consists of two main activities: discovery and justification. Design science research is composed of an iterative build-and-evaluate loop. Meanwhile, the action research methodology allows the researcher to be dynamically involved in the project, collaboratively change experiments, and actively apply knowledge obtained in one iteration to the next (Baskerville, 1999). We followed the action research framework of Baskerville (1999). Baskerville's action research framework is a two-stage process. In the first stage – the diagnostic stage – the project team observes the problems, conducts a focus group, and involves the stakeholders to identify the specific problems. The outputs of this stage are a set of user requirements. In the second stage – the therapeutic stage – the project team designs and develops software based on the user requirements obtained during the previous stage and iterates the changes when needed to improve the situation. The results of each phase are studied to provide the inputs for the next phase. Meanwhile, Baskerville (1999)'s action research cycle has five iterative stages: diagnosing, action planning, action taking, evaluating, and specifying learning.

Baskerville (1999) defined a project infrastructure as agreements that specify the responsibilities of host clients and researchers as well as their legitimate actions. Hence, the project infrastructure constitutes the working environment. During the period of study, there were 115 graduate students (most of whom are part-time students who live off-campus), five full-time faculty members, three staff members, and over 600 alumni. In this study we consider current students, faculty members, and alumni as the main stakeholders of the system.

The development team used a Community-Centered Development (CCD) (Lazar & Preece, 1999) approach to build the artifact. CCD is a five-step approach to development. In the first step in this approach, the project team assesses the community needs. Next, based on the community's needs, the project team selects technology that would best foster sociability within the community according to its needs. The third step is to prototype. During this step, the project team goes through several iterations of design, implementation, and testing using small subsets of the community. User feedback is gathered to form a clearer and more refined picture of the community's needs, in order to better address them in the next iteration. After prototyping, the next step is the large-scale testing of the prototype reached in the previous step in order to fine-tune the system. The final step is deployment, where the project team maintains, publicizes, and supports the system across the community. It is the project team's responsibility to generate awareness of the system to new users and nurturing them as they learn to use the system.

Phase I: Prototyping Phase and Initial Deployment

First, the project team attempted to diagnose the situation and assess the community's needs. The first step in the action research cycle is defining the primary problems. In the socio-technical model of action research, the stakeholders – that is, the actual students and faculty that it is hoped will benefit from our artifact – should have a chance to identify their own problems or design new improvements (Mumford, 2001; Lindgren, Henfidsson and Schultze (2004). Through hour-long focus groups conducted within the labs, the team got students to discuss what they felt was

lacking within the community and even suggest their own solutions for the proposed new system. The first focus group was attended by a total of eleven participants: two faculty members, one staff member, two alumni, and six current students (including two of the students with a long campus commute). The participants shared their opinions and discussed the possibility of using blogs as the main tool to improve communication among members. A student stressed:

"This is a really good idea for our school to have this type of system. I live and work in Northridge and sometimes, I can't beat the traffic to attend the Edge seminar on Friday afternoon. Also to be able to keep track of who's doing what research would be helpful to me as a researcher."

The team analyzed which social technologies would be best suited to combat the problems identified within the community. Several technologies were suggested in the focus group:

"A Blog is a good idea, but what about chat and instant messenger? What if I want to communicate with others instantly?"

Hundreds of man-hours were spent in conversation and observation with various community members. Interview data was gathered from meeting minutes, informal interviews, weekly meetings, informal conversation, notes taken during conversations, transcripts from interview recordings, etc. on an ongoing basis with community members and on a weekly basis with other SL^2 members. In all, the project team obtained positive feedback coupled with constructive suggestions. A faculty member who attended the focus group suggested a unique and distinctive name, SISATSpace.

According to Baskerville and Wood-Harper (1996) and Baskerville (1999), action research needs to present the theoretical framework as a premise to link theory and practice. According to

Kohli and Kettinger (2004, p. 369), using established theories can structure the problem situation and better guide the researcher to a successful project conclusion. Social Presence Theory was used as a lens through which the project team could analyze the problems' context. The team's goal was to reduce the students' feeling of isolation in the school and enhance a feeling of community and affiliation. Social presence theory, when applied in an online community setting, considers how individuals' perceptions affect their participation in the community. Social presence can be achieved in a sufficiently rich communication medium, such as audio communication (telephone conference) and text-based communication (e-mail, blog, wiki, and instant messenger).

Wagner and Bolloju (2005) compared the relatively modern social technologies of blogs and wikis with relatively older social technology, such as discussion forums, and concluded that even though forums are the most popular technology, different types of communities require different tools to serve their particular purposes. They stated that in order to get the most benefit from each type of technology, it was important to take into account the technology-related and behavior-related issues. Based on this, and upon the general consensus among community members, four Web 2.0 technologies appeared best suited to the community's problems: Blogs, wikis, social bookmarks, and podcasts.

Blogs, a contraction of the term "web log," are a personal online diary used to foster asynchronous discussion. Similar to message boards, blogs are more personalized and individualized. Blog owners can keep a log of their experiences by posting blog entries, meanwhile readers are free to post their own comments on each entry. These comments are left on the blog for everyone else to see and similarly comment on. Some of the advantages of using blogs is that blog-based websites tend to be updated more regularly and more often than other types of websites (Wilcox, Cameron, Ault, & Agee 2003; Trammell 2004). Also, blogs are

better suited to establishing a sense of ownership in whoever maintains it. Since a blog is owned by an individual or – in some cases – a small group of owners, their personality and identity is more strongly affixed to it. As such, a blog's readership identifies with that online persona, further motivating the owner to be honest and trustworthy about all posted content (Callison 2001). Blogs have the potential to foster asynchronous discussion and dissemination of tacit knowledge without any significant technological barriers. Due to the user-friendliness of most blogging software, initial learning costs would be kept to a minimum. Brown, Collins, & Duguid (1989) talk about a community of practice's need for a repository for the community's collective wisdom, e.g. the tacit knowledge shared during informal conversations. Blogs were seen as a way for community members to keep a constant diary of their "war stories," and as a way for other members to discuss these stories, compare them with their own stories, and in the process gain new tools for their conceptual toolboxes. The community of bloggers is often referred to as the "blogosphere."

Contrasted to blogs, "a wiki is a work made by a community. The blogosphere is a community made by its works" (Cunningham, 2006, p. 6). In other words, with blogs, a community forms from the content posted by its users. Meanwhile, content in a wiki is generated from a pre-existing community. Derived from the Hawaiian word, "wikiwiki" (meaning "fast"), a wiki is "a freely expandable collection of interlinked Web pages, a hypertext system for storing and modifying information – a database where each page is easily editable by any users with a forms-capable web browser client" (Leuf & Cunningham 2001, p. 14). Users are free to post, edit, and deleted any content posted to the site. Wiki technology was considered by the project team as a means of providing students with a tool for collaborative writing.

Social bookmarks were also considered to provide a shared repository of links and Internet resources to the community. Social bookmarking sites, such as digg.com or Del.icio.us, allow users to post links to online resources and categorize them via tags into a loose folksonomy to make browsing and searching for resources easy for other users. A folksonomy is a bottom-up classification generated by users (Smith 2008). A tag is a user-defined keyword that allows others to easily search for and find these bookmarks.

Podcast technology was considered to disseminate video content to the community members. A portmanteau of iPod™ and broadcast, podcasts refer to audio or video content that distributed automatically via the Internet to the users' PC or MP3 player (Geoghegan & Klass 2005). A podcast does not have to be audio/video content. A podcast can represent any type of file, such as a Word document or a PowerPoint presentation, as long as it is defined in an XML format for the same purpose. Originally used primarily to allow users to receive radio or television content, podcasts have also been used in education. An example is how some universities allow students to download podcasts of lectures or class sessions. This video content we wished to disseminate included recordings of campus events, such as guest lectures, research seminars, or other presentations that some students might not have been able to attend. This content also included FacultyCasts, StudentCasts, ResearchCasts, and AlumniCasts, collectively referred to as "Casts." Casts were what the development team used to refer to recorded interviews with students, faculty members, alumni, which were disseminated via SISATSpace to foster a sense of community and increase familiarity within the department. While most Faculty, Student, and AlumniCasts featured interviews with members of the community, ResearchCasts included recordings of events, lectures, and seminars on campus that many students would have otherwise missed due to schedule conflicts.

Next, the project team had to decide on how such technologies would be utilized. Blogs were central to the vision from the start. Blogs are a tool wherein a community grows and develops from its content. The informal style of communication found in blogs creates a comfortable atmosphere for sharing information. With the freedom to write his or her own page, the blog owner can add what he or she knows to the sum total of knowledge, be it industry and product knowledge, valuable insights on specific subjects, or personal stories (Cohen & Clemens, 2005; Ojala, 2004). Unlike the discussion found in message boards, where discussion is of a more 'public forum' type, a blog provides a personal and intimate alternative for disseminating information and expressing ideas over which blog owners have full control, such as issues, restriction of authorized viewers, and deletion of undesirable comments. There are many tools and technologies for supporting blogs, such as trackback, blogroll, permalink, as well as really simple syndication, also known as rich site summary (RSS), that provide convenience for users and encourage knowledge sharing (Cayzer, 2004). The project team also wanted users to feel a sense of ownership to their own content.

The team decided to use two types of blogs in SISATSpace: A Main Blog, and Individual User Blogs. The wiki and social bookmarks, linked to from the Main Blog, would be used to provide a knowledge repository for the department. The Main Blog would be the first thing users see when they visit SISATSpace, and would be used to disseminate important campus news and events. Previous studies have been conducted on the possibility of using blogs to generate a sense of community. Williams and Jacobs (2004) look at the use of blogs in higher education settings. Roger (2006) relied on informality and reader engagement to create a sense of community with a news blog. Roger's study emphasized the importance of having online social presence. Communication that fosters social presence is "friendly, uses personal examples, uses first names, asks questions, uses humor, uses personal pronouns, discloses personal information, and uses verbal expressions that express emotion such as emoticons or punctuation marks" (Menzie, 2006 p. 38). Blogs are well suited to this kind of communication, as personality and informality is typical to the sort of communication found in most blogs (Sallnas 1999). Menzie (2006) and Roger (2006) both found that levels of sense of community are cumulative, that creating a community blog can attract readership, and that reading such a blog frequently can lead to increased levels of sense of community. Perschbach (2006) used blogs to encourage social learning within a community college setting. Bourgeois and Horan (2007) looked at social networking software to build social capital at Biola University. Podcasting would be used to disseminate Casts via the Main Blog.

Each user would have his or her own Individual User Blog linked to from the main page. Their blog would be something they could update and customize according to their whim. Individual User Blogs were the agreed upon "best-fit" with the five dimensions of social presence identified by Cameron and Anderson (2006). A sense of ownership would be achieved by giving each student their own personal online space that they could control. A sense of focus would be achieved by allowing each students to control the subject matter and discuss what interested them in their own personal space. Being free to lead this discourse and customize all aspects of their own blog would instill a sense of identity and style. For example, several themes and templates would be made available to students so that they could customize the layout, look, and feel of their personal space. Finally, privacy controls would instill a sense of safety. It was hoped that giving each community member their own blog would lead to a perceived symmetry of social presence, allowing us to achieve an intersubjective level of social presence (Biocca and Harms, 2002).

After deciding on which Web 2.0 technologies would be used for SISATSpace, and how SISATSpace would use them, the project team next had to go about deciding which specific software packages to use to develop the system.

In deciding which tools to use for SISATSpace, the project team aimed for ease-of-use and cost. Ease-of-use was a factor, because a high level of usability would less likely frustrate new users, and would help the system adopt and hold onto users. To address costs, the project team aimed for open source software packages with a vibrant user community. For this reason, WordPress MU, an open-source variant of the popular WordPress blogging platform, was selected to become the backbone of SISATSpace. The WordPress user community had developed several plug-ins for WordPress to enhance and extend functionality. Examples of plug-ins the project team used included a plug-in that allowed users to upload photo slideshows. Another example was a plug-in that allowed users to embed YouTube videos within their blogs. This feature also supported the project team's podcasting goal. Casts were disseminated through SISATSpace by first uploading the videos to YouTube, and then embedding the video into a post on the Main Blog. Another important plug-in was a tracking tool called SlimStat, used only by the project team for the purpose of collecting important web stat data, including the number of posts made by community members, the number of comments made by community members on other blogs (including the main page), and the number of unique site visits per day SISATSpace received.

The Artifact

From the start of the prototyping process, there were two key elements to SISATSpace: The main page, and the individual User Blogs. These elements can be seen in Figure 1. The main page served to disseminate important department and campus events, as well as Casts, through the Main Blog. At the top of the page were a Search feature and several tabs. The tabs were labeled:

- Home: Takes the user back to the Main Blog.

Figure 1. SISATSpace

- FacultyCast: Displays all FacultyCasts in chronological order, starting from the most recent.
- StudentCast: Similarly displays all StudentCasts.
- ResearchCast: Similarly displays all ResearchCasts.
- SISAT Bookmarks: Took the user to the Social Bookmarks page.
- SISAT Wiki: Took the user to the Wiki page.
- HelpCast (added at the very end of Phase I): Takes the user to the Help Page, where video tutorials for all of SISATSpace's features could be found.

The main page was divided into two different sections: The Main Blog, on the right, and the sidebar, on the left. Students were free to comment on any post published to the Main Blog (Figure 2). The sidebar contained several useful features. The first was "Faces of SISATSpace." Clicking on this link took users to a linked directory of all the students in the department. Below that was a section called Most Recent Posts/Comments (Figure 2). This section was added partway into Phase II based on user feedback, and on the research of Nowak and Biocca (2003), which stated that anthropomorphism enhanced social presence in online communities. This section contained the 10 most recent posts or comments, along with what was usually a 2 sentence preview of the post and a link to the post itself. Below this was a section called "Most Active Blogs" (Figure 3), which displayed the 20 most prolific bloggers (including their profile picture and a link to their blog). As with Most Recent Posts/Comments, "Most Active Blogs" was a feature added later on based on user feedback. At the bottom of the sidebar was a Calendar where users could find Main Blog posts by what day they were posted.

"Faces of SISATSpace" was SISATSpace's name for the directory of students (Figure 4). This

Figure 2. The comments section for a blog post. Also in the screenshots are the most recent posts/comments section of the sidebar

feature displayed links to each and every student's SISATSpace blog, sorted by number of posts (in descending order). Each link also displayed pictures of each student's face (hence the name) and the number of posts they have made in their Individual User Blog.

The Individual User Blogs were up to the user to customize. Users were able to customize their blogs from a diverse preset list of templates

(Figure 5). The static feature of each Individual User Blog was the sidebar, which contained a Search feature, a Calendar to find posts, links to the user's Pages, and their Blogroll. The Pages were posts separate from a student's blog. Usually this was reserved for a short biographical post including information such as research interests. The Blogroll was a set of customizable links that users could post to their sidebar. Students were

Figure 3. Most active blogs (left) and an example of a "This week in SISAT" post (right), a feature added partway into phase II to put the spotlight on standout blog posts from the prior week

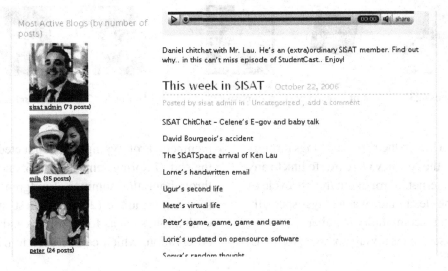

Figure 4. Faces of SISATSpace

encouraged to link to their friends' blogs through this feature, although they were free to link to any page on the Internet. Throughout the life cycle of the project, the Dean's blog was always especially popular amongst community members.

The first users of the initial prototype were SL[2]

members. Prototyping was conducted starting at the end of Spring semester 2006, and continued throughout the summer. Lindgren, Henfridsson, and Schultze (2004) suggest methods for evaluation, such as focus groups and participant observation, which can be used to triangulating the results. Focus groups (usually with an attendance of between 11 to 15 students and faculty members) were carried out, and online interactions were observed closely by the development team. The prototype was updated based on feedback from other lab members. The team went through several iterations in the process of building the prototype. This is the nature of the prototyping approach which, as proposed by Baskerville (1996), must be carried out through the process of iteration, reconstruction, and user evaluation until arriving at full functionality. As a clear vision for SISATSpace began to form, invitations were sent out to community members – current students and faculty – to create their own blogs and read and comment on content posted by their peers. During this summer session, 63 of the 115 current students, ten alumni, and two faculty members signed up to create their own blog. Feedback was gathered via face-to-face interviews and workshops conducted throughout summer. From the feedback, the project team gathered that users were curious about the new system, but suggested that tutorials be provided to help new users learn how to use the system. Thus, the project team decided to create a "HelpCasts" link on the main

page, which would provide users with video and text tutorials on how to utilize all the features of SISATSpace. Concerns about the usefulness of the wiki and social bookmarking features also arose from the focus groups. Despite the encouragement of professors within the department teaching during the summer session to use these features for their courses, students made little use of the social bookmarks page, and far less use of the wiki. Since these technologies did not contribute much to neither community building nor any of the dimensions of social presence identified by Cameron and Anderson (2006), the project team decided to focus more on the technologies that did, such as the blog and podcasting features. New students were seen as a likely group of first adopters for the system, so with the finalized tool, and existing content generated from use throughout the summer, the project team decided to unveil SISATSpace at the New Student Orientation for the Fall 2006 semester.

Evaluation of Phase I

For analysis, the project team employed qualitative analysis of blog post and comment content

Figure 5. Examples of individual user blogs

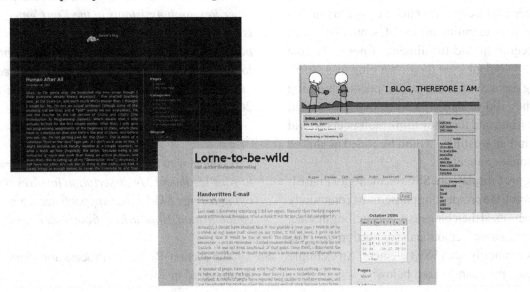

Figure 6. SSCI data for Phase I

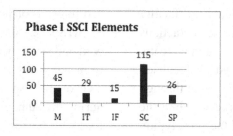

throughout SISATSpace's lifecycle using the School Sense of Community Index (SSCI) proposed by Wright (2004). Again, the five elements of Wright's SSCI are membership (M), influence and trust (IT), integration and fulfillment of needs (IF), shared emotional connection (SC), and sense of purpose (SP). Although somewhat subjective, the project team would collaborative go over each post and comment and quantified each post for SSCI elements. To give an example of each, a blog post where a new student introduced themselves to the community would be coded as a membership element. A comment that indicated that the student felt he or she influenced or was influenced by the community (i.e. following a suggestion made by a fellow student) would be coded as an influence and trust element. A post or comment where a student uses SISATSpace to fulfill a need, such as letting others know they are attending a certain event, or trying to find out who else is attending the event, would be coded as integration and fulfillment of needs. A post where a student used their own blog as a story-telling device – relating to their peers something that they did or participated in that they found interesting, and that they think their peers would also find interesting – would be coded as shared emotional connecting.

Figure 6 displays the SSCI elements for Phase I:

During the prototyping phase, most community members used their blogs as a story-telling device. As such, shared emotional connection was the most commonly seen SSCI element. An example of such a post can be seen below:

"You may be wondering how it is that I am able to write papers and get them accepted. Well, let me share my current day's efforts with you. I have spent the last 2 hours trying to make a scrollbar (in a scrollpane in a Java applet) a different color. My subjects on Monday said it was difficult to see, and I concurred. I was fighting with the code for quite a while until I came across this link, which has solved my problem. Thank goodness for other coders out there. Now, to make text bold in an HTML displaying JEditorPane...back to that problem. Lest you think all Research Assistantships are glamorous..."

The second most commonly seen element was membership, as many participants also used their blog to introduce themselves:

"Hello Everyone, I'm ... a 3rd year PhD student in IS&T. I'm working currently with Dr. Horan and other Research Assistants in the Kay Center. This is an awesome opportunity and I'm happy to be a part of the research going on at the Kay Center. I look forward to seeing the new faces and reconnecting with familiar faces as we start the Fall 2006 semester."

"Hi I am new to the SISAT blog and look forward to your feedback. My dissertation involves developing a Trust Model that supports secure ad hoc collaboration. Hope to hear from some of you soon.

The Action Research Process for Phase I is summarized in Table 1.

Table 1. Summary of the action research process for phase I

Diagnosing	• Analyze social technologies and their impact on the problems identified in the community. • Design and build a prototype. • Conduct focus groups among stakeholders (two faculty members, one staff member, two alumni, and six current students)
Action Planning	• Features that should be included in the first prototype: a community blog, individual blogs for each student, podcasts, wiki, online directory of students, and social bookmarks.
Action Taking	• SL² members are the first group of users. • Send out email invitations to community members.
Evaluating	• 63 of the 115 current students, ten alumni, and two faculty members sign up and create an individual blog and provide feedback via face-to-face interviews. • Weekly meetings with SL² to evaluate the initial prototype and their impacts • Track usage statistics
Specifying Learning	• Concerns about some of the requirements and problems of the initial design, namely the wiki and social bookmarking features. • Users seems to be curious about the new system. • Tutorials on how to use the software would be helpful.

Phase II: Official Deployment and Maintenance of Community

The official release of SISATSpace launched in Fall 2006, after modifications were made to the initial prototype in line with participant feedback. Andrews, Preece, and Turoff (2001) claim that a "tangible touch" event is an important first-step to take when attempting to start an online community. A tangible touch event is an event meant to jumpstart a community and create a critical mass for participation. The development team decided to use the Fall Orientation to provide this tangible touch event. Attempting to use the incoming student body as first adopters, a workshop was held during the orientation to introduce SISATSpace and its goals to the new students, and demonstrate some of its features. Thirteen new students, including a few of the students with long commutes, attended the one-hour workshop. The project team provided a brochure, gave a description of SISATSpace, and encouraged the students to sign up. Establishing credibility is an important step in ensuring that a system can generate behavioral or attitude changes within a community (Fogg 2003). Reputed credibility is a kind of credibility established by a reputable third

party. According to Fogg, Soohoo, Danielson, & Marable (2002), one of the ways to garner reputed credibility is to have the site recommended to a community by a reputable or respected person or website. The project team used the tangible touch event to garner this kind of credibility by having the Dean of SISAT, a professor from within the department, and the University President lobby in SISATSpace's favor in front of the new student body.

During the following three-month period, 83 of the at-the-moment 115 student population at SISAT created blogs in SISATSpace. A follow-up workshop was held two weeks into the semester to reintroduce SISATSpace to the community members, face-to-face. The goal of this workshop was to ensure that community members knew about the system. Another important aspect of earning credibility is responding to user feedback (Fogg et al. 2002). During the second workshop, a student made the following comment:

"I can't see the update in others' blogs on the main page. I don't have time to go to every blog to check if they update their contents or not. There ought to be a feature that notifies users that a blog has been updated."

Although the key of social presence theory is the ability of community members to effectively participate, interact, and collaborate within their group, SISATSpace had a problem with a lack of group awareness in the system. Group awareness is an important factor which promotes success in collaboration. Wang and Chee (2001) found that students have difficulties in collaborating with others when a collaborative learning system cannot adequately support group awareness between users. A fundamental requirement of group interaction is that participants need to recognize other members' activities, or in our case, they need to be aware of when other participants post or update their blogs.

To address the user's complaint, the project team implemented the Most Recent Posts/Comments (Figure 2) and Most Active Blog (Figure 3) features. Motivation for this feature was twofold. In addition to addressing user feedback, Social Comparison theory states that people will have more motivation to adopt a target behavior – in the case of SISATSpace, more active participation within the community – if they are given information via computing technology on how their performance compares with that of their peers (Fogg 2003, pg. 198). Most Active Bloggers lets the user know how often his or her peers are posting. The additional purpose of the Most Active Bloggers list is to provide users with information about their peers, "information that helps shape decisions and behaviors" (Fogg 2003 pg. 199). Most Active Bloggers also added an element of competition into SISATSpace. Competition is a group-level intrinsic motivator, a motivator that originates from an inherently rewarding activity (Malone & Lepper 1987, Fogg 2003). Not only did the Most Active Bloggers list display how many posts each person had, but depending on how many posts one had published to their blog, it was possible to get booted off the list if one stopped posting and others overtook them by updating more often.

Further feedback suggested that some International students had trouble with English as a language barrier:

"I don't know what to write; my English is not good. I wish I could post a video blog about my hobby"

Additional feedback gave suggestions for how the system could be improved and better fulfill the needs of students:

"It would be convenient to be able to upload and store our files within SISATSpace, instead of uploading them to WFS [i.e., CGU's web file sharing system] first and then come back to SISATSpace."

To latter suggestion was easy enough to implement, however the first suggestion requested a feature, video blogging, that SISATSpaces already supported. To address this, halfway into the semester, at the end of October, a third workshop was held to teach and publicize the more advanced features of SISATSpace. By this time, the number of Individual User Blogs had reached 90. An e-mail invitation was sent out to the department ahead of time, and ultimately 21 participants showed up: 13 current users, 8 new or inactive users. Most of the attendees at the workshop were international students. At the workshop, the project lead students on a walkthrough of several advanced features, such as the ability to upload video or slideshow content.

When not conducting workshops, the project team devoted much of Phase II to publicizing and supporting the system amongst the community members. Always having new content on a site is a highly effective way of establishing surface credibility (Fogg et al. 2002), and thus, the project team would strive to publish new material to the Main Blog at a rate of at least one post per day, and one Cast (be it StudentCast, FacultyCast, ResearchCast, etc.) per week. In addition, support for features that users neglected and which provided little value to establishing a stronger sense of community (the wiki and social bookmarks) was silently cut off, while new features to encourage more active participation were implemented, such as "This Week in SISATSpace" (Figure 3). This feature utilized "recognition," another group-level intrinsic motivator (Malone & Lepper 1987, Fogg 2003). "This Week in SISATSpace" was a recurring feature wherein the project team would publish on the Main Blog a weekly digest of the standout blog posts students had posted throughout the previous week. Those who had posted the previous week would have their achievements and musings publicly recognized.

Recognition was also the main idea behind Casts. During the podcasted interviews with students and faculty, interviewees would be asked about their background, their research, their accomplishments, and their hobbies. SISATSpace offers up public recognition upon that student, and give the SISAT community the opportunity to do the same by posting comments. Students would be motivated to come to SISATSpace and watch the Casts to better know their peers, classmates, and professors

To get a better picture of the background of the community members and how they feel about the social presence on campus, the project team provided a questionnaire halfway into the school year to learn how familiar users were with social technologies, how often they used SISATSpace, and how they felt about social networks and communities of practice. The project team received 46 usable responses to the survey. From this snapshot

of the blogging student body, it was discovered that most were male (61%), and nearly half (48%) were international students. Most of the respondents were under 40, with 20 students between the ages of 20-29, 13 between the ages of 30-39, 8 between the ages of 40-49, and 4 over the age of 50 (with one student declining to answer). Questionnaire items pertaining to system use are displayed in Table 2 (the full questionnaire can be found in Appendix A:

From the questionnaire results, it was learned that only 17% of the student population updated their blogs on a regular basis. The project team came to the realization that students were not feeling like they were recognized as individuals, and were not feeling a strong sense of connectedness with the group. An environment where students' input does not seem to be valued may result in a reduced motivation to participate.

While SISATSpace had satisfactory readership, the level of active participation was problematic. There are two kinds of participation: passive participation, and active participation. Active participation refers to users who both read others' content and contribute their own content. Passive participation refers to users who only read content posted by others while posting little or not content of their own. In an online community, those who mainly engage in passive participation are referred to as "lurkers." Preece, Nonnecke, and Andrews (2004) identify several reasons why lurkers do not actively participate: they simply do not feel the need to contribute, they lack sufficient knowledge about the community, they think that it actually helps the community for them to remain quiet,

Table 2. System use

1 = None, 3= Somewhat, 5 = Everyday					
	1	2	3	4	5
How often do you read SISATSpace main blog site?	20%	43%	30%	4%	2%
How often do you read others' blog?	20%	46%	26%	4%	4%
How often do you update your blog?	41%	41%	15%	0%	2%

they have problems or issues with the software, or they simply have issues with the community or its members. Lurking is a widespread pattern in virtually every online community (Nonnecke and Preece, 2000). Ebner and Holzinger (2005) looked at lurking in an online educational environment and found that the lurking process begins with a decrease in the amount of active participation while passive participation increases or remains the same throughout the course. Furthermore, they determined that passive participation is the most prevalent kind of participation in an online community, and that both active and passive participants in an online community will generally read more content than they contribute. They also found that while a lurking student may not actively participate in online discussion, they participate just as much as active participants in terms of reading other students' content, similar to how in brick-and-mortar classrooms, there are students who play an active role in class discussion while others never speak up – just because the students do not speak up does not mean they are not a part of the community. Thus, passive participants are just as important to an online community as active participants, in terms of building a sense of community.

Passive participation in SISATSpace consisted of reading posts and comments made by others, and watching Casts. Since there was a face-to-face component to the community, when students met on campus, SISATSpace had some forms of "active passive participation," in that this form of participation was only considered passive in that students did not post content to the site, but could not exactly be considered lurking either. Examples of "active passive participation" included students discussing content posted on SISATSpace through face-to-face communication, or attending events that they or others learned of from announcements on the Main Blog. Nevertheless, the project team still sought out to address the issue of low levels of active participation.

Design science is an inherently iterative process (Hevner et al. 2004), and effective design is oftentimes a search process for an effective artifact, iteratively identifying shortcomings in an artifact and creatively developing solutions that address these shortcomings (Markus, Majchrzak, & Gasser 2002, as cited in Hevner et al. 2004). To get a stronger grasp at the problem at hand and the shortcomings in the system, the project team engaged in several interviews with various community members – formally and informally, in workshops, lab meetings, and around campus – to determine how to facilitate more active participation. One user provided the following idea:

"I think people would discuss about something they care about and not just a bunch of research seminars or short interview videos. You could run a feature on one specific student and promote the interaction that way."

To this end, the project team created a set of activities – dubbed Interventions – to encourage more user participation with the system and reinforce a sense of community. Gunawardena (1995) demonstrated that in an online community, the impetus falls to the community moderators to create a sense of online community in order to promote interaction. The project team planned two Intervention activities, one in July and one in August 2007. These Interventions were, respectively, Student Appreciation Week and Magid Igbaria Remembrance Week. Each activity would be held for one week to allow community members to join and participate. As per the user's suggestion, these Interventions would each run a feature on one specific member of the SISAT community to promote participation and affiliation. Reaching back to the literature on motivation to participate, Bock, Zmud, and Kim (2005) demonstrated that an organizational climate with a strong sense of affiliation would have a positive effect on the subjective norms towards participation and the community members' intention to participate. Thus, affiliation would be the theme for the first two interventions.

Interventions

The first Intervention was titled, "Student Appreciation Week." The goal of this intervention was to allow community members to get to know the specific student to appreciate at a personal level, as well as allow them to share their story and well wishes to their fellow students, thus reinforcing the level of community via demonstrating a social climate with a strong sense of affiliation. The project team picked one student who was involved in several activities around campus, and who happened to have a birthday at the end of the week, to become the focal point of the Intervention. Students were encouraged to send public birthday wishes to the student via their blogs, and others recorded their own StudentCasts where they wished the individual a Happy Birthday.

Appreciation Week ran for the week of July 23-July 29, 2007, beginning one day after the selected student's birthday, thus giving community members an opportunity to give him their belated birthday wishes. Email announcements were sent to all current community members, encouraging them to participate by posting their well wishes or to make comments on blog posts. During Appreciation week, the researcher created several StudentCasts where students recorded their Happy Birthday massage for the selected student.

The Intervention turned out to be a success. Participation and traffic saw a spike, and the overall system traffic for the month of July 2007 was the highest out of any month in SISATSpace's lifespan. After the first activity week, the research team met with SL² members and received feedback on the first intervention. Many were satisfied with the lively conversation and participation generated from the intervention:

"I really like [Student Appreciation] week. I didn't know that [he] did so many things outside of school."

Although feedback was generally positive, there was some concern with the subject chosen for Student Appreciation Week: Some community members who did not know this specific student could care less about SISATSpace featuring this individual. This could lead to a sense of isolation from the rest of the community during the Intervention week for those who would not care for this type of Intervention. To get more involvement from disinterested community members, one user suggested:

"Maybe SISATSpace could feature a faculty appreciation week. That way, more people will be more involved."

One of the lessons learned from the first intervention was that alumni are as much of a major stakeholder in the community as its current members. Since SISAT boasted more than 600 alumni worldwide, the project team decided to conduct an Intervention that would appeal to both current students and alumni. At the behest of his fellow colleagues, the project team decided that the second Intervention should be week of remembrance for a deceased faculty member, Dr. Magid Igbaria. Thus, the week of August 9-16, 2007 was dedicated to Dr. Igbaria as "Magid Igbaria Remembrance Week." The week of the Intervention marked the fifth anniversary of Dr. Igbaria's passing due to complications from cancer. The project team sent emails to all stakeholders, including Dr. Igbaria's wife Afaf Igbaria, current community members (student and faculty members), alumni, and friends of the community such as Dr. Igbaria's colleagues. His fellow faculty, as well as students who had taken his classes, were encouraged to share their recollections and memories of the professor through blog posts or podcasts. The goal of this intervention was to focus on how Dr. Igbaria influenced the SISAT community, and to generate a sense of community and affiliation on a much deeper level than with the first Intervention.

While Remembrance Week did not produce as much activity or traffic as with the first Intervention, the comments left by community members qualitatively demonstrated a stronger sense of community and affiliation with the school:

"I don't remember the date of when we last communicated via email but I do remember the contents of his last email message to me. It was full of encouragement and of course, a reminder of his mantra for me. To this day, I still hear his words and remember his wisdom. It inspires and guides me. It's not easy to carry out his mantra to the letter, but I'm getting better at it! Thank you, Magid."

"He inspired me to live a good and meaningful life and serve as a role model to accomplish my goals in the future. He's a man I look up to, and taught me great lessons in life. I took IS340 (E-commerce) with him, which also benefits me greatly for my work at Tesco Lotus. He's truly missed..."

"Magid was a genius when it comes to academic publishing. He set a high standard for himself, and for all of us. I miss him! I was a PhD student at Drexel when Magid was there. This was a career change for me, and I was and still am, inspired by Magid's work ethic and insights. While not with us as a physical being, he lives on through his colleagues, friends, and family and of course his legacy of printed work."

"But the real benefit of an intellectual life is a kind of immortality — I am still actively using Magid's (and his doctoral students') research in my own work in IT Economics and E-Commerce."

Furthermore, feedback on using SISATSpace as a community tool was mentioned by some users:

"This week really has shown the power of SISAT-Space to connect students, faculty, alumni, and friends of the community. Kudos to all involved. Best wishes to [Dr. Igbaria's wife] Afaf and [his son] Mohammad."

"I'm so impressed with this week in SISATSpace. It's very touching. Although I never meet him before but I believe that he's a great person."

Evaluation of Phase II

One of the major lessons learned from Phase II was that in an online community in a graduate educational setting, the admin must play a vital role, not just in producing and distributing content such as Main Blog posts or podcasts, but also in conducting Intervention-like activities. Phase II also taught the project team how effective Intervention-like activities are for generating participation and a sense of affiliation within the community. The months of the two interventions, July and August 2007 respectively, saw the highest traffic rates in SISATSpace's lifecycle. Figures 7a-c summarizes the SSCI elements for Phase II, the SSCI elements for the week of Intervention I, and the SSCI elements for the week of Intervention II:

By now, as students start to familiarize with each other, occurrences of membership elements drop, and conversation moved onto that of one based on trust and influence. Shared emotional connection saw a boost from the two Interventions as users expressed a sense of membership through their shared connection with the student from Appreciation Week and with Dr. Igbaria. Remembrance Week in particular, which generated more shared emotional connection elements, was effective at drawing readership and active participation from alumni and off-campus students.

Figure 7. (a) SSCI data for phase I. (b and c) SSCI data for interventions I & II

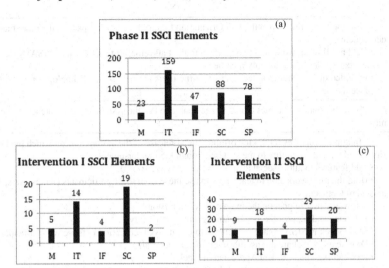

One major surprise for the project team was that SISATSpace served as an effective recruitment tool for prospective students. SISATSpace was able to generate subjective-level social presence (Biocca and Harms, 2002) within members outside the community. Early in the Fall 2006 semester, SISAT's Director of Recruitment suggested showing SISATSpace to prospective students and incoming students in order for them to obtain a clear picture of what the SISAT community is like. For example, one incoming student who had been directed to SISATSpace by our faculty was able to make connections with current SISAT students after finding out that they shared similar interests and opinions from perusing their blogs. One student who entered the program Fall 2007 semester said she felt like she had already known some of the students before joining SISAT from reading their blog posts and seeing pictures of them posted on the Main Blog. Another student who came in Fall 2007 favorably compared SISATSpace to student portals at other universities. She said the websites for departments at other universities only talked about the academics and not the people. At most, other websites would give a one-paragraph blurb about each professor and their research interests. However, SISATSpace gave her a clearer picture

of what the community of SISATSpace was really like, and – because some faculty members often blogged about their extra-academic interests and hobbies – a clearer picture of what the people of SISATSpace were really like.

The Action Research Process for Phase II is summarized in Table 3.

Phase III: Transfer of Control

The first two Interventions were a success that breathed new life into the system. However, while the Interventions did promote a sense of affiliation across the department, it did not promote student networking or centrality. Going back once again to the literature on fostering active participation, Wasko and Faraj (2005) determined that centrality, or the number of personal connections a community member has within a community, determined his or her motivation to participate. At this point, it was decided that the SISATSpace project would be consolidated into the campus-wide Claremont Conversation Online (CCO) initiative proposed by the University President at the start of the Winter 2008 semester, and that control of the project would be handed over to those leading CCO. During this period, the project team decided to conduct two

Table 3. Summary of the action research process for phase II

Diagnosing	• Held the first workshop at the Fall Orientation to introduce SISATSpace to the new students entering the department. • Held a follow up workshop two weeks into the Fall semester to reintroduce SISATSpace and its more advanced features to the community members. • Provided questionnaires to learn how familiar users are with social technology and how they feel about social presence in school.
Action Planning	• Plan Intervention activities to encourage people to use the system and generate a stronger sense of community.
Action Taking	• "Tangible Touch" event to kick off the official release of the system, during which the Dean and the University President lent credibility to the system through their endorsement. • Add features to allow social awareness (Most Active Blogs). • Hold the third workshop to teach how to use the system to 21 participants (8 new users, 13 current users) at the end of October. • Allow any user to post on the main page's Main Blog. • Publicize and support the system amongst the community. • "This Week in SISATSpace": Publicize tool and give recognition to those who participate • Drop features that are not useful (wiki, social bookmark). • First Intervention: Student Appreciation Week. • Second Intervention: Dr. Magrid Igbaria Remembrance Week.
Evaluating	• Use SlimStat to keep tabs on blog posts, blog comments, traffic logs. • Get prospective students to join.
Specifying Learning	• Major increase in activity during the two Intervention weeks. • The admin must play a vital role in maintaining the main blog page and in conducting Intervention activities.

more Interventions focusing on centrality rather than affiliation.

The first Intervention in Phase III was "Welcome New Members Week," held in the final week of August 2007. For the new incoming student body, the project team made a brief presentation at Orientation, asking new students afterwards to make a quick StudentCast recording, introducing themselves to the community. In addition, faculty and ISSC members also introduced themselves and explained the nature of SISATSpace to new students, further solidifying the legitimacy of the community. Participation was voluntary. In addition, emails were sent, inviting current members to participate by welcoming the new members. Ten of the fifteen new students participated in the activity. Each student recorded a short video introducing themselves to the community. Although traffic remained light during the week of the Intervention, the amount of participation by new users through the community posts was high. Two of the current members posted a welcome video message, voicing their hospitality towards

the new community members, and there were lively exchanges between current and new students through blog comments.

Continuing the pattern of using student suggestions and feedback as the kernel from which to develop new Intervention ideas, the project team looked to suggestions from the new students for ideas on the last Intervention of Phase III. Feedback from the new students demonstrated a demand for social integration.

"My semester started on a good note hope to continue it till the end of semester!!! Also, please tell me from where can I check if there is an activity going on in the university... is there a forum or something???"

This echoed posts from current students throughout the system's lifecycle seeking information on how to socialize with other members. To fulfill the users' need for achieving social integration, the researcher suggested to the SISAT Student Council officers the idea of using SISATSpace as a portal where members could sign up for a team-based activity during the Annual SISAT Fall Barbeque, a social gathering held each year in late September for all SISAT community members. An ISSC officer suggested creating three teams, led by faculty members, that would play against each other at the barbeque. This Intervention would focus on both centrality (students both old and new network with each other in a competitive setting) and – to a lesser extent – affiliation and membership (students sign up for teams led by faculty members). Guided by Nowak and Biocca (2003) the project team created a digital anthropomorphic avatar for each professor. As individuals signed up, the teams were updated on the Main Blog. Again, the researcher sent out an email to inform users about joining one of the professors' teams. Site traffic demonstrated a sizeable spike during this Intervention week, leading up to the day of the barbeque, though traffic levels did not reach those seen in Phase II's Interventions. A few members could not attend the barbeque, but expressed via blog comments their well wishes toward other members who had already signed up.

Following these two interventions, the project team continued to publish content and maintain the system in preparation for its transfer to the campus-wide Claremont Conversation Online initiative.

Evaluation of Phase III

Figures 8a-c summarizes the SSCI elements for Phase III, the SSCI elements for the week of Intervention III, and the SSCI elements for the week of Intervention IV:

Membership was the most commonly seen element in Phase III and Intervention III, as new users used SISATSpace to introduce themselves to the community. Intervention IV accounted for over half the instances of integration and fulfillment of needs elements found in Phase III, as many participants in Intervention IV would add a personal comment when signing up for teams:

"I'm a good player. Please count me in. Although I can't come to play because I have class from 4-7pm, I'd like to be a Prof. Lorne's team member."

Figure 8. (a) SSCI data for phase I. (b and c) SSCI data for interventions I & II

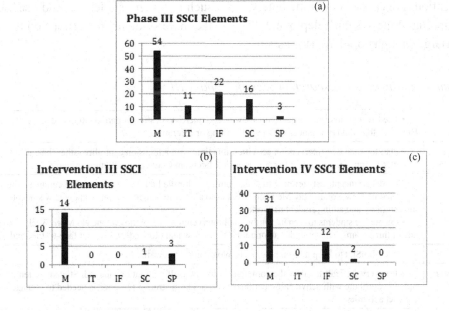

"I can't miss this team. I wanna be a brave soldier for Prof. Ryan in this war. Fight! Fight! Go Go!! Team Terry!!"

The Action Research Process for Phase III is summarized in Table 4.

FUTURE RESEARCH DIRECTIONS

Currently, SISATSpace is being integrated into CGU's Claremont Conversation Online initiative. It remains to be seen whether such techniques like the intervention activities would be applicable to different populations. SISAT is one of the smaller departments on campus, whose population usually hovers between 65-120 students. Possible future research directions include replicating this study in different academic populations. How will the results differ if a similar study is conducted at a larger academic department? How will the results differ if a similar study is conducted at a department where students are not as tech savvy? If a similar study is conducted across the entire university, across multiple departments? Could such a system support transdisciplinary academic networking? How will the results differ if techniques similar to our Interventions are carried out immediately, from the beginning of the system's deployment? If there was a large enough population to sustain a communal critical mass, would it do away with the community's reliance on a strong administrative presence or a need to conduct activities like our interventions? Facilitating active user participation was an issue with SISATSpace, future research can also be done on the attitudes and motivations for students who would rather read the contributions of their peers than contribute themselves.

It also remains to be seen if results would have differed with a different set of technologies. SISATSpace abandoned early on the use of wiki and social bookmarking technology. Since SISAT-Space's lifecycle, plugins have been developed for WordPress MU, such as BuddyPress, that can be used to more effectively turn WordPress MU into a social networking platform.

Future research possibilities include conducting similar studies that emphasize learning more than just student networking and community. Blogs and Web 2.0 technologies have much to offer to for education, and a system similar to SISATSpace could be set up to promote both learning and communal affiliation. Since with SISATSpace, each user had their own individual blog in which they could publish posts or pages, it is easy to conceive of a similar system being used to support e-Portfolio functionality. Within such a system, students could use their blogs to facilitate students' reflections on their learning.

Table 4. Summary of the action research process for phase III

Diagnosing	• The first two Intervention activities saw a large increase in student participation and sense of community. However, they did not promote student networking or centrality.
Action Planning	• Plan for final two Intervention activities, this time with a focus on centrality rather than affiliation. • Plan to transfer the system to campus-wide Claremont Conversation Online initiative.
Action Taking	• Produce StudentCasts for new students coming in for the Fall 2007 semester and conduct a third Intervention – "Welcome New Community Members Week" –to allow old students to get to know new students, thus increasing centrality and aiding student networking. • Encourage students to sign up for the final Intervention – "Bowling Alone No More Week" – to participate in any of three teams. This provides an opportunity for new and old students to meet face-to-face and network.
Evaluating	• Use SlimStat to keep tabs on blog posts, blog comments, traffic logs.
Specifying Learning	• It is very difficult to allow the community sustain itself without outside aid. Students oftentimes do not have time to contribute with active participation. A strong administrative presence is needed to manage the content and conduct activities.

Table 5. Summary for the study (adapted from Kohli and Kettinger (2004))

Phase	Time Period	Functionality	Technologies Characteristics	Motivation
1	May–August 2006	Community-Based Social Networking system	Blog system using Wordpress MU. Wiki system using MediaWiki Social Bookmarking system using Scuttle	Testbed for the new system. During this time, prototypes of the system were unveiled in a series of focus groups, workshops, and stakeholder meetings to gather feedback and change system accordingly.
2	September 2006 – August 2007	Maintain, publicize, and support the system. Generate awareness of the system, nurture users	Open source Wordpress plug-ins allowing users to upload YouTube and Google Video content and Flickr photo slideshows to their blogs	Official release of the system. Using blogging and podcasting software to eliminate the need for same-time same-place environments for scholarly conversation, and to develop a stronger sense of community within the department.
3	September-December 2007	Motivate users to participate more and engage in discussion		Active participation has reached a low level towards the end of the school year. A new approach is needed to motivate users to participate. A series of interventions are held to encourage users to participate

CONCLUSION

The three Phases of the SISATSpace project are summarized in Table 5.

The main lesson learned was the difficulty in maintaining a healthy level of active participation within an online community without a strong administrative presence. A small system such as ours with a limited number of active participants would be in peril without such a presence to sustain interest, provide content, and generate motivation to participate. This administrative presence was needed to constantly publish new material to the main blog, whether it be in the form of blog postings or podcasts. Many students lack the time and are too tied down with other commitments to regularly contribute and actively participate in online community. Rather, these students participate passively, reading and watching content posted by others without making their own contribution. Even when the demographic expanded during the later stages of SISATSpace's lifecycle, the number of active bloggers – around 15 out of 90 – for the most part remained the same. To facilitate participation and aide the system in its goal of enhancing the sense of community and conversation of the department, the project team carried out a series of interventions activities to sustain a desired level of interactivity. The two months in which the first three interventions were carried out saw traffic rates double that of the previous month's. Figure 9 graphs the traffic levels throughout SISATSpace's lifespan.

These interventions had to be carried out at a rate of around once per month, as after the final intervention, SISATSpace traffic dropped back to average levels.

For other researchers developing their own intellectual community at the university level, our study provides several design principles (which will be used to improve the intellectual community at CGU by expanding SISATSpace to the entire

Figure 9. System traffic per month (in terms of hits)

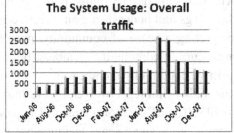

campus as part of the Claremont Conversation Online initiative). First, a strong administrative is required to disseminate a constant stream of content, in order to maintain user interest and draw and sustain readership. With a steady rate of one blog post on the Main Blog per day and one Cast on the Main Blog per week, the project team was only able to generate average levels of readership throughout most of Phase II (as indicated through student responses to our questionnaire). It could be that more content that what was provided would have been necessary to increase readership. Secondly, interventions or intervention-like activities, possibly done once or twice a month, are an extremely effective method of nurturing participation, both active and passive. Corollary to this is that interventions must be driven by theory. Our study showed that interventions that fostered a strong sense of communal affiliation or a shared emotional connection could motivate more members to participate. Intervention II in particular was able to draw readership and active participation from alumni and off-campus students. To a lesser extent, motivation to participate can also be achieved with interventions that supported centrality and connection building for participants amongst their peers. Next, the system should support awareness. Awareness means knowing what actions others are taking. Without awareness, keeping track of who has updated his or her blog becomes a cumbersome activity and users quickly lose motivation. Finally, blogs and podcasts can be effectively used as a recruitment tool, and a means to foster a sense of membership within a community in individuals prior to their entrance into the community. This was seen in SISATSpace's use as a recruitment tool. Used as we did, blogs and podcasts are an effective tool for projecting a sense of community, not only amongst current community members, but also prospective community members.

Our study is limited, however, by the uniqueness of SISAT, and Claremont Graduate University in general, as a small-scale technically-savvy graduate-only educational environment. While we suspect awareness is still an important factor no matter what the variables of a particular online environment are, it remains to be seen whether it would be easier or more difficult to foster active participation in a larger department, a different field, or a campus with a non-graduate-exclusive setting, using the levels of content dissemination or intervention strategies that we used. Finally, we suspect that SISATSpace's ability to project a sense of community to outsiders as a recruitment tool is not something specific to SISAT. However, that is a topic for future research.

REFERENCES

Andrews, D., Preece, J., & Turoff, M. (2001). *A conceptual framework for demographic groups resistant to online community interaction.* Paper presented at the 34th Hawaii International Conference on System Sciences.

Baskerville, R. L. (1999). Investigating information systems with action research. *Communications of the Association for Information Systems, 2*(19), 1–32.

Baskerville, R. L., & Wood-Harper, A. T. (1996). A critical perspective on action research as a method for information systems research. *Journal of Information Technology, 11*(3), 235–246. doi:10.1080/026839696345289

Biocca, F., Burgoon, J., Harms, C., & Stoner, M. (2001). *Criteria and scope conditions for a theory and measure of social presence.* Paper presented at PRESENCE 2001, Philadelphia, PA.

Biocca, F., & Harms, C. (2002). Defining and measuring social presence: Contribution to the networked minds theory and measure. In. *Proceedings of PRESENCE, 2002,* 7–36.

Biocca, F., Harms, C., & Burgoon, J. K. (2003). Toward a more robust theory and measure of social presence: Review and suggested criteria. *Presence (Cambridge, Mass.)*, *12*(5), 456–480. doi:10.1162/105474603322761270

Bock, G., Zmud, R. W., & Kim, Y. (2005). Behavioral intention formation in knowledge sharing: Examining the roles of extrinsic motivators, social-psychological forces, and organizational climate. *Management Information Systems Quarterly*, *29*(1), 87–111.

Bourgeois, D. T., & Horan, T. A. (2007). A design theory approach to community informatics: Community-centered development and action research testing of online social networking prototype. *The Journal of Community Informatics*, *3*(1).

Brown, J. S., Collins, A., & Duguid, P. (1989). Situated cognition and the culture of learning. *Educational Researcher*, *18*(1), 32–42.

Callison, C. (2001). Do PR practitioners have a PR problem?: The effect of associating a source with public relations and client-negative news on audience perception of credibility. *Journal of Public Relations Research*, *13*, 219–234. doi:10.1207/S1532754XJPRR1303_2

Cameron, D., & Anderson, T. (2006). *Comparing weblogs to threaded discussion tools in online educational contexts*. Instructional Technology & Distance Learning.

Cayzer, S. (2004). Semantic blogging and decentralized knowledge management. *Communications of the ACM*, *47*, 47–52. doi:10.1145/1035134.1035164

Chavis, D. M., & Newbrough, J. R. (1986). The meaning of "community" in community psychology. *Journal of Community Psychology*, *14*(4), 335–340. doi:10.1002/1520-6629(198610)14:4<335::AID-JCOP2290140402>3.0.CO;2-T

Chipuer, H. M., & Pretty, G. M. H. (1999). A review of the sense of community index: Current uses, factor structure, reliability, and further development. *Journal of Community Psychology*, *27*(6), 643–658. doi:10.1002/(SICI)1520-6629(199911)27:6<643::AID-JCOP2>3.0.CO;2-B

Cohen, T., & Clemens, B. (2005). *Social networks for creative collaboration*. Paper presented at the Proceedings of the 5th conference on Creativity & Cognition.

Cole, R., Purao, S., Rossi, M., & Sein, M. K. (2005). Being proactive: Where action research meets design research. In *Proceedings of the 26th International Conference on Information Systems* (pp. 325-336).

Corey, S. (1953). *Action research to improve school practice*. New York: Teachers College, Columbia University.

Cress, U., Barquero, B., Schwan, S., & Hesse, F. W. (2007). Improving quality and quantity of contributions: Two models for promoting knowledge exchange with shared databases. *Computers & Education*, *49*(2), 423–440. doi:10.1016/j.compedu.2005.10.003

Cunningham, W. (2006). *Design principles of Wiki: How can so little do so much?* Retrieved February 20, 2008, from http://c2.com/doc/wikisym/WikiSym2006.pdf

Daft, R., & Lengel, R. (1986). Organizational information requirements, media richness, and structure design. *Management Science*, *32*(5). doi:10.1287/mnsc.32.5.554

Dourish, P., & Bellotti, V. (1992). *Awareness and coordination in shared workspaces*. Paper presented at the ACM Conference on Computer Supported Cooperative Work, Toronto, Ontario.

Drucker, P. (1993, March). According to Peter Drucker (Interview). *Forbes*, 90–95.

Ebner, M., & Holzinger, A. (2005). Lurking: An underestimated human-computer phenomenon. *IEEE MultiMedia, 12*(4), 70–75. doi:10.1109/MMUL.2005.74

Ellemers, N., Spears, R., & Doosje, B. (Eds.). (1999). *Social identity: Context, commitment, content*. Oxford, UK: Blackwell.

Ellemers, N., Spears, R., & Doosje, B. (2002). Self and social identity. *Annual Review of Psychology, 53*, 161–186. doi:10.1146/annurev.psych.53.100901.135228

Fishbein, M., & Ajzen, I. (1975). *Beliefs, attitude, intention and behavior: An introduction to theory and research*. Reading, MA: Addison-Wesley Publishing Company.

Fogg, B. J. (2003). *Persuasive technology: Using computers to change what we yhink and do*. San Fransisco: Morgan Kaufmann Publishers.

Fogg, B. J., Soohoo, C., Danielson, D., & Marable, L. (2002). *How do people evaluate a web site's: Results from a large study (A consumer reports WebWatch research report)*. Standford, CA: Standford University, Stanford Persuasive Technology Lab.

Geoghegan, M., & Klass, D. (2007). *Podcast solutions: The complete guide to audio and video podcasting*. Berkeley, CA: Friends of ED.

Gunawardena, C. (1995). Social presence theory and implications for interaction and collaborative learning in computer conferencing. *International Journal of Educational Telecommunications, 1*(2-3), 147–166.

Gunawardena, C., & Zittle, F. (1997). Social presence as a predictor of satisfaction within a computer mediated conferencing environment. *American Journal of Distance Education, 11*(3), 8–26. doi:10.1080/08923649709526970

Hevner, A. R., March, S. T., Park, J., & Ram, S. (2004). Design research in information systems research. *Management Information Systems Quarterly, 28*(1), 75–105.

Hiltz, S. R., & Wellman, B. (1997). Asynchronous learning networks as a virtual classroom. *Communications of the ACM, 40*, 44–47. doi:10.1145/260750.260764

Ijsselsteijn, W., Baren, J. V., & Lanen, F. V. (2003). *Staying in touch: Social presence and connectedness through synchronous and asynchronous communication media*. Paper presented at the 10th International Conference on Human-Computer Interaction. Lawrence Erlbaum.

Kimmerle, J., & Cress, U. (2008). Group awareness and self-presentation in computersupported information exchange. *International Journal of Computer-Supported Collaborative Learning, 3*(1), 85–97. doi:10.1007/s11412-007-9027-z

Kimmerle, J., Wodzicki, K., & Cress, U. (2008). The social psychology of knowledge management. *Team Performance Management, 14*(7/8), 381–401. doi:10.1108/13527590810912340

Kohli, R., & Kettinger, W. J. (2004). Informating the Clan: Controlling Physicians' Costs and Outcomes. *Management Information Systems Quarterly, 28*(3), 363–394.

Kraut, R. E., Fish, R. S., Root, R. W., & Chalfonte, B. L. (Eds.). (1990). *Informal communication in organizations: Form, function, and technology*. Beverly Hills, CA: Sage Publications.

Kuwabara, K., Watanabe, T., Ohguro, T., Itoh, Y., & Maeda, Y. (2002). Connectedness oriented communication: Fostering a sense of connectedness to augment social relationships. *Information Processing Society of Japan Journal, 43*(11), 3270–3279.

Lazar, J., & Preece, J. (1999). *Implementing service learning in an online communities course.* Paper presented at the 1999 Conference of the International Association for Information Management.

Leuf, B., & Cunningham, W. (2001). *The Wiki way: Quick collaboration of the Web.* Reading, MA: Addison-Wesley Professional.

Lindgren, R., Henfridsson, O., & Schultze, U. (2004). Design principles for competence management systems: A synthesis of an action research study. *Management Information Systems Quarterly, 28*(3), 435–472.

Long, D. A., & Perkins, D. D. (2003). Confirmatory factor analysis of the sense of community index and development of a brief SCI. *Journal of Community Psychology, 31*, 279–296. doi:10.1002/jcop.10046

Malone, T., & Lepper, M. (1987). Making learning fun: A taxonomy of intrinsic motivation for learning. In Snow, R. E., & Farr, M. J. (Eds.), *Aptitude, learning, and instruction.* Hillsdale, NJ: Lawrence Earlbaum.

Markus, M. L., Majchrzak, A., & Gasser, L. (2002). A design theory for systems that support emergent knowledge processes. *Management Information Systems Quarterly, 26*(3), 179–212.

McGrath, J. E., & Hollingshead, A. B. (1994). *Groups interacting with technology.* Thousand Oaks: Sage Publications.

McMillan, D. W. (1996). Sense of community. *Journal of Community Psychology, 24*(4), 315–325. doi:10.1002/(SICI)1520-6629(199610)24:4<315::AID-JCOP2>3.0.CO;2-T

McMillan, D. W., & Chavis, D. M. (1986). Sense of community: A definition and theory. *Journal of Community Psychology, 14*(1), 6–23. doi:10.1002/1520-6629(198601)14:1<6::AID-JCOP2290140103>3.0.CO;2-I

Menzie, K. A. (2006). *Building online relationships: Relationship marketing and social presence as foundations for a university library blog.* Lawrence, KS: The University of Kansas.

Mumford, E. (2001). Advice for an Action Researcher. *Information Technology & People, 14*(1), 12–27. doi:10.1108/09593840110384753

Nonnecke, B., & Preece, J. (2000). Lurker demographics: Counting the silent. In *Proceedings of Special Interest Group on Computer-Human Interactions (SIGCHI) Conference* (pp. 73-80). New York: ACM Press.

Nowak, K. L., & Biocca, F. (2003). The Effect of the agency and anthropomorphism on users' sense of telepresence, copresence, and social presence in virtual environments. *Presence (Cambridge, Mass.), 12*(5), 481–494. doi:10.1162/105474603322761289

Ojala, M. (2004). *Weaving weblogs into knowledge sharing and dissemination.* Nord I&D, Knowledge and Change. Retrieved October 13, 2006, from http://www2.db.dk/NIOD/ojala.pdf

Perschbach, W. J. (2006). *Blogging: An inquiry into the efficacy of a web-based technology for student reflection in community college computer science programs.* Dissertation, Dissertation Abstracts International. (3206012)

Preece, J. (2000). *Online communities: Designing usability, supporting sociability.* New York: John Wiley & Sons.

Preece, J., Nonnecke, B., & Andrews, D. (2004). The top 5 reasons for lurking: Improving community experiences for everyone. *Special Issue of Computers in Human Behavior: An Interdisciplinary Perspective, 20*(2).

Putnam, R. D. (2000). *Bowling Alone. The collapse and revival of American community.* New York: Simon and Schuster.

Rettie, R. M. (2003a). *A comparison of four new communication technologies*. Paper presented at the HCI International Conference on Human-Computer Interaction, New Jersey.

Rettie, R. M. (2003b). *Connectedness, awareness and social presence*. Paper presented at the 6th International Presence Workshop, Aalborg, Denmark.

Rice, R. (1993). Media Appropriateness; using social presence theory to compare traditional and new organizational media. *Human Communication Research*, *19*(4), 451–484. doi:10.1111/j.1468-2958.1993.tb00309.x

Roger, R. (2006). *Creating community and gaining readers through newspaper blogs*. Chapel Hill, NC: The University of North Carolina at Chapel Hill.

Sallnäs, E. L. (1999). *Presence in multimodal interfaces*. Paper presented at the Second International Workshop on Presence, Colchester, UK.

Sarason, S. B. (1974). *The psychological sense of community: Prospects for a community psychology*. San Francisco: Jossey-Bass.

Sarbaugh-Thompson, M., & Feldman, M. (1998). Electronic mail and organizational communication: Does saying 'Hi' really matter? *Organization Science*, *9*(6), 685–698. doi:10.1287/orsc.9.6.685

Schroeder, R. (2002). Social interaction in virtual environments: Key issues, common themes, and a framework for research. In R. Schroeder (Ed.), The Social Life of Avatars; Presence and Interaction in Shared Virtual Environments (1-18). London: Springer-Verlag.

Shih, L., & Swan, K. (2005). Fostering social presence in asynchronous online class discussions. *Paper presented at the 2005 Conference on Computer Support for Collaborative Learning*.

Short, J., Williams, E., & Christie, B. (1976). *The social psychology telecommunications*. London: John Wiley and Sons.

Simon, H. (1996). *The sciences of the artificial*. Cambridge, MA: MIT Press.

Smith, E., & Mackie, D. (2000). *Social psychology*. New York, USA: Psychology Press.

Smith, G. (2008). *Tagging: People-powered metadata for the social web*. Berkeley, CA: New Riders.

Stacey, E. (2002). Social presence online: Networking learners at a distance. *Education and Information Technologies*, *7*(4), 287–294. doi:10.1023/A:1020901202588

Trammell, K. D. (2004). *Celebrity blogs: Investigation in the persuasive nature of two-way communication regarding politics* (Additional Readings). Unpublished doctoral dissertation, University of Florida, Florida.

Tran, M. H., Raikundalia, G. K., & Yang, Y. (2006). Using an experimental study to develop group awareness support for real-time distributed collaborative writing. *Information and Software Technology*, *48*(11), 1006–1024. doi:10.1016/j.infsof.2005.12.009

Tu, C., & McIsaac, M. (2002). The relationship of social presence and interaction in online classes. *American Journal of Distance Education*, *16*, 131–150. doi:10.1207/S15389286AJDE1603_2

Tu, C. H. (2002). The measurement of social presence in an online learning environment. *International Journal on E-Learning*, *1*(2), 34–45.

Wagner, C., & Bolloju, N. (2005). Supporting knowledge management in organizations with conversational technologies: Discussion forums, weblogs, and wikis. *Journal of Database Management*, *16*(2), i–viii.

Walther, J. B. (1996). Computer-mediated communication: Impersonal, interpersonal, and hyperpersonal interaction. *Communication Research, 23*, 3–43. doi:10.1177/009365096023001001

Wang, H., & Chee, Y. S. (2001). *Supporting workspace awareness in distance learning environments: Issues and experiences in the development of a collaborative learning system.* Paper presented at the ICCE/SchoolNet 2001--Ninth International Conference on Computers in Education. Seoul, South Korea.

Wasko, M. M., & Faraj, S. (2005). Why should I share? Examining social capital and knowledge contribution in electronic networks of practice. *Management Information Systems Quarterly, 29*(1), 35–57.

Wellman, B., Salaff, J., Dimitrova, D., Garton, L., Gulia, M., & Haythornthwaite, C. (1996). Computer networks as social networks: Collaborative work, telework, and virtual community. *Annual Review of Sociology, 22*, 213–238. doi:10.1146/annurev.soc.22.1.213

What is Enterprise 2.0? (n.d.). Retrieved October 15, 2008, from http://www.e2conf.com/about/what-is-enterprise2.0.php

Wilcox, D. L., Cameron, G. T., Ault, P. H., & Agee, W. K. (2003). *Public relations: Strategies and tactics.* Boston: Allyn and Bacon.

Williams, J. B., & Jacobs, J. (2004). Exploring the use of blogs as learning spaces in the higher education sector. *Australasian Journal of Educational Technology, 20*(2), 232–247.

Wright, S. P. (2004). *Exploring psychological sense of community in living learning programs and in the university as a whole.* Dissertation, Digital Repository at the University of Maryland, Maryland.

ADDITIONAL READING

Alem, L., & Kravis, S. (2005, January). Design and evaluation of an online learning community: A case study at CSIRO. *ACM SIGGROUP Bulletin, 25*(1).

Baker-Eveleth, L., Sarker, S., & Eveleth, D. M. (2005). *Formation of an online community of practice: An inductive study unearthing key elements.* Paper presented at the 38th Hawaii International Conference on System Sciences.

Butler, B., Sproull, L., Kiesler, S., & Kraut, R. (2002). Community effort in online groups: Who does the work and why? In Weisband, S., & Atwater, L. (Eds.), *Leadership at a Distance* (p. 11).

Collins, A., Brown, J. S., & Newman, D. (1989). Cognitive apprenticeship: Teaching the craft of reading, writing, and mathematics. In Resnick, L. B. (Ed.), *Knowing, learning, and instruction: Essay in honor of Robert Glaser* (pp. 453–494). Hillsdale, NJ: Lawrence Erlbaum Associates.

Crosta, L., & McConnell, D. (2006). Action research and tutoring in the learning community: New implications for online adult education. *Networked Learning.* Retrieved from http://www.networkedlearningconference.org.uk/past/nlc2006/abstracts/pdfs/P43%20Crosta.pdf

Dafoulas, G. A. (2005). *Enhancing computer mediated communication in virtual learning environments.* Paper presented at the Fifth IEEE International Conference on Advanced Learning Technologies.

Du, Y. (2006). *Modeling the behavior of lurkers in online communities using intentional agents.* Paper presented at the International Conference on Computational Intelligence for Modeling Control and Automation, and International Conference on Intelligent Agents, Web Technologies and Internet Commerce.

Duffy, T. M., & Jonassen, D. H. (1992). *Constructivism and the technology of instruction: A conversation*. Hillsdale, NJ: Lawrence Erlbaum Associates.

Garrett, N., Thoms, B., Soffer, M., & Ryan, T. (2007). *Extending the ELGG social networking system to enhance the campus conversation*. Paper presented at Second Annual Design Research in Information Systems (DESRIST), Pasadena, California.

Grabowski, B. (1990). Social and intellectual value of computer-mediated communications in a graduate community. *Educational & Training Technology International, 27*(3), 276.

Gunderman, R. (2008). Are we building intellectual community? *Journal of the American College of Radiology, 5*(9), 1007–1009. doi:10.1016/j.jacr.2008.02.011

Jonassen, D. H. (1991). Objectivism versus constructivism: Do we need a new philosophical paradigm. *Educational Technology Research and Development, 39*(3), 4–14. doi:10.1007/BF02296434

Kankanhalli, A., Tan, B. C., & Wei, K. (2005). Contributing knowledge to electronic knowledge repositories: An empirical investigation. *Management Information Systems Quarterly, 29*(1), 113–143.

Klitgaard, R. (2006, September 20). *More Like Us*. Retrieved from http://www.cgu.edu/pages/4421.asp

Klitgaard, R. (2008, February). Universities have the responsibility to Tackle the World's Toughest Problems. *The Chronicle of Higher Education, 54*(21), A1.

Lave, J., & Wenger, E. (1991). *Situated learning: Legitimate periperal participation*. Cambridge, UK: Cambridge University Press.

McConnell, D. (2002). Action Research and Distributed Problem-Based Learning in Continuing Professional Education. *Distance Education, 23*(1), 59–83. doi:10.1080/01587910220123982

McElrath, E., & McDowell, K. (2008). Pedagogical Strategies for Building Community in Graduate Level Distance Education Courses. *Journal of Online Learning and Teaching, 4*(1).

Nonnecke, B., & Preece, J. (2001). *Why lurkers lurk*. Paper presented at the Americas Conference on Information Systems.

Raman, M., Ryan, T., & Olfman, L. (2005). Designing knowledge management systems for teaching and learning with wiki technology. *Journal of Information Systems Education, 16*(3), 311–320.

Rogoff, B., & Lave, J. (1984). *Everyday cognition: Its development in social context*. Cambridge, UK: Cambridge University Press.

Scardamalia, M., Bereiter, C., Mclean, R. S., Swallow, J., & Woodruff, E. (1989). Computer supported intentional learning environments. *Journal of Educational Computing Research, 5*, 51–68.

Thoms, B., Garrett, N., Soffer, M., & Ryan, T. (2007) *Resurrecting graduate conversation through an online learning community*. Paper presented IADIS Multi Conference on Computer Science and Information Systems, Lisbon, Portugal.

Tran, M. H., Yang, Y., & Raikundalia, G. K. (2006). *Extended radar view and modification director: Awareness mechanisms for synchronous collaborative authoring*. Paper presented at the 7th Australasian User Interface Conference, Hobart, Australia.

Wenger, E. (1998). *Communities of practice: Learning, meaning, and identity*. Cambridge, UK: Cambridge University Press.

Wenger, E., McDermott, R., & Snyder, W. M. (2002). *Cultivating communities or practice: A guide to managing knowledge*. Boston: Harvard Business School Press.

Wenger, E., White, N., Smith, J., & Rowe, K. (2005). *Technology for communities.* Retrieved from http://technologyforcommunities.com/CE-FRIO_Book_Chapter_v_5.2.pdf

APPENDIX

This is a summary of the responses given to the questionnaire handed out at the end of the Fall 2006 semester.

Table 6. Technology familiarity

1 = Not Familiar With, 3= Somewhat Familiar, 5 = Very Familiar With						
	1	2	3	4	5	Average number of hours per week
Podcasting	30%	7%	35%	14%	14%	1.216
Blogging	14%	7%	25%	25%	30%	1.892
Social Networks	27%	14%	18%	20%	20%	2
Social Bookmarking	48%	17%	21%	5%	10%	0.581
Wiki	9%	16%	18%	34%	23%	2.776

Table 7. System Use

1 = None, 3= Somewhat, 5 = Everyday					
	1	2	3	4	5
How often do you read SISATSpace main blog site?	20%	43%	30%	4%	2%
How often do you read others' blog?	20%	46%	26%	4%	4%
How often do you update your blog?	41%	41%	15%	0%	2%

Table 8. Social Networks and Community of Practices

1 = Strongly Disagree, 2 = Disagree,3 = Neutral, 4 = Agree, 5 = Strongly Agree					
	1	2	3	4	5
I am comfortable communicating electronically	0%	0%	9%	35%	57%
I am willing to actively communicate with my SISATspace users electronically	4%	15%	30%	20%	30%
I feel comfortable communicating in written communication in English	2%	0%	11%	22%	65%
I feel that face-to-face contact with my friends and colleagues is necessary for learning to occur	0%	9%	39%	15%	37%
I can discuss and collaborate with other colleagues during Internet activities outside of class	0%	2%	17%	37%	43%
I can identify my colleagues when I see them	0%	7%	17%	35%	41%
I am interested in what my colleagues have to say about themselves	0%	2%	28%	35%	35%
I am interested in what my colleagues have to say about me	2%	13%	24%	35%	26%
I am interested in academic activities such as research seminar events within our community	2%	4%	13%	35%	46%
I am frequently kept up with the extra activities happening within our community	2%	24%	28%	37%	9%
Overall, I believe building relationship with my colleagues will improve my well-being within the community	2%	2%	9%	37%	50%
I attempt to express my interests and share them with my colleagues	2%	7%	24%	41%	26%
I frequently share my knowledge with others in the community	2%	9%	33%	33%	24%
I make a conscious effort to spend time engaged in activities that contribute knowledge to the community	4%	20%	33%	26%	17%

Other community members find my knowledge-sharing contributions to be useful	7%	10%	50%	31%	2%
My contributions to the community enable others to develop new knowledge	2%	17%	43%	29%	10%
Overall, I feel the frequency and quality of my knowledge-sharing efforts are of great value to me and our community	2%	14%	30%	36%	18%
Currently, I believe the community is interested in my well-being	4%	7%	47%	29%	13%
Currently, I believe the community is genuine and sincere	4%	7%	18%	38%	33%
Currently, I believe the community is a competent and effective source of expertise	2%	7%	26%	41%	24%
Currently, I believe the community performs its role of sharing knowledge very well	2%	13%	33%	37%	15%

Section 2
Technologies

Chapter 4
Collaborative Knowledge Construction with Web Video Conferencing:
A Work Based Learning Approach

Stylianos Hatzipanagos
King's College London, UK

Anthony Basiel
Middlesex University, UK

Annette Fillery-Travis
Middlesex University, UK

ABSTRACT

This chapter explores how web-based video conferencing (WVC) can be used to create and support learning environments within a work based learning context. Computer mediated communication interactions through WVC can support collaborative knowledge construction by encouraging dialogical processes in communities of learners and practitioners. We position our field of exploration within the educational landscape defined by socio-economic changes, resulting from the development of the knowledge economy, and the explosive growth of information and communication technologies to serve it.

INTRODUCTION

Work-based learning (WBL) gives employed learners the opportunity to achieve academic credit for real-life learning experiences in the workplace (Armsby, Costley, & Garnett, 2006). It provides a framework for the development and acknowledgement of knowledge within and about practice and

hence is a well evidenced vehicle for this type of flexible and context based development.

It is now accepted that distance learning within WBL should be provided through a blended approach (Basiel, 2008). Computer based learning environments engage multimedia to motivate learners and to improve metacognitive skills; however they lack in social interaction. Social interaction, with the corresponding increase in trust and security

DOI: 10.4018/978-1-61520-937-8.ch004

for the individuals, can have an impact on deeper exploration and sharing of learning.

Videoconferencing technology allows people at different locations to see and hear each other and to share computer applications such as internet pages, documents or software (Greenberg, 2004). A synchronous web-based videoconferencing (WVC) set-up consists of computers fitted with a camera and appropriate software.

The chapter will discuss how to embed successfully WVC into the WBL curriculum design; it builds on our on-going research on WVC and its pedagogical affordances (Hatzipanagos, Commins & Basiel, 2007). Models of implementation will be discussed in conjunction with underpinning technology enhanced learning theories. Two case studies will illustrate the theoretical background and the affordances of the technology. We have used an action research approach, with an emphasis on the pedagogic shift in thinking of the tutor and professional learner practitioners. Finally, we have identified a number of specific issues whose explicit discussion allows a smooth progression from initiation/induction via the appropriate use of technology through to e-collaborative knowledge construction.

KNOWLEDGE ECONOMY AND COMMUNICATION TECHNOLOGIES

The development of the knowledge economy in organisations, and the use of communication technologies to serve it, has:

- Increased the ability to respond quickly to emerging opportunities and threats. (Morey, Maybury & Thuraisingham, 2002).
- Led to restructuring and made hierarchical levels manageable, away from a conventional organisational hierarchy towards flatter more networked systems, where

authority and responsibility is devolved further downstream.

- Altered expectations of individual employees who must have the appropriate knowledge and authority to perform. They must be able to continually adapt and develop if they are to maintain their position in organisations seeking to achieve the responsiveness and innovation they need to prosper within rapidly changing markets (Jarvis, Lane & Fillery-Travis, 2006).

It was this need to harness individuals' learning and development for the benefit of the whole organisation which led to the concept of the 'learning organisation', as envisaged by Senge (1990) and this driver remains at the centre of a range of both national and European government initiatives.

The expansion of information resulting from the new economy and changing work practices has placed strain on traditional organisational systems, bringing to light new required capabilities to fully evolve and take advantage of the opportunities and effects they provide. Knowledge management is the umbrella term for these new capabilities and has been an established discipline since 1995 (Stankosky, 2005). As its name implies, it attempts to bring together the various strands of thought and practice relating to:

- Intellectual capital and the knowledge worker (Drucker, 1973)
- The learning organisation (Senge, 1990)
- The formation of organisational communities, such as Communities of Practice (Wenger, 1998)
- Technologies such as knowledge bases and expert systems, help desks, corporate intranets and social software, such as organisational wikis.

Originally, knowledge management was seen as an investment in organisation–wide systems such as intranets which would allow individuals to store, share and manage their knowledge. Thus, for many, knowledge management became synonymous with information systems and infrastructure. It soon became clear that to be effective, the overall organisational management perspective needed to be attuned to knowledge management as well. The behaviour of people was equally important as the choice of systems, and could be guided to enhance knowledge activity and hence effectiveness. The terms explicit and tacit knowledge (Polanyi, 1966) came into use, identifying some of the real challenges of codifying all the knowledge within an organisation. Explicit knowledge can be relatively easily captured and written down; examples include manuals and research findings. Tacit knowledge is more nebulous as it is the 'unspoken understanding' held by an individual about a topic (Cong & Panya, 2003). It is considered more valuable, as it is contextualised and imbibed with both personal and professional experience.

The central hub of this construct, however, is the learning of the individual. The challenge for the organisation is how best to promote, and indeed exploit, such learning for its own benefit. WBL is one way by which this learning is made explicit, shared and acknowledged to the benefit of both learners and the organisation (Reeve & Gallacher, 2000).

WORK BASED LEARNING AND KNOWLEDGE CONSTRUCTION

The term WBL has been used to describe a range of provision, where learning within work is incorporated within a university programme. In this chapter we restrict our discussion to the type of WBL, where there is an explicit partnership between the university and the organisation, based upon the assumption that employees are continually developing and use knowledge over and above that acknowledged by the credentials

they may already have (Armsby, Costley & Garnett, 2006). WBL refers specifically to the achievement of planned learning outcomes derived from the experience of performing a work role or function. This learning can then be accredited by a university towards the attainment of foundation through to doctorate degrees. Currently there is a range of WBL provision within the UK HE sector and similar provision is available within US and Australia. This method of acknowledging learning within the workplace has also been popular with professional bodies as a recognised accessible route for the attainment of professional designations.

In terms of efficacy; these programmes are required to meet all the conventional academic quality standards in relation to the development of the individual but must also achieve impact within the candidate's work role. The evaluation of the impact goes beyond the immediate value of the results of the project work undertaken and impacts upon the motivation and professionalism of the individual and the initiation of change in the broader organizational context (Lester & Costley, 2009).

WBL provides the opportunity for full-time employed or volunteer professionals to explore and develop their professional knowledge, acquired through their practice, within the workplace. It provides a means to gain higher education degrees by the acknowledgement of that learning and can be delivered through distance learning programmes. It is probable that this learning will be transdisciplinary (involving more than one discipline and incorporating the experience of the individuals involved) and contextualised but still able to comply with the learning outcomes required for university level accreditation.

Learning will also be, to some extent, unique to the individual, their background and role. At first sight this level of complexity - in essence an individualised 'curriculum' - would seem to resist any attempt to codify it into a generalisable university programme. WBL programmes circumvent such issues by treating each programme for what it is - an individual programme of study - and place the responsibility with the learner to negotiate the content, level and final award for their programme with the university and, to an appropriate extent, their organisation. At postgraduate level this results in a 'Programme Plan', explicitly agreed and signed by the candidate, their organisation and the university. It identifies what learning the individual has already developed (and for which they are seeking accreditation) and what learning they are looking to develop within their programme - usually as part of a research project. This research project must be focused upon the working practice of the candidate and the results must have impact upon their own practice, their profession and/or their organisation. In effect the project will encompass both practitioner research and its development into practice. In this way the focus of learning is shifted away from the accumulation of knowledge to the identification, consolidation and development of work based knowledge in which the individual learner already has significant expertise. The shift is one from a defined curriculum to learning which is self directed by the candidates themselves. The respect accorded to the expertise of the learner in this case is reflected by the use of the term candidate as opposed to student. The term student has connotations of novice whereas candidate implies a person of achievement seeking accreditation of their expertise.

The benefits of such an approach are clear. The candidate has the opportunity to develop their learning within their work or professional practice, to achieve a university award and the organisation benefits from targeted research and development by in-house practitioners which meets their defined objectives. The effort expanded by the individual in achieving their own development also benefits the organisation in a direct and tangible outcome. The challenges are also clear - specifically the development, assessment and management of the programmes.

The assessment framework addresses significant considerations, namely: who should assess and using what criteria and what assessment tasks should be undertaken to evidence learning in which professional element.

The initiation and management of these programme also requires considerable investment. Conventional university procedures and protocols are designed for students who are attending classes within a designated timeframe following a set curriculum. The flexibility required for professional candidates working on individual programmes at a distance is substantial. The transdisciplinary nature of it also 'departs substantially from the disciplinary framework of university study' (Boud, 2001) and hence requires a change in appropriate pedagogical methodologies and practices.

In this chapter we consider the support the candidates require, and specifically how that support can be provided in an appropriate work based context. In the following section we identify a model of engagement of the candidate with the advisor which draws heavily upon coaching and mentoring theory. The model is not advisor/tutor centred, as it empowers the learner. The context of WBL allows the adoption of self regulated attitudes that are essential to any WBL undertaking.

WBL CANDIDATE ENGAGEMENT

The role of tutor or supervisor in such a programme is complex as they are not an expert per se (although they may have an academic subject specialism). They will not have full knowledge of the context in which the candidate is working. Neither are they 'in control' of the learning that their candidate achieves. Rather they work at a meta-level as a facilitator of learning or, in essence, a learning coach (Jarvis, Lane & Fillery-Travis, 2006). They do provide some direct advice and expertise in academic processes, such as assessment and reporting but the majority of their work with a candidate will be the facilitation of the learning the candidate has chosen to undertake. This change in role from expert knowledge provider to facilitator of learning is denoted by a corresponding change in title from supervisor/tutor to advisor.

The mode of interaction with the candidate is not confined to the familiar classroom activity. The candidate's learning is in the workplace so the facilitation of that learning within a classroom in a remote campus at a time to suit academic norms is inappropriate and inconsistent with the philosophy of the engagement. The advisor, candidate and peers are free to interact in a variety of ways – face-to-face meetings, phone calls etc. The location and timing of the candidate /advisor interaction is also flexible and must reflect the context within which the candidate is working. The advisor must also be attuned to the candidate's workplace culture and mode of working.

In some ways the physical presence of the advisor in the workplace would be desirable but it is impractical for an advisor dealing with a significant number of individual candidates. In the past we have formed cohorts of candidates where there is a shared profession or workplace, but in general candidates approach their programmes on an individual basis. It was not surprising that in seeking to reconcile these requirements of advisor responsiveness and flexibility that we turned to WVC as a method of engagement.

THE WVC LEARNING EXPERIENCE

Hatzipanagos, Commins & Basiel (2007) have looked at and charted the attributes of WVC that make it suitable as a learning tool. This classification of attributes comprises:

a. Interactivity, to enhance the social experience of participants by allowing a new form of real time communication aligned to more traditional forms of communication. Users are generally more comfortable with this form of communication, rather than other forms of computer mediated communication, as it is similar to interactions they encounter daily in the 'real world'.

b. Technology, as a significant pre-requisite, keeping in mind that it is the learning outcomes that will determine the technology used and not vice versa.

c. Student centred learning, as WVC has the potential to reduce the isolation of remote learners, by providing opportunities to interact with peers/experts and engage intellectually and emotionally (Smyth, 2005).

d. Multiple learning styles, which WVC can accommodate. Irele (1999) has pointed out that the inclusion of WVC and associated technologies can increase the range of learning styles that can be accommodated.

e. Role changes, as the change of medium dictates different approaches and roles for the teaching practitioners. The instructional set-ups when WVC technology is introduced are substantially different from a face-to-face setting, as are the roles of the educators involved in the learning process.

In addition, other studies have shown the impact of WVC as a web based learning tool that can engender self-directed collaborative work (Ertl, Reiserer & Mandl, 2005). Learners get the opportunities to construct and acquire new knowledge in such environments that engage both conceptual and socio-cognitive support measures (Ertl, Fischer & Mandl, 2006).

The following WBL case study identifies some of the issues involved in establishing a learning relationship between advisor and candidate using this technology. We have sought in this work to explore rapport building between participants when using WVC.

Figure 1. Web video conference set ups

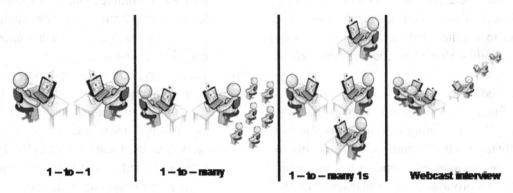

|1 – to – 1|1 – to – many|1 – to – many 1s|Webcast interview|

CASE STUDY 1: DEVELOPMENT OF ADVISOR/CANDIDATE ONLINE RELATIONSHIP

We have drawn heavily upon the executive coaching literature as a framework for this exploration, as it has specifically investigated the factors impacting upon the development of such learning relationships (Fillery-Travis & Lane 2006). Within this literature the most consistently identified positive factor contributing to the success of a coaching engagement was the quality of the relationship established between the coach and candidate, as identified by their rapport (Assay & Lambert 1999; Thach 2002).

There are several web video conferencing set-ups (Figure 1) depending on the number of participants involved. In the 1-to-1 set-up the web cam frames a single person. The 1-to-many model has a single facilitator moderating a face-to-face group. The 1-to-many 1s links many individuals in a two-way interaction. The webcast interview has two face-to-face people interacting with many individuals. These models can be adapted and applied to a variety of technology enhanced learning situations addressed later in this chapter.

The work was undertaken at an international Institute for WBL, based in a UK university. The Institute has led the development of WBL as a field of study and offers undergraduate and postgraduate programmes. Historically, within the Institute

programmes, the rapport between advisor and candidate has been formed face-to-face, through text based computer mediated communication (email/web based fora) and via the telephone. Candidates are increasingly geographically dispersed with reduced time for physical meetings. Anecdotally, they report that they value continuous professional development but have limited resources, in terms of time and study leave, to follow it. The advisor/candidate relationship is a key component to their programme of study, and our challenge has been to develop it within virtual environments in a manner capable of meeting the learners' needs in terms of timeliness, immediacy and rapport.

We have developed our research question into 'does WVC provide the rapport development essential for candidate progression within the WBL programme?' The aims and objectives of the case study were to:

- Identify if this technology can be accessed easily by candidates with basic computer skills
- Obtain their perceptions of its usefulness, compared to phone and text based communication
- Identify any barriers (technological or psychological) to its use and experiment with possible solutions
- Explore the use of the technology to engender collaborative knowledge construction.

The WVC system used within this programme was a blended one using a web based phone system for audio and software to simulate a virtual room for the meeting containing features such as a whiteboard, file/desktop sharing and PowerPoint slide viewing.

WVC and Digital Literacies

Currently a total of eight Master and Doctorate candidates have been tutored via the WVC system over two years. They have all been competent in Windows Software and have reasonable typing skills but none had an interest in computers or used computers within their leisure interests. It was originally thought that the technological context of the project would cause the most difficulty to candidates. However, in just the three years we have been working on computer mediated communication systems, the level of sophistication of the candidates in terms of their use of these technologies has improved dramatically. It is common today to have a passing knowledge of instant messaging and the majority of people have been on some kind of social networking site. Web cams are now standard features of PCs. The result is that the level of 'technophobia' has decreased enormously and no candidate expressed concern about their ability to use the technology. Simultaneously, the time candidates can put aside for tutorials away from work tasks has decreased. A significant number of our professional candidates must arrange cover for their work through colleagues or locums if they are absent from their practice. A specific discussion of these issues at the initial (contracting) stage of the relationship inevitably meant that there was a willingness to try WVC. In the following section the rapport building that WVC engendered will be discussed.

Rapport Building through WVC Systems

Once the candidates were logged onto the system it was the interpersonal communication, its ease and structuring, which impacted upon the perceived success of the relationship building. For everyday face-to-face communication the 'rules of engagement' have been learnt from experience, are implicit and (usually) well used by participants. However, there are a range of factors which we generally take for granted e.g. people's tendency to express feelings, needs, and thoughts by means of indirect messages and behavioural impacts. According to much cited research (Mehrabian and Ferris, 1967), 55% of impact is determined by body language--postures, gestures, and eye contact, 38% by the tone of voice, and 7% by the content or the words used in the communication process. It is not surprising that in relationship building we wish to see the other person but when this 'seeing' is indirect, such as through WVC, then it quickly becomes clear that the implicit rules needed to be amended and made explicit – in effect we needed to frame the conversation (NCSL, 2006).

Conversation Frame

A frame can provide a road map for all within the conversation – the candidates as well as the tutor. To achieve this remotely requires the establishment of behavioural norms or an etiquette which allows the candidate to know that their concerns and issues will be heard. Below is a frame which has evolved for the programme.

1. Preparation - The tutor must set up the 'room' well in advance of the tutorial time. All materials should be posted and available for use. For the tutor a quick technology check (by logging in as a guest via another computer close by before the candidate 'arrives') will allow to identify that the room is available and working well.

2. Greeting - Once the candidate has entered the 'room' it is critical that the tutor is waiting for them and is easily seen via their web cam. This is equivalent to the expected communication upon entering a physical room. From that point onwards it is critical that tutors face the web cam and talk directly to the candidate i.e. that they behave as though they have stepped into a physical room with them. For the tutor to ignore or appear disinterested with the candidate once they have entered the virtual room is equivalent to ignoring them within a physical room. The candidate will become anxious and feel slighted. For instance, the tutor may be trying to fix a fault but unless they state what they are doing and ask permission to 'go offline' the candidate will not know. Re-engaging with the candidate will not be easy as trust has in effect broken down.

3. Set-up - When the candidate enters the 'room' then normal social rules apply and some 'checking in' is expected i.e. connecting on a social level. Once that is complete, the tutor can facilitate induction, helping the candidate with the setting up process. They have by this time settled themselves into the process of seeing each other on the screen and responding to discussion prompts. They have become familiar enough with the system to be able to follow the commands to set their camera up etc. Usually this will only take a few minutes and then WVC is established with both sides seeing each other. If a technical issue persists (firewalls at the candidates' side is a common issue) then it is not appropriate to appear flustered or upset. WVC can proceed as long as the candidate can see the tutor.

4. Contracting - Once WVC is established the rules of engagement should be agreed i.e. pre-arranged process for the unexpected (i.e. if a connection breaks down then a phone number for them to call to ask for help) and when breaks will be taken. The agenda for the meeting can then be agreed with each participant explicitly stating what they would like to achieve within the meeting. For the candidate this may be clarity on assessment criteria for a particular module and for the tutor a review of the candidate's progression.

5. Dialogue - The business of the meeting is developed.

6. Closing - Bringing WVC to an end successfully is often problematic as the standard classroom social cues, such as gathering equipment and getting ready to rise from your chair, are missing. The tutor needs to be cogniscent of this and make a definite ending by ensuring that each participant feels that their needs have been met within the meeting before formally bringing it to a close.

Evaluation

All the candidates who have used the system have identified that the ability to see the tutor at the same time as hear them was extremely useful. The immediacy of the interaction allowed the development of an understanding between the tutor and candidates. The facial expressions and body language were apparent and allowed the rapport to be more easily established.

In all cases the supervision sessions were identified as effective by the candidates although all agreed that this technology should complement face-to-face supervision which was still the preferred method overall.

It is of note that in one session an additional supervisor sat in on the supervision and this was the only unsatisfactory session. The additional supervisor was not trained in the use of the technology and the candidate commented that she was distracted and found establishing rapport difficult. It may be that further 'rules of engagement' are required when more then two people are in the meeting.

Pre-loading of the 'room' with a range of resource material (the majority of which may not be used) added significant value to the meeting and was identified by candidates and advisors as a major benefit of working online. As both were still working at their own PC or Mac they were able to react spontaneously to the need for additional resources or illustrative material. This provided an enjoyable and stimulating perspective to the interaction.

This case study illustrated a tutorial model whose focus was the joint knowledge building of two collaboration partners. The following section will describe the context of a WVC model known as Work Based Learning Wednesdays.

CASE STUDY 2: WORK BASED LEARNING WEDNESDAYS

The aims of the WBL Wednesdays project (Figure 2) were two-fold. First, real-time academic support is provided to current or prospective candidates. Secondly, we provide an online marketing opportunity through live guest interviews. An outcome of this on-going event has been audio and video records which are also used to produce collaboratively a frequently-asked-questions (FAQ) type of resource for candidates.

The strategy was to run a 'soft launch' internally within the university before promoting it to the general public. In this way, technical or logistical issues were identified early on in the project.

Our plan was to start with an hour long web cast show on the first and second Wednesday of each month. The first half of the show was for call-ins from anyone with queries related to the WBL programme. The second half hour was focused on interviewing the guest speaker. They would tell their story in the context of WBL and discuss at the end any 'student tips to success'. This pedagogic design was adapted from a related technology enhanced learning research project for

offline induction (Basiel, 2009). The collaborative knowledge construction model in this example was dynamic, flexible, and scalable to meet the needs of the candidates.

Each guest speaker would be asked for their opinion of what 'student tips-for-success' could be offered to current or prospective WBL candidates for their profession or occupation. This would also support continuing professional development activity. These recommendations would then be added to the dynamic FAQ resource.

There were several technical considerations that needed to be addressed. The aim was to be as accessible to the target audience as possible. To that end, we devised a set of complementary technologies to support the session. Our blended systems approach used audio conferencing in addition to the WVC environment. The live face-to-face event in the studio was also recorded with a digital camcorder.

In addition to WVC and audio, features included were live text-chat, a white board mark-up tool for Flash PowerPoint slides, an online survey tool and file and desktop sharing. The event was also captured for streaming or downloading. A transcription service (a voice to text feature to generate text files of the spoken dialogue) allowed us to make the resources search optimised for web 2.0 tagging.

The pedagogic considerations of WBL Wednesdays are linked to an emerging technology enhanced learning design known as PAP (Pre-At-Post) model. In brief, this approach attempts to take advantage of the temporal quality of a real-time e-learning event. This can be illustrated by a before, during and after sequences to show the progression of time in relation to the learning experience. The synchronous nature of the event is challenged when 'live' events can be captured or recorded to be viewed any time. The following table summarises these design considerations:

In a related study on digital video, ethical considerations were highlighted. We established the need to formally declare in advance that the session

Figure 2. The WVC learning environment

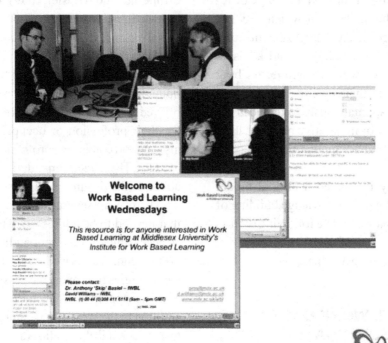

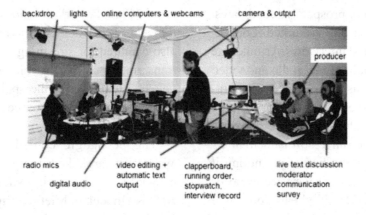

would be recorded and made available on our web site. This policy and procedure also released the intellectual property rights to the university for any technology enhanced learning content generated from the WBL Wednesday events.

To increase participation, a promotional strategy was needed. A scalable approach was used starting off with just the Institute staff as participants for feedback. The next stage included members of the university. When we became confident with the robustness of the WVC system, we included an external audience.

Linked to our choice of past successful alumni as guests was the 'associated audience' connected to the speaker, such as work colleagues of the guest speaker, who could 'tune in' our web casts to provide a rich, collaborative exchange. Other more traditional techniques were also used such

Table 1. PAP model for WVC events

Timeline of the event	Pedagogic considerations and supportive online tools
PRE -	• Set up WBL Induction resources (e.g. Captivate Simulations, Presentation PowerPoints, PDF files, etc.) • Establish email booking system (e.g. used to create distribution lists for up-coming events) • Disseminate Ethics release and disclaimer to record live sessions • Preview clips of past events to be used during the session (if appropriate) • Provide access to FAQs – searchable text and/or video
AT -	• Use structured approach to guide discussions • Share interactivity protocols for participant identification through various media (e.g. phone call-in, pod casts, text chat, etc.) • Use live text to reflect and support audio and video exchanges • Gather recommendations provided by the guest at the end of each session to become FAQ resources
POST -	• Provide access to online survey tool (e.g. – session feedback at the end of each web cast session) • Enable candidate search, access and replay of past sessions (for review or for candidates that missed the session) • Establish links to other related network events
Evaluation	• Build in evaluation opportunities for each WBL Wednesday event • Get user evaluations to encourage reflective feedback via an online survey tool

as advertisements in university publicity and intranet, Google Adwords (an online content targeted advertising service) and search optimisation techniques such as linking our web pages to partner organisations' web sites. We also used a distribution list to inform past audiences of new guests and events.

Evaluation

The outcomes of the evaluation and the lessons learnt from this project were:

- The debriefing sessions after each WVC event helped to conceptualize the collaborative knowledge construction.
- Organizational perspectives were a significant priority for the success of the sessions.
- Technical perspectives dictated the use of a controlled studio environment rather than an open access room.
- To encourage reflective feedback, users should be given the opportunity to provide feedback via an online survey tool.

The following section will explore the implications of the case studies to provide recommendations for knowledge construction with WVC.

DISCUSSION

In the two case studies, digital resources and technology set-ups were used to create an environment that facilitated computer mediated communication. WVC was introduced to replace and compensate for the absence of face-to-face contact. However, mere replication of the face-to-face experiences was not possible and in the context of this communication (many to many, one to many and one to one), the medium and the learning set-up created a different enriched code of communication between learners and tutors.

WVC integrates video, text chat or voice and web applications into a converged communications environment. WVC requires an orchestration and preparation that is not negligible to facilitate learning. However, this complex environment of media that replace and complement face-to-face communication serves an important purpose:

to enhance the communication aspect and to facilitate collaborative knowledge construction. Tutor moderation tasks in these environments are labour intensive but more intuitive and richer than in environments such as virtual discussion fora, where text based communication is the only available medium to use.

Attributes that enrich these environments are:

- An etiquette that is subversive as it reinvents face-to-face communication principles, putting emphasis on the significant and not on the trivial, on the reflective and participatory rather than on the transmissive aspect of teaching.
- A reversal of roles where the WBL candidate is empowered to negotiate with the tutor/advisor, in a flexible and transdisciplinary environment.
- Opportunities for candidates to engage in small group collaborative activities and to expose knowledge and beliefs, independently of a tutor/advisor.
- A collaborative creation of artefacts of knowledge, (a) indirectly, by using and sharing 'snapshots' of the communication, in the form of transcripts, extracts of video, audio or text records or (b) directly, encouraging collaborative creation of artefacts in a collective knowledge construction, where the emphasis is on collaborative rather than co-operative activities.

WBL was not chosen as a 'backdrop' in discussing WVC. It provides a robust framework for the acknowledgement and development of knowledge. The use of WVC within this context goes beyond simply providing a networking opportunity – it provides the environment where coaching can develop skills by direct interactions between the tutor/coaches, peers and faculty. Adult learners need peer interaction and feedback to go beyond surface learning and attain levels

of analysis and synthesis necessary for deeper learning at professional levels.

The ways in which educational institutions build relationships with employers and respond to their needs and how technology can support this by enabling complex analyses of data are highlighted as being both useful and complex and so warrant further debate and exploration.

CONCLUSION

In this chapter we described the manner by which WBL, a route for individual and organisational development, enables learning to be made explicit and hence shared for the benefit of the individual and the organisation. We described two case studies in which WVC can be used to meet the needs of learners.

The chapter explored and analysed the ways WVC can be used in creating and supporting learning environments. It explored two scenaria for implementation of e-collaborative knowledge construction. The chosen scenaria were underpinned by an exploration of the theoretical background (WBL and WVC as systems to support distance learning). Last but not least the technical perspectives to consider before implementing e-collaborative knowledge construction in WVC scenaria were discussed.

Online support models are emerging from this chapter: through the WVC systems and the associated pedagogic frameworks professionals can access expert consultancy and construct new media learning artefacts.

REFERENCES

Armsby, P., Costley, C., & Garnett, J. (2006). The legitimisation of knowledge: a work-based learning perspective of APEL. *Lifelong Learning and Education*, *25*(4), 369–383. doi:10.1080/02601370600772368

Assay T.P., & Lambert, M.J. (1999 February) The empirical case for the common factors in therapy: qualitative findings. *Training Magazine*.

Basiel, A. (2008). The media literacy spectrum: shifting pedagogic design. In *Proceedings of World Conference on Educational Multimedia, Hypermedia and Telecommunications 2008* (pp. 3614-3630). Chesapeake, VA: AACE. Retrieved June 5, 2009, from http://www.editlib.org/p/28887

Basiel, A. (2008). *Offline Project*. Retrieved June 5, 2009, from http://www.mhmvr.co.uk/iwblcoursecd/iwblcoursecd/video/tips4802.html

Boud, D. (2001). Creating a work-based curriculum. In Boud, D., & Solomon, N. (Eds.), *Work-based Learning: a new higher education*. Buckingham, UK: Society for Research into Higher Education / Open University Press.

Cong, V., & Panya, K. (2003). Issues of knowledge management in the public sector. *Electronic Journal of Knowledge Management, 1*(2).

Drucker, P. F. (1973). *Management: Tasks, Responsibilities, Practices*. New York: Harper & Row.

Ertl, B., Fischer, F., & Mandl, H. (2006). Conceptual and socio-cognitive support for collaborative learning in videoconferencing environments. *Computers & Education. Communication Information, 47*(3), 298–315.

Ertl, B., Reiserer, M., & Mandl, H. (2005). Fostering collaborative learning in videoconferencing: the influence of content schemes and collaboration scripts on collaboration outcomes and individual learning outcomes. *Education Communication and Information, 5*(2), 147–166.

Fillery-Travis, A., & Lane, D. (2006). Does Coaching Work or are we asking the wrong question? *International Coaching Psychology Review, 1*(1).

Greenberg, A. (2004). *Navigating the sea of research on video conferencing-based distance education: A platform for understanding research into the technology's effectiveness and value*. Retrieved June 5, 2009 from http://wainhouse.com/files/papers/wr-navseadistedu.pdf.

Hatzipanagos, S., Commins, R., & Basiel, A. (2007). Web-based video conferencing in transnational higher education: pedagogies and good practice. In Hug, T. (Ed.), *Didactics of Microlearning: Concepts, Discourses and Examples*. New York: Waxmann Publishing Co.

Irele, M. (1999). *Relative Effectiveness of Distance Learning Systems*. Lucent Technologies and the World Campus, Pennsylvania State University Press.

Jarvis, J., Lane, D., & Fillery-Travis, A. (2006). *The Case for Coaching - Making Evidence -based decision on coaching*. CIPD London.

Lester, S., & Costley, C. (2009). *Work-based learning at higher education level: value, practice and critique*. Retrieved June 2, 2009 from http://www.sld.demon.co.uk

Mehrabian, A., & Ferris, S. R. (1967). Inference of Attitude from Nonverbal Communication in Two Channels. *Journal of Counseling Psychology, 31*, 248–252.

Morey, C., Maybury, M., & Thuraisingham, B. (Eds.). (2002). *Knowledge Management: Classic and Contemporary Works*. Cambridge, MA: MIT Press.

National College for School Leadership. (2006). *Learning Conversations in Learning Networks*. Cranfield, UK: NCSL.

Polanyi, M. (1966). *The Tacit Dimension*. New York: Doubleday.

Reeve, F., & Gallacher, J. (2000). *Researching the implementation of work-based learning within higher education: questioning collusion and resistance*. Paper presented at the AERC, Vancouver, Canada.

Senge, P. (1990). *The Fifth Discipline: The Art and Practice of the Learning Organization.* New York: Doubleday.

Smyth, R. (2005). Broadband videoconferencing as a tool for learner-centred distance learning in higher education. *British Journal of Educational Technology, 36*(5), 805–820. doi:10.1111/j.1467-8535.2005.00499.x

Stankosky, M. (Ed.). (2005). *Creating the Discipline of Knowledge Management.* Oxford, UK: Butterworth- Heinemann.

Thach, E. C. (2002). the impact of executive coaching and 360 feedback on leadership effectiveness. *Leadership and Organization Development Journal, 23*(4), 294–306. doi:10.1108/01437730210429070

Wenger, E. (1998). *Communities of Practice: Learning, Meaning, and Identity.* Cambridge, UK: Cambridge University Press.

KEY TERMS AND DEFINITIONS

Web-Based Videoconferencing: A synchronous computer mediated communication set-up which consists of computers fitted with a camera and appropriate software.

Work-Based Learning: Gives employed learners the opportunity to achieve academic credit for real-life learning experiences in the workplace.

Chapter 5
Supporting Case–Based Learning Through a Collaborative Authoring System

Bo Hu
Universität der Bundeswehr München, Germany

Klaus Gollin
Fachhochschule für Oekonomie und Management, Germany

ABSTRACT

A web based collaborative authoring system is deployed to support collaborative and case-based learning projects. Using the versioning and logging data provided by the system a high utilization intensity can be partially ascertained. Reducing plagiarism constitutes a further utilization potential of the collaborative authoring system.

INTRODUCTION

Studying while holding a full-time job has enjoyed increasing popularity in Germany in the past years. The number of students at the University of Applied Sciences of Economics and Management in Essen (FOM) which focuses its study programs for such students have more than quadrupled between the Fall Semester 2001 and the Fall Semester 2006 (Destatis, 2008). Facing such a high average annual growth rate of up to 30 percent it has to be guaranteed that students continue to get interactive feedback from their teachers regarding their learning progress. Such feedback is an essential instrument of control and

motivation in teaching (Sesink, Geraskov, Göller, Rüsse, & Trebing, 2005). This applies in particular to supervising thesis papers as well as conducting group and case based studies.

These group and case based studies can be considered as an attempt to adapt the approach of collaborative knowledge construction (Mandl, & Krause, 2001; Fischer, 2001). Benefiting from their different vocational experiences and skills on the one side, based on a taught process model on the other side, the students are instructed to organize themselves to find solutions in some specific problem cases. Each student group has to interview the "client", to write a scientific paper collaboratively and to carry out a final presentation. The teacher acts not only as the "client" who engages the teams to

DOI: 10.4018/978-1-61520-937-8.ch005

solve some management problems, but also helps the students achieve their objectives by defining milestones and giving feedback.

It is well known though that such a formative method causes a teacher's workload to be five times higher than if using the classical summative one. Merely through use of online technologies this additional expenditure can be kept within limits (Low, 2005). Moreover, due to their full-time jobs these students have fewer opportunities to communicate face-to-face between both each other and to the supervisors, compared to students at most other universities. An online technology based learning scenario helps students proceed with their case-based learning projects independently of time and space, while keeping a proper work-life balance.

Collaborative learning environments (Howard, 2005; Jia, 2005) and especially collaborative authoring systems (CAS) are such online technological platforms. Besides various approaches perfecting synchronous CAS (Shen, & Sun, 2004; Raikundalia, & Zhang, 2005) several successful projects deploying XML and web based asynchronous systems have been reported (Kim, 2002; Luzi, Ricci, Fazi, & Vignetti, 2003; Weng, & Gennari, 2004). XML or Extensible Markup Language is a simple, very flexible text format which plays an increasingly important role in the storage and exchange of data on the Web and elsewhere (W3C, 2009).

The usage of a collaborative authoring system does not only require a continuous evaluation of the system in a live environment but supports this by its inherent functionality. Many studies have been made to present comprehensive concepts (Steves, & Scholtz, 2005; Adler, Nash, & Noël, 2006) or to carry out research work using diverse experimental setups (Wells, & Sevilla, 2003; Krowne, & Bazaz, 2004; Emigh, & Herring, 2005; Linde, 2005; Masoodian, Bouamrane, Luz, & King, 2005; Zander, 2005).

Since mid of 2005 an XML and web based asynchronous collaborative authoring system has

been provided at the Study Centre Munich of the FOM University of Applied Science. This system was first published in 2004 (Hu, & Lauck, 2004) and has been developed continuously (Hu, 2006). Using this system the students should not only streamline their document creation in distributed working groups but also develop their collaboration skills while applying collaboration techniques. The system also facilitates diverse capabilities for teachers to conduct group based and distributed learning projects.

In this chapter we look at how this XML and web based asynchronous CAS can be used to support case-based learning. The aim of this chapter is to

- Outline the specific needs of these kind of students
- Explain what functions this system provides to support these needs
- Report the actual extent of the system's usage by the students
- Debate the pros and cons of the system
- Evaluate the deployment potential of the existing collaborative authoring system
- Motivate further specific improvements in the system.

PROBLEM SITUATION FACED BY STUDENTS AND TEACHERS

As a compulsory subject students at FOM have to carry out two case-based learning projects in self-organized teams. The course is organized on a semi-distance learning basis. Each team consists of normally four or five members. The case-based learning projects require that each team produces a conclusive document that complies with the requirements on academic papers. The goal of such projects is communicated clearly as a combined training of both hard and soft skills. Unlike many other universities FOM students are employed and studying besides job, many of them are parents. Time spent for face-to-face sessions is thus a crucial factor. Coordinating team work over distance and reducing workload becomes a real challenge.

To provide a picture of the situation a survey (Gollin, & Hu, 2008) was carried out among about 500 students and alumni of FOM in 2007. This survey should clarify how the case based studies were accomplished, what tools were used and how the students managed the problem that they were living on different locations. 134 answered the survey. For text processing Microsoft WORD is the most popular software package, used by 93 percent of students for their case-based studies. With respect to the techniques used to communicate and coordinate their collaborative authoring process nearly hundred percent of the participants reported that they used e-mails. Telephone ranked on the second place, followed by other systems like instant messengers. 65 percent did meet more than two times additionally to the compulsory face to face sessions. Less than 10 percent of participants organized themselves over social networks or Microsoft SharePoint services. Most students have thus to manage different versions of his/her own document fragments, but also many fragments of the other team members manually. One third said that the amount of work was increased because of different word processors or different versions of the same package causing problems when merging the different fragments into a single document. In spite of this, more than 50 percent of the students reported that they merged the document more than two times during the entire project. More than 70 percent of the participants reported that the predominant part of workload finalizing the document laid on one team member.

From the teachers' point of view it is very crucial to accompany the students from the very beginning of the writing process. That includes supporting to find a subject, refining the structure and giving concrete advices on how to write an academic paper with respect both to the content and to the form. It is important to be aware of the progress of each of the learning projects. Every time when answering a question raised by a student it is important to place the question and the answer into the right context of the case-based learning project. This context, however, cannot be achieved through sending the entire project documents to the supervisor via e-mails. Firstly the learning group would have to merge their fragments manually more frequently than necessary. Secondly the supervisor would have to read the entire document whilst only some parts of the document are really new or changed. Finally the work flow within the learning group would be affected since the supervisor would not always be able to response timely since more than one group is supervised at the same time.

Conventionally a document is handled as a single (and complex) object. When writing a document collaboratively, distributed team members often make their local copies of the document and work on them using standard word processors like Microsoft WORD or OpenOffice.org. In addition to the main document to be created collaboratively there are various other documents containing ideas, drafts and data sheets and so on. To get the collaborative process going all those files are sent back and forth via email. It has been said that e-mail is a poor man's workflow management system (Dulaney, 2003). E-mail includes usually intensive human interventions in composing and reading. It is a major challenge not only to reduce the effort and mistakes both for students and teachers, but also to establish a well-defined knowledge management process within the course, facilitating a centralized communication and collaboration platform beyond e-mail (Radjou, Schadler, Ciardelli, & Smith, 1999).

Even when a centralized project file storage is established it is still a hard work to manage and to merge different versions and fragments to the final document manually. As a matter of fact many problems described above are mainly caused by this kind of process and technical systems that do not provide substantial support to collaborative teams.

Figure 1. Process oversight of the XML and web-based CMS

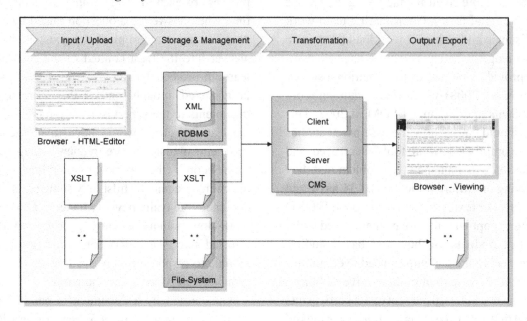

A BRIEF PRESENTATION OF THE COLLABORATIVE AUTHORING SYSTEM

As an alternative a document can also be processed as a collection of numerous content objects. A collaborative authoring system (CAS) is then used to manage these objects on a web server and merge them into a single document automatically when necessary. Different team members working collaboratively on a single document are provided with write access to different parts of the document simultaneously. They have read access to the most recent version and the only copy of the entire document so that the collaborative writing process is kept visible for all team members.

Generally speaking the core of the CAS is a content management system (CMS); more precisely it is a web-based content management system (WCMS). It provides the functions used to create and to manage web pages, to upload and to manage additional files (e.g. images, audio or video streams etc.) and to define authorization and authentication mechanisms. All functions are available via web browsers. A widely used function of such CMS is the separation of content from its presentation. The content of this system is stored in XML format and the presentation as web pages is carried out using XSLT technology which is one of the recommendations made by W3C for defining XML document transformation and presentation (W3C, 2009a). Using XSLT technology it is more easily to adapt the user interfaces of the system under consideration to meet the teaching and learning requirements. Fig. 1 gives an oversight of the system.

As mentioned above the input of text contents of a web page is handled by a web-based HTML editor (Knabben, 2009). Each web page is treated as an object of the CMS. Besides styling and formatting functions known from the standard text processors, the editor provides functions to integrate images (which are stored within the file system) and to define hyper links that can be established to refer to other CMS web pages or to any external web sources. Headlines, illustrations and tables can be numbered automatically and referenced within the document to the corresponding numbers. Once finished the text content is stored in XML format within a relational data-

Figure 2. The hierarchical concept of the CMS and a CAS document

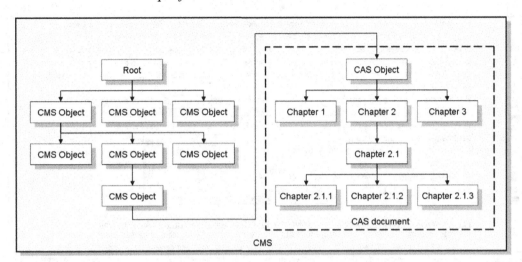

base management system (RDBMS). The CMS supports versioning by creating a new version of an object each time the object is stored together with a time stamp and the name of the user who produced the version. When reading a CMS web page, the system transforms the content of the RDBMS and the file system either through the client's capability producing HTML by combining XML and the XSLT template, or - if the client's browser does not support this transformation - the server generates the HTML output. Also files from the file system can be downloaded by means of the browser's functionality.

The objects in the CMS are organized hierarchically. This is the same way how objects of a complex and comprehensive document can be organized by the CAS. The CAS provides a set of functions to expand the capability of the CMS. Each section of a document corresponds to an object that is defined in a hierarchical structure by a structuring item. Fig. 2 depicts the data structure of the CMS and a CAS document as a part of the entire data structure. Whilst each object of a complex document is handled separately, the entire document including all sections, footnotes, figures and numbered chapters, etc. can be presented in a separate window using a single mouse click. From

this window the user can copy the entire document to a word processor or even print it directly. The CAS supports MS WORD, OpenOffice.org and LaTeX as output format.

Different user roles can be applied based on the authorization concept that includes various authentication methods. The authorization concept is applicable to each of the objects in the CMS and thus also in the CAS. Each user can be member of various groups and act independently of the other users within the system. Members can create, delete and edit objects, as well as invite other registered users in the CMS to join their group. Even non-registered users (guests) can be admitted to the team by e-mail and they receive a temporarily limited access to the system via an invitation code.

One of the central functions of the CAS for the awareness support (Gross, & Koch, 2007) is the commenting function. Comments can be created, edited or deleted by the supervisor as well as by the group members. The depicted large (yellow) comment field in figure 3 can be positioned and anchored at any location in the text. It is also possible to mark one or more words of the text and comment or delete them. Such marked comments are highlighted by a colored background;

Figure 3. The comment function of the CMS / CAS

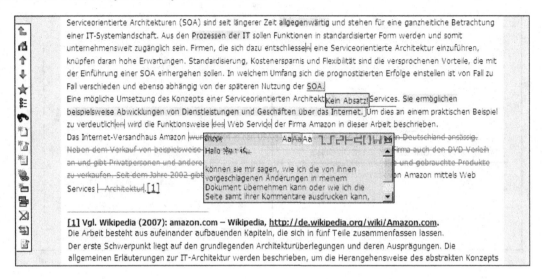

the reader can move the mouse cursor over it and receives the information behind it in an appearing text box. Proof-readers' marks can also be used (Kuhrt, 2002) as they are depicted here in the upper right corner of the commenting field. In addition to the commenting function discussion forums can be established in parallel to a CAS document. Both the commenting function and the forums can be used to facilitate discussions and feedbacks by both instructors and students.

For scientific papers reference management is one of the key functions. In contrast to many bibliography software programs which are mainly designed for stand-alone usage or usage in local networks the CAS bibliographic information is managed on the server and can be shared within a group or even across different groups. From within the editor this database can be accessed to create citations. When using this function a list of cited literature with all necessary information is produced at the end of the document.

An interesting feature is the possibility to define content templates. Those content templates are not only used by the students to create document fragments according a taught process model. In the sense of "Conversational Framework" (Laurillard, 2002) the teachers are also able to improve the templates as a part of "teachers' constructed environment" continuously. Since the templates can be created and updated online the new or updated templates are provided to the students automatically without any delay.

DEPLOYMENT: A REPORT OF OUR EXPERIENCES

One of the central functions of the CAS presented in this work is to provide an automatic versioning management at section level. That is to say, it is possible to restore and continue to work on any preceding version of a section, which has been saved within the system. For any altered version of a section, the point in time of saving and the author can be determined. In addition to this, the period of time that was required for editing the section is taken down in a journal. The results of the analysis of these tracking data are being elucidated in the following sections.

Extent of the Utilization by the Students

So far the system presented in the previous section has been made available to 104 students or 24 study groups of normally four or five participants carrying out case-based learning projects since its introduction in mid 2005. Each group is required to create 17 individual specification documents according to an established process model as well as a joint paper in a related area. The total volume of the written paper shall amount to approximately 50 pages depending on the number of the members of the group.

Additionally more than 40 students writing their Diplom theses have also been provided access to this system. 26 of them have meanwhile concluded their works. Generally a volume of 70 pages is set as the usual target. Whilst the collaborative aspect between students is generally irrelevant when writing a Diplom thesis, the importance of online supervision remains.

As the usage of the system has been recommended but not mandated, the students can be assigned to one of the four subsequent categories with reference to the utilization intensity.

Thirteen project groups built by totally 59 persons are among the category "high". Additionally nine more students writing their theses also join them. In this category the documents were created consistently according to the hierarchical concept of the collaborative authoring system. By means of the versioning and logging functions of the system the utilization extent can be represented in numerical values (Table 1). Thus, the members of each project group of the category "high" have spent in median terms a period of almost 24.8 hours alone in the editing mode of the system. For a student of this category, writing Diplom thesis, this value amounts to 17.0 hours. During this time, in median terms 773 or 859, respectively, content objects are created, deleted or replaced by a new version. At the end, in median terms approximately 200 objects remain in the case of a case-based learning group as well as for a Diplom thesis. These content objects do not only give an account of the hierarchically structured thesis or study documents, but they are also forum postings which are, together with numerous comments, at least a part of the "persistent conversation" (Erickson, & Herring, 2005) with respect to these works. A comparison of the system usage between students writing their Diplom theses an those doing case studies reveals primarily that the commenting function has been used more frequently for case studies. Obviously, this function has been used for coordination within the group, too. Some random samples of the comments' contents confirm this assumption.

Among the students writing Diplom theses there are four persons who were concerned with some tasks of the development of system directly or indirectly, so that the intensities of their system usage is even beyond the category "high". These four persons are categorized in a separate group called "experts", as shown in the table below.

The category "low" is located at the other end of scale of the utilization intensity. Within this category the collaborative authoring system is only used sporadically by the students for Diplom theses or case-based studies, respectively. It is noticeable that the median number of the e-mails sent to the supervisor by students writing Diplom thesis, is higher than the ones of other categories. In contrast to this, the students working on case studies of this category have sent fewer e-mails to the supervisor than the ones of the two other categories.

Between both categories mentioned above lies the category "moderate". For the case study students the collaborative authoring system is no prominent working system but a central repository which holds a certain coordination function. For instance, some task lists are inter alia created online and updated in accordance with the progress of the project work.

Table 1. Identification data for various categories of the utilization intensity

Median	Case-based learning groups			Students writing Diplom thesis			
	high	moderate	low	experts	high	moderate	low
Comments	96	23	1	86	62	41	0
E-mails sent to supervisor	8	5	5	75	13	7	19
Edits	773	331	72	3084	859	437	65
- Deleted objects	128	42	13	177	88	52	5
- Updates	493	191	29	2412	562	272	36
- Objects	171	70	31	401	204	126	25
Online edit time	24,8	10,9	1,7	123,0	17,0	4,9	0,3
Workgroups	13	7	4	4	9	7	6
Persons	59	31	14	4	9	7	6

Workload Distribution within the Learning Groups

The significant difference between the various study groups with respect to the utilization intensity of the collaborative authoring system follows clearly from the previous section. This difference exists at the same time within the study group. As described in 2nd section of this chapter, 98 of 132 persons questioned (74,2%) have answered in the affirmative that a single member of the group was burdened with the entire workload to merge the separate fragments to a single document. The data obtained by the versioning and logging function (see below) confirm this opinion at least partly even when using a collaborative authoring system. In the winter semester 2007, for instance, it was possible to use those data to identify one person in each of the three case study groups whom approximately half of the online editing time and half of the edits of the respective group can be assigned to.

Since all interim versions of the collaborative documents are stored in the collaborative authoring system, the individual contributions made by several team members can be determined for each section by comparing the different versions (Hu, Lauck, & Scheffczyk, 2005). Figure 4 demonstrates the result of such a calculation. There are all in all eleven different versions of the section to be scrutinized. As it is apparent from the table's third column, four members of the group have been working on this section. By comparing two successive versions with one another (columns 5 and 7), the second and fifth alterations may be identified as elaborate. The difference of an interim version with regard to the final version "N" (columns 4 and 6) provides moreover the effective contribution to the final result. Moreover Figure 4 reflects that Anton and Chris are the two more diligent persons (according to column 7, they have caused the most extensive alterations with respect to the preliminary version in line 2 and 5), while Chris and Doris have yielded the more effective contributions (the effectiveness is judged by the increase of the bar in the sixth column, i.e. line 5 and 6). Björn has worked in this case even counter-productively, since in comparison with the preliminary version, the similarity of his version to the final version has been reduced (in line 4 of column 6, the bar became shorter than it had already been before).

To reduce unbalances of workload within a team Salomon et al referred to some factors like "intergroup (rather than intragroup) competition" and "intergroup differential expertise" (Salomon, & Globerson, 1989). These factors have been already taken into account by design of our group

Figure 4. Comparison of the versions demonstrates the individual contributions of several team members (all names have been changed) with respect to one segment

No.	Time	User	Diff.	R.	Simularity to the end version	Difference to the previous version
1	24.11.2007 13:24:23	Anton	116	0		
2	24.11.2007 13:25:16	Anton	105	80		
3	24.11.2007 13:25:48	Anton	104	1		
4	01.12.2007 16:37:53	Björn	124	11		
5	01.12.2007 16:59:13	Chris	38	88		
6	02.12.2007 18:32:32	Doris	12	15		
7	03.12.2007 14:24:18	Anton	12	4		
8	09.12.2007 18:12:44	Doris	6	10		
9	09.12.2007 18:15:52	Anton	2	4		
10	09.12.2007 18:17:16	Anton	1	2		
N	09.12.2007 18:20:26	Anton	0	1		

and case based studies. Using the platform's analyze function both the instructors and the team members have additionally the possibility to have some objective data about the real workload of the different team members and their individual contributions to the team's project. This may help team members reorganize their task to rebalance their workload.

In this context it is also to be stated that an objective evaluation of the actual student's expenditure is significant for the development of Bachelor and Master courses for which the workload serves as a basis of assessment. An objective evaluation is in addition to this of fundamental significance for a breakdown of workload between the students within a group of learners and boosts in the end also the co-operation in learning.

DISCUSSION: FURTHER POTENTIAL FOR IMPROVEMENT AND DEPLOYMENT

The technical objective of the presented CAS is, as mentioned before, to avoid local copies of a document which is being edited collaboratively by distributed group members. A document is written online and collaboratively. Once finished the entire document can be exported into WORD or OpenOffice.org for final processing, using the export functions provided by the system. The best practice is that the workload of final processing is reduced dramatically from several days to several minutes.

However, it has been turned out as the most important argument against the usage of CAS that writing online is not always possible or desired by all users. Habit and a loose feeling of uncertainty are often referred to as reasons, when inquired. The persons questioned feared that they might be hampered in their continuity of writing in case of lacking internet connectivity or server availability. Many students prefer to write their texts offline, although they appreciate the advantages of the CAS. In order to make use of these advantages they wish to have the opportunity to export their documents drawn up in WORD into the CAS periodically. As long as the interval between two such data interchanges is kept short this method can be seen as a "second best" and should also be supported by the system. An approach to provide more sophisticated import function from WORD or from OpenOffice.org into the CAS document is provided by the XML technique. Since the presented collaborative authoring system is an XML orientated application, an adoption of an

XML document allows to be accomplished relatively easily by means of the functions available for XML. An import filter for OpenOffice.org (ISO, 2006) is already being worked on within the framework of a Diplom thesis. An import filter for Microsoft Office 2007 (Rice, 2006) shall follow. In a current case study even a prototype of an offline editor for this system is being defined and implemented. With this, the acceptance for the collaborative authoring system can be further increased.

The estimation of workload by analyzing computer data is an important starting point for analyzing the extent of the utilization of the system under consideration. However, because the data are collected from a real world rather than in a laboratory setup, it is possible to pretend a higher workload while some meaningful activities like searching in web and even reading of text passages written by other team members are not even recorded. Further research work and refined software development are necessary to overcome these limitations.

A point in favor of the deployment of a collaborative authoring system in teaching is a further, hitherto not considered reason: To reduce plagiarism. Various studies and reports show that there is a high level of willingness to plagiarize among the students (Sergiou, 2004; Jones, 2006; Strünkelnberg, 2008; Maier, 2003). Regardless of whether the actual extent of this problem has thereby been given an exact account of, the significance and urgency of combating plagiarism is an undisputable fact. Every University is responsible for this within the framework of its statutory mission (HRK, 1998).

In addition to various manual strategies to discover or avoid plagiarism numerous software solutions which compare a submitted paper automatically with text sources from the internet to expose potential plagiarism have been in existence for a lengthy period (Weber-Wulff, 2002). Most of the methods fail, however, if the original text which was copied from is not available or does not exist in a form that can be processed digitally. For example, if the original text is a purchasable paper or if a translation plagiarism (Weber-Wulff, & Wohnsdorf, 2006) is committed.

A special way of reducing plagiarism denoted "portfolio assessment" is capable of resolving the matter in this context decisively: instead of merely assessing the final result, the entire process of writing shall be considered and accompanied by the lecturer (Baume, 2001). Ultimately, it is not the final result, but the process of creation that makes the difference between original and plagiarism. An individual supervision results in a personalization of the creation process which encourages the students to contribute their authentic ideas and their own efforts (Irons, 2004). Starting from the train of thought, via structuring and diverse references found useful for the work, up to various interim versions, the learner shall document the intermediate steps and submit them to the teacher for commentary and assessment. The fact that "nobody simply sits down and writes ready for publication, but that one has to work, in order to structure and formulate a text clearly and logically" is taken into account, so that an attempt of plagiarism can be made more difficult even in the initial stages (Weber-Wulff et al., 2006).

From the authors' points of view, the collaborative authoring system described here may represent primarily an effective platform for portfolio assessment, since students are already instructed to use the platform during the entire writing process. They also benefit from the portfolio assessment and from the platform if the teacher are capable not only to control but also to motivate the learning process by timely feedbacks and by providing more content-oriented structuring supports (Weinberger, Reiserer, Ertl, Fischer, & Mandl, 2003), for instance, some predefined milestones and templates which are still to be developed.

SUMMARY

Studying while holding a full-time job does not only stand for more students' commitment but also requires a more comprehensive support using online technologies, especially for collaborative case-based learning projects. A survey shows that standard word processors do not support collaborative work properly. This contribution presents a web based collaborative authoring system which has been developed and deployed to meet this need at the Study Centre Munich of the FOM since the middle of 2005.

Using the versioning and logging data of the system high utilization intensity can be ascertained among approximately 60% of the students which the access to the system is provided. Furthermore, the data analysis confirms in a certain way that the workload of the written paper is unevenly divided up within a case-based learning group even when a collaborative authoring system is used. As expected, a seamless import function from standard word processor can even increase the acceptance of the collaborative authoring system. Further research work and refined software development are necessary to achieve more precise result of workload measurement. An intensive utilization of the collaborative authoring system may be of benefit for a more effective reduction of plagiarisms as well as for a better conduction of case and group based learning projects.

REFERENCES

W3C. (2009). *Extensible Markup Language (XML)*. Retrieved May 2009, from http://www.w3.org/XML/

W3C. (2009a). *The Extensible Stylesheet Language Family (XSL)*. Retrieved April 2009, from http://www.w3.org/Style/XSL/

Adler, A., Nash, J. C., & Noël, S. (2006). Evaluating and implementing a collaborative office document system. *Interacting with Computers, 18*(4), 665–682. doi:10.1016/j.intcom.2005.10.001

Baume, D. (2001). A Briefing on Assessment of Portfolios. *LTSN Generic Centre*. Retrieved May 2009, from http://www.palatine.ac.uk/files/973.pdf

Destatis (2008). Statistik der Studenten. *GENESIS-Online,* Wiesbaden: Statistisches Bundesamt Deutschland. Retrieved Feb. 2008, from http://www-genesis.destatis.de/

Dulaney, K. (2003). Wireless E-Mail Is Driving the Real-Time Enterprise. *Gartner Research Note, Technology, T-19-5799*. Retrieved March 02, 2009, from http://www.bus.umich.edu/ KresgePublic/Journals/Gartner/research/114000/114015/114015.pdf

Emigh, W., & Herring, S. C. (2005). Collaborative Authoring on the Web: A Genre Analysis of Online Encyclopedias. In *Proceedings of the 38th Hawaii International Conference on System Sciences*.

Erickson, T., & Herring, S. C. (2005). Persistent Conversation: A Dialog Between Research and Design. In *Proceedings of the 38th Annual Hawaii International Conference on System Sciences (HICSS'05) - Track 4,* Big Island, Hawaii (pp. 106).

Fischer, F. (2001). *Gemeinsame Wissenskonstruktion – Theoretische und methodologische Aspekte. Forschungsbericht, 142*. München: LMU, Lehrstuhl für Empirische Pädagogik und Pädagogische Psychologie.

Gollin, K., & Hu, B. (2008). *Organisationsform und Betreuungsaspekte bei der Durchführung von gruppenbasierten Fallstudien in berufsbegleitenden Studiengängen. 1. Wissenschaftliche Tagung Hochschulpolitik und Hochschulmanagement*. Essen: FOM.

Gross, T., & Koch, M. (2007). Computer-Supported Cooperative Work. In Herczeg, M. (Ed.), *Interactive Medien*. München, Germany: Oldenbourg Wissenschaftsverlag.

Howard, C. (2007). *Collaborative E-Learning Systems - Increasing the Pace of E-Learning Development at Norfolk Southern*. Case Study, Bersin & Associates. Retrieved April 20, 2007, from http://www.bersinassociates.com/free_research/ ns_case_study_1.8.pdf

HRK. (1998). Zum Umgang mit wissenschaftlichem Fehlverhalten in den Hochschulen. *Empfehlung des 185. Plenums,* Hochschulrektorkonferenz. Retrieved Feburary 29, 2008, from http://www.hrk.de/de/beschluesse/109_422.php

Hu, B. (2006). Correction Marks and Comments on Web Pages. In *Proceedings Intelligent Tutoring Systems: 8th International Conference, ITS 2006, Springer Lecture Notes in Computer Science* (pp. 784 - 786). Berlin: Springer.

Hu, B., & Lauck, F. (2004). Prototype of a Web and XML Based Collaborative Authoring System. In *International Conference on Computing, Communications and Control Technologies (CCCT'04), Proceedings,* Austin, USA (Vol. 4, pp. 79-84).

Hu, B., Lauck, F., & Scheffczyk, J. (2005). How Recent is a Web Document? *Electronic Notes in Theoretical Computer Science, 157*(2), 147–166. doi:10.1016/j.entcs.2005.12.052

Irons, A. D. (2004). Using portfolios in assessment to reduce plagiarism. In *Proceedings of the Plagiarism: Prevention, Practice and Policy Conference,* Northumbria University.

ISO/IEC 26300:2006. (2006). *Information technology -- Open Document Format for Office Applications (OpenDocument) v1.0. Abstract.* International Organization for Standardization.

Jia, Y. (2005). Building a Web-Based Collaborative Learning Environment. In *ITHET 6th Annual International Conference, Session F2D (7-9)*. Juan Dolio, Dominican Republic: IEEE.

Jones, M. (2006). Plagiarism Proceedings in Higher Education – Quality Assured? In *Proceedings of 2nd International Plagiarism Conference.*

Kim, H.-C. (Ed.). (2002). From Comments to Dialogues: A Study of Asynchronous Dialogue Processes as Part of Collaborative Reviewing on the Web. In *Proceedings of the 35th Hawaii International Conference on System Sciences (HICSS-35'02).*

Knabben, F. C. (2009). *FCKeditor - The text editor for Internet.* Retrieved February 1, 2009, from http://www.fckeditor.net/

Krowne, A., & Bazaz, A. (2004). Authority Models for Collaborative Authoring. In *Proceedings of the 37th Hawaii International Conference on System Sciences.*

Kuhrt, N. (2002). *Korrekturzeichen nach DIN 16511.* Grundlagen und Anwendung. Retrieved February 29, 2008, from http://www.ewrite.de/mg/downloads/data/pdf/ewrite/ korrekturzeichen.pdf

Laurillard, D. (2002, January/February). Rethinking Teaching for the Knowledge Society. *EDUCAUSE Review, 37*(1), 16–25.

Linde, G. d. (2005). The Perception of Business Students At PUCMM Of The Use Of Collaborative Learning Using The BSCW As A Tool. In *ITHET 6th Annual International Conference, Session F2D* (pp. 10-15). Juan Dolio, Dominican Republic: IEEE.

Low, S. M. (2005). Reduction of Teacher Workload in a Formative Assessment Environment through use of Online Technology. *ITHET 6th Annual International Conference, Proceedings, F4A (18-21).* Juan Dolio, Dominican Republic: IEEE

Luzi, D., Ricci, F. L., Fazi, P., & Vignetti, M. (2003). The Clinical Trial Collaborative Writing: A New Functionality of the WITH System. *IADIS International Conference e-Society 2003, (799-803)*. IADIS.

Maier, T. (2003). Unis wollen Internet-Abschreibern an den Kragen. *Heise Online News*. Retrieved February 29, 2008, from http://www.heise.de/newsticker/meldung/34467

Mandl, H., & Krause, U.-M. (2001). *Lernkompetenz für die Wissensgesellschaft. Forschungsbericht, 145*. München: Ludwig-Maximilians-Universität, Lehrstuhl für Empirische Pädagogik und Pädagogische Psychologie.

Masoodian, M., Bouamrane, M.-M., Luz, S., & King, K. (2005). Recoled: A Group-Aware Collaborative Text Editor for Capturing Document History. In *IADIS International Conference on WWW/Internet 2005* (pp. 323-330).

Radjou, N., Schadler, T., Ciardelli, A. J., & Smith, S. (1999). Collaboration Beyond Email. *The Forrester Report*.

Raikundalia, G. K., & Zhang, H. L. (2005). Newly-discovered Group Awareness Mechanisms for Supporting Real-time Collaborative Authoring. In M. Billinghurst & A. Cockburn (Hrsg.), *6th Australasian User Interface Conference (AUIC2005)* (Vol. 40, pp. 127-136). Newcastle: Australian Computer Society, Inc.

Rice, F. (2006). Introducing the Office (2007). Open XML File Formats. *MSDN, Microsoft Corporation*. Retrieved February 29, 2008, from http://msdn2.microsoft.com/en-us/library/aa338205.aspx

Salomon, G., & Globerson, T. (1989). When teams do not function the way they ought to. *International Journal of Educational Research, 13*(1), 89–99. doi:10.1016/0883-0355(89)90018-9

Sergiou, K. (2004). Why do students plagiarise? In *Proceedings of the Plagiarism: Prevention, Practice and Policy Conference,* Northumbria University.

Sesink, W., Geraskov, D., Göller, S., Rüsse, W., & Trebing, T. (2005). Transformation einer Vorlesung durch E-Learning-Elemente. In Sesink, W. (Ed.), *MedieanPädagogik - Online-Zeitschrift für Theorie und Praxis der Medienbildung, 10 Medien in der Erziehungswissenschaft II (2005)*.

Shen, H., & Sun, C. (2004). Improving real-time collaboration with highlighting. [Amsterdam: Elsevier Science Publishers B. V.]. *Future Generation Computer Systems, 20*(4), 605–625. doi:10.1016/S0167-739X(03)00176-6

Steves, M. P., & Scholtz, J. (2005). A Framework for Evaluating Collaborative Systems in the Real World. In *Proceedings of the 38th Hawaii International Conference on System Sciences - 2005*.

Strünkelnberg, T. (2008). Studie - Neun von zehn Studenten zu Plagiat bereit. *Mitteldeutsche Zeitung*. Retrieved Feburary 28, 2008, from http://www.mz-web.de/servlet/ContentServer?pagename=ksta/page&atype=ksArtikel&aid=1202045354659&openMenu=1013083806226& calledPageId=1013083806226&listid=1018881578460

Weber-Wulff, D. (2002). *Aufdeckung von Plagiaten: Suchen im Internet für Lehrkräfte*. Retrieved February 29, 2008, from http://www.f4.fhtw-berlin.de/~weberwu/papers/plagiat.shtml

Weber-Wulff, D., & Wohnsdorf, G. (2006). Strategien der Plagiatsbekämpfung. [Deutsche Gesellschaft für Informationswissenschaft und Informationspraxis e.V.]. *Zeitschrift IWP, 2/06*, 90–98.

Weinberger, A., Reiserer, M., Ertl, B., Fischer, F., & Mandl, H. (2003). *Facilitating collaborative knowledge construction in computer mediated learning with structuring tools. Research reports, 158*. München: LMU, Department of Psychology, Institute for Educational Psychology.

Wells, T. D., & Sevilla, C. (2003). Evaluation of Collaborative Document Creation. In *IADIS International Conference e-Society 2003* (pp. 681-684).

Weng, C., & Gennari, J. H. (2004). Asynchronous collaborative writing through annotations. In *Proceedings of the 2004 ACM conference on CSCW* (pp. 578 - 581). Chicago: ACM Press

Zander, P.-O. (2005). The Role of Collective Subjects in Appropriation - An Evaluation of a Collaborative Writing Project. In *IADIS International Conference on Cognition and Exploratory Learning in Digital Age (CELDA 2005),* (pp. 285-292).

Chapter 6
Knowledge Access and Interaction Evolution in Virtual Learning Communities

Maria Chiara Caschera
Institute of Research on Population and Social Policies (CNR-IRPPS), Italy

Alessia D'Andrea
Institute of Research on Population and Social Policies (CNR-IRPPS), Italy

Fernando Ferri
Institute of Research on Population and Social Policies (CNR-IRPPS), Italy

Patrizia Grifoni
Institute of Research on Population and Social Policies (CNR-IRPPS), Italy

ABSTRACT

Interaction among members in Virtual Learning Communities influences the communities' evolution. Starting from this consideration, this chapter provides a discussion on the more widely used software systems that support interaction between virtual communities' members and virtual learning environment underlining the advantages and the disadvantages considering the several processes that characterize the VLCs. Moreover in education environments interactions are important in order to facilitate the learning process, and this chapter describes how the intelligent agent approaches can bean interesting alternative to a human facilitator. The analysis of intelligent agents describes how they allow both analysing interaction and improving the level of participation of members of a Virtual Learning Community.

INTRODUCTION

The Web has been transformed from a place with many readers and few publishers, into a space where everyone can have a voice via tools such as forums and blogs or communities of users that can collaboratively create a body of knowledge about some concrete topic. This evolution of the Web has produced the Web 2.0 or Social Web, and it promises to boost human collaboration capabilities on a worldwide scale, enabling individuals to rendezvous, share information and collaborate by means of read-write web and user generated content.

DOI: 10.4018/978-1-61520-937-8.ch006

A great number of these new forms of communication arise and attract increasing numbers of users from different social backgrounds. This indicates that people's information usage in daily life is changing. Correspondingly, learning processes are facing this change greatly as well. Its impact on e-learning leads to the so-called e-learning 2.0, in which Virtual Learning Communities (VLCs) have paid more attention than common learning repositories or learning management systems.

A VLC is defined as "a particular type of virtual learning environment that must allow learners to engage each other intentionally and collectively in the transaction or transformation of knowledge" (Schwier, 2004). VLCs are emerging as alternatives to classroom-based training. They are similar to Virtual Communities of Practice (VCPs) but are not based on a set of practices. Rather, they are based on the desire of members to learn from each other. VLCs emerge over time as members interact and negotiate so they are products of social interaction (Schwier, 2001). The social interaction enables members to reach their goals. These can be goals for building knowledge, working together or solving problems that require more than one person to solve.

The VLC can be considered as a structure for groups that have the purpose of learning and exchanging ideas, knowledge, skills, experience, and competencies. The communication and the collaboration in VLCs are efficiently supported by the use of technology results and the development of more efficient forms of education.

The use of technological media and tools is focal in VLCs due to the fact that have the purpose to provide a Virtual education (Kurbel, 2001) that refers to instruction in a learning environment where teachers and learners are separated by time and/or space. In this environment the teachers provides course content through course management applications, multimedia resources, videoconferencing, and other computer mediated communication systems.

The Virtual education takes place in a virtual learning environment that can be viewed as a software system designed to support teaching and learning in an educational environment by tools, such as discussion forums, blogs and whiteboards.

This chapter provides a discussion on the more widely used software systems that support interaction between virtual communities' members and virtual learning environment underlining the advantages and the disadvantages considering the several processes that characterize the VLCs.

The main goal of this chapter is to describe how VLCs represent an effective support tool for social interaction, knowledge management and learning promotion among learners analysing how existing technological systems and approaches are able to support these goals. The study will be focused on computer-mediated systems analysing how different types of systems regulate the activities of participants of the learning community.

Moreover in education environments interactions are very important in order to facilitate the learning process, and the intelligent agent approaches can offer an interesting alternative to a human facilitator. Starting from this consideration, this chapter will provide a discussion about intelligent software agents (Lieberman, 1997) that can be viewed as a metaphor or an abstraction tool for the design and the definition of distance-learning systems. The discussion will focuses on how they can be used for both analysing and improving the interaction process among members for supporting users in different way by contributing to gradually improve the level of familiarity of each user with the system and the level of participation.

The paper is organised as follow. After a short introduction, which deals with some issues of categorization and definition of VC and VLCs (section one), the chapter describes the essential elements of a VLC (section two). Considering the interaction process, in section three the chapter describes the most common computer-mediated communication systems used by members of a

VLC while section four presents an exposition about how the agent-based approach can be used for both analysing and improving the interaction process among members of the VLC. Section five concludes the chapter.

BACKGROUND

A VC can be defined as an information source or the place of the knowledge creation in which people share interests and information. The participants of the community have different knowledge or expertise and they can exchange useful information by communicating with each other (Kurabayashi et al., 2002).

There are many definitions of VCs that depend upon the perspective from which they are considered, that can be sociological, technological, economic etc..

From the sociological perspective VCs are defined based on their physical features or the strength and type of relationship. Etzioni & Etzioni (1999) view VCs from the perspective of bonding and culture and define it as having two attributes: (i) a web of affect-laden relationships encompassing group of individuals (bonding) and commitment to a set of shared values, mores, meanings and (ii) a shared historical identity (culture). Romm et al. (1997) define them as groups of people who communicate with each other via electronic media, such as the Internet and share common interests unconstrained by their geographical location, physical interaction or ethnic belonging. Ridings et al. (2002) define VCs as groups of people with common interests and practices that communicate regularly and for some duration in an organized way over the Internet through a common location or mechanism.

The technological perspective refers to VCs based on the software supporting them such as list servers, newsgroups, bulletin boards and Internet Relay Chats (IRC). These software technologies support the communication within the network (Lazar et al., 1999).

Balasubramanian & Mahajan (2001) take an economic perspective and define a VC as any "entity" that is "an aggregation of people, who are rational utility-maximizers, who interact without physical collocation in a social exchange process, with a shared objective".

In all of these definitions VCs are described as social entities comprised of individuals who share information and collaborate. The notion of information refers to the fact that membership of a VC is linked to the possibility of gaining access to specific information regarding areas or issues of interest, whilst the notion of collaboration refers to the search for moments of interaction during which one can share with others, passions, interests, experiences and knowledge.

The popularity of VCs, combined with the widespread diffusion of e-learning practices, has given rise to the phenomenon of VLCs. VLCs represent just a new organizational form of cooperation that uses information and communication technologies (ICTs) for a collaborative learning environment. Schwier (2002) defines VLCs as "particular types of virtual learning environment". A learning environment must allow learners to engage each other intentionally and collectively in the transaction or transformation of knowledge. It is not enough that material is presented to people and they interact with it. It is not enough that the learners interact with instructors to refine their understanding of material. Instead, for a VLC to exist, it is necessary for individuals to take advantage of, and in some cases invent, a process for engaging ideas, negotiating meanings and learning collectively. Jobring (2002) describes VLCs as "learning atmospheres, a context providing a supportive system from which sustainable learning processes are gained through a dialogue and collaborative construction of knowledge by acquiring, generating, analysing and structuring information". Pea (2002) describes the three components (virtual, learning and community) separately. The term virtual is defined as "the medium for communication and community formation are computer and related web-based technologies" while the term learning "identifies the objective of activity in this context". Finally the term community refers to "a group of participants who have something in common". Luppicini (2003) identifies different categories of VLCs:

- Knowledge building;
- Inquiry;
- Practice;
- Culture;
- Socialization;
- Counselling and development.

Members of knowledge building communities work independently or in groups with the aim to create and share knowledge rather than to construct specific products or to complete particular tasks. VLCs of inquiry bring members together with a common purpose. Each member shares his/her own responsibility to contribute content conducive to achieve that purpose. VLCs of practice provide a means to practice a role or learning a skill or profession. They are mainly used for professional practices. VLCs of culture bring together members with similar histories that share ethical and cultural values, and customs in an informal learning setting. Members of VLCs of socialization focus on members with common interests who seek to socialize with others. Finally VLCs of counselling and development provide groups support. Their purpose is to facilitate individual growth.

ESSENTIAL ELEMENTS OF VIRTUAL LEARNING COMMUNITIES

A VLC is characterized by a strong and frequent use of ICT tools, for enhancing the "meeting opportunities" and the interactions among its members. Three fundamental elements are shared by all members:

- A domain,
- A community composed of a group of people,
- Learning, practice, skills and knowledge among members of that domain.

The domain represents the common ground of interest in something that brings members together to join the community (topics on focus). Recognizing and understanding the domain is important since it makes it feasible to understand the reason behind the existence of the community and its role and value to its members. It also allows members to distinguish between the topics that will be interesting to the other members and the topics that are not (what matters & what matters not).

The community implies the process of bringing those who have interest in specific domain and remove interaction barriers, to build trust and relationships among the members of the community, to commence the learning process. In creating a community each member develops her/his own identity in relation to the community. The members' interactions over time help members in creating a network of trustees, composed of those who feel confident and comfortable with. This in return creates a reference source to ask for help when it is necessary. An important factor in forming a community is the mutual engagement among the community members. Members whether joined the community voluntarily or were obliged to join cannot be forced to contribute to it. They rather can be encouraged to participate by understanding the value a community generates to them.

Finally, the sharing of learning practice is the process of capturing, developing, sharing and maintaining learning knowledge inside a community. It is the set of ideas, tools, information, actions, documents, learning activities knowledge bases and other repositories that members share. Successful learning practice involves both the codification and interactions of the tacit and explicit knowledge inside a community. Members share and explore their knowledge based on mutual

Table 1. Classification proposed by Fleming

TECHNOLOGY	SYNCHRONOUS/ ASYNCHRONOUS
Chat room	S
Video (conference)	S
Audio (conference)	S
Video/animation (recorded)	A
Hypertext/Web pages	A
Whiteboards	S
Electronic mail	A
Newsgroups	A
Discussion boards	A
Audio + shared spaces	S
Simulation/visualization	Both

activities, and produce documents or tools for example based on the lessons learned.

To support users during the learning activities several computer-mediated communication systems are used. In the following section these systems are described in detail.

COMPUTER-MEDIATED COMMUNICATION SYSTEMS

With the rapid development of the contemporary Internet technologies, a very large amount of information can be accessed in the Web if users formulate queries with the appropriate key words. At the same time, with the Web 2.0 technologies rising, computer-mediated communication systems have become a mainstream of online media. Computer-mediated communication systems refer to virtual environments that support users to interact, compose, store, deliver and process information and communication providing functionalities for searching and browsing information (Reid, 1991).

The use of computer-mediated communication systems in VLCs facilitates collaboration and communication among members.

Fleming (2004) classifies the different computer-mediated communication systems used in

VLCs, in synchronous and asynchronous (Table 1). Synchronous systems allow "a real-time communication that brings learners together with or without their instructor at a specific time and place" (Lavooy & Newlin, 2003) while, asynchronous systems allow a "communication that does not occur at regular intervals and generally describe communications in which data are transmitted intermittently"(Madjidi et. al., 1999).

Starting from the classification proposed by Fleming, in the following paragraph we describe in particular the most used: (i) discussion forums, that provide members with the ability to post and reply to messages in a common area, (ii) whiteboards, that allow users to brainstorm together and draw graphical objects into a shared window (iii) video/audio conferencing systems, that allow users to talk, send video and audio signals, take polls or view online presentations over the Internet (iv) newsgroups that enable people exchange ideas, discuss, communicate and even make friends. Moreover we add to this classification also blogs because they are considered as more typical communication tools now.

All these systems are analysed according to their functionalities to improve the level of participation and involvement of each member and to support the learning process.

Figure 1. Graphical representation of a discussion board

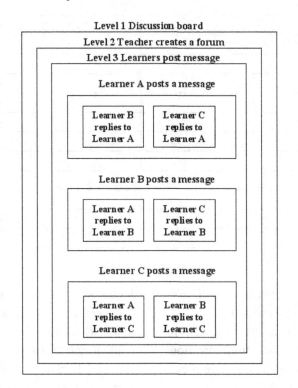

Discussion Forums

Discussion forums, also called discussion boards, message boards and/or online forums, are "asynchronous environmental tools that provide an opportunity for each individual learner to post a statement as well as to respond to the postings of other learners; thus, creating a discussion" (Markel, 2001). Many VLCs contain a discussion board for its ability to restrict both who can participate and read the discussion. Discussions boards have the potential to enhance interactions between learners and teachers in an asynchronous format by allowing them to:

- Communicate in a global manner;
- Build peer to peer relationships;
- Discuss relevant topics.

Figure 1 shows a graphical representation of a discussion board.

If a teacher chooses to use a discussion board in a VLC, typically she/he will post a topical question (by creating a forum) that learners have to answer. The act to collect learners' answers and sending them to the discussion board is referred to as a post. A series of posts with the same subject are referred to as a thread. The exchange of posts among learners has the potential both to promote collaborative learning and to develop effective knowledge construction. According to Harman & Koohang (2005) the knowledge creation process in a discussion board (Figure 2) begins by presentation of a real-world problem, which a learner, by deriving goals and objectives, is encouraged to solve. A learner is also encouraged both to use her/his own previous experience(s) and to empathise elements such as "higher-level thinking skills", exploration, and use of primary sources of data and apply them to the problem. Afterwards learners, in a collaborative and cooperative setting, create discussions engaging herself/himself in dialogue

Figure 2. Knowledge creation process in discussion boards

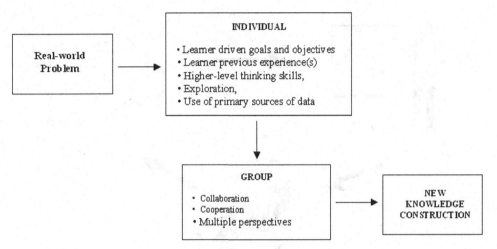

with others members of the VLCs. This permits to create social interactions that allow learners to reinforce their own ideas and in some cases even to change their own original thinking. She/he will build a combined knowledge with multiple perspectives that construct a new knowledge.

According to Higgison & Harris (2002), the use of discussion boards in learning practices presents a lot of advantages but also limitations (Table 2).

The greatest advantage of discussion forums is that they represent a very useful tool to share discussions, collaborate and archive individual comments. They allow to link members across time and space by reducing the need to have place for learning activities. Moreover their asynchronous nature affords more time for learners to reflect on problems and to react them. Asynchronicity also allows to set non-linear hyper-talk through which learners contribute to different threads of discussion without the need to fight for "airtime". On the other hand, asynchronous discussion presents also a very important limitation. The members "lose feedback through non-verbal cues; they must thus make conscious efforts to 'verbalise' a thought" (Lim & Tan, 2001).

Whiteboards

The whiteboard is a means of chat, sharing notes and drawings over the Internet as an effective support tool for communication and distance learning among learners from different parts of the globe. Generally it is possible to classify whiteboards into tree categories:

* Standalone copy whiteboard: where the content can be scanned and printed out;

Table 2. Advantages and limitations of discussion boards in learning practices

ADVANTAGES
• Time and place independence
• No need to travel to the place of learning
• Time between messages allows for reflection
• Speakers of other languages have added time to read and compose answers
• All students have a voice without the need to fight for 'airtime', as in a face-to-face situation
• The lack of visual cues provides participants with a more equal footing
• Many to many interaction may enhance peer learning
• Answers to questions can be seen by all
• Discussion is potentially richer than in a face to face classroom
• Messages are archived centrally providing a database of interactions
• Process of learning more visible to all.

Figure 3. Whiteboard's components

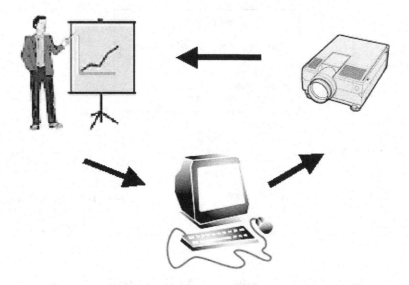

- Peripheral whiteboard: where information, in the form of digital files, is transferred to a connected computer;
- Interactive whiteboard: where large touch-screen monitors, synchronized to a connected computer, allow users to interact with the display.

Fully-functioning whiteboards usually involves three components: a computer, a projector, and a display panel (Figure 3).

The computer is connected with the projector and the computer monitor image on the whiteboard. Additional components can be also used that includes handheld keypads to gather individual responses and interactive white whiteboard tablets.

According to Brown (2004) the use of whiteboards in the learning practices presents a lot of advantages but also disadvantages (Table 3).

As teaching tools, whiteboards have considerable potential to change teaching. The interaction with electronic and multimedia contents allows

Table 3. Advantages and disadvantages of whiteboards in learning practices

ADVANTAGES
• They can help even technophobic teachers to use this medium with ease for presentations from the front of the room.
• They help in broadening the use of e-learning because they rapidly demonstrate the potential of alternative modes of delivery.
• They make it easy for teachers to enhance presentation content by easily integrating a wide range of material into a lesson, such as a picture from the internet, a graph from a spreadsheet or text from a Microsoft Word file, in addition to student and teacher annotations on these objects.
• They allow teachers to create easily and rapidly customised learning objects from a range of existing content and to adapt it to the needs of the class in real time.
• They allow learners to absorb information more easily.
• They allow learners to participate in-group discussions by freeing them from note taking.
• They allow learners to work collaboratively around a shared task or work area.
• When fully integrated into a VLE (virtual learning environment) and learning object repository there is potential for widespread sharing of resources.
• When used for interactive testing of understanding for the entire class, they can rapidly provide learner feedback.

learners and teachers to perform different learning activities in a supportive learning environment. In particular they can:

- Use text and images for graphical presentations;
- Write notes in digital inks;
- Save notes for review;
- Make electronic lesson (with templates and images);
- Use presentation tools as learning materials.

All these activities benefit of learner motivation and engagement and teachers expectations. With respect to learners the use of whiteboard appeals to both intrinsically and extrinsically motivated them. Learners are intrinsically motivated because they enjoy in demonstrating their own knowledge on the interaction while they are extrinsically motivated by the enjoyment in using the technology. Moreover learners are more likely to engage in learning due to the surprise element that is offered through the large visual cues offered through the presentation format. Considering teachers they have the possibility to make lessons memorable, by using digital resources that allow maintaining dynamic interaction with the entire class. Moreover whiteboards are seen by teachers as technologies that afford creativity and enable to provide learning experiences that meet the needs of all learners.

Video/Audio Conferencing Systems

Video/audio conferencing systems refer to synchronous (live) meetings and applications sharing over the web. They involve the transmission of image (video) and speech (audio) between physically separated locations (Lensegrav & Pearce, 2002). During a video/audio conferencing participants can see whatever is on the presenter's screen, and simultaneously share applications and discuss mat-

ters of common topic. The combination of video data with voice interaction makes possible to:

- Collaboratively perform activities in different parts of the world;
- Provide mentoring or homework help.

One of the most used video/audio conferencing systems is *Skype* a program that allows users to communication with voice, video/audio conference, or chat for free between computers. The Skype program allows supporting existing learning approaches. It facilitates learner's engagement with its easy way to communicate. Interacting with people from the whole wide world can help learners to understand cultural differences, fine-tune foreign language skill and learn about social norms. Virtual learning becomes as important as traditional "real learning" because it integrates its functionalities overcoming the walls of the classroom.

Williamson (2003) underlines the possible applications of Skype program in the range of electronic learning. According to the author "one possible application could be to visit via Skype other classes all over the world in online video-audio conferences. This leads as well to the possibility to establish various cross-cultural projects, virtual student exchange programs".

Moreover Skype allows "learners to create a personal profile, expert-networks can be build up by finding the needed expert with the help of an intelligent profile search. This allows consulting experts on a certain problem". Another application is the search for other learners with similar interests; so Skype might be "a medium for an interesting cross-cultural exchange in which learners are able to build up a social or theme-based network of peers from a variety of backgrounds and nationalities, eventually initiated by a course teacher or a e-learning project manager".

The use of video/audio conferencing systems such as Skype creates an interactive environment

Table 4. Advantages and disadvantages of Video/ audio conferencing systems in learning practice

ADVANTAGES
• Relatively inexpensive • Reach more people since uses available telephone technology • Appeals to audio learner • Familiar technology • Interactive medium, allows direct learner and facilitator participation • Can combine with other media for example print, video, computers • Site coordinator not needed • Technology fairly reliable • Timely, shorter lead time to schedule • Accessibility

for the online learning activities. This interaction between teachers and learners, and between learners themselves, is found to be at the heart of effective on-line learning (Lewis, 2006).

According to Frey & Overfield (2002) the use of video/audio conferencing systems presents a lot of advantages but also disadvantages (Table 4).

The most important benefits that video/audio conferencing systems bring to the learning practices consist of their capacity to increase the dialogue both with in an individual learner environment and within a collaborative learner environment. The virtual presence of participants creates a sense of social presence, although it does not add much in cognitive terms (Coventry, 1995). This allows transferring traditional learning practices out of a limited space into a wide-ranged distributed learning environment.

Newsgroups

A Newsgroup represents a repository of messages posted by many users from different locations. It can be considered as a virtual space where people exchange ideas, discuss, communicate and even make friends (Roberts, 1998).

The use of newsgroups in learning practices allows carrying out different learning activities such as:

- To pose questions;
- To collaboratively discuss and write;
- To post procedure and calendars;
- To post web pages.

According to Au et al. (1999) in using the newsgroup, learning is conceptualised as three levels of involvement. The first is the individual involvement. It refers to the extent learner interact with other ones. The second level is the interpersonal involvement. This pertains to learner-to-learner interaction in which relationships and friendships are formed. The third level of involvement is societal. This notion extends from the immediate social groups around a learner to the community as a whole to exercise the politics of democratic societies to the authority.

To determine the involvement in newsgroups a very important aspect to consider is the motivation of participants. In particular two different kinds of motivation have to be considered. Extrinsic motivation is originated from the desire to obtain social approval and attain at social-solidarity goals. Intrinsic motivation refers to the participants desire to learn new things. The more the learners are motivated by achievement, the more likely that they will be involved in the newsgroup (Maehr & Braskamp, 1986).

According to the Uppsala University (2001) the use of newsgroups presents a lot of advantages but also disadvantages (Table 5).

Newsgroups provide an infinite number of possibilities to participants. They can be used to access information, post questions or commentar-

Table 5. Advantages and disadvantages of newsgroups in learning practices

ADVANTAGES
• They allow to categorized topics that match users interests are easy to find. • They permit to join public and private discussions. • Depth of discussions can go far if many learners have common topics to discuss.

ies about different topics. Postings can give a sort of "pulse" of the learners and allow teachers to see what types of issues learners from particular topics are concerned about. Newsgroup also allow participants to take the time to reflect their responses more carefully than when they are under pressure of a face-to-face discussion. In this sense newsgroups are able to create a "de-centered" dialogue among learners and between learners and teachers.

Blogs

A blog provides a forum for communication, collaboration, knowledge building, information gathering and publishing.

Many educators use blogs as effective learning tools. Many are the studies on their potential to promote learning. Oravec (2002) observes "blogs have many dimensions that are suited to learners 'unique voices', empowering them, and encouraging them to become more critically analytical in their thinking". Writing a blog supports this because "it forces the learner to confront his/her own opinions and contemplate how his/her view might be interpreted and reflected upon by others" (Williams. & Jacobs, 2004). Also the study conducted by Ferdig & Trammel (2004) is significant to assess the educational value of blogs. The authors argue that "the discursive nature of knowledge construction is best addressed by the immediacy and commentary based system of blogging". They observe that "there will be a natural tendency for reflection and analysis on the part of the student, given feedback systems are integral to the blogging interface, but also note that the contextualisation of learning through hypertext links to other materials encourages revisiting and revising of learned concepts, enriching the learning experience". Many are the advantages that blogs offer to learning activities (Table 6). They can be used to support all the major processes involved in traditional learning such as: knowledge shar-

ing, knowledge organization, thinking over the content and discussion over the content. In fact blogs help in organizing notes, publishing notes, providing course, posting content and information with annotated links to online resources, discussing learning material and so on. This would reposition the teacher and communication central to the learning process.

According to Tseng (2008) despite of their advantages, blogs also present some disadvantages. The first concerns the teachers' workload when making corrections. As learners can post a lot of messages on the blogs, it increases teachers' workload to correct all the writing materials. Then blogs present the problem of privacy. It is a place for learners to express comments but it is also a place that everyone can browse. There is no limitation or restriction to block those who intentionally leave inappropriate and annoying comments. Moreover, the language used in blogs often is playful and deliberate and this can create problems. Finally another problem is the time-investment. A significant number of hours is required to maintain a successful blog. Many blogs fail because it is difficult for people to find enough time to update a blog everyday (Wiebrands, 2006).

STUDY INTERACTION IN VIRTUAL LEARNING COMMUNITIES BY USING AN AGENT-BASED APPROACH

The considered computer-mediated communication systems have the purpose to support both the interaction process and the learning process in a virtual learning environment. An important interaction aspect to consider in the VLCs is the social interaction among its members. Social interaction means exchanging "group experiences or establishing some relevant collective learning". This helps the learner to acquire "appropriate social skills and assists team building in reaching joint learning objectives" (Ryu & Parsons, 2009).

Table 6. Advantages and disadvantages of blogs in learning practices

ADVANTAGES
• Learning is independent of time and place
• Education is demand-oriented
• Learners are encouraged to be active through the course period
• Learners improve their writing competencies
• Changes in thinking are captured
• People are invited to collaborate
• Education is more informal
• External people are involved
• The use of images is facilitated
• Costs are reduced
• People continuously try thinks out

Moreover the interactions among members of a VLC evolve during the time, and the community influences those interactions at the same time defining the direction, strength and content of a particular interaction providing an evolution of the VLC (Zhang and Tanniru, 2005). For this reason the study of the dynamic interaction process helps to understand the evolution of VLCs and to manage this evolution. To analyse this process and improve the interaction aspects is focal to consider the different learners' background knowledge and skills (Weber, 1999). In fact, individual or tailored instruction based on learners' needs and background should be analysed for facilitating online learning, based on learners' backgrounds and individual differences. Some studies have analysed psychological variables affecting the quality of online learning considering several aspects such as: demographic variables (Biner et al., 1995), field dependence and independence variables (Brenner, 1997) and learning styles (Cox and Huglin, 2000). These pieces of information incorporate domain-related data and information about personal attributes, such as capabilities and preferences; they are used to build user models, having an important role during the interaction process in the VLC (Milne et al. 1996).

Starting from these consideration the social ability, the intelligent decision-making capabilities, concurrent execution and mobility capabili-ties of intelligent agents are important features for enhancing and supporting learning models so they have become alternatives to traditional client-server computing (Wooldridge and Jennings, 1995).

Agents in VLCs have been employed: i) for assisting people in personal activities; ii) for monitoring and upgrading resources, tools and system in VLCs; and iii) for supporting teaching/learning related activities.

Considering these functionalities this section is mainly focused on the third point, providing a discussion about how intelligent agents can be used for both analysing and improving the interaction process among members for supporting teaching/learning activities.

The agent-based approaches allow to better understand the evolution of communities and to manage this evolution (Jones et al., 2002) (Schrott & Beimborn, 2003).

An important definition of intelligent agent has been given by Lieberman (Lieberman, 1997): *"An intelligent agent is any program that can be considered by the user to be acting as an assistant or helper, rather than as a tool in the manner of a conventional direct manipulation interface. An agent should as well display some, but perhaps not all, of the characteristics that are associated with human intelligence: learning, inference, adaptability, independence, creativity, etc."*

An intelligent agent is efficient to support user-focused e-learning content because it presents characteristics that support the social interface metaphor (Selker, 1994) as the following table describes.

Therefore autonomous, communication, and proactive features of intelligent agents support Web-based distributed learning providing co-operative and adaptive learning (Mamdani et al., 1999). In this environment each agent has a specialized task managing resource components that are assigned to it. The control of the learning process is distributed over the agent hierarchy so each agent works at a specific level making

Table 7. Intelligent agent characteristics

INTELLIGENT AGENT CHARACTERISTICS	
Autonomy implies that an agent pursues goals in different ways:	*Goal-oriented*: agent accepts high-level requests indicating the requests of the user and it is responsible for deciding how and when to satisfy user requests
	Collaborative: agent does not blindly accept commands but can modify requests asking clarification questions, or in specific case it can refuse to satisfy requests
	Flexible: agent is able to dynamically decide which actions to invoke, and in what sequence, according to the state of its external environment
	Self-starting: agent can understand changes in its environment and it decides when to act
Temporal continuity implies that an agent is a continuously running process that is persistent in its pursuit of goals	
Personality implies that an agent has a well-defined personality that facilitates interaction with users	
Communication ability implies that agent can interact with other agents and people in order to obtain information for achieving its purposes in a networked environment	
Adaptability implies that agent can automatically customizes itself to the preferences of its user according to previous experience adapting itself to changes in its environment	
Mobility implies that agent can transport itself across different system architectures and platforms	

specific decisions, and it generates specialized dynamic view.

In virtual learning environments, intelligent agents provide three types of services (Ganzha, 2008): helping students to complete innovative activities; stimulating social interactions among students; and providing teachers clear, objective information about students' performance.

In regard to these considerations, the following paragraphs present descriptions of the agent-based approach on considering how this allows both analysing interaction and improving the level of participation of members of a VLC.

Analysing Interaction by Using an Agent-Based Approach

The agent-based approach can be usefully applied to analyse interactions in VLCs because it only needs an understanding of essential characteristics and basic interaction rules for modelling the VLC. In fact, this approach allows modelling the characteristics of the VLC members, the rules that

characterize the interaction among members, and the consequences of the interaction.

The intelligent agents are well suited to study interactions in VLCs because a VLC can be viewed as composed of agents representing its members. Using the agent-based approach, members of the VLC are modelled as agents and simulations on the model are defined in order to analyse interactions.

Each member is modelled by an agent with particular cognitive and social features (Zhang and Tanniru, 2005). These features include:

- Autonomy that defines the possibility of a member to join the VLC;
- Interaction with other members;
- Reactivity to the environment of the VLC that is due to the fact each member learns and adapts to the new environment at individual level;
- Persistence to keep continuous interaction.

Modelling members by these features, agent-based approaches are applied to study relationships between users individual behaviours and the overall development of VLCs, modelling participants as agents and analysing interactions among them. In detail, interactions that have been studied in literature concern interactions for improving the members' knowledge and skills, by learning, discussing and sharing.

Agents have their own knowledge and they are able to communicate with each other. Similarly to participants of the VLCs, agents communicate exchanging their individual knowledge and cooperate for solving problems and for reaching collective or individual goals (Huhn and Stephens, 1999). Agents can be members of several VLCs and they can ask and send information to the community.

Participants of VLCs can have different roles in the community, such as managers or moderators. According to this claim, in (Lee and Chong, 2003) each agent is structured in order to have a different role in the community. Lee and Chong (2003) propose a learning management system where each agent interacts with others and acts according with its role, which can be: i) a learner agent that is an expert on a specific learner variable (such as learning behaviours); ii) a learner agent manager that is a manger of the learner agents; iii) a learner management system that is a decision-maker on user's adaptive learning considering information provided by specialized agents, such as learner agents. Similarly, Maret and Calmet (2009) propose a community where the community leader agent has created the community to achieve purposes in the domain of interest and member agents that exchange messages obeying policies that define the community. The interaction among member agents is also monitored by leaders that receive all the messages sent by the members, and they control the access to the community (Maret and Calmet, 2009).

The agents manage the knowledge in the communities and they can dynamically modify the course of learning content and presentation over time according with information about learner's cognitive behaviour.

Moreover, studies about interaction in VLCs that apply intelligent agents have underlined important aspects related to participants with high activeness interaction level in VLCs (Zhang and Tanniru, 2005). These studies evidence that the most active participants tend to move from a VLC to another more significantly than others. In fact, if the contribution of the active members of the VLC is not appreciated or the number of members decreases, the active members reduce their contributions or leave the VLC (Zhang and Tanniru, 2005). Moreover the number of members decreases if there is a negative correlation between the expertise level and the activeness level. If active members give advices too easily, members who require that pieces of information be mislead and confused because pieces of information may distract the original focus of the discussion too (Jones et al., 2002).

The following section will provide a discussion about how agent-based approach can compensate the interaction problems improving the level of participation of members in a correct manner.

Improving the Level of Participation by Using an Agent-Based Approach

As well as to analyse interaction in VLCs, intelligent agents can be usefully applied to understand how improve the level of participation of members to a VLC.

Considering the characteristics of intelligent agents (Table 6), they allow supporting users in different way by contributing to gradually improve the level of familiarity of each user with the system and her/his level of participation.

Therefore, intelligent agents are programs that can help and assist users during the learning process. In detail, they can improve the learning effectiveness and learner satisfaction reducing costs (Thaiupathump et al., 1999). Studies, accomplished in (Thaiupathump et al., 1999), have proved that agents' activities during the online learning of students stimulate people for completing their works and improve the retention rate of students. This fact is related to the positive correlation between the number of times that users use intelligent agents and the number of their tasks completed has been demonstrated (Thaiupathump et al., 1999).

For these reasons an intelligent agent can be viewed as a motivational tool. In fact, studies about motivation on virtual learning environment (Bourne, 1998) have indicated that intelligent agents efficiently contribute in encouraging e-mail, immediate feedback, and motivating the participants to complete the assignments.

These characteristics of agents cause benefits in the virtual learning environment. For example the immediate feedback stimulate the learners to be focused on completing the assignments, and the agents' characteristics to give explicit directions on how to face problems in an task is a useful feature for learners.

Moreover, agents facilitate the users' enjoyment of the learning situation because a social relationship is established between user and pedagogical agent and this mechanism promotes learning in Web-based learning environment.

Considering the support of their interaction process, intelligent agents encourage users to reflect for improving the achievement of knowledge connected to their interests, abilities and performance styles supporting the planning of users' actions better for achieving their goals. The agent-based approach increases interactions among members of the community providing mechanism for stimulating discussions and people-to-people interactions.

Adopting intelligent agents into the learning environment allows moving online learning paradigms away from a traditional learning environment focusing the learning process on a user's individual needs, and supporting students to progress toward or learn-while-doing approach.

Moreover, in educational environment intelligent agents have been also used in order to discover if the content of the course materials of a particular course has significantly been updated or modified in order to provide a notification to the students taking the course. Moreover they have been applied to also monitoring hyperlinks connected to the course materials in order to inform the course teacher to remedy the problem (Lin and Poon, 2004).

In addition, intelligent agents support the use of the system reducing the search cost for value creation by locating and suggesting the exploration of the system.

DISCUSSION AND CONCLUSION

This chapter has proposed a discussion about VLCs on analysing in particular how these represent an effective support tool for social interaction, knowledge sharing, management and learning promotion and how existing technological systems and approaches are able to support these goals.

In the first part the chapter provides the main definitions given in literature and the main features that characterize a VLC.

Then the chapter has provided a description of the most common computer-mediated communication systems used to promote interaction and collaboration. In particular, we described: (i) discussion forums, that provide members with the ability to post and reply to messages in a common area, (ii) whiteboards, that allow users to brainstorm together and draw graphical objects into a shared window (iii) video/audio conferencing systems, that allow users to talk over the Internet, send video and audio signals, view online presentations over the Internet (iv) newsgroups that enable people exchange ideas, discuss, communicate and even make friends (v) blogs that provide a forum for communication, collaboration, knowledge building, information gathering and publishing.

The different computer-mediated communication systems have been analysed on considering the advantages and disadvantages that each of them brings to the learning process. By comparing the analysed systems, some advantages and disadvantages appear to be in common among them. The results of this comparative analysis are presented in Table 8.

As shown in the Table 8, computer-mediated communication systems have considerable potential to change learning activities. Education becomes more informal and participant-oriented since learners construct knowledge through the shared experiences they bring to the collaborative discussions. Discussions can occur in different places and times due to time and place in which learning and teaching take place. The use of computer mediated communication systems to negotiate and construct knowledge is an example of using the technology as a cognitive tool and not simply as another kind of one-way communication method. According to (Jonassen, 1998) "cognitive tools stimulate learning strategies and critical thinking, learners engaged with course content in discussions and group work with other learners engage in generative processing of information". In particular the author describes the generative processing as "deeper information processing results from activating appropriate mental models, using them to interpret new information, assimilating new information back into those models, reorganizing the models in light of the newly interpreted information, and then us-

ing those newly aggrandized models to explain, interpret, or infer new knowledge".

In summary computer mediated communication systems are able to create a more dynamic environment oriented to innovation and knowledge sharing among learners. In this perspective, they amplify openness, interoperability, scalability, and extensibility of traditional learning tools.

However they present also very important limitations. They allow setting non-linear hyper-talk through which learners contribute to different threads of discussion without the need to fight for "airtime" therefore context and reference of massages may be unclear and misunderstanding may occur. On the other hand, learners lose feedback through non-verbal cues; they must thus make conscious efforts to verbalise a thought. Moreover computer mediated communication systems present the problem of privacy and plagiarism since there is no limitation or restriction to block those people who intentionally leave inappropriate comments.

The description of the existing systems has underlined the importance of the interaction process in the learning process. For this reason the focus of the chapter has been moved on the intelligent agent techniques, considering how they allow both analysing interaction and improving the level of participation of members of a VLC. The analysis of the agent-based models has underlined that they are able to understand essential characteristics and basic interaction rules that characterize the interaction among members. This chapter has underlined how these types of information allow studying the dynamic interaction process, to understand the evolution of VLCs and to manage this evolution.

The analysis has underlined the importance of agent technology for supporting the interactions in educational environment due to the fact that it efficiently simulate a human facilitator to give immediate responses in an on-demand learning environment.

It is possible to conclude that the use of intelligent agents can be significantly associated with

Table 8. Advantages and disadvantages the different tools have in common

ADVANTAGES
• Education is more informal
• Time and place independence
• Collaborative interaction may enhance peer learning
• Process of learning more accessible to all
• Education is participant-oriented

learner progress giving personalized instruction and support human-to-human interactions.

REFERENCES

Au, K. Y., Ng, A. L., & Ho, F. K. (1999). Using newsgroups to prepare students for the virtual business community: A technological, pedagogical, and motivational analysis. In James, J. (Ed.), *Quality in Teaching and Learning in Higher Education: A collection of refereed papers from the first conference on Quality in Teaching and Learning in Higher Education* (pp. 192–199). Hong Kong: The Hong Kong Polytechnic University, Educational Development Centre.

Balasubramanian, S., & Mahajan, V. (2001). The Economic Leverage of the Virtual Community. *International Journal of Electronic Commerce, 5,* 103–138.

Barton, M. (2004, May 21). *Embrace the wiki way!* [Electronic version]. Retrieved February 11, 2007, from http://www.mattbarton.net/tikiwiki/tiki-print_article.php?articleId=4

Biner, P., Bink, M., Huffman, M., & Dean, R. (1995). Personality characteristics differentiating and predicting the achievement of televised-course students and traditional-course students. *American Journal of Distance Education, 9*(2), 46–60. doi:10.1080/08923649509526887

Bourne, J. R. (1998). Net-Learning: Strategies for On-Campus and Off-Campus Network-enabled Learning. *Journal of Asynchronous Learning Networks, 2*(2), 70–88.

Brenner, J. (1997). An analysis of student's cognitive styles in asynchronous distance education courses at a community college. In *Third International Conference on Asynchronous Learning Networks.*

Brown, S. (2004). *Interactive Whiteboards in Education.* San Bruno, CA: TechLearn.

Coventry, L. (1995). *Video Conferencing in Higher Education.* Retrieved from www.man.ac.uk/MVC//SIMA/video3/two1.html

Desilets, A., Paquet, S., & Vinson, N. (2005). Are wikis usable? In *WikiSym 2005 Conference,* October 16-18, San Diego, CA, USA.

Ebersbach, A., Glaser, M., & Heigl, R. (2005). *Wiki: Web Collaboration.* Berlin, Germany: Springer.

Etzioni, A., & Etzioni, O. (1999). Face-to-face and computer-mediated communities; a comparative analysis. *The Information Society, 15*(4), 241–248. doi:10.1080/019722499128402

Ferdig, R., & Trammell, K. (2004, February). *Content delivery in 'Blogosphere.' Technological Horizons in Education Journal.* Retrieved from http://www.thejournal.com/articles/16626

Fleming, S. (2004). *Virtual Learning Communities – Supporting Learning through Interaction.* Technical Report OUCS-2004-13.

Frey, B., & Overfield, K. (2002). Audio Professional Development Workshops Less Glamorous More Cost Effective. In *New Horizons. Adult Education, 16*(2).

Ganzha, M. (2008). E-learning with Intelligent Agents. *IEEE Distributed Systems Online, 9*(2), 4. doi:10.1109/MDSO.2008.6

Harman, K., & Koohang, A. (2005). Discussion Board: A Learning Object. *Interdisciplinary Journal of Knowledge and Learning Objects.*

Higgison, C., & Harris, R. (2002). *Online tutoring: the OTiS experience.* Retrieved from http://otis.scotcit.ac.uk

Huhn, M., & Stephens, L. (1999). Multiagent systems and societies of agents. In *Multiagent Systems: A Modern Introduction to Distributed Artificial Intelligence* (pp. 79–120). Cambridge, MA, USA: MIT Press.

Jobring, O. (2002). *Online Learning Community Research website (English)*. Retrieved from http://www.learnloop.org/olc

Jonassen, D. (1998). *Technology as cognitive tools: Learners as designers*. IT FORUM Paper 1. Retrieved from http://itech1.coe.uga.edu/itforum/paper1/paper1.html

Jones, Q., Ravid, G., & Rafaeli, S. (2002). An Empirical Exploration of Mass Interaction System Dynamics: Individual Information Overload and Usenet Discourse. In *35th Annual Hawaii International Conference on System Sciences (HICSS'02)*, Big Island, Hawaii.

Kurabayashi, N., Yamazaki, T., Yuasa, T., & Hasuike, K. (2002). Proactive Information Supply for Activating Conversational Interaction in Virtual Communities. In *the IEEE International Workshop on Knowledge Media Networking (KMN'02)* (pp.167-170).

Kurbel, K. (2001). Virtuality on the Students and on the Teachers Sides: A Multimedia and Internet Based International Master Program (ICEF). In *Proc. on the 7th International Conference on Technology Supported Learning and Training* (pp. 133-136).

Lamb, B. (2004, September/October). Wide open spaces: Wikis, ready or not. *EDUCASE Review, 39*(5), 36-48. Retrieved November 2006, from http://www.educase.edu/pub/er/erm04/erm0452.asp?BHEP=1

Lavooy, M., & Newlin, M. (2003). Computer mediated communication: online instruction and interactivity. *Journal of Interactive Learning Research, 14*(9), 157.

Lazar, J. R., Tsao, R., & Preece, J. (1999). One foot in cyberspace and the other on the ground: A case study of analysis and design issues in a hybrid virtual and physical community. *Web Net Journal: Internet Technologies. Applications and Issues, 1*(3), 49–57.

Lee, Y., & Chong, Q. (2003, January). Multi-agent systems support for Community-Based Learning Interacting with Computers. *Interacting with Computers, 15*(1), 33–55. doi:10.1016/S0953-5438(02)00057-7

Lensegrav, P., & Pearce, K. (2002). *The responsiveness of elementary students to the use of video conferencing*. Retrieved from http://www.bhsu.edu/education/edfaculty/lq>earce/Responsiveness%20ofl'ib20Elementarv%20Students%20to%20Video%20Conferencing.htm

Lewis, C. C., & Abdul-Hamid, H. (2006). Implementing Effective Online Teaching Practices: Voices of Exemplary Faculty. *Innovative Higher Education, 31*(2), 83–98. doi:10.1007/s10755-006-9010-z

Lieberman, H. (1997). Autonomous Interface Agents. CHI 97 Papers (pp. 22-27).

Lim, C. P., & Tan, S. C. (2001). Online discussion boards for focus group interviews: An exploratory study. *Journal of Educational Enquiry, 2*(1), 50–60.

Lin, F., & Poon, L. (2004). *Integrating Web Services and Agent Technology for E-learning Course Content Maintenance* (pp. 848–856). IEA/AIE.

Luppicini, R. (2003). Categories of virtual learning communities for educational design. *The Quarterly Review of Distance Education, 4*(4), 409–416.

Mader, S. (2006). *Using Wiki in education, the book*. Retrieved November 2006, from http://www.wikiineducation.com.

Madjidi, F., Hughes, H., Johnson, R. & Cary, K. (1999). *Virtual learning environments*.

Maehr, M. L., & Braskamp, L. A. (1986). The motivation factor: A theory of personal investment. Lexington, MA: Lexington.

Mamdani, A., Pitt, J., & Stathis, K. (1999). Connected Communities from the Standpoint of Multi-agent Systems. *New Generation Computing, 17*(4), 381–393. doi:10.1007/BF03037244

Maret, P., & Calmet, J. (2009). Agent-based knowledge communities. *International Journal of Computer Science and Applications, 6*(2), 1–18.

Markel, S. (2001). Technology and education online discussion forum: it's in the response. *Online Journal of Distance Learning Administration, 4*(2). Retrieved November 17, 2008, from http://www.westga.edu.ezproxy1.lib.asu.edu/%26sim;distance/ojdla/summer42/marke142.html

Milne, S., Shiu, E., & Cook, J. (1996). Development of a model of user attributes and its implementation within an adaptive tutoring system. *User Modeling and User-Adapted Interaction, 6*(4), 303–335. doi:10.1007/BF00213186

Oravec, J. (2002). Bookmarking the world: Weblog applications in education. *Journal of Adolescent & Adult Literacy, 45*(7), 616–621.

Pea, R. (2002). Learning Science Through Collaborative Visualization over the Internet. *Nobel Symposium (NS 120), Virtual Museums and Public Understanding of Science and Culture,* May 26-29, 2002, Stockholm, Sweden.

Reid, E. M. (1991). Electropolis: Communication and Community on Internet Relay Chat. *Intertek, 3*(3), 7–15.

Ridings, C. M., Gefen, D., & Arinze, B. (2002). Some antecedents and effects of trust in virtual communities. *The Journal of Strategic Information Systems,* (11): 271–295. doi:10.1016/S0963-8687(02)00021-5

Roberts, T. (1998). Are newsgroups virtual communities? In The SIGCHI conference on Human factors in computing systems (pp.360–367).

Romm, C., Pliskin, N., & Clarke, R. (1997). Virtual communities and society: Toward an integrative three phase model. *International Journal of Information Management, 17*(4), 261–270. doi:10.1016/S0268-4012(97)00004-2

Ryu, H., & Parsons, D. (2009). Designing Learning Activities with Mobile Technologies. In *Handbook Innovative Mobile Learning.* Techniques and Technologies.

Schrott, G., & Beimborn, D. (2003). *Informal Knowledge Networks: Toward a Community-Engineering Framework.* Presented at International Conference on Information Systems.

Schwier, R. A. (2001). Catalysts, Emphases, and Elements of Virtual Learning Communities. Implication for Research. *The Quarterly Review of Distance Education, 2*(1), 5–18.

Schwier, R. A. (2002). *Shaping the Metaphor of Community in Online Learning Environments.* Unpublished Manuscript, University of Saskatchewan.

Schwier, R. A. (2004). Virtual learning communities. In Anglin, G. (Ed.), *Critical issues in instructional technology.* Portsmouth, NH: Teacher Ideas Press.

Selker, T. (1994). Coach: A Teaching Agent that Learns. *Communications of the ACM, 37*(7), 92–99. doi:10.1145/176789.176799

Thaiupathump, C., Bourne, J., & Campbell, J. (1999). Intelligent agents for online learning. *Journal of Asynchronous Learning Networks, 3*(2). Retrieved May 17, 2004, from http://www.sloan-c.org/publications/jaln/v3n2/pdf/v3n2_choon.pdf

Tseng, M. C. (2008). The Use of Blogs in English Classes for Medicine-Related Majors. *Journal of Humanities and Social Sciences, 1*(1), 167–187.

Uppsala University. (2001). *A comprehensive study of using sap in a university environment.* Report, 2001.

Weber, G. (1999). *Adaptive learning systems in the World Wide Web*. In *Proceedings of the Seventh International Conference User Modeling (UM99)* (pp.371-377). Wien, Austria: Springer.

Wenger, E. C., & Snyder, W. M. (2000). Communities of Practice: The Organizational Frontier. *Harvard Business Review, 78,* 139–144.

Wiebrands, C. (2006). Creating community: The blog as a networking device. In *ALIA 2006 Biennial Conference*, Perth. Retrieved July 12, 2007, from http://espace.lis.curtin.edu.au/archive/00001015/03/Click06_Wiebrands_blogging.pdf

Williams, J. B., & Jacobs, J. (2004). Exploring the use of blogs as learning spaces in the higher education sector. *Australasian Journal of Educational Technology, 20*(2), 232–247.

Williamson. B. (2003). *Skype-ing work*. Retrieved from http://www.guardian.co.uk.

Wooldridge, M., & Jennings, N.v. (1995). Intelligent agents: Theory and practice. *The Knowledge Engineering Review, 10*(2), 115–152. doi:10.1017/S0269888900008122

Zhang, Y., & Tanniru, M. (2005). *An Agent-based Approach to Study Virtual Learning Communities*. HICSS-2005 (best paper award in collaboration track).

Chapter 7
E–Collaboration Between People and Technological Boundary Objects:
A New Learning Partnership in Knowledge Construction

Sandra Y. Okita
Columbia University, USA

ABSTRACT

Computerized instruction has become more common over the years. Students can now learn from computerized images of people in virtual environments. A new learning partnership can develop with a Technological Boundary Object (TBO) that simultaneously belongs to mutually exclusive categories. The TBOs may have human-like appearance and behavior that naturally elicit a social response. As learning environments become more human-like, should TBOs maintain a boundary-like state or aim for perfect human mimicry? The challenges to high fidelity seem to outweigh the benefits. Three common categories in TBOs: animate and inanimate, real and virtual, and self and other, are exemplified through empirical studies. The findings draw attention to the different learning partnerships that can be developed with TBOs and their future potential.

INTRODUCTION

People learn from various sources. Traditional sources involve learning from people or objects. Recently, people have started to learn more from computerized instructions that blends the natural properties of people and objects. For example, virtual environments include computerized people. Learning can even occur with life-sized humanoid robots.

The chapter proposes a new learning partnership between people and Technological Boundary Objects (TBO). TBOs are artifacts that simultaneously belong to mutually exclusive categories. For example, a robot dog would simultaneously reside in categories of animal and machine. TBOs that involve human-related categories typically have a human-like appearance and behavior. Appearance and behavior elicit strong social responses in TBOs that invite active engagement and can develop peer-learning relationships. Ideally, TBOs will support

DOI: 10.4018/978-1-61520-937-8.ch007

factual learning, knowledge construction, and the development of metacognitive skills.

The chapter begins by introducing TBOs. The chapter then organizes learning environments into categories of socially indifferent, socially implicit, and socially explicit. As learning environments become more human-like should TBOs aim for higher fidelity to the point that no boundary-like state remains? The challenges and issues to high fidelity seem to outweigh the benefits. Three common TBO combinations – animate and inanimate, real and virtual, and self and other – have been mapped to empirical studies to measure the effects of TBOs. The studies draw attention to the different possible learning partnerships that can be developed. The chapter will then share possible future work, and concludes with a summary. The objective of this chapter is to shine light on new potentials with TBOs, and provide some initial evidence to this interest.

TECHNOLOGICAL BOUNDARY OBJECTS (TBO)

The term "Boundary Object" was originally introduced by Susan L. Star and James R. Griesemer (1989). Boundary objects referred to ideas that serve as an interface across different communities of practice. For example, "affordance" in ecological psychology (Gibson, 1977, 1979) means all action possibilities of the environment for a specific organism. In Human-Computer Interaction (Norman, 1988), the concept of "affordance" is relational, and refers to perceived action possibilities such as "to suggest" or "to invite". People in the two communities can use the word "affordance" to communicate, despite the different theoretical commitments hidden behind the term.

Here, the term "boundary object" is used differently. Boundary objects refer to artifacts that simultaneously belong to mutually exclusive categories. For example, Frankenstein belongs to categories of both alive and dead. Boundary objects often elicit strong responses that bewilder the beliefs in them. People acknowledge quite easily that Frankenstein and Werewolf are fictional, or that what they see "is only a movie", but they continue to be afraid of the idea. Similarly, visiting Disney's haunted mansion, or watching a vampire movie, generates affective responses regardless of one's beliefs. Many combinations of categories trigger similar responses that elicit primitive reactions, often fear, despite people's beliefs. Ideally, technology should be able to design and create boundary objects that capitalize on their atypical cognitive status but are geared toward learning, not fear.

Technological Boundary Objects (TBO) are subsets of boundary objects. TBOs involve technological devices such as computers and robots. For example, a robotic dog is a machine that can take on similar forms and motions as a real dog. Therefore, the robotic dog resides in categories of both animal and machine. TBOs can be "physically real" like humanoid robots, or "virtually real", like a game character in the computer. Most TBOs are interactive, which increases their potential for engagement.

Interactive and human-looking TBOs naturally elicit a social response. The human-like appearance is appealing and attention grabbing. Human-like interactions often involve movements that give an animate impression. Movements like looking, talking, or body language, invite social interaction, and suggest a possible method of communication. For example, children may try to communicate by "showing" if a TBO is looking, by "speaking" if a TBO is talking, and by "gesturing" if a TBO shows body language. Human-like appearance and behavior can also trigger familiar schemas and responses. Familiarity taps into people's prior knowledge and experience. Familiarity may easily trigger affective responses, attributions, and stereotypical behaviors. For example, a learner may recognize a familiar gesture from a robotic cat (stretch), make attributions toward them (cat must be sleepy), and elicit familiar behavior (pet cat). An essential factor in designing a TBO involves controlling the appearance and behavior, which in turn controls social interaction and familiarity with humans.

LEARNING ENVIRONMENTS AND TECHNOLOGICAL BOUNDARY OBJECTS

Computerized learning environments can be described on a dimension with "socially indifferent" and "socially indistinguishable" at separate ends. Socially indifferent systems reside fully in the category of machine – they do not partake in the category of social. Socially indistinguishable systems reside fully in the category of humans. They do not fully exist yet. However, researchers have increasingly incorporated human-like elements to elicit social interaction. Whether or not socially indistinguishable systems can be realized, human-like elements naturally elicit social responses. In-between socially indifferent and socially indistinguishable are learning environments that partake of both machine-like and human-like features. These are TBOs. Systems in this middle ground can be socially implicit – they draw on social patterns of interaction without trying to lead the learner to think in terms of humans. They can also be socially explicit – they explicitly try to cue learners to think of social interaction, for example, by having a character interact with the student.

Socially Indifferent

Programmed learning environments in the early days were more machine-like with no social interaction. Some computerized instructions and practical applications demand interaction with no social response. For example, statistical applications and word processors have no direct social exchange with the user. The learning environment is "socially indifferent" because there are no so-

cial functions, social interests, or social abilities designed as part of the learning environment. An early example of a learning environment with no social interaction was Sidney Pressey's Testing and Teaching Machine. Developed in the 1920's (Pressey, 1932), the student studied a subject and turned to the machine for a multiple-choice test. The interaction involved moving to the next problem if the answer was correct or pressing a different button if the answer was incorrect. In 1954, Skinner created a machine that taught arithmetic, where a sequence of math problems appeared on the top of a machine box. This sequence called "Programmed Instruction" guided the learner (Skinner, 1986). The Teaching Machine was successful for some time, resulting in 250 programmed courses placed in elementary, secondary, and college mathematics throughout the United States.

Socially Implicit

Socially implicit systems tacitly draw on social schemas for interaction, but usually do not include a real social presence or metaphor. Computer tutors, for example, incorporate interaction patterns known to be effective for tutoring, but they usually have a command line for interaction and no visual representation of a tutor character to elicit social responses.

Anderson, Boyle, and Reiser (1985) developed an intelligent tutor called the "Cognitive Tutor" which was a computational model that represented student thinking and cognition. Cognitive Tutors draw on the idea of tutors helping and correcting students through the learning process. The tutor is usually a disembodied text on a screen. There is no visual character maximizing the social metaphor of a tutor. Students have no discernible social relationship with the computer as they would with a human tutor. In a large-scale study, Cognitive Tutors were used to teach algebra in two thousand U.S. schools (Koedinger & Corbett, 2006). Results showed students who used the Cognitive

Tutor course scored twice as high on open-ended problems, than students in the traditional algebra course.

A number of cognitive models on human thinking have been successfully implemented as learning environments. In fact, one of the primary benefits of the tutors has been their value in doing research on basic cognitive processes for learning. For example, Anderson, Corbett, Koedinger and Pelletier (1995) manipulated whether students received immediate or delayed feedback when they made errors. If the feedback was immediate, students needed only half the time to reach a criterion, compared to the time for delayed feedback. Interaction manipulations such as the timing of feedback can reveal much about cognition and learning even without a strong social component. Recent versions of Cognitive Tutors have sophisticated features that monitor students, adjust to students cognitive needs, and provide reinforcement and feedback at the appropriate time (Koedinger & Corbett, 2006).

Socially Explicit

The third type of environment builds on explicit social metaphors of interaction and appearances to invite social interaction. Learning environments in this category differ in the degree that they emphasize the TBO aspects of the system. For example, a simple bitmap tutor in the corner of the screen is a social metaphor. However, the bitmap does not maximize social quality to a level that can gain strong social responses (Mayer & Anderson, 1992). Socially explicit systems usually consist of features that maximize social metaphors and social presence so an affective social interaction can take place.

Teachable Agents (Biswas, Schwartz, & Bransford, 2001), is a socially explicit pedagogical computer agent that students teach. Teachable Agents are TBOs created on the premise that teaching others is highly motivating and powerful (Bargh & Schul, 1980). The agent takes what the student

teaches and answers questions using simple artificial intelligence techniques. The system allows students to learn by teaching and observing how the agents behave once the teaching is complete. In a more recent work (Schwartz, Blair, Biswas, Leelawong, & Davis, 2007), students create the agent's "brain" as represented by nodes and links. Students interact with the "Betty's Brain" agent through a concept map that they created with links such as "increases", and "decreases". Using qualitative reasoning techniques, the agent could chain through the links to derive conclusions using animations. This learning environment allows the learner to structure their thoughts through social interaction with the agent. Though students know the teachable agent is not really a live person, students behave as though the agent is somewhat alive. In some cases, students attribute responsibility to the agent (Chase, Chin, Oppezzo, & Schwartz, in press). Results show that the learners who teach the agent develop more complex causal models of science.

Another example of a socially explicit TBO is a humanoid robot. Humanoid robots are machine-looking robots that model a human form. Some examples of humanoid robots in fictional movies are C-3PO from *Star Wars* (Lucas, 1977), and Sonny from *I, Robot* (Davis, Dow, Godfrey, Mark, & Proyas, 2004). The character Andrew from Chris Columbus's *Bicentennial Man* (Barnathan, Columbus, & Katz, 1999), shows the humanoid robot Andrew becoming an android as technology advances.

A real life example is Honda's ASIMO robot (Sakagami, Watanabe, Aoyama, Matsunaga, Higaki, & Fujimura, 2002). ASIMO uses human-like movement and has cognitive models that invite social interaction (Okita, Ng-Thow-Hing, & Sarvadevabhatla, 2009; Ng-Thow-Hing, Thórisson, Sarvadevabhatla, & Wormer, 2009). Humanoid robots appear mechanical, but consist of biologically inspired features, and show intelligent behavior. Robot technologies are now moving from industry into homes as personal social companions for adults and children. ASIMO is capable of complex interactions, and can perform human-like motor tasks like walking up and down the stairs (See Figure 1). Humanoids usually have features that resemble (or partly resemble) a human form. In many cases, the robot will have arms, legs, and a head to take on similar motions as real humans. ASIMO can carry out familiar human tasks such as serving coffee, and placing a cup on the table. Humanoids may not carry out the task in the same way as human do, because mechanical bodies are built differently than humans. Humanoids often aim for better performance than perfect human mimicry.

Socially Indistinguishable

The category of socially indistinguishable, which has not yet been realized, will occur when technology achieves perfect human mimicry. The learning environment will no longer need to rely on social metaphors or "pretend" beliefs. The high fidelity appearance and behavior will make the system indistinguishable from humans. Future development seems to be moving toward this goal of achieving perfect human mimicry.

For example, Ishiguro (2007) has been using technology to replicate humans as androids. Androids are human-looking robots designed to act like people, and have identical appearance as humans. Androids exhibit human-like consciousness, intelligence, personalities and emotions. Androids have become quite familiar in science fiction movies such as the character Data in *Star Trek* (Gresh & Weinberg, 1999), David from Steven Spielberg's movie *Artificial Intelligence A.I.* (Spielberg, Kubrick, Harlan, Kennedy, Parkes, & Curtis, 2001), and Rachael from *Blade Runner* (Deeley & Scott, 1982). Science fiction movies have made the public more familiar with the idea of social interaction with artificial robotic people.

Many robot researchers agree that there are several material and design challenges that still need to be addressed to reach the realistic level of

science fiction movies, but research on creating androids are progressing rapidly. Androids are usually created by physically copying another human. The process of making a human copy starts with shaping foam to mold from real humans, and creating plaster casts. Actuators and robotic skeletons are then embedded inside the plaster casts to generate human-like behavior. Multiple sensors are put inside to achieve human-like perceptions. Ishiguro has been successful to some extent in copying the human body and muscle movement. Hashimoto, Hiramatsu, and Kobayashi (2006) studied human facial expressions of androids. Actuators in the android's head pull partial areas of the face to make facial expressions. Hashimoto has roughly imitated face muscle structures, but is still far from perfect human mimicry. Material challenges include creating the wet surface of eyes, realistic skin and natural movement. Design challenges including integrating natural language processing, free will, emotions, and implementing theory of mind to androids. However, the true challenge lies in connecting such reasoning to the real world (Roese & Amir, 2009).

Ishiguro (2007) conducted a study to see if people could tell the difference between a human and an android. Twenty subjects briefly saw an android behind a curtain. The curtain was pulled back for two seconds and participants were asked what color she (android) was wearing. Participants were questioned to see if they recognized that the presentation was an android. In one condition, the android exhibited micromovements like shifting, and leaning. In the other condition, the android made no movement. In the micromovement condition, the results showed seven out of ten subjects thought the android was a human, compared to only three people viewing the no-movement condition. As the display time increased, Ishiguro found that more participants identified the android.

The pursuit of perfect human mimicry currently focuses on copying external appearance and movement. However, perfect mimicry should also include internal mechanism such as human-like emotions. Some researchers stress the importance of implementing emotions into robots, so human-robot interaction can be more natural and comfortable (Bellman, 2002; Maes, 1987). Other researchers fear that emotion-sensing technology will be used in patronizing ways (Muir, 2009). Androids are nowhere close to effectively linking behavior to internal human thinking, emotion, agency, or preference. As learning environments move closer to achieving perfect human mimicry, should TBOs also pursue higher fidelity to a point where no boundary-like characteristic remains?

MAINTAINING A BOUNDARY-LIKE STATE OVER HIGHER FIDELITY

The section explores the benefit in maintaining a boundary-like state for TBOs and why pursuing

either extreme of socially indifferent or socially indistinguishable is unfavorable. The issues surrounding high fidelity such as the uncanny valley seem like a difficult challenge that outweighs the benefits. Differences and similarities of TBOs in relation to the uncanny valley will be discussed.

Intentionally Middle is Good for TBOs

The previous sections examined whether TBOs should consider becoming more socially indifferent as in machine-like instruction, or become socially indistinguishable to attain perfect human mimicry. There is a third option where TBOs maintain a boundary-like state. The TBOs that overlap in varying degrees of machine-like and human-like features can be socially implicit and/or socially explicit in feature.

Figure 1. Humanoid robot ASIMO from Honda motors co. ltd. (A) ASIMO walking down the stairs (B) ASIMO as a social companion within the home (C) ASIMO attending to guests serving coffee

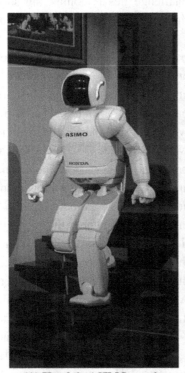

(A) Honda's ASIMO coming
down the stairway

(B) ASIMO social companion in the home

(C) ASIMO attending to guests

The boundary-like nature seems to offer a little wiggle room for both imagination and creativity. Familiarity in a TBO can trigger imagination and creativity. Imagination can trigger imitation, mental simulation, and monitoring that can help the learner develop deeper understanding, knowledge construction, and metacognitive skills. The imagination and creativity triggered from familiarity may make the learning process and experience more original to the learner.

This section gives examples of different socially implicit and explicit TBOs that show learning benefits when maintaining a boundary-like state. The examples are organized as psychological and practical benefits.

Psychological Benefits

The psychological benefits of a boundary-like state can generate imagination and creativity. Socially implicit and socially explicit examples illustrate the effectiveness of a boundary-like state.

Socially Implicit TBOs

The text-based Multi-User Domain (MUD) is a successful TBO that is socially implicit. Text-based MUDs elicit a powerful sense of space (Gordon & Hall, 1997), and provide learners with rich visual imagery. According to Gordon and Hall, this simple text-based construction has a greater effect than graphical Virtual Environments (VE). In the non-graphical VE, MUD learners build environments with their own imagination. Learners share a deep sense of presence with others through their own creations that invite social interaction.

Another socially implicit TBO is the classic text-based computer program ELIZA (Weizenbaum, 1966). ELIZA was one of the early natural language processing programs that enabled communication between humans and machines. ELIZA posed as a psychiatrist, took user responses and rephrased the statements as questions. For example, if the user said, "I am very upset with what happened today", ELIZA would respond, "Why are you upset with what happened today?" Many users believed that ELIZA was a real person even after Weizenbaum explained how the computer program worked.

Socially Explicit TBOs

A simple cartoon character on a screen can be a TBO, if the image is simple. In his book *Understanding Comics*, McCloud (1993) demonstrated that simpler cartoon figures leave more room for interpretation and elicit greater empathy from the audience. McCloud believes that the cartoon's simplicity and iconic form is close to the way people understand their own internal shapes. McCloud found as figures take on more detail, the more the figure becomes a representation of an "other" that is difficult for the learner to identify with.

Another socially explicit TBO is the distributed simulation in VE for military training exercise. In the past, VE military exercises mostly involved flight simulators. Current applications include combat training, negotiation with foreign civilians in the Middle East, and the treatment of Post-Traumatic Stress Disorder (PTSD) for soldiers (Rizzo, Difede, Rothbaum, Johnston, McLay, Reger, Gahm, Parsons, Graap, & Pair, 2009). Phobia training includes fear of heights (Hodges, Anderson, Burdea, & Hoffmann, 2001), spiders (Juan, Alcaniz, Monserrat, Botella, Banos, & Guerrero, 2005), and eating disorders (Riva, Bacchetta, Baruffi, Rinaldi, & Molinari, 1999). Treating PTSD and phobia involves a delicate balance of virtual and real, where familiarity is important, but cannot be too real or too fake. The learning environment has to have just enough familiarity to trigger a response and let the learner imagine and "fill in the blanks".

Practical Benefits of a Boundary-Like State

The practical benefits are how the boundary-like state can manipulate learning environments to fit a learner's needs. Socially implicit and socially explicit TBOs are good examples to show the effectiveness of the boundary-like state.

Socially Implicit TBOs

The text-based Multi-User Domain (MUD) is a successful TBO that is socially implicit and provides practical benefits. Text-based MUDs allow people to easily create and revise their VE, which is not easily accomplished in graphical environments. This is a powerful feature in TBOs that invite social interaction. The learners do not exist in the same graphical representation, but can still share and develop a strong connection, even if the VE is purely imaginative. Along with spatial skills, text based environments can develop mental simulation and imagery skills in the learner.

Socially Explicit TBOs

Graphical virtual environments can be powerful TBOs because the learner environment can be manipulated. Seating in virtual classrooms can be positioned based on the learner's attention level (Bailenson, Yee, Blascovich, Beall, Lundblad, & Jin, 2008a). Knowing or not knowing that there might be a real person behind the avatar teacher can affect learner engagement. The teacher can also be represented differently (e.g., with or without eye contact) to communicate with the learner in the most optimal way (Beall, Bailenson, Loomis, Blascovich, & Rex, 2003). Real life teachers can set up quests for learners (Barab, 2006) in VE, or engage in interactive stories with story-telling agents in VE (Ryokai, Vancelle, & Cassell, 2002).

In another study (Bailenson, Bailenson, Patel, Nielsen, Bajscy, Jung, & Kurillo, 2008b), a participant learns physical actions (e.g., Tai Chi movements) in VE. The learner can see the instructor by using their avatar and performing the Tai Chi movement. The learner engages in the same physical action through their avatar. The learner is able to overlap their avatar (self) onto the instructor's avatar (other) and adjust their movements in real-time. The use of this TBO (Instructor's avatar and learner avatar) allows the learner to experience both self and other in the Tai Chi movement.

Socially Indifferent Learning Environments

The TBO should not become socially indifferent for both practical and psychological reasons. Socially indifferent means eliminating human-like features that elicit social responses. Social interaction plays an important role in learning (Vygotsky, 1978). Such elimination will be unfortunate since social interaction has proven to be quite effective in collaborative learning, peer learning, reciprocal teaching, tutoring, and behavior modeling (Chi, Roy, & Hausmann, 2008; Bransford, Brown, & Cocking, 1999; Webb, 1989; O'Donnell & Dansereau, 1992; O'Donnell, 1999; Bandura, 1977; Bandura,1995). Eliminating social interaction may limit the learning methods and testing methods that can be used. For example, Skinner and Pressley's teaching machines mostly involve drill and practice or testing, using non-social measures like multiple-choice questions.

Psychologically, eliminating characters that elicit social response may be difficult. The work by Reeves and Nass (1996) found that when the users spent a fair amount of time with computers, people started to treat computers in the same way as humans. It was possible that content triggered social reaction, or humans were just social by nature. To eliminate social responses, the use of machine-like systems may be restricted.

Socially Indistinguishable Learning Environments

The TBOs should not pursue higher fidelity for several practical and psychological reasons. Achieving perfect fidelity is difficult when general perceptions of human-likeness evolve. For example, what used to be a human characteristic like being able to calculate problems can easily be reduced over time as being "mechanical" like a calculator. Hayes and Ford (1995) mention that evaluation can easily shift between a test of "cognitive status" to a test of "ability of the human species".

Another practical reason why TBOs should not pursue socially indistinguishable learning environment is because there are no good measures to determine partial progress. For example, in the Turing Test (Turing, 1950) a human judge engaged in natural language conversation with a human participant and a machine through teletype communication. The participant and the machine tried to convince the judge that they were human. If the judge failed to identify correctly, the machine was considered intelligent. Hayes and Ford (1995) were concerned that the Turing Test could only test for complete success, and had no way to measure partial progress toward a goal (French, 2000). Even if there were progress, the Turing Test measure would evaluate partial progress as "unstable" and label it as a failure. Expert systems with Artificial Intelligence had been successful in their intended domain, but evaluated unfairly as being brittle, because of the expectancy remaining from the Turing Test.

Another practical reason is that creating perfect mimicry may limit advancement in technology. In examining what aspects are important, it makes sense to copy from nature or the "original". The idea of flying started with making a machine that flies like a bird, since birds were the only examples around at the time. Hayes and Ford (1995) refer to the early gliders as copying the bird's anatomy. Attempting to mimic the original led to years of unsuccessful trials. Progress was made in flight technology only when mimicking nature was abandoned. Hayes and Ford mentioned that development did not come from imitating nature, but was found only when engineers abandoned that naive notion. He mentioned that engineers sought to identify general principles of their goals (e.g. stable flight), and developed machines based on those principles. Mimicry usually limits the usage of technology to one purpose. Technology developed from general principles can be applied to other usage. Hayes and Ford gave an example where, instead of explicitly selling "intelligence", or a limited version of "expertise", engineers incorporated what might be called cognitive functionality into their products (e.g., camera, copiers, automobiles, laptop, and operating systems). They moved on to develop a "general science of cognition" focusing more on restricted areas of cognition (e.g., vision, generalization, and categorization abilities). As a result, instead of creating a perfect mimicry of humans, the shift led to the creation of multiple artificial systems that amplify and support the cognitive abilities of humans.

The psychological reason is the difficulty in overcoming the "uncanniness" to achieve perfect human mimicry. The challenge is external appearance and behavior. As robots became more human-like, Mori (1970) says that people would find them appealing. However, there is a point where the robots become "almost human-like, but not quite", where people will suddenly be so distracted by the way the robot was "not human", they will start to find them creepy instead of appealing. Mori calls this realization the "Uncanny Valley". Mori created a hypothetical graph that depicted the correlation between familiarity and human-likeness. The graph shows the first curve that suddenly dips just before reaching perfection in human mimicry. That dip is the uncanny valley. The second curve moves up again as the robot once again aims for refined perfection in terms of human mimicry (Bartneck,

Kanda, Ishiguro, & Hagita, 2007). As the second curve moves upward, the artifact once again becomes appealing and evokes positive empathetic responses, thus achieving perfect human mimicry.

Another challenge in overcoming uncanniness is the complexity of movement. Mori found that a highly influential factor in the correlation between familiarity and human-likeness was movement. Movement can have both a positive and negative effect on familiarity. For example if the TBO is highly realistic in appearance, adding movement may trigger an awkward response. Mori stresses that a slight variation in movement can cause a robot, android, puppet or prosthetic hand to plunge into the uncanny valley. MacDorman (2005) mentions the difficulty is not about creating the right appearance and physical proportions of a human, but rather the timing and character movement when interacting with people. Garau, Slater, Vinayagamoorhty, Brogni, Steed, and Sasse (2003), also found that increasing photographic realism of an avatar could actually cause a decrease in social presence if behavioral realism was not also increased.

Movement in androids is created by capturing real human movements with precise 3D motion capturing system and then adjusting the position of the actuators by hand. Actuators are mechanical devices that assist movement. Currently, imitating human movements in androids is challenging because actuators work differently from human muscles.

Mori mentions that there is a far greater risk of falling into the uncanny valley if developers aim for the second peak, which is perfect human mimicry. Mori predicts that time may be better spent to create a robot that can produce familiarity even if it is less human-like.

The TBO in Relation to the Uncanny Valley

The section focuses on the relation between TBOs and the uncanny valley. Many systems that attempt perfect human mimicry fail to overcome the uncanniness, and fall into the uncanny valley. Uncanniness is a feature that TBOs share, and most systems that fall into the uncanny valley are a form of TBO, but differences exist. The differences are best described by comparing a "fallen" android to a humanoid. The two are different in their creation process, expectation, and goal.

The goal of the humanoid developer is not to copy a human, but to create robots with a mixture of human and non human-like features. The purpose may vary, but humanoids are currently used to improve robot human interaction, perform specific tasks, or become a social partner. The goal for the android developer is perfect human mimicry. Hayes and Want mention that copying from the original may seem like a good start, but certain limitations cannot be solved from such copying. Again, identifying general principles instead of mimicry, and creating instead of copying, may lead to more flexibility in the application of the system. The designer's point of view differs between humanoids and androids because the fallen android is a "copy design" of an actual human, and a humanoid is an original "creative design" of a general human form.

The expectations toward a fallen android and humanoid robot are also different. The expectation is somewhat clear for the fallen android, namely to copy a human. The expectation for the humanoid is still undefined and open to possibilities.

The distinction between a successful and unsuccessful TBO is difficult to say because the user makes the judgment. For example, the classic movie *The Exorcist* displayed uncanny movements of the body, creating fear in viewers. This was a successful TBO if the intention was to scare people, but unsuccessful as a learning system. The concept of "Fight or Flight", and the consequent behavior may determine if the TBO is successful for learning. If the learner shows a fight response by attempting to understand, communicate, or engage in social interaction, the TBO is successful. This is because the TBO has elicited a social response that triggered the learner to engage in social interaction that may lead to learning. If a flight response occurs, there is little chance for social interaction or learning.

Age may also have an effect on whether a TBO is successful or not. A study by Itakura, Kanaya, Shimada, Minato, and Ishiguro (2004) looked at how age can have an effect on familiarity with androids. The results showed that adults could identify the androids. One- year old infants were attracted to androids, while three- and five- year olds were afraid and refused to look at the androids. In this case, the android was an unsuccessful TBO for young children and infants. Unsuccessful for infants because the android had achieved perfect human mimicry, and was thus not a boundary object. The flight response in young children implied that the TBO was unsuccessful as a learning environment. For adults, the android was a successful TBO for learning. Ishiguro found that adults treated androids as a human even if they knew or consciously recognized that it was an android. If the adults had engaged in social interaction to test the android's capabilities, the TBO was successful as a learning environment.

COMMON CATEGORIES AND EMPIRICAL STUDIES THAT USE TBO

There are three mutually exclusive categories that overlap in features commonly seen in the TBO learning environment. The features are animate and inanimate, virtual and real, and self and other. For each of the three overlapping categories, relevant empirical studies are introduced. The TBOs in these studies overlap in varying degrees of machine-like and human-like features and will have socially implicit and/or socially explicit features. To help highlight the three categories, the section emphasizes them separately, but all three are usually at play in each situation.

Category of Animate and Inanimate

The ancient ambition to make something "come alive" as in the Greek myth of Pygmalion still exists, but now people rely on technology to accomplish that feat. The category animate and inanimate shares this fascination. Robotic pets that were once a fantasy now exist in reality taking on similar form and motion as real animals and exhibiting intelligent behaviors (Bar-Cohen & Breazeal, 2003).

The learner's interpretation of animate and inanimate may differ based on the TBOs. For example, a robotic animal can take a realistic approach, where the robot looks like a real cat (See Figure 2A, a realistic robotic cat). In this case, the animate and inanimate distinction may be whether the robot is indistinguishable from a real live cat. In the machine-like approach, the robotic dog looks like a mechanical dog taking on similar form and motion as a real dog. In this case, the learner does not compare with a real dog, but sees the robot as an active machine and possibly animate (See Figure 2B, a machine-like robotic dog). In the familiarity approach, the robot looks like a real animal that is somewhat familiar, but uncommon, such as a baby seal. Because the animal is uncommon, it is difficult for the learner to make a detailed comparison with a real baby seal (See Figure 2C, a familiar animal robot). Therefore, the learner may be more generous in labeling the robot seal as animate.

The TBO that overlaps in the categories of animate and inanimate has properties that are both lifelike, and not lifelike. The boundary of animate and inanimate can overlap at different magnitudes. In some cases, the boundary-like feature may show a stronger emphasis toward one of the categories. For example, a robotic cat with the realistic approach will have a stronger emphasis on a lifelike appearance, while the robotic cat with the machine-like approach will have a stronger machine appearance that is not at all lifelike.

Figure 2. (A)Realistic robotic cat from Omron corporation, (B) machine-like robotic dog from Sony corporation, and (C) robotic baby seal based on a familiar animal but uncommon in everyday life from National Institute of Advanced Industrial Science and Technology

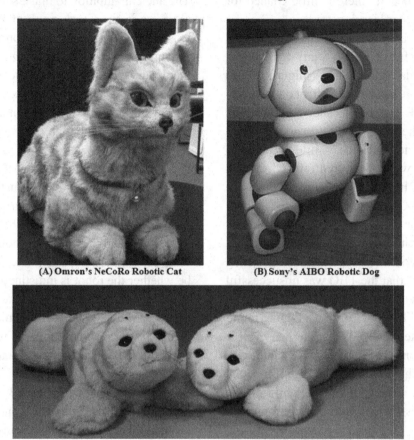

(A) Omron's NeCoRo Robotic Cat (B) Sony's AIBO Robotic Dog

(C) AIST's PARO Robotic Baby Seal

Animate and Inanimate Study: Young Children's Understanding of Animacy and Robotic Animals

The section briefly introduces a set of studies by Okita and Schwartz (2006) which involve TBOs that overlap in animate and inanimate. This study examined the inferences children made toward robotic animals, and whether robots had potential for use in learning.

The first study conducted at a local preschool, involved thirty-two children between the ages 3- to 5- years in a one-to-one, 10–15 minute session. The study examined whether children made animistic intuitions based on the robots'

appearance and actions. Young children unfamiliar with robots observed three robotic animals each hidden under a box. The three robots were Sony's Aibo with different machine-like appearance. The experimenter lifted each box, and the robot performed a behavior. The box was then lowered, and the experimenter revealed the next robotic dog. Behaviors included find and kick the ball, dance to music, or turn off no behavior. After observing the three robots and their behavior, children answered a total of nine questions that probed their attributions on biology, intelligence, and agency. For example, the biology questions would ask, "Do you think any of these dogs can grow? (if yes) which one?", an intelligence question would ask, "If I grab this leash, do you think any of these dogs would know that it's time to go for a walk? (if yes) which one?", and an agency question would ask, "If I forget my remote control, do you think any of these dogs would move? (if yes) which one?"

One implication of the result was that children brought a set of existing beliefs to robots and developed the category "robot" slowly in a piecemeal fashion (Keil, 1989; Wellman, 1990). Rather than replacing one theory with another, they changed discrete beliefs based on facts they had acquired about technology, that differed from living things. For example, children inferred that growing things need "soft" exteriors and that robots need a remote control to move. However, this belief did not prevent them from believing that robots ate food or that they could be bad dogs and jump on the couch when no one was looking. The study found that the complex nature of these boundary objects challenged children's beliefs and invited serious thinking when asked to make inferences about biological properties. Another implication was that children's attributions of biology, intelligence and agency only somewhat connected to robot behavior. For example, there was no difference in attribution made on intelligence between the robot that kicked the ball, and the robot that was turned off.

In a second study, sixty-one children between the ages 3- to 5- years participated in a one-to-one, 10–15 minute session. The study addressed interests from the first study. One interest was whether having an interactive experience with a more or less responsive robot influenced children's attributions. Children only interacted with one robot out of four that varied in realistic appearance and intelligence. The second interest was to explore the inconsistent pattern of biological attributions focusing on biological rather than intelligence questions. A third interest asked children if the robot was alive, or whether they were just playing pretend that the robot was alive (Taylor, 1999; Mitchell, 2002). Asking about animacy attempted

to unravel how biological attributions differed when children believed the robot was alive or not (Inagaki & Hatano, G. 2002). Children answered six questions that probed their biology and sensory attributions towards the robot in addition to the animacy question.

The results showed that for older children, the intelligent responsiveness of the robot had a modest but non-significant effect on their attributions. Improving the realism of robots did not have a significant effect on the child's conceptual beliefs (Carey, 1985). However, this did not mean that the realism of the robot had no other effects. This work questioned an important theoretical position in developmental psychology. One of the findings was that children did not have a well-developed concept of what it meant to be animate. Many scholars believed that young children had a theory of "aliveness" (Gelman & Gottfried, 1996; Fox & McDaniel, 1982). The study showed that children did not have cogent theories, but they did have "scripts" about familiar events through which they could develop a relationship. For children, it is not the "realism" or "aliveness" of these boundary objects that is important, but possibly the scripts that reference familiar routines such as a "preparing for a tea party" that help build a relationship with technology. Therefore, robots have the potential to become a learning companion or instructional tool, but learning may be most effective when interactions are organized around a familiar script.

Category of Real and Virtual

In the past, people engaged in the two separate worlds, real and virtual (see Figure 3A). Video game characters in standalone VEs, did not affect the real world. As Internet accessibility grew, the interaction became a mixture of real and virtual (Figure 3B). Today, people interact with virtual people such as avatars and agents, but the people behind the graphic characters may or may not be a real person. Mobile gaming devices have become a virtual gate or an access point that moves with people. People can now access the VE to play against an avatar controlled by a person walking down the street (Figure 3C). Virtual environments are also an extension of the real world. The TBOs with embedded devices such as physiological sensors can now exchange conscious and unconscious information. For example, Bailenson et. al. (2008b) used sensor devices to record physical actions (e.g., Tai Chi movements) in the real world, and mapped the movements onto an avatar in the virtual world. The learner and the instructor of Tai Chi were physically in different locations, but together in the virtual environment. The movement from the sensors allowed the learner to overlap their avatar (self) onto the instructor's avatar (other) and self correct movements in real-time. As various TBOs develop, very little distinction is left between real and virtual worlds (Figure 3D).

The TBO that overlaps categories of real and virtual has properties that lie in-between the real physical world and the VE. The boundary of real and virtual can overlap at different magnitudes. In some cases, the boundary-like feature may show a stronger emphasis toward one of the cat-egories. For example, an avatar situated in VE, shows stronger virtual traits, but is operated by real humans via computer.

Real and Virtual Study: The Belief in Social and Social Action

This section introduces a set of studies by Okita, Bailenson, and Schwartz (2008) that tacitly draw on the social schemas of interaction. The VE permits novel investigations of what it means to be social, by providing unique ways to examine the effects of social interaction on learning. The VE allow students to interact with TBOs such as agents and avatars in a highly controlled environment.

The study consisted of thirty-five college students, examining whether believing a virtual representation was an agent or an avatar affected learning. A student read a passage on the mechanisms that sustained a fever. The student then played a game in the real world with a confederate named Alyssa. In the agent condition, Alyssa was sent into a separate room to participate in a different experiment. The student was told to stay in the room and interact with a computer

Figure 3. Real and virtual worlds (A) two separate worlds, (B) mixed world where people can stay in the real world but interact in the virtual world through avatars, (C) communication devices act as access points where people can go in and out of both worlds, (D) no distinction between the two worlds. Virtual is an extension of the real world

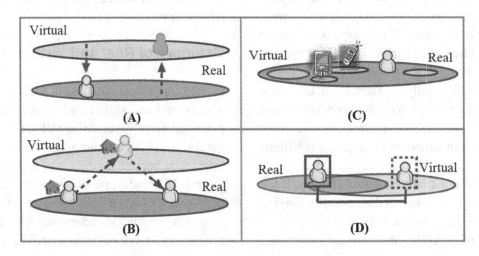

agent in VE. In the VE, the student saw a virtual desk, computer screen, and a computer character behind the table. A question appeared on the computer screen, and the student was asked to read the question to the computer character. The students in the agent condition were told to say, "Computer program" before reading each question to the agent. For example, "Computer-Program, do you know what we are doing?" In the avatar condition the students were told that Alyssa would meet them in VE (See Figure 4). The students in the avatar condition were told to say, "Alyssa" before reading each question to the computer character. For example, "Alyssa, can you hear me?" Otherwise, the conditions were identical and the student always interacted with the computer agent.

In both conditions, participants spoke identical words when asking questions and the computer character provided identical pre-recorded verbal and nonverbal responses. In this way, all interactions and information were constant across conditions. The experiment was able to isolate "social belief" from other aspects of social interactions in learning.

There were two dependent measures: learning and arousal. The learning data was collected in the post-test session outside of VE. Students answered the same nine questions and answers heard in VE, plus six new questions they had not heard. The total fifteen questions comprised of equal numbers of factual, inference, and application problems. Factual questions such as, "Why do your hands and feet get cold during a fever?" could be answered directly from the passage read earlier. Inference questions such as "Why is shivering not enough to cause a fever?" required integrating information from across the passage. Application questions such

Figure 4. Photogrammetric software creating the avatar Alyssa or computer program, and the experimental setting in the virtual environment

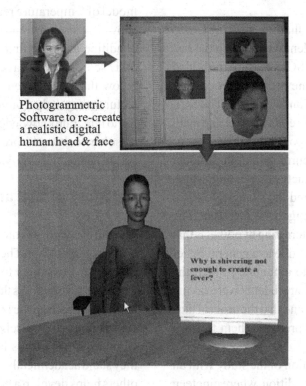

as, "Why does a dry nose mean a dog might have a fever?" required explaining familiar, real world facts about fever.

Two coders independently scored the student's answers: 0 points for a wrong or no answer, 0.5 points for a partial answer such as describing one of two mechanisms, and 1 point for a complete answer. The coders had 97% agreement. The prerecorded response from the computer agent was very limited and any similar response given by the student was not counted toward the final score.

The study found that "belief" of interacting with a real person in the avatar condition resulted in a significant learning gain and higher arousal measures (i.e., physiological sensors that measure skin conductance level-SCL) relative to the agent condition. In general, higher levels of arousal were associated with better answers. For problems where the student had high SCL during the VE interaction with the avatar or agent, the student was likely to score high on the same problem on the post-test. The correlation between learning and arousal (SCL) was the same across conditions, despite the overall condition difference.

The study also found that the peak SCL was the highest when the student was reading the last portion of a question. The SCL measures provided some indication of the time course of processing during each question and answer event. The SCL scored during reading were also correlated with learning. This suggested a possibility that the locus of the learning effect occurred when the student took the socially-relevant action of reading, which may have, in turn, prepared the students to learn more deeply when listening to the response. The SCL data suggested the interesting hypothesis that the learning effect was not due to a general belief that they were listening to a human. Rather, the effect may be the belief that students were taking a socially relevant action, and that the arousal during this action was what prepared them to learn from the response.

This led to the replication of the study with an additional avatar-silent condition, where nineteen new students read the questions silently rather than aloud to the avatar. In this way, they could not take any socially relevant action. If students only listen passively to an avatar, they might not learn as well and their arousal signatures (SCL measures) might stay low. If so, this might help explain some of the common wisdom that just listening is not always as good as interacting. This study explored whether it was the social action, or potential for social action, that prepared one to listen to the response.

The scores of the avatar-silent condition along with the previous avatar and agent subjects was broken out by the three question types, factual, inference, and application. The results showed successful replication of the avatar and agent condition from the previous study, where the avatar conditions (i.e., avatar, avatar-silent) led to superior learning than the agent condition. However, the avatar condition started to show moderate advantage over the avatar-silent condition as the problem progressed to harder inferential questions that required the development of a fuller model of temperature regulation. The SCL scores showed a similar trend for the avatar and agent condition as in the first study, but found that the SCL scores for the avatar-silent condition was below that of the agent. Passively listening to a lecturer may help you learn factual knowledge, but to integrate knowledge and transfer knowledge to solve real-world problems, a relevant social action seems necessary.

Category of Self and Other

The third category is the overlapping characteristics of self and other. The categories overlap when people turn to others to understand themselves. There are several ways that others may help people learn (Okita & Schwartz, 2006). Learning can occur by comparing ourselves to others. For example, comparing test scores helps people learn where they stand academically. Another way is observing others helps develop a better understanding of the self. For example observing others solve a math problem helps you learn how to solve problems. A third way is controlling other's behaviors may help control your own behavior. An example may be learning to self-monitor by monitoring others, where catching other's calculation mistakes may help people catch their own calculation mistakes. An ideal TBO for this learning environment would be an interactive pedagogical agent designed to solve math problems that would engage the students in catching mistakes and monitoring agent behavior.

Self and Other Study: Learning to Self Monitor by Monitoring Projective Pedagogical Agents

Children may find it difficult to be attentive to their own mistakes when they are concentrating on a problem or task (Markman, 1977). However, they may find it relatively easy to find inconsistencies in other people's work. An on-going study examines whether children learn to self-monitor by monitoring others. The task of catching the agent's calculation mistakes, may help the child

learn the skill of monitoring, making it easier to eventually self-monitor. An ideal TBO for this learning environment would be an interactive pedagogical agent that openly displays its reasoning while solving math problems. Children can then correct the agent's mistakes and continue to monitor agent behavior (See Figure 6).

In the first study, thirty-one elementary school students between the ages 10- to 11- years participated in a one-to-one sixty-minute session. The session included two within-subject treatment sessions of self-monitoring and self-other monitoring. A new technology called Projective Pedagogical Agent, "ProJo," provided a testing environment where students practiced monitoring the agent's performance on the math skill while checking for potential mistakes. One treatment session taught the reordering skills for addition, and another treatment session taught divisibility rules for multiplication problems (See Figure 5). For example, the addition math skill on reordering involved taking the problem 23+35+17+72+15+8= and reordering the numbers 23+17+35+15+72+8=, so that the addition process can be grouped (23+17)+(35+15)+(72+8)=, mak-

Figure 5. Addition and multiplication math trick used during the treatment session

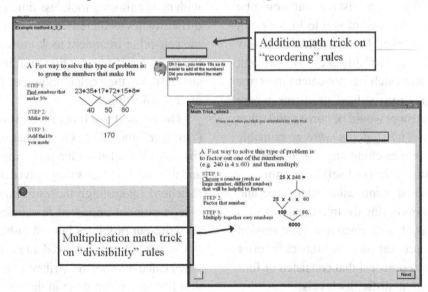

Figure 6. ProJo environment where child monitors ProJo for calculation mistakes

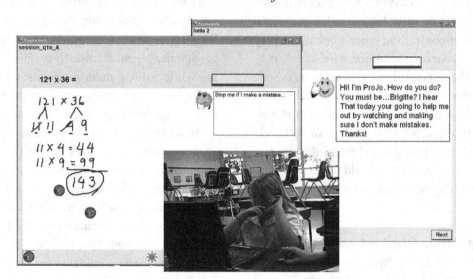

ing the calculation 40+50+80= easier for students. Each treatment session was either addition or multiplication. The self-monitoring treatment consisted of six trials with one problem per trial, where students solved math problems on their own. In the self-other monitoring treatment, students took turns with ProJo. The students had three trials solving the problem on their own, and three trials monitoring ProJo solve problems. ProJo would say, "I think I learned a lot by watching you play. Let me try. I don't like mistakes, so if you can catch me when I make a mistake that would be great, since I wouldn't want you to lose a point because of my mistake." ProJo would make a few intentional "slow motion" mistakes so the student could monitor and catch (or not catch) the error (See Figure 6). ProJo solved problems where sometimes the answer would be correct and other times incorrect. The students were responsible for monitoring and catching any mistakes ProJo made. The relative effects of self-other monitoring were evaluated using calculation time and accuracy measures during the treatments, as well as pre-test and post-tests. Each treatment session consisted of one pre-test question to check for prior knowledge, and a post-test that consisted of four problems varying in difficulty levels.

The study was a first attempt to examine the question of whether monitoring a task as simple as watching a computer agent play a math game elicit better learning. The results showed that students under the self-other treatment slowed down their calculation speed after monitoring "others". Three different calculation times are shown in figure 7, the calculation time of the "other" agent, the calculation time of students in self-treatment, and the calculation time of students in self-other treatment. The students in the self-treatment with no monitoring took less time even when the difficulty level increased, whereas students in the self-other treatment took more time to solve the problems. Students that monitored the agent slowed down their calculation speed immediately after monitoring.

The posttest had four problems with two parts ("In Head" and "Write Out") where students were first asked to calculate the problems in their head, and then write out how they solved the problem in their head. Interestingly the results showed that self-other treatment improved the student's accuracy on write-out problems but not in-head problems. Self-other treatment showed a relative advantage when calculations were written-out, but a relative disadvantage when done in the head (See Figure

Figure 7. Slow down effect between conditions when solving easy, medium and hard math problems

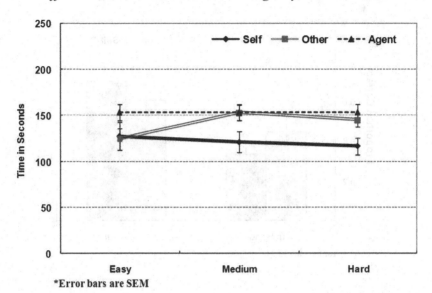

*Error bars are SEM

8). This meant that monitoring "others" affected subsequent paper and pencil task more than in-head problem solving. One possible interpretation was that their own external representation of writing the calculations out was a form of representing the "other" that helped them apply monitoring. Students may learn to monitor external behaviors first, and then learn to monitor their own thinking through this write-out process. Being able to monitor one's own outward performance would presumably be a way to internalize the process of problem solving and monitoring. Another interpretation might be that students monitored when calculating problems in their head, which caused them to slow down, and temporarily perform poorly. However, this is speculative.

The initial thought was that students in the self-other treatment would "slow down" when solving problems on their own. Instead, students in both treatments solved problems faster. The difference was how quickly they solved the problems. The students in the self-other treatment showed a more gradual decrease in time than the self-treatment (See Figure 9B). The students in the self-treatment increased calculation speed immediately after the first trial. Students in both treatments spent the most time on the initial problem, possibly because it was the first one they solved. The effect of accuracy and time was short lived where the two treatments showed little difference by the posttest. Comparing calculation time and accuracy across the trials, results showed that students in the self-other treatment gradually picked up speed and improved in accuracy over time (Figure 9A). Students in the self-treatment immediately picked up speed and did worse over time.

The second study built on findings from the first study. Forty elementary school students between the ages 10- to 11- years participated in a one-to-one forty-five minute session. The students participated in one treatment session, the self-monitoring treatment or the self-other monitoring treatment. Self-other treatment was compared directly to self-treatment as a between subjects design. This new design increased the number of trials and gave a better estimate for long-lasting effects.

The second experiment also involved adding a working memory measure. Working memory refers to the ability people have to temporarily encode, manage and retrieve information in carrying out cognitive tasks. For example, mental arithmetic or other cognitive tasks that involve

Figure 8. The external first effect where monitoring improved write out problems

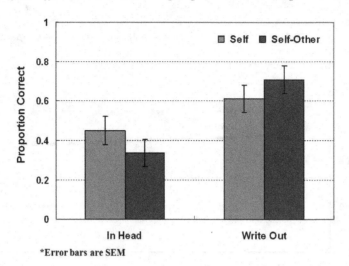

Figure 9. (A) Accuracy Score on trials where children solved math problems on their own, (B) Time taken to solve math problems on their own

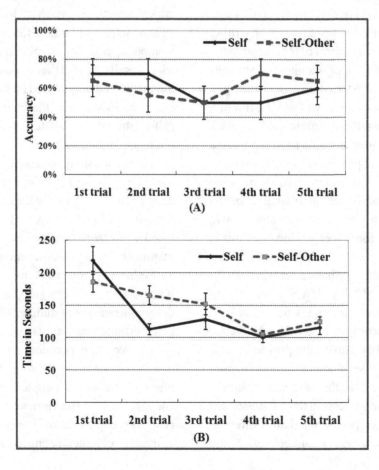

Figure 10. First few trials during the treatment session. High working memory (WM) students in the self-monitoring condition take more time, and perform the worst

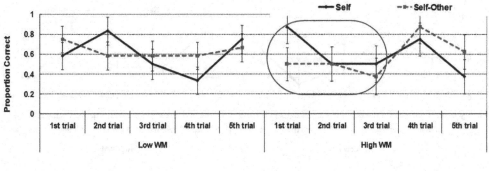

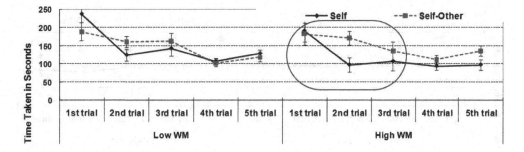

learning, reasoning, and comprehension activities use working memory.

Monitoring one's own problem solving was thought as a dual task demand (monitoring as one task, and solving the problem as another task) that placed a heavy burden on working memory. Therefore, a strong working memory would facilitate the ability to monitor, especially for the students in the self-other treatment that had the opportunity to practice on an external plane. A slightly different prediction was that monitoring somebody else while solving a problem increases the burden on working memory more. This would presumably occur because the individual needs to monitor the computer agents's problem solving process while also computing on their own to check the agent's answer. The computer agent displays the reasoning behind the problem solving so the student can follow the agent's "lead" and check the answer. In other words, the computer agent's performance collapses monitoring and problem solving. The overall prediction was that working memory would

not influence effectiveness of other monitoring, but it would facilitate the acquisition and ability to monitor oneself in the self-other treatment.

Students also took a digit span task to see if working memory capacity affected their learning. The standard digit span task involved an examiner reading a list of random numbers and asking the student to recall the numbers in order. After the digit span task, students were randomly assigned to their treatment condition. The tasks were all multiplication problems with ten trials in each treatment. In the self-other treatment, the student took turns with the agent, and solved five trials on their own and monitored the agent for five other trials. The students were assigned to high and low working memory conditions post-hoc for statistical analyses.

Regardless of working memory level, students varied in accuracy across trials. The only descriptive effect to note was that the high working memory students in the self-other treatment took more time, and showed the lowest accuracy in the

Figure 11. Last few trials during same treatment session as seen in Figure 10. High working memory (WM) students in the self-other condition take less time and perform higher accuracy

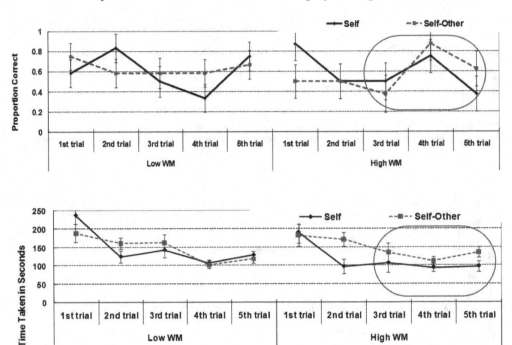

beginning (See Figure 10 circled area), and later on took less time and increased accuracy (See Figure 11 circled area).

The slow down was relatively stable for the students in the self-other treatment (See Figure 11). Interestingly, high working memory students in the self-other treatment sustained the slow down for longer than the high working memory students in the self-treatment. The same slow down pattern was found in the first study. In both studies, students early on take more time and show the lowest accuracy. One possible interpretation is that students are working the hardest on internalizing the other monitoring into their own problem solving, which cashed out on later problems. The results are not sufficiently strong to guarantee this interpretation, but they are consistent with the pattern seen in the first study.

The high working memory students in the self-treatment took less time to solve the problem than low working memory students in the same

treatment. The high working memory students in the self-other treatment took more time than students with low working memory in the same treatment. One possible interpretation for this effect was that students with a high working memory were trying to self-monitor after they monitored the agent. The burden of completing this dual task might have only been attempted by students with high working memory (See Figure 11).

Prior to the second study, a math test was conducted to see what kinds of calculation mistakes students made. This pre-test data was used for ProJo to make similar mistakes as students. There were five pairs of problems. The students in the self-treatment solved all problems on their own, while students in the self-other treatment took turns with the agent. During monitoring, the agent ProJo would always make three mistakes and correctly solve two problems. The three mistakes included two similar mistakes as the child (mix-up procedure and losing track in procedure), and one general calculation mistake (different from the student's mistake). The results showed that similar mistakes were difficult to catch, while students had no trouble catching general mistakes. The students also had no trouble acknowledging when the ProJo solved the problems correctly.

For the mix-up problems, students found it easier to solve it on their own than monitor the agent's mistake. For the general calculation problems, students were able to catch the agent making a mistake more than they could catch their own mistake. Overall, students with low working memory did well compared to students with high working memory (See Figure 13). For the lose track problems, students found it easier to solve it on their own than catching the agent's mistake. In summary for general calculation problems, students are better at catching errors than solving the problems on their own. For similar mistakes of mix-up and lose track problems, the students are worse at catching errors, and do better solving the problems on their own. One possible explanation for this result is that the general calculation errors are matters of fact. Students can remember their math facts and compare them to the agent's computation. In contrast, for the mix-up and lose

track problems, the errors are procedural, and students need to follow the procedure and check it against their own answer. This may be more difficult because procedures are new, whereas math facts are well known. An alternative explanation is that the calculation errors are different from the mistakes the students would make, so it is easy for them to catch.

The limitation of solving problems with procedural mistakes was that monitoring could be worse than solving the problem on your own. Students still seemed to benefit from monitoring general calculation problems. This was an interesting finding, but further exploration needed. The critical limitation was that the ProJo agent was successful at replaying errors, but unsuccessful in making the students notice their own mistakes.

Overall, the evidence that children learn to self-monitor by monitoring others was suggestive but not definitive. The two studies demonstrated four effects. The "Slow-Error effect" and "Late-Gain effect" found that students in the self-other treatment slowed their problem solving and made more errors after initially monitoring the agent (See Figure 10), and more so for the high working memory students. These results suggested students

Figure 12. Overall accuracy score in monitoring ProJo solving problems where some are solved correctly and others incorrectly

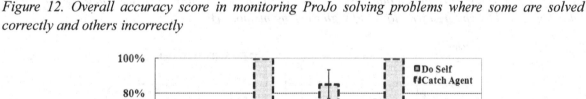

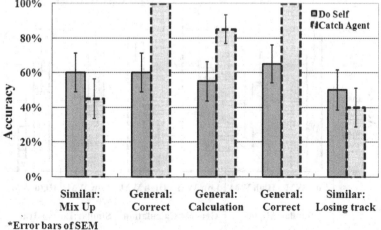

were trying to monitor themselves, but because monitoring added new complexities to the task, they were inefficient. However, over time, they became faster and more accurate than students in the self-monitoring condition, which suggested they had learned to self-monitor through a U-shaped curve of performance (Karmiloff-Smith, 1979).

The "External First effect" occurred in the first study (See Figure 8). On the post-test children in the self-other treatment showed a relative advantage on problems when they could write out the answers, but not for problems done in their head. In the second study, children with high working memory in the self-other treatment exhibited a post-test advantage for problems that they had to solve completely in their head. In the first study, perhaps writing the calculations out became an external representation of the "other" and helped them apply monitoring. Students may learn to monitor their external behavior first, before they can monitor their own thinking. In the second study, students with higher working memory may have been able to better manage the dual cognitive demands of completing the problem and monitoring their thinking. Therefore, they did not need to depend on the external representation of working

out the problem on paper to apply self-monitoring.

The "Catch You not Me effect" indicated that students found it difficult to catch mistakes of the agent that were similar to their own, but they were successful at catching the mistakes if the errors were unlike their own (See Figure 12). The pattern was the same for children with both high and low working memory. Even though students did not always catch the agent when the mistakes were similar to their own, seeing ProJo's errors still had a modest benefit for student learning. This was seen in the post-test where the students solved problems on their own, away from ProJo. If students made an error on their own problem, and then monitored ProJo make a similar error, the students were less likely to make the error on the post-test. If the students had not made an error, but saw ProJo make a mistake on a similar problem, this tended to hurt the student's post-test performance. Students in the self-monitoring treatment who made an error, but did not get to monitor ProJo make a similar error, were likely to make a similar error on the post-test. These tentative results suggest a practical hypothesis that if a student gets a problem right, then the student should solve another problem on their own.

Figure 13. Accuracy score in catching mistakes of ProJo that are similar to their own, or general mistakes separated by children with low and high working memory (WM)

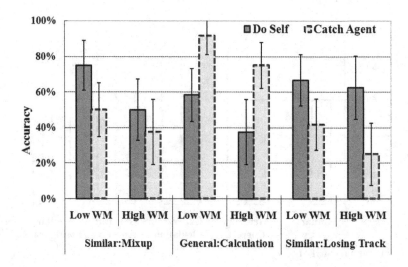

Figure 14. The learning partnership triangle between TBOs and learner. Interaction (A) between learner and TBO, interaction (B) psychological researcher learns by observing interaction between learner and TBO, and interaction (C) engineering researcher learns by observing interaction between learner and TBO

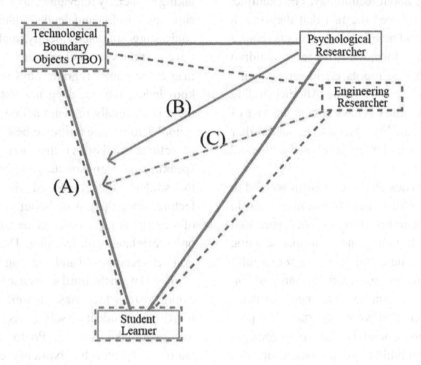

If the student gets a problem wrong, have them monitor an agent. A more sophisticated version of ProJo could be designed where the system makes real-time decision to have the student monitor an incorrect ProJo, a correct ProJo, or simply continue working on their own.

The studies provided initial evidence that self-other treatment using a TBO ProJo may be an effective way to help students develop self-monitoring skills and learn better. The studies were short in duration and used only mental math techniques as the content. The studies were designed to see if there were any short term effects of self-other monitoring. A larger intervention that lasts several months could determine if more sustained practice at monitoring over several topics would lead to stronger effects and improved learning.

The present measures of Slow-Error effect and Late-Gain effect fall short in determining whether the students were monitoring or just copying behavior. Nevertheless, the short duration

and small sample studies did provide a template for larger more ambitious studies, and the results appeared to indicate that self-other monitoring a computer agent was changing behavior in ways that merits follow up.

DISCUSSION

The three empirical studies demonstrated the use of TBOs as a learning environment. The TBO used in each study consisted of a boundary-like state that varied in degree of machine-like and human-like features. This section briefly reflects the findings, and discusses the different learning partnerships possible between humans and TBOs.

The TBO in the first study was a robotic animal used to probe what children know. The robots helped researchers learn that children brought a set of beliefs to robots. Knowledge construction of "robots" developed slowly in a piecemeal fashion instead of replacing theories (Keil, 1989; Wellman, 1990). Children changed discrete beliefs based on known facts about technology. For example, older children ignored the fact that they saw a moving robot, and mentioned that robots require a remote control to move. The same children later suggested that robots could jump on the couch when no one was looking. Another finding was that children did not have cogent theories of "aliveness", but did have "scripts" about familiar events through which they developed a "lively" social relationship.

In relation to design, robot realism seemed to be more in the child's beliefs and ideas than in the realistic appearance of robots. The feature that enabled the child to activate a familiar schema, through which s/he could sustain a social relationship, was far more important than realism. It was not the "realism" or "aliveness" of these boundary objects that were important, but possibly the scripts around familiar play routines that helped them build a social relationship with technology. Unlike a doll or a stuffed animal, robots are responsive to the child, meaning that the child's ability to pretend is constrained by what the robot will do in response. Until robots have the intelligence or flexibility to respond to young children's interactive bids, children will have to follow a well-known script, such as planning a birthday party, or playing house. In doing so, children can be sure to stay within the repertoire available to the robot. Robots have potential in becoming a learning companion or tool for young children, but learning may be most effective when designing social interactions organized around a familiar script.

The TBO in the second study was an avatar and agent in a VE setting. The study isolated the social element from a relevant action, to explore whether it was the student's mere belief of being social, or taking a socially relevant action that contributed to learning. The boundary-like nature helped manipulate student's beliefs of interacting with a

human avatar or a computer agent. As a result, the mere belief of "being social with a human", and taking a "socially relevant action" led to students' superior learning and deeper understanding. The study suggests that evidently, making them believe that the virtual character is a person rather than a computer program, buys students factual knowledge, but not deep understanding unless there is a socially relevant action involved. In a school setting, one rationale behind the benefits of lectures over books is that there is a real person speaking. A complementary explanation may be that students are not aroused when listening to a lecture, since there is no belief in the possibility of social action. However, in these studies arousal only correlates with learning. The specific relation between arousal and learning is still unclear.

The TBO in the third study used a pedagogical agent ProJo, which was a learning environment used to train students to self-correct by monitoring the agent make mistakes. ProJo helped students learn to monitor by explicitly displaying the reasoning during calculation. Children found it relatively natural to catch agent's errors, more so than their own. ProJo provided a testing ground to practice monitoring. ProJo was also an environment where self-other monitoring could be compared directly to self-monitoring. Some promissory evidence showed that self-other monitoring could be an effective way to develop metacognitive skills. The present measures fall short in determining whether the students are monitoring or just copying behavior. Nevertheless, the short duration and small sample studies did provide a template for larger more ambitious studies..

Learning Partnerships

Different learning partnerships can develop between people and TBOs. The three studies described earlier also had different learning partnerships. However, this section will mainly focus on three learning partnerships; student and

TBO partnership, psychological researcher and TBO partnership, and engineer researcher and TBO partnership.

Interestingly, student, psychological researcher and engineer researcher can share the same learning environment, but have different learning experiences and goals. The next section describes each of the learning partnerships in detail (See Figure 14).

Student and TBO Partnership

The learning partnership between the student and TBO is similar to a peer-learning relationship (See Figure 14 interaction A). The student learns through observation and interaction with the TBO. The goal of the student is learning with deep understanding, knowledge construction, and developing metacognitive skills.

One kind of learning is learning with deep understanding. Learning occurs when students refer to and use their own knowledge to understand unfamiliar objects (Meltzoff & Gopnik, 1993). When interacting with TBOs, the student's first attempt is to understand the situation using prior knowledge and personal experience. If unsuccessful, they move on to confront cases of conflict by comparing with prior knowledge. Another attempt may be mental experimentation. Students begin to think of ways to test and reason about the TBO. For example, in an online environment, the student interacts with an avatar that is a computer graphic character. The student believes another human player is controlling the avatar, until a series of awkward behaviors occur. The student may reflect back on past encounters (confront cases of conflict), attempt to come up with challenging questions to distinguish human from computer (mental experimentation), or realize that they are now more interested in the avatar than before. As a result, the student may listen carefully, be more attentive, reflect more, and may perform better recall.

Another kind of learning is knowledge construction. Learning occurs when the student engages in joint play with TBOs. Students with no prior knowledge attempt to gain knowledge by interacting with the unfamiliar object (Goldman, 2005). For example, a young child with no prior knowledge of robots may imitate robot behavior to gain knowledge.

Another kind of learning is developing metacognitive skills (Brown, 1987). Learning occurs when the experience of monitoring the TBO turns inward, and helps self-monitoring. For example, a student monitors the TBO skip counting, and is asked to catch any mistakes the TBO makes. The child learns to monitor both self and other, and with time may help self-monitoring (Gelman & Meck, 1983).

Another kind of learning is developing mind-reading skills. Learning occurs when the student picks up certain features from the TBO to engage in joint play. A form of joint play is role-play. In role-play, if the TBO has familiar features to the child, a small set of movement or sound from the TBO may be enough to suggest or trigger the child into role-play. For example, a sound of a honking horn may suggest to the child to gesture driving a car. In another role-play, the child may imitate the robot, notice a few features, and then ignore what they see, and proceed to carry out what the child believes to be the goal (Harris & Want, 2005). For example, the child sees a robot sitting in the chair, notices the hard surface and mechanical appearance, and imitates a robot pilot getting ready to fly. In the first example, the child is attempting to mind-read by using the feature as a hint to carry out TBO's intentions. The second example is using certain TBO features to guess what the TBO's goals are, and carrying them out.

Another kind of learning is developing mental simulation skills. Learning occurs when the student encounters a situation with the TBO, maps the situation to a similar situation from the past, and experiences the interaction from the TBO's point of view. For example, the child sees the robotic dog accidentally hit the wall, and the child puts a hand over their forehead and says "ouch!"

Psychological Researcher and TBO Partnership

The learning partnership between the researcher and TBO is similar to observational learning. The researcher learns by observing the student and TBO interact (See Figure 14 interaction B). The goal of the researcher is to understand how people interact with TBOs, and understand the causal mechanism that determine which properties in TBO lead to changes in learning and behavior.

One kind of learning that occurs in the researcher is learning what the student knows. If observation is not enough, the researcher uses probing and scaffolding techniques to explore what the learner is thinking. For example, the researcher can observe the student's reaction when the robotic dog fetches a ball. The researcher can then ask probing questions, "Do you think Chai can tell between a real bone and a pretend bone?" to see if robot behavior affects the learner's response. The findings may help understand if robot behaviors link to reasoning.

Learning occurs if the researcher designs a joint play session that turns into a learning session. For example, a robot plays an imitation game where it shows and explains the gestures to a child. Some children will have a robot with a human voice, while other children will have a robot with a robotic voice. The researcher can see if voice has an effect on how much detail the children remember. The researcher can also see if the speed or type of the gesture influences learning.

Engineer Researcher and TBO Partnership

The learning partnership between the engineer researcher and TBO may be a mixture of obser-vational learning and computer-human interaction design. The engineer researcher learns by observing the student and TBO interact, but from a different perspective than that of the psychological researcher (See Figure 14 interaction C). Sheridan (2002) describes the partnership well by mentioning that "design engineers have to be taught that the object is not design of a thing, but design of a relationship between a human and a thing"(pg.162). The goal of the engineer researcher is to figure out how the learner can become part of the system, part of the design, and to produce cognitive artifacts that can be things to think with, communicate, plan, play, and argue.

One kind of learning that occurs is learning what people do with TBOs. Learning occurs when the developer observes the student's reaction and interaction with TBOs. For example, a child encounters a human-like avatar with very realistic features. The child runs away from the computer even before any interaction begins. The researcher learns that even with a human-like appearance, not all human-like features invite social interaction.

Another kind of learning that occurs is identifying learner needs and technical needs. Improving technology and human productivity is a delicate balance. Learning occurs when the researcher realizes the different goals for the TBO and the student. Researchers often strive to create the best, and automate features for convenience. Researchers often forget to question whether the enhanced feature addresses learner needs. Salomon, Perkins, and Globerson (1991) warn that once tools become sufficiently intelligent, people may lose sight of their unique contribution because everything is automated. An example is an expert medical diagnostic system where the system's expertise is refined. There is nothing for the novice physician to do, or to improve his skills. There is a serious need to find ways to accurately evaluate and monitor the process of learning. Performance success with technology does not imply successful knowledge construction, and outputs can often mask learning.

FUTURE RESEARCH DIRECTIONS

Much extensive empirical work and a larger sample size are needed to develop a successful learning partnership. There are two types of research studies for future work. One type involves learning studies that determine if TBO leads to effective learning. The second type involves causal studies that try to determine which properties in TBO lead to changes in learning and behavior.

Future work in technical development is to create mechanisms where the learning process can be better monitored, so that the system can make real-time decisions. For example, ProJo should monitor a student's progress in real-time, and design interactions according to student history and potential.

On a more general note, research and technical development in e-collaboration between humans and technology is currently an exciting area of research across various fields. There is much to be learned about the human partner in relation to the technical partner. Possibly the next step in this partnership between people and technology, is to figure out how the learner can become part of the system and part of the design. This in turn may produce TBOs that think with students, communicate, plan, play, and argue with students.

CONCLUSION

In summary, the chapter introduced a new learning partnership between learners and TBOs. The TBO has human-like appearance and behavior that naturally elicits a social response effective for learning. One concern is whether TBOs maintain a boundary-like state or aim for perfect human mimicry. The challenges to high fidelity seem to outweigh the benefits. Three common TBO combinations – animate and inanimate, real and virtual, and self and other – were mapped to empirical studies to measure the effect of TBOs. The studies drew attention to the different possible learning

partnerships that could be developed. Some studies showed evidence in support of TBOs, while other studies showed only promissory evidence for learning. The findings however did draw clear attention to the different learning partnerships that can develop with TBOs. Multiple partnerships can exist in one shared learning environment, but have different learning experiences and goals.

In summary, it is important to note that successful collaboration and educational interventions between people and TBOs do not depend on a single learning mechanism or innovative technology. It is important to remember that successful partnerships depends on situations that bring together a well-chosen confluence of effective learning resources and technology that help unfold the student's potential knowledge.

REFERENCES

Anderson, J. R., Boyle, C. F., & Reiser, B. J. (1985). Intelligent tutoring systems. *Science*, *228*, 456–468. doi:10.1126/science.228.4698.456

Anderson, J. R., Corbett, A. T., Koedinger, K. R., & Pelletier, R. (1995). Cognitive tutors: Lessons learned. *Journal of the Learning Sciences*, *4*(2), 167–207. doi:10.1207/s15327809jls0402_2

Bailenson, J. N., Patel, K., Nielsen, A., Bajscy, R., Jung, S., & Kurillo, G. (2008b). The Effect of Interactivity on Learning Physical Actions in Virtual Reality. *Media Psychology*, *11*, 354–376. doi:10.1080/15213260802285214

Bailenson, J. N., Yee, N., Blascovich, J., Beall, A. C., Lundblad, N., & Jin, M. (2008a). The Use of Immersive Virtual Reality in the Learning Sciences: Digital Transformations of Teachers, Students, and Social Context. *Journal of the Learning Sciences*, *17*, 102–141. doi:10.1080/10508400701793141

Bandura, A. (1977). *Social learning theory*. Englewood Cliffs, NJ: Prentice-Hall.

Bandura, A. (1995). Social learning. In Manstead, A. S. R., & Hewstone, M. (Eds.), *Blackwell Encyclopedia of Social Psychology* (pp. 600–606). Oxford, UK: Blackwell.

Bar-Cohen, Y., & Breazeal, C. L. (2003). *Biologically Inspired Intelligent Robots*. Washington: SPIE Press.

Barab, S. (2006). Design-Based Research, A Methodological Toolkit for the Learning Scientist. In *The Cambridge Handbook of The Learning Sciences* (pp. 153–169). New York: Cambridge University Press.

Bargh, J. A., & Schul, Y. (1980). On Cognitive Benefits of Teaching. *Journal of Educational Psychology*, *72*(5), 593–604. doi:10.1037/0022-0663.72.5.593

Barnathan, M., Columbus, C., & Katz, G. (Producer) & Columbus, C. (Director). (1999). *Bicentennial Man* [Motion picture]. United States: Touchstone Pictures

Bartneck, C., Kanda, T., Ishiguro, H., & Hagita, N. (2007). Is the Uncanny Valley an Uncanny Cliff? In *Proceedings of 16th IEEE International Conference on Robot & Human Interactive Communication*. New York: IEEE Press

Beall, A. C., Bailenson, J. N., Loomis, J., Blascovich, J., & Rex, C. (2003). Non-zero-sum mutual gaze in immersive virtual environments. In *Proceedings of HCI International* (pp.1108-1112). New York: ACM Press.

Bellman, K. L. (2002). Emotions: Meaningful Mappings Between the Individual and Its World. In Trappl, R., Pettta, P., & Payr, S. (Eds.), *Emotions in Humans and Artifacts* (pp. 149–188). Cambridge, MA: The MIT Press.

Biswas, G., Schwartz, D. L., & Bransford, J. (2001). Technology Support for Complex Problem Solving. In Forbus, K. D., & Feltovich, P. J. (Eds.), *Smart Machines in Education: The coming revolution in educational technology* (pp. 71–97). Menlo Park, CA: AAAI Press.

Brandsford, J. D., Brown, A. L., & Cocking, R. R. (1999). *How People Learn: Brain, mind, experience, and school. Committee on Developments in the Science of Learning Commission on Behavioral and Social Sciences and Education. National Research Council*. Washington, DC: National Academy Press.

Brown, A. (1987). Metacognition, executive control, self-regulation and other more mysterious mechanisms. In Weinert, F. E., & Kluwq, R. H. (Eds.), *Metacognition, Motivation and Understanding*. New Jersey: Lawrence Erlbaum Associates.

Carey, S. (1985). *Conceptual Change in Childhood*. Cambridge, MA: MIT Press.

Chase, C., Chin, D. B., Oppezzo, M., & Schwartz, D. L. (in press). Teachable agents and the protégé effect: Increasing the effort towards learning. *Journal of Science Education and Technology*.

Chi, M. T. H., Roy, M., & Hausmann, R. G. M. (2008). Observing tutorial dialogues collaboratively: Insights about human tutoring effectiveness from vicarious learning. *Cognitive Science*, *32*, 301–341. doi:10.1080/03640210701863396

Davis, J., Dow, T., Godfrey, W., & Mark, L. (Producer) & Proyas, A. (Director). (2004). *I, Robot* [Motion picture]. United States: Twentieth Century Fox.

Deeley, M. (Producer) & Scott, R. (Director). (1982). *Blade Runner* [Motion Picture], United States: The Ladd Company.

Fox, R., & McDaniel, C. (1982). The perception of biological motion by human infants. *Science*, *218*, 486–487. doi:10.1126/science.7123249

French, R. M. (2000). The Turing Test: The First Fifty Years. *Trends in Cognitive Sciences*, *4*(3), 115–121. doi:10.1016/S1364-6613(00)01453-4

Garau, M., Slater, M., Vinayagamoorhty, V., Brogni, A., Steed, A., & Sasse, M. A. (2003). The impact of avatar realism and eye gaze control on perceived quality of communication in a shared immersive virtual environment. In *Proceedings of the SIGCHI Conference on Human Factors in Computing Systems* (pp. 529-536). New York: ACM Press.

Gelman, R., & Meck, E. (1983). Preschoolers' counting: Principles before skill. *Cognition, 13*, 343–359. doi:10.1016/0010-0277(83)90014-8

Gelman, S. A., & Gottfried, G. M. (1996). Children's causal explanations of animate and inanimate motion. *Child Development, 67*, 1970–1987. doi:10.2307/1131604

Gibson, J. J. (1977). The Theory of Affordances. In Shaw, R., & Bransford, J. (Eds.), *Perceiving, Acting and Knowing*. Hillsdale, NJ: Erlbaum.

Gibson, J. J. (1979). *The Ecological Approach to Visual Perception*. Boston: Houghton-Mifflin.

Goldman, A. (2005). Imitation, Mind Reading, and Simulation. In Hurley, S., & Chater, N. (Eds.), *Perspectives on Imitation: From Neuroscience to Social Science*. Cambridge, MA: The MIT Press.

Gordon, A., & Hall, L. (1997). *Collaboration with Agents in a Virtual World. Technical Report, NPC-TRS-97-3*. Department of Computing, University of Northumbria.

Gresh, L. H., & Weinberg, R. (1999). Data. In Gresh, L. H., & Weinberg, R. (Eds.), *The Computers of Star Trek* (pp. 105–125). New York: Basic Books.

Harris, P., & Want, S. (2005). On learning what not to do: The emergence of selective imitation in young children's tool use. In Hurley, S., & Chater, N. (Eds.), *Perspectives on Imitation: From Neuroscience to Social Science*. Cambridge, MA: The MIT Press.

Hashimoto, T., Hiramatsu, S., & Kobayashi, H. (2006). Development of face robot for emotional communication between human and robot. In *Proceedings of IEEE International Conference on Mechatronics & Automation*. New York: IEEE Press.

Hayes, P., & Ford, K. (1995). Turing Test considered harmful. In *Proceedings of the Fourteenth International Joint Conference on Artificial Intelligence, 1*, 972-977.

Hodges, L. F., Anderson, P., Burdea, G. C., & Hoffmann, B. O. (2001). Treating Psychological and Physical Disorders with VR. *IEEE Computer Graphics and Applications, 21*(6), 25–33. doi:10.1109/38.963458

Inagaki, K., & Hatano, G. (2002). *Young Children's Naive Thinking about the Biological World*. New York: Psychology Press.

Ishiguro, H. (2007). Scientific Issues Concerning Androids. *The International Journal of Robotics Research, 26*(1), 105–117. doi:10.1177/0278364907074474

Itakura, S., Kanaya, N., Shimada, M., Minato, T., & Ishiguro, H. (2004). *Communicative behavior to the android robot in human infants*. Poster paper in International Conference on Developmental Learning.

Juan, M. C., Alcaniz, M., Monserrat, C., Botella, C., Banos, R. M., & Guerrero, B. (2005). Using augmented reality to treat phobias. *IEEE Computer Graphics and Applications, 25*(6), 31–37. doi:10.1109/MCG.2005.143

Karmiloff-Smith, A. (1979). Micro- and macro-developmental changes in language acquisition and other representational systems. *Cognitive Science, 3*, 91–118. doi:10.1207/s15516709cog0302_1

Keil, F. C. (1989). *Concepts, Kinds, and Cognitive Development*. Cambridge, MA: MIT Press.

Koedinger, K. R., & Corbett, A. (2006). Cognitive Tutors, Technology Bringing Learning Science to the Classroom. In Sawyer, R. K. (Ed.), *The Cambridge Handbook of The Learning Sciences* (pp. 61–75). New York: Cambridge University Press.

Lucas, G. (Producer & Director). (1977). *Star Wars* [Motion picture]. United States: Twentieth Century Fox.

MacDorman, K. F. (2005). Androids as an experimental apparatus: Why is there an uncanny valley and can we exploit it? In Cognitive Science 2005 Workshop: Toward Social Mechanisms of Android Science, (pp.106-118).

Maes, P. (1987). *Computational Reflection. MIT Technical Reports, 87-2*. Cambridge, MA: MIT AI Laboratory.

Markman, E. (1977). Realizing that you don't understand: Elementary school children's awareness of inconsistencies. *Child Development, 48*, 986–992. doi:10.1111/j.1467-8624.1977.tb01257.x

Mayer, R. E., & Anderson, A. B. (1992). The instructive animation: Helping students build connections between words and pictures in multimedia learning. *Journal of Educational Psychology, 84*, 444–452. doi:10.1037/0022-0663.84.4.444

McCloud, S. (1993). *Understanding Comics*. Amherst, MA: Kitchen Sink Press.

Meltzoff, A., & Gopnik, A. (1993). The role of imitation in understanding persons and developing a theory of mind. In Baron-Cohen, S., Tager-Flusberg, H., & Cohen, D. (Eds.), *Understanding other minds, perspectives from autism* (pp. 335–366). Oxford, UK: Oxford University Press.

Mitchell, R. W. (2002). Imaginative animals, pretending children. In Mitchell, R. W. (Ed.), *Pretending and Imagination in Animals and Children* (pp. 3–22). Cambridge, UK: Cambridge University Press. doi:10.1017/CBO9780511542282.003

Mori, M. (1970). Bukimi no tani [The Uncanny Valley]. (K. F. MacDorman & T. Minato, Trans.). *Energy, 7*(4), 33–35.

Muir, H. (2009). Emotional robots: Will we love them or hate them? *New Scientist, 2715*. Retrieved July 1, 2009, from http://www.newscientist.com/article/mg20327151.400-emotional-robots-will-we-love-them-or-hate-them.html

Ng-Thow-Hing, V., Thórisson, K. R., Sarvadevabhatla, R. K., & Wormer, J. (2009). Cognitive Map Architecture: Facilitation of Human-Robot Interaction in Humanoid Robots. *IEEE Robotics & Automation Magazine, 1*(16), 55–66. doi:10.1109/MRA.2008.931634

Norman, D. A. (1988). *The psychology of everyday things*. New York: Basic Books.

O'Donnell, A. M. (1999). Structuring dyadic interaction through scripted cooperation. In O'Donnell, A. M., & King, A. (Eds.), *Cognitive Perspectives on Peer Learning* (pp. 179–196). Mahwah, NJ: Erlbaum.

O'Donnell, A. M., & Dansereau, D. F. (1992). Scripted cooperation in student dyads: A method for analyzing and enhancing academic learning and performance. In Hertz-Lazarowitz, R., & Miller, N. (Eds.), *Interactions in cooperative groups: Theoretical anatomy of group learning* (pp. 120–141). Cambridge, MA: Cambridge University Press.

Okita, S. Y., Bailenson, J., & Schwartz, D. L. (2008). Mere Belief of Social Action Improves Complex Learning. In S. Barab, K. Hay, & D. Hickey (Eds.), *Proceedings of the 8th International Conference for the Learning Sciences,* Utrecht, The Netherlands. New Jersey: Lawrence Erlbaum Associates.

Okita, S. Y., Ng-Thow-Hing, V., & Sarvadevabhatla, R. K. (2009). Learning Together: ASIMO Developing an Interactive Learning Partnership with Children. In *Proceedings of the 18th IEEE International Symposium on Robot and Human Interactive Communication* (RO-MAN), Toyama, Japan.

Okita, S. Y., & Schwartz, D. L. (2006). Young Children's Understanding of Animacy and Entertainment Robots. [IJHR]. *International Journal of Humanoid Robotics, 3*(3), 393–412. doi:10.1142/S0219843606000795

Okita, S. Y., & Schwartz, D. L. (2006). When Observation Beats Doing: Learning by Teaching. In S. Barab, K. Hay & D. Hickey (Eds.), *Seventh International Conference of the Learning Sciences* (Vol. 1, pp. 509-516). Mahwah, NJ: Erlbaum.

Pressey, S. L. (1932). A Third and Fourth Contribution Toward the Coming Industrial Revolution in Education. *School and Society, 36*, 934.

Reeves, B., & Nass, C. (1996). *The media equation: How people treat computers, television, and new media like real people and places.* Cambridge, UK: Cambridge University Press.

Riva, G., Bacchetta, M., Baruffi, M., Rinaldi, S., & Molinari, E. (1999). Virtual reality based experiential cognitive treatment of anorexia nervosa. *Journal of Behavior Therapy and Experimental Psychiatry, 30*(3), 221–230. doi:10.1016/S0005-7916(99)00018-X

Rizzo, A. A., Difede, J., Rothbaum, B. O., Johnston, S., McLay, R. N., & Reger, G. (2009). VR PTSD Exposure Therapy Results with Active Duty OIF/OEF Combatants. In Westwood, J. D., Westwood, S. W., Haluck, R. S., Hoffman, H. M., Mogel, G. T., & Phillips, R. (Eds.), *Medicine Meets Virtual Reality, 17- Next Med: Design for the Well Being.* Amsterdam: IOS Press.

Roese, N. J., & Amir, E. (2009). Human-Android Interaction in the Near and Distant Future. *Perspectives on Psychological Science, 4*(4), 429–434. doi:10.1111/j.1745-6924.2009.01150.x

Ryokai, K., Vaucelle, C., & Cassell, J. (2002). *Literacy Learning by Storytelling with a Virtual Peer.* Paper presented at the meeting of Computer Support for Collaborative Learning.

Sakagami, Y., Watanabe, R., Aoyama, C., Matsunaga, S., Higaki, N., & Fujimura, K. (2002). The intelligent ASIMO: System overview and integration. In *Proceedings of IEEE/RSJ International Conference on Intelligent Robots and Systems* (pp. 2478–2383).

Salomon, G., Perkins, D. N., & Globerson, T. (1991). Partners in Cognition: Extending Human Intelligence with Intelligent Technologies. *Educational Researcher, 20*(3), 2–9.

Schwartz, D. L., Blair, K. P., Biswas, G., Leelawong, K., & Davis, J. (2007). Animations of thought: Interactivity in the teachable agent paradigm. In Lowe, R., & Schnotz, W. (Eds.), *Learning with animation: Research and implications for design.* Cambridge, UK: Cambridge University Press.

Sheridan, T. B. (2002). *Humans and Automation: System Design and Research Issues.* New York: John Wiley & Sons, Inc.

Skinner, B. E. (1986). Programmed Instruction Revisited. *Phi Delta Kappan, 68*(2), 103–110.

Spielberg, S., Kubrick, S., Harlan, J., Kennedy, K., Parkes, W. F., & Curtis, B. (Producer), & Spielberg, S. (Director). (2001). *A. I. Artificial Intelligence* [Motion picture], United States: Amblin Entertainment.

Star, S. L., & Griesemer, J. R. (1989). Institutional Ecology, Translations' and Boundary Objects: Amateurs and Professionals in Berkeley's Museum of Vertebrate Zoology, 1907-39. *Social Studies of Science, 19*(4), 387–420. doi:10.1177/030631289019003001

Taylor, M. (1999). *Imaginary Companions and the Children Who Created Them.* New York: Oxford University Press.

Turing, A. (1950). Computing machinery and intelligence. *Mind*, 433–460. doi:10.1093/mind/LIX.236.433

Vygotsky, L. S. (1978). *Mind in society: The development of higher psychological processes.* Cambridge, MA: Harvard University Press.

Webb, N. M. (1989). Peer interaction and learning in small groups. *International Journal of Educational Research, 13*, 21–39. doi:10.1016/0883-0355(89)90014-1

Weizenbaum, J. (1966). ELIZA, A computer program for the study of natural language communications between men and machines. *Communications of the ACM, 9*, 36–45. doi:10.1145/365153.365168

Wellman, H. M. (1990). *The Child's Theory of Mind.* Cambridge, MA: MIT Press.

ADDITIONAL READING

Anzai, Y., & Simon, H. A. (1979). The theory of Learning by doing. *Psychological Review, 86*(2), 124–140. doi:10.1037/0033-295X.86.2.124

Azmitia, M. (1996). Peer interactive minds: developmental, theoretical, and methodological issues. In Baltes, P. B., & Staudinger, U. M. (Eds.), *Interactive Minds: Life-span perspectives on the social foundation of cognition* (pp. 133–162). Cambridge, UK: Cambridge University Press.

Bailenson, J. N., & Blascovich, J. (2004). Avatars. In W.S. Bainbridge's (Eds.) Encyclopedia of Human-Computer Interaction (pp. 64-68). Great Barrington, MA: Berkshire Publishing Group

Bailenson, J. N., Iyengar, S., Yee, N., & Collins, N. (2008). Facial similarity between voters and candidates causes influence. *Public Opinion Quarterly, 72*(5), 935–961. doi:10.1093/poq/nfn064

Bailenson, J. N., Yee, N., Patel, K., & Beall, A. C. (2008). Detecting digital chameleons. *Computers in Human Behavior, 24*(1), 66–87. doi:10.1016/j.chb.2007.01.015

Bowker, G. C., & Star, S. L. (1999). *Sorting Things Out. Classification and Its Consequences.* Cambridge, MA: The MIT Press.

Bruner, J. (1964). *The process of education.* Cambridge, MA: Harvard University Press.

Campione, J. C., Brown, A. L., Ferrara, R. A., & Bryant, N. A. (1984). The zone of proximal development: Implications for individual differences and learning. In Rogoff, B., & Wertsch, J. V. (Eds.), *Children's Learning in the "Zone of Proximal Development".* San Francisco: Jossey-Bass.

Clark, E. V. (1995). Later Lexical Development and Word Formation. In Fletcher, P., & MacWhinney, B. (Eds.), *The Handbook of Child Language* (pp. 393–412). Cambridge: Basil Blackwell.

diSessa, A. A. (1988). Knowledge in pieces. In Forman, G., & Pufall, P. (Eds.), *Constructivism in the Computer Age* (pp. 49–70). Hillsdale, NJ: Lawrence Erbaum Associates.

Flavell, J. H. (1976). Metacognitive aspects of problem solving. In Resnick, L. B. (Ed.), *The nature of intelligence.* NJ: L. Erlbaum.

Fortunato, I., Hecht, D., Tittle, C. K., & Alvarez, L. (1991). Metacognition and problem solving. *The Arithmetic Teacher, 7*, 38–40.

Garner, R. (1987). *Metacognition and reading comprehension.* Norwood, NJ: Ablex Publishing Corporation.

Gopnik, A., & Meltzoff, A. N. (1997). *Words, Thoughts, and Theories. Cambridge, MA.* Bradford: MIT Press.

Landauer, C., & Bellman, K. L. (1999). Computational Embodiment: Agents as Constructed Complex Systems. In Dautenhahn, K. (Ed.), *Human Cognition and Social Agent Technology.* New York: Benjamins.

Massey, C. M., & Gelman, R. (1988). Preschooler's ability to decide whether a photographed unfamiliar object can move itself. *Developmental Psychology*, *24*, 307–317. doi:10.1037/0012-1649.24.3.307

Newell, A., & Simon, H. A. (1972). *Human problem solving*. Englewood Cliffs, NJ: Prentice Hall.

Sagotsky, G., Patterson, C. J., & Lepper, M. R. (1978). Training Children's Self-Control: A Field Experiment in Self-Monitoring and Goal-Setting in the Classroom. *Journal of Experimental Child Psychology*, *25*, 242–253. doi:10.1016/0022-0965(78)90080-2

Schober, M. F., & Clark, H. H. (1989). Understanding by Addresses and Overhearers. *Cognitive Psychology*, *21*, 211–232. doi:10.1016/0010-0285(89)90008-X

Schoenfeld, A. H. (1987). What's all the fuss about metacognition? In Schoenfeld, A. H. (Ed.), *Cognitive science and mathematics education* (pp. 189–215). Hillsdale, NJ: Lawrence Erlbaum Associates.

Schunk, D. H. (1983). Progress Self-Monitoring: Effects on Children's Self-Efficacy and Achievement. *Journal of Experimental Education*, *51*, 89–93.

Seifert, C. M., & Hutchins, E. L. (1992). Error as Opportunity: Learning in a cooperative task. *Human-Computer Interaction*, *7*, 409–435. doi:10.1207/s15327051hci0704_3

Simon, H. A. (1987). Computers and society. In Kiesler, S. B., & Sproul, L. S. (Eds.), *Computing and change on campus* (pp. 4–15). New York: Cambridge University Press.

Sleeman, D. H., & Brown, J. S. (1982). Intelligent Tutoring Systems: An Overview. In Sleeman, D. H., & Brown, J. S. (Eds.), *Intelligent Tutoring Systems* (pp. 1–11). London: Academic Press.

Sloman, A. (1997). Synthetic Minds. In W. L. Johnson (Ed.), *Proceedings of the First International Conference on Autonomous Agents, ACM SIGART* (pp.534-535). New York: Associations for Computing Machinery.

Vygotsky, L. S. (1978). *Mind in society: The development of higher psychological processes*. Cambridge, MA: Harvard University Press.

Wertsch, J. V. (1978). Adult-child interaction and the roots of metacognition. *Quarterly Newsletter of the Institute for Comparative Human Development*, *1*, 15–18.

Section 3
Outlook

Chapter 8
From Instructional Design to Setting up Pedagogical Infrastructures:
Designing Technology–Enhanced Knowledge Creation

Minna Lakkala
University of Helsinki, Finland

Liisa Ilomäki
University of Helsinki, Finland

Kari Kosonen
University of Helsinki, Finland

ABSTRACT

Changes in society and working life have led educationists to propose that educational practices should pay special attention to advancing skills for knowledge creation, collaboration, and expert-like working with knowledge supported by modern technology. Classic models of instructional design mainly concentrate on individual content learning and are based on the strict pre-structuring of activities. The pedagogical design of collaborative knowledge construction is more indirect, focusing on establishing the underlying conditions in the learning environment to enhance desired practices. This creates new challenges for pedagogical design. Building on such views, a pedagogical infrastructure framework, including technical, social, epistemological, and cognitive components, is introduced as a conceptual tool to be used in evaluating the implementations of technology-enhanced collaborative knowledge practices in education. Three course examples are described using the introduced framework to demonstrate its applicability for examining pedagogical designs.

DOI: 10.4018/978-1-61520-937-8.ch008

INTRODUCTION

A widely experienced concern in western societies is how to prepare present-day students to cope with the demands of the knowledge-based society and their future working lives. An obvious educational challenge is the need to train citizens to use modern information and communication technologies that constitute the most visible part of the knowledge society. It appears, however, that the skills for using the new technology or basic information skills are not enough, and that people need more advanced skills for working with knowledge, using it meaningfully in different contexts and collaborating with others. Educational experts are proposing that educational practices should pay special attention to improving competencies necessary for expert-like knowledge work and co-construction of knowledge instead of mere content mastery in specific subject domains (Bereiter, 2002; Paavola & Hakkarainen, 2005). These viewpoints relate to the increasing interest in the *socio-cultural paradigm*, in which human activities in general are seen as socially mediated, which entails that learning is also regarded as embedded in social processes rather than being an individual venture (Vygotsky, 1978; Jonassen & Land, 2000).

Within current educational literature, the pedagogical practices that researchers recommend and emphasize as important, have very similar characteristics to each other. These characteristics typically include solving of authentic ill-defined problems, usage of various knowledge sources, collaboration in groups, usage of web-based technology for collaboration, the creation of new knowledge and concrete products as a result of the working process, and critical self-reflection (see, e.g., Scardamalia 2002; Winn 2002; Kozma, 2003; Ilomäki, Lakkala, & Paavola, 2006). Paavola and Hakkarainen (2005) suggested that such viewpoints represent an emerging epistemological approach to learning, which they call the *knowledge creation metaphor*. This suggestion

extends the well-known idea of two metaphors of learning – *knowledge acquisition* and *participation* – introduced by Sfard (1998), and emphasizes the role of collaboratively developed knowledge artifacts (ideas, solutions, models, products) as mediating elements and driving forces for learning and development.

The knowledge creation metaphor presents educators with new challenges since the goals and practices emphasizing creative work around knowledge objects assume changes in the conventional ways of designing educational settings in a detailed and carefully pre-structured manner (Lowyck & Pöysä, 2001; Palincsar & Herrenkohl, 2002). The processes and outcomes emerging in collaborative knowledge creation are shaped by somewhat unpredictable joint activity and interaction between the participants and, therefore, cannot be fully designed or structured in advance (Dillenbourg, 2002). And yet, many practitioners and researchers have witnessed that free, unguided, or unstructured collaborative work does not necessarily result in productive activity or meaningful learning (Kreijns, Kischner, & Jochems, 2003; Winn, 2002). Therefore, new approaches for pedagogical design are required that provide midway solutions between too strictly structured and fully self-directed activities.

The purpose of the present article is to introduce a research-based conceptual framework for examining pedagogical design efforts, explicating some essential components in supporting *technology-enhanced collaborative knowledge creation. A pedagogical infrastructure framework* is developed especially for providing researchers and educators with a conceptual tool for structuring the creation, description, and analysis of pedagogical designs of complex collaboration settings. The framework is supposed to be generic enough to be applied to various kinds of educational settings representing collaborative knowledge creation practices.

First, some existing approaches concerning the pedagogical design of collaborative settings are discussed and questioned, after which the new framework is introduced with a description of the studies through which it was developed. The application of the framework is demonstrated by examining the pedagogical design of three higher education courses that all represent technology-enhanced collaborative knowledge creation practices. Finally, some concluding remarks of the utility of the framework are presented.

PREVIOUS APPROACHES TO THE OVERALL DESIGN OF TECHNOLOGY-ENHANCED COLLABORATIVE LEARNING

In this section, we first comment on the insufficiency of existing notions and approaches meant for designing pedagogical support for complex settings representing collaborative knowledge creation and usage of technology.

Instructional Design Models

The research related to the design of educational settings and learning materials has predominantly been based on the models of *instructional design*. The instructional design approach has it roots in cognitive psychology, which considers learning as an individual process of acquiring new knowledge. The models mainly concentrate on the learning outcomes of individual students; they are commonly based on detailed pre-structuring of content and strict sequencing of activities, and they aim at creating a learning environment that supports the acquisition of a specific content or skill (Häkkinen, 2002; Jonassen & Land, 2000). Classic models of instructional design overlook the socio-cultural perspectives of orchestrating socially mediated activities; therefore, they are not very applicable for designing educational practices relying on collaboration and creation of new knowledge together (Gagne & Merrill, 1990).

In recent studies, the instructional design models are revised to be more suitable for designing complex, authentic tasks which are believed to result in qualitatively better learning outcomes. For instance, Merriënboer, Kirschner, and Kester (2003) suggested such design strategies as supporting whole-task practice (sequencing simple-to-complex classes of equivalent tasks; using worked-out examples), and just-in-time information presentation (linking supportive information to task classes; presenting procedural information precisely when it is needed during task performance). However, these strategies still concentrate on designing educational settings mainly from the individual students' viewpoint, in situations where the learning of certain pre-defined content is the primary aim and through somewhat mechanical structuring of the process progression.

Scripting

One approach especially developed for designing the pedagogical support for technology-enhanced collaborative learning is using structured *scripts*, typically embedded in a technological learning environment. Scripts are a detailed set of guidelines, rules, and functionalities that support collaborative learning by constraining the co-learners' activities and thereby supporting coordination between distributed actors as well as guiding them through the collaborative learning process (Dillenbourg, 2002). Based on an analysis of existing scripts, Kollar, Fischer and Hesse (2006) concluded that scripts usually represent two kinds of support: a) those that provide support on a content-related or conceptual level and b) those that provide support related to the interactive processes between the collaborators. For example, Weinberger, Ertl, Fischer and Mandl (2005) designed *epistemic scripts* to facilitate students' knowledge creation activities and *social scripts* to structure the interaction of learners in a collaborative learning setting.

The design approach of scripting acknowledges the social dimension of learning but it is still mainly focused on supporting and stimulating individual learners' content acquisition via structuring of collaboration. Scripts are often designed for a special context and purpose, such as creating trust between the collaborators, as in the study of Mäki-talo, Weinberger, Häkkinen, Järvelä, and Fischer (2005). As Dillenbourg (2002) stated, scripts may disturb natural interaction and problem solving processes and may lead to the introduction of fake collaboration and arbitrary and superficial activity. In a later article, Dillenbourg and Tchounikine (2007) made a distinction between *micro-scripts* that support the interaction process in itself at a detailed level, and *macro-scripts* that set up higher-level conditions in which collaborative activity should occur. We maintain that scripts are not the all-round solution for designing an entire educational setting, but that they may provide an additional means for supporting learners in some specific epistemic or social aspects of the eligible activity. However, the support should be appropriately integrated with the overall design of an educational setting.

Distributed Scaffolding

A noteworthy perspective for designing complex, technology-enhanced collaborative learning settings is the notion of *distributed scaffolding*, introduced by Puntambecar and Kolodner (2005). They proposed that the support for students in complex classroom settings should be distributed, in an integrated manner, across various tools and agents constituting students' learning environment, such as material resources, task structures, social arrangements, and technological tools, as well as teacher guidance. Examples of the elements that could be designed to actualize such distributed scaffolding are certain kinds of task sequencing, timely teacher interventions, and templates and prompts embedded in tools.

The notion of distributed scaffolding calls pedagogical designers to develop learning settings that integrate various means to support partici-

pants' learning activities. For instance, Hannafin, Hill, and McCarthy (2002) distinguished four types of potentially useful scaffolds embedded in tools to support knowledge creation activities: *conceptual* scaffolds assist the user in recognizing relationships and deciding what to consider; *metacognitive* scaffolds help learners to reflect on the goal or problem, relating prior knowledge and decision making in complex, ill-defined problems; *procedural* scaffolds assist learners with navigating in the implemented learning environments; and *strategic* scaffolds offer support to approach a task and reflect on existing expertise in the target domain.

Distributed scaffolding appears a promising idea for examining pedagogical support, but perhaps the concept of *scaffolding* is too narrow to describe the whole design challenge that educators face when designing educational units for collaborative knowledge creation. As Pea (2004) argued, the special meaning of the scaffolding concept should be maintained. Originally, the metaphor of scaffolding was used to describe adapted guidance provided by a more competent adult to help an individual learner in a problem-solving task that was otherwise beyond his or her skill (Wood, Bruner, & Ross, 1976). Further, the support was meant to be given only for as long as needed, until independent performance was achieved. The pedagogical design of an entire educational unit includes a wider scope than only the design of temporary support that the learners need for specific tasks and situations. For instance, the web-based environment that is used in some educational settings does not only scaffold participants' cognitive or collaborative learning efforts temporarily but also provides central cultural tools that are essential mediating elements throughout the collaborative knowledge creation process. Hence, the role of tools is broader than only a way for providing scaffolding, and this overarching role and relevance of tools in the enacted activities should be taken into account in the set-up of the whole educational unit.

Design Principles

One recent solution for designing complex learning settings is to define generic *design principles* that explicate central features of some pedagogical approaches to guide the designer (Kali, 2006). Design principles aim at guiding the construction of an educational setting with guidelines based on a specific learning theory; in this sense they can be regarded as normative, defining conditions for "ideal learning". A noteworthy example of applying this approach is the specification of knowledge building principles by Scardamalia (2002). Lee, Chan, and van Aalst (2006) investigated how students themselves may benefit from the usage of knowledge-building principles as criteria for a collaborative portfolio; their results witnessed that explicitly stated principles as guidelines fostered the deepening of inquiry and collaborative knowledge advancement.

In the context of an international KP-Lab project (Knowledge Practices Laboratory: www. kp-lab.org), a set of design principles were developed for a "trialogical" approach to learning, aiming at fostering knowledge creation practices that center around co-construction of knowledge objects through technological tools (Paavola & Hakkarainen, 2009). The trialogical design principles have so far been applied for transforming the designs of current higher-education courses towards improved support for expert-like knowledge creation practices (Ilomäki & Paavola, 2008).

According to Bell, Hoadley, and Linn (2004), design principles are mediating generalizations between research findings and unique examples that emerge in practice, and they are meant for informing innovative educational practice rather than for falsifying scientific laws. They provide a good means to explicate which type of learning or knowledge practices a certain pedagogical approach is aiming at. This uniqueness of each set of design principles can also be regarded as a limitation of this approach, if the aim is to define generic, descriptive frameworks to be used widely in the examination of various kinds of educational settings, based on different pedagogical goals or assumptions.

CONSIDERING PEDAGOGICAL DESIGN AS THE BUILDING OF APPROPRIATE INFRASTRUCTURES

It appears that another kind of solution than scripting, distributed scaffolding or design principles is required to structure the examination of technology-enhanced collaborative knowledge creation pedagogues. Gavriel Salomon, an acknowledged pioneer in research on technology in education, had already written in 1992:

what matters is not just the design of a computer tool or program, not even the design of a single task or curricular unit. Rather, the cultivation of minds, which itself requires mindful engagement in a social process of meaning appropriation, requires that the whole learning environment, not just the computer program or tool, be designed as a well orchestrated whole. This includes curriculum, teachers' behaviors, collaborative tasks, mode of peer collaboration and interaction, tasks, learning goals, and the like. (p. 64, emphasis from the original reference).

Jones, Dirckinck-Holmfeld and Lindström (2006) stated that the set-up of computer-supported collaborative learning settings is based on *indirect design*, where the pedagogical conditions provide basic supporting structures that foster collaborative activity, but do not prescribe the exact activities or outcomes.

We suggest using the notion of *infrastructure* as a metaphor to illustrate how the pedagogical design of any collaborative learning setting resembles the construction of physical infrastructure, providing underlying support for desired activities (see also Guribye, 2005; Lipponen & Lallimo, 2004). We adopted the original idea from Bielaczyc (2006) who introduced the *social infrastructure* concept, stating that characteristic of successful computer-supported collaborative learning experiments is the building of an appropriate social infrastructure around technical infrastructure, such as classroom culture and norms established, classroom practices and online activities in the process, and the use of technology for collaboration and communication. Usually, infrastructure refers to technical or physical elements embedded in the system that are deliberately built into a society to provide for adequate functioning of people in their ordinary lives (Star, 1999). It appears a suitable notion also for describing the set of basic conditions that should be designed to shape and support collaborative activities in educational settings. According to Star, infrastructure is learned as part of membership and thus mediates cultural conventions for novices. Similarly, in a complex learning setting, the elements that build affordances for students' actions, designed by the teacher or based on the conventions of the educational institution, can be said to consist of components that form a *pedagogical infrastructure* that mediates cultural practices and directs students' learning activity both explicitly and implicitly (Lakkala, Muukkonen, Paavola & Hakkarainen, 2008).

The Pedagogical Infrastructure Framework

Based on several studies (see the next section), we have identified that educational settings that especially aim at fostering technology-enhanced collaborative knowledge creation should consist of deliberately designed *technical*, *social*, *epistemic*, and *cognitive* support structures. These critical components constitute the *pedagogical infrastructure framework*, meant to be used for constructing, examining, and evaluating the set-up of educational settings. One may argue that various other aspects should also be taken into account

in pedagogical design, for instance motivational elements. However, we maintain that the chosen components highlight aspects that are essential, particularly, for promoting collaborative knowledge creation practices, and that are not necessarily systematically considered in conventional pedagogical practices.

The framework itself is not normative; it does not prescribe how the technical, social, epistemological, or cognitive components of an educational setting should be designed (Lakkala, Muukkonen et al., 2008). The individual design solutions that would build up an appropriate and effective pedagogical infrastructure in each case depend on the goals and the intended nature of activity that the specific educational setting is supposed to promote; the framework just helps in examining, in a structured fashion, the basic features that are considered applicable for various types of cases. In Table 1, each component of the pedagogical infrastructure framework is briefly explained, together with the specification of design principles or criteria that would especially account for expert-like knowledge work and knowledge creation practices.

We maintain that the pedagogical infrastructure framework can be used to classify, design, analyze, and compare the elements of various educational settings. The separate components exist in parallel and intertwined with each other, and in a successful educational setting, aiming at collaborative knowledge creation, all aspects are taken care of in an integrated way: technology works and is used appropriately, deliberate collaboration is built in the tasks and activities, the object of students' activity is genuine construction and elaboration of knowledge (not just individual internalization of certain content), and students' autonomy and the development of metaskills are supported by explicit cognitive modeling and reflection of expert-like practices.

Table 1. The pedagogical infrastructure framework and recommended features of each component for educational settings aiming at collaborative knowledge creation

Component	Definition	Features promoting knowledge creation practices
Technical	The providing of technology and technical advice to the participants; organizing and orchestrating the use of technology; the functionality of the tools provided; and their appropriateness for the desired activity	a. Providing of technology that enables and facilitates co-construction and elaboration of shared knowledge artifacts and coordination of the collaborative process; b. Easy access to technology in all phases of the process; c. Face-to-face and technology-mediated activities are highly integrated; d. Availability of guidance for using technology for expert-like knowledge practices.
Social	The combination of designed individual or collaborative student activities and required outcomes and actual arrangements to organize students' collaboration and social interaction	a. The whole process is openly shared between the participants; b. Students' assignments aim at truly collaborative co-construction of knowledge objects; c. Shared activities and responsibilities are explicitly regulated and defined; d. A supportive and constructive communication atmosphere is deliberately promoted; e. Students may have direct collaboration with professionals in the target field.
Epistemo-logical	The ways of operating with knowledge and the nature of knowledge processing that the assignments promote; nature of knowledge resources used; and the role of participants and information resources while working with knowledge.	a. Students are engaged in solving complex, ill-defined problems through practices that explicitly and purposefully aim at creating new knowledge; b. Students use various knowledge sources; c. Knowledge is produced also for subsequent use; d. Students may be engaged in the real practices of a target field.
Cognitive	Designed tasks and artifacts or tools performing a modeling and reflective function for promoting students' self-regulative competencies to work in an intended way	a. Explicit modeling of expert-like knowledge practices through concrete models and templates; b. Methods used to promote self-reflection; c. Guidance provided for students about effective working strategies; d. Explicit scaffolding for collaborative knowledge creation processes embedded in tools.

Research Resulting in the Pedagogical Infrastructure Framework

As mentioned earlier, the first inspiration for developing the infrastructure approach for pedagogical design came from Bielaczyc (2006) who introduced the social infrastructure concept as complementary to *technological infrastructure* for collaborative learning. For instance, a study investigating the effects of technology mediation on students' engagement in collaborative inquiry (Muukkonen, Lakkala, & Hakkarainen, 2005) indicated that the scaffolding provided by the web-based collaboration software together with the possibility for dialogue through technology, supported practices of problem-setting, self-

reflection, and collaborative development of ideas. In a subsequent study by Lakkala, Ilomäki and Palonen (2007), the implementation of distance learning through collaborative inquiry practices in a lower secondary school was investigated. The results indicated that the *social* arrangements (distance working and virtual collaboration in teams) as such were not the problem in the setting. The most difficult challenge for the students – and also for the teachers – appears to have been to understand the epistemic nature of the inquiry process and find effective ways to actualize it in practice. Also the web-based system used in the case did not have sophisticated tools for sharing or co-authoring of knowledge products, and this imperfect technical infrastructure appears to have discouraged sharing the entire, epistemic process-progression among the participants. The results highlighted the requirement for the teachers to explicitly influence students' attitudes towards knowledge work and practices of inquiry through systematic pedagogical support for *epistemic* actions. As Paavola, Lipponen, & Hakkarainen (2002) stated, innovative knowledge creation practices are fostered by an appropriate *epistemological infrastructure*, referring to individual and collective practices of working with knowledge, treating knowledge as something that can be shared and developed, and deliberate efforts to engage in knowledge-creating inquiry.

In another study (Lakkala, Lallimo, & Hakkarainen, 2005), eight computer-supported collaborative inquiry projects in elementary and lower and upper secondary schools were compared using the technical, social, and epistemological infrastructures as categories for analyzing the designs. Social infrastructure was defined to include the social nature of activities (individual or collaborative activities and individual or collaborative products) and the structuring of collaboration (open collaboration or scaffolded collaboration). Epistemological infrastructure was specified to consist of the epistemic nature of activities (task-accomplishment, the sharing of ideas, or purposeful inquiry) and the structuring of activity (rigidly structured activity, open inquiry, or scaffolded inquiry). The results indicated that productive collaboration and inquiry strategies were not sufficiently guided and modeled for students, which was a clear weakness in the actualized designs, also reported by the participating teachers themselves. Therefore, explicit structuring and modeling of effective knowledge creation *strategies* was concluded to be a separate design task that requires special attention from the teacher. These results led to the first ideas of deliberately designed *cognitive infrastructure* needed for supporting students' intentional knowledge creation, in addition to technical, social and epistemological infrastructures. If one wants students to improve their competencies in collaborative knowledge creation, educational

settings should include elements that explicitly advance students' self-regulative competencies and metaskills for monitoring and regulating individual, collaborative, and knowledge-related aspects of the process (Bolhuis & Voeten, 2001; Muukkonen & Lakkala, 2009). Appropriate support could be provided by concrete *conceptual tools*, such as guidelines, models, templates, and scaffolds for planning, monitoring, and reflecting the work, or by *metacognitive tasks*, such as requirements for explicit justification of actions or reflection on the produced knowledge and processes (Choi, Land, & Turgeon, 2005; White & Fredriksen, 2005).

In the study by Lakkala, Muukkonen et al. (2008), the complete pedagogical infrastructure framework was specified and applied in the retrospective analysis of a design-based research effort consisting of four consecutive university courses applying collaborative inquiry. The framework helped to account for the characteristics of the design in each course through unifying terms and to compare the design features with the outcomes of the students' inquiry activity and self-reported experiences. Perhaps the most noteworthy benefit of the framework was that it provided a means to present an overview of various design features in a concise form, thereby facilitating the examination of the interplay between the components in each setting.

In a recent study, Muukkonen, Lakkala, and Paavola (in press) used the pedagogical infrastructure framework to compare the knowledge creation practices in two higher education courses. One was an applied cognitive psychology course in which the collaborative inquiry approach was implemented to replace conventional lecturing. The other was a course about organizational psychology in which students produced solutions for the knowledge problems of real clients, working according to a virtual teamwork model. The analysis of these two quite different settings through the framework revealed some consistent challenges that open-ended collaborative problem-solving assignments presented for students.

In summary, the pedagogical infrastructure framework has proven to be applicable for analyzing specified pedagogical designs in greater depth, but also more generally and from different perspectives, comparing separate designs.

EVALUATING THREE COURSE DESIGNS THROUGH THE PEDAGOGICAL INFRASTRUCTURE FRAMEWORK

In this section, three higher education courses from different subject domains are described through the pedagogical infrastructure framework to illustrate its usage for examining educational settings aiming at promoting collaborative knowledge creation mediated by technology. For each case, first the specific pedagogical approach and goal of the course is described, and then the elements of the course design, using the technical, social, epistemological, and cognitive components, are defined through the features that are considered essential for knowledge creation pedagogy (see Table 1). In addition, suggestions are made to improve the pedagogical design of each course, in order to better foster collaborative knowledge creation practices. The descriptions are based on explorative and interpretative analysis of multiple data collected from the courses for research purposes (observations, teacher interviews, database content, etc.). Some results of the courses are reported by Kosonen, Ilomäki, and Lakkala (2008) concerning Case 2 and by Lakkala, Kosonen, Bauters, and Rämö (2008) concerning Case 3.

Case 1: Question-Driven Knowledge Creation Through Wiki

The case includes a course titled "Emerging research themes in Psychology", conducted in the Autumn of 2008 and targeted at undergraduate and post-graduate students of the Faculty of Behavioral Sciences in the University of Helsinki,

Finland. The language of the course was English and therefore about half of the participants were international exchange students. The course lasted one study period of seven weeks with two hour weekly lecture meetings followed by one hour voluntary hands-on practicing in a computer lab. In addition, students had two weeks' time to submit their final reports after the last meeting.

Objectives: The objective of the course was to introduce emerging research themes in psychology that are not taught in regular courses of the department and, hence, offer fresh perspectives on psychology as a science.

Pedagogical approach and course activities: Students were introduced to research themes (e.g., transactive memory, knowledge creation approach to learning, user experience in digital gaming) in seven lectures held by expert researchers presenting their own investigations. The course was based on expert lecturing, but conventional lecture course practices were transformed and enriched by collaborative virtual inquiry assignments between the weekly lectures. Students were engaged in critical reflection on the introduced research themes and methodologies through joint question-generation and co-construction of written explanations through a wiki application. Each theme was first discussed vividly during the course meetings. After each lecture, participants posted questions regarding the lecture in a shared wiki area, and the teacher categorized and structured the questions for joint writing. There was the possibility for hands-on work in a computer lab with the help of the teachers after each lecture. Before the next lecture, participants wrote their own viewpoints concerning the created questions, building on each others' writings on the wiki. To enhance productive collaboration, students were first directed to introduce themselves on the wiki through an introductory text. As a final task, students produced a written final report from a chosen question or theme individually or in pairs, and submitted the reports to the shared wiki.

Table 2. Analysis of the pedagogical infrastructure in Case 1

Component	Essential design features of the setting	Shortcomings in the design and suggestions for improvements
Technical	a. Wiki application as a tool instead of more familiar discussion forum to engage students in co-construction activities that go beyond discussion-type communication; wiki offered proper tools for co-editing of textual objects; b. Easy access to wiki through Internet; c. Wiki activity was an integrated continuation of discussions in lectures; d. A possibility for hands-on practicing with tutor offered after each lecture.	Wiki was inflexible for linking and rearranging created content items. A better tool for explicating mutual relationships and enabling rearrangement of created questions, concepts, and explanations would support more advanced knowledge construction.
Social	a. Shared question and explanation formulation; b. An assignment for building on others' viewpoints in wiki; c. Freedom to produce final reports individually or in pairs; d. Acquainting students with each other through an explicit task to introduce oneself; promotion of spontaneous face-to-face discussion during the lectures; e. Lecturers were professional researchers presenting their authentic studies.	Not enough time for discussions during the lectures; participants reported it to be challenging to start formulating questions on a new theme alone. Each lecture should be shorter, reserving more time for collaborative reflection. Apart from one pair, all students produced their final reports alone. Pair or group work should be compulsory if the goal is to engage students in collaborative knowledge construction.
Epistemo-log-ical	a. Question-driven inquiry through wiki promoted questioning and critical examination of the themes; no fixed content to be mastered as such; b. Various scientific resources were shared with students; students were also expected to search for additional references themselves; c. Wiki texts used for writing the final reports but no systematic plans for exploiting the material after the course; d. Atypical course content: lectures resembled scientific conference presentations more than teaching lectures; contents was challenging for those not familiar with the topics beforehand.	Joint question-formulation and elaboration of viewpoints succeeded well within each theme but more overarching (methodological or theoretical) questioning and reflection across the themes remained modest. Individual final reports were high level in terms of examining some themes deeper but their mutual integration was not achieved.
Cognitive	a. Written guidelines for course practices and basic template for final reports provided; b. Students were engaged in a reflection activity after the course through writing about issues that were significant, important, interesting, or central for them in the course experience. c. The teachers, as experts in the field, supported question-driven knowledge creation by categorizing students' questions, structuring the theme areas and contributing to the joint writing; teachers gave written feedback on the final reports through the wiki; d. No built-in scaffolding in the tools.	The question-formulation and co-writing activities through the wiki were experienced challenging because the way of working was new for the students; more time should be reserved practicing the working strategies during meetings, for instance in small groups guided by the teachers. Reflection on practices and outcomes remained an individual venture (even though shared through the wiki) and some students did not do it at all; reflection should be organized as a compulsory, joint activity.

Technology used: A version of Confluence wiki, available for all university students, was used as a shared virtual space for the course. The teachers carried out the basic structuring of the pages.

Case 2: Qualitative Methods Seminar

The course was a seminar about qualitative research methods, conducted in the Autumn of 2006 at the Department of Psychology in the University of Helsinki, Finland. It was targeted at students preparing their master thesis (or starting their doctoral studies) but who did not have much formal education about qualitative methods. The course lasted one study period of seven weeks with two hour weekly meetings and virtual work between the meetings.

Objectives: The aim was to support students' research practices, especially using qualitative methodology, in the concrete context that the students' own master theses provided. Typically research methods in higher education include lecturing complemented by small-scale practical exercises; such general method courses do not usually match with students' needs in their own research processes.

Pedagogical approach and course activities: The activities during the seminar simulated the knowledge practices of a real research community; the participants were at the same time in the role of a student learning research methods and novice researchers conducting their own studies. The pedagogical model consisted of interrelated elements, jointly contributing to the building of a comprehensive knowledge base and competencies for justifying and applying methodological choices in research practice: 1) conceptualization of domain concepts through constructing and revising concept maps in pairs; 2) conducting authentic research by applying the methods in real, personal research cases regarding students' own theses; 3) participating in a research community by arguing and defending methodological solutions, guided by more experienced researchers, and using authentic research examples, journals, and handbooks as information sources. Students explored qualitative methods and defined a specific methodological question, essential and important for their own study at that time. The content of the seminar meetings was constructed around students' presentations of their own questions. During the meetings, students worked in pairs; each pair shared the same methodological interest. Concept maps related to their interests were revised in each meeting according to new viewpoints that students got from other presentations. During the periods between the meetings, the students prepared their presentations in pairs, shared materials related to the presentations in the web-based environments, and conducted some discussions there concerning qualitative methods. Each student also continued working on their own thesis individually.

Technology used: Specific software, Cmap-Tools (http://cmap.ihmc.us/conceptmap.html), was used for enabling and facilitating the creation and iterative modification of the concept maps in pairs. A web-based collaboration environment, FLE3 (http://fle3.uiah.fi), was used for sharing the process (background materials, presentation documents, discussions, and commenting) between course participants both during and between the seminar meetings. In addition, ordinary office applications, such as e-mails, word processing, and presentation tools, were used by the students.

Case 3: Collaborative Design Course for Engineering Students

The case was a compulsory term project in the domain of media engineering, conducted in the Spring of 2007 and targeted at third year media technology students in EVTEK (later Metropolia) University of Applied Sciences, Espoo, Finland. The course lasted about four months, including four joint meetings and several team meetings among the students and with the customers.

Objectives: The goal of the course was to learn collaborative design practices and project-based working methods for solving the practical problems of media technology. An engineering education should prepare students for professional design and software development practices of the present day and for their future working lives. One sophisticated solution is to create possibilities for true cross-fertilization of expertise between students and professionals in workplaces.

Pedagogical approach and course activities: Through a so-called term project, students gradually improved their knowledge practices in managing projects and dealing with real situations. Students were meant to conduct a realistic design task for a real client (e.g. a multimedia product or a website application), using professional design project models, methods, and multimedia tools. Students communicated directly with the representatives of the client organization and

Table 3. Analysis of the pedagogical infrastructure in Case 2

Component	Essential design features of the setting	Shortcomings in the design and suggestions for improvements
Technical	a. CMapTools was particularly designed for creating and revising concept maps. FLE3 enabled saving and sharing presentations and concept maps, and scientific resources provided by the teacher; it also enabled communication between the meetings; b. Seminar meetings held in a computer lab with portable computers and access to basic office applications, internet connections and scientific databases. CMapTools and FLE3 available through internet; file management system accessible only in university premises; c. Same tools and systems used both during and between meetings; d. The teacher and a tutor guided students in seminar meetings.	The implementation of two different technical systems and a separate university file management system used through portable computers created technical problems for the students; it was not possible to easily integrate materials in separate systems. Applications that would enable all activities to be conducted in one place or highly integrated tools that are easy to use would better support the course activities.
Social	a. Course participants worked as a community in face-to-face and virtual discussions, sharing ideas and solutions; b. Students coming to the course had individual research problems based on their own theses; pairs (or individuals) prepared methodological presentations; c. Pairs were formed of students with the same methodological interests; concept maps about qualitative methods were also created and revised in pairs. d. A supportive and constructive communication atmosphere was deliberately promoted by the teacher; e. The teacher of the course was a professional researcher giving examples from her own studies.	Students contributed to other participants' research efforts by discussing and reflecting on them in meetings and experienced a supportive atmosphere. More considered commenting and reflection efforts on others' work could, however, be added in the activities, e.g., by explicit tasks to comment on others' presentations and concept maps virtually between the meetings.
Epistemo-logical	a. The content of the course was based on the questions introduced by the participants; b. Scientific resources (articles, handbooks) were provided by the teacher and sought by the students themselves; c. Activities integrated tightly with the students' own research; the participants were also intended to apply and elaborate on the knowledge and skills in their personal theses after the course; d. Students' presentations about methodological issues resembled those in scientific conferences and workshops, and the teacher's presentations and case examples shared and demonstrated expert practices.	A visit of an external professional researcher discussing qualitative methods from the perspective of his or her expertise was conceived in the course scenario. The visit did not actualize because of practical obstacles. Such a visit would have complemented the role of the teacher as a professional researcher, showing cross-fertilization between study practices and professional research practices.
Cognitive	a. Students received templates and guidelines of scientific standards concerning the construction of a methods section in a scientific article; b. Reflection on one's own understanding of qualitative research methods by preparing and iteratively developing conceptual models (concept maps) and reflection on methodological solutions through discussions based on the research cases of the participants were expected; c. Teacher as an expert researcher demonstrating professional problem-solving through commenting on the participants' research cases; d. No built-in scaffolding in the tools.	Usually students produced from two to five versions of the concept maps to reflect their models of qualitative methods. However, some students produced only one map; more deliberate attention should be paid to direct and motivate all students to put efforts into this conceptualization and reflection activity.

developed their drafts and final products through close collaboration and joint meetings with them. The final products were actually used in the client organizations after the course; therefore, students had to take into account the real needs of the clients' domains. The students had the freedom to conduct the project alone or in teams and to choose the customer and project objective from those that the teacher offered or to source them themselves. Some students were paid for their project work by the customer. In one lecture, a former student presented "lessons learnt" viewpoints and guidelines for avoiding the pitfalls of project work. At the end of the course, each team presented their project to the other course participants. The main part of the course consisted of project work periods, during which the teams worked independently among themselves and with the client, as well as posting the specified project documents, such as a project plan, a prototype, or a final report, onto

Table 4. Analysis of the pedagogical infrastructure in Case 3

Component	Essential design features of the setting	Shortcomings in the design and suggestions for improvements
Technical	a. OVI-portal was used for administrative course management issues; NetPro system served for uploading and sharing finalized project documentation materials and for the teacher to keep track of the project progression; b. OVI-portal and NetPro were available through the internet; on university premises, the students had access to professional multimedia applications for producing the multimedia products; c. Design work in teams was conducted mainly through face-to-face meetings and email; web technology was used for sharing finalized documents; d. Technical support was available in the university for professional tools if needed.	Tools were not used for elaboration, commenting, or editing of the design objects or coordinating the collaborative process; mainly e-mail was used for internal communication. More sophisticated tools for co-construction of knowledge objects (e.g. wiki, file versioning) should be provided. Sharing of the design process virtually with the client was not possible due to the lack of extranet services. Special attention should be paid to providing technological systems that would enable virtual collaboration with external customers.
Social	a. Outcomes from separate projects were shared through finalized documents and oral presentations; b. The assignment of designing a multimedia product for a customer created a strong shared object in project teams; c. The responsibilities inside the teams were divided between the members by assigned roles (e.g. project manager); course grading was based on both team outcomes and personal learning logs; d. Course activities were mainly based on team work; each team was responsible for creating their own working atmosphere; e. Project teams took care of direct collaboration with the client; the teams were supposed to meet the clients on a regular basis.	The project model taught to the engineering students appeared to follow the conventions of dividing the labor and responsibilities between the team members. The models should explicitly enforce collaborative development of design documents, e.g. by defining explicit milestones for reviewing and contributing to shared documents. Students had the freedom to conduct the project alone and collaborate only with their individually arranged client; not all project teams maintained regular contacts with their clients. If the goal is to practice collaborative design, team work and contacts with clients should be compulsory.
Epistemo-logical	a. The authentic design task required students to apply prior domain knowledge and new knowledge in a versatile way; b. The process involved such knowledge activities as surveys on existing solutions for similar design problems, creation of prototypes, and evaluations of these intermediary products with the client; c. Final products were created for real use by the client; d. The students were supposed to find out their clients' needs and expectations and convert this knowledge into user requirements directing the design process.	A four month-long course period turned out to be a short time for such a complex, iterative assignment; the teacher had to be flexible with the deadlines for delivering the project outcomes; this problem relates also to institutional-level decisions for organizing study programs.
Cognitive	a. Professional project work models and document templates provided guidelines for explicating design solutions and organizing the process; an alumni student lectured about lessons learnt in project work; b. There was an intermediate review of each team with the teacher and a final plenary review session of all projects; students were directed to reflect on the design process both individually and in teams; c. The teacher actively participated in the meetings with clients in some projects, acting as an expert and providing situation-specific guidance for the students; d. File sharing space of the NetPro system was structured according to the professional project documentation model.	The project teams mainly created the documentation afterwards, simultaneously with the delivery of the final product; the students did not appear to realize the role of explicit planning and reflection of design work throughout the process. More systematic planning and monitoring practices and delivery of documents on time should be required by the teacher. The guidance for the project teams was somewhat arbitrary – the teacher followed and supervised some teams closely but left other teams and their outcomes unattended.

the shared virtual system. Each student and each team was given the assignment of writing a self-evaluation at the end of the course.

Technology used: An intranet system, OVI-portal, generally used in all courses in EVTEK, was used as a forum for arranging the students' course participation, announcements, materials, and task assignments. All lectures and presentations conducted during the course were videotaped and made available for the participants through the web afterwards. The teacher organized the delivery, sharing, and monitoring of the project teams' documentation through a special, web-based project tool, NetPro, developed in EVTEK. In addition, the students were provided with various professional multimedia tools for creating the multimedia products designed in their teams.

CONCLUDING REMARKS

In our previous studies, the pedagogical infrastructure framework was mainly applied to analyze fairly identical pedagogical practices following the collaborative inquiry approach. In the present article, the educational settings used as examples represented more varying pedagogical approaches, albeit all following the practices of collaborative knowledge creation. The use of the framework in the cases was descriptive, based on interpretative analysis of the specific, unique features in each setting. Although the introduced framework is abstract and generic, we maintain that it provided a novel perspective for examining the course designs, and offered conceptual means to focus on some fundamental aspects in the designs, especially related to promoting collaborative knowledge creation practices.

An applicable methodology for examining the design of complex learning settings appears to be the combination of a descriptive framework and prescriptive design principles: the generic pedagogical infrastructure framework explicates what elements to concentrate on or to incorporate into

the analysis, and the design principles or criteria define what characteristics those elements should have or include in order to reach the goals of the chosen pedagogical approach. Such a strategy enabled the explication of some shortcomings and suggestions for improvements in the presented cases concerning knowledge practices, such as suggestions to provide participants with techno-logical tools with more flexible and appropriate affordances for co-construction of knowledge objects than the existing tools, or to require more explicit and deliberate collaborative activity in shared tasks and outcomes.

In the scope of the present article, we found that it was somewhat difficult to rise above in-dividual cases and to compare the settings with each other, or to more systematically explicate some overarching features in a similar way for all cases. The pedagogical infrastructure framework was primarily introduced as a tool for analyzing and evaluating existing designs, but it may also support educational practitioners when they imple-ment a collaborative knowledge creation approach in their educational practices. For that purpose, a more detailed and specific framework including explicit guidelines or categories and examples would be needed. An interesting and fruitful endeavor could be a research and design project, conducted together with some knowledgeable educators, testing whether the framework helps them to evaluate their course designs in more systematic way, and working with the educators to develop and concretize the framework further.

REFERENCES

Bell, P., Hoadley, C. M., & Linn, M. C. (2004). Design-based research in education. In Linn, M. C., Davis, E. A., & Bell, P. (Eds.), *Internet environments for science education* (pp. 73–85). Mahwah, NJ: Erlbaum.

Bereiter, C. (2002). *Education and mind in the knowledge age*. Hillsdale, NY: Erlbaum.

Bielaczyc, K. (2006). Designing social infrastructure: Critical issues in creating learning environments with technology. *Journal of the Learning Sciences, 15*(3), 301–329. doi:10.1207/s15327809jls1503_1

Bolhuis, S., & Voeten, M. J. M. (2001). Toward self-directed learning in secondary schools: What do teachers do? *Teaching and Teacher Education, 17*, 837–855. doi:10.1016/S0742-051X(01)00034-8

Choi, I., Land, S. M., & Turgeon, A. J. (2005). Scaffolding peer-questioning strategies to facilitate metacognition during online small group discussion. *Instructional Science, 33*(5-6), 483–511. doi:10.1007/s11251-005-1277-4

Dillenbourg, P. (2002). Over-scripting CSCL: The risk of blending collaborative learning with instructional design. In Kirschner, P. A. (Ed.), *Three worlds of CSCL: Can we support CSCL?* (pp. 61–91). Heerlen, The Netherlands: Open Universiteit Nederland.

Dillenbourg, P., & Tchounikine, P. (2007). Flexibility in macro-scripts for computer-supported collaborative learning. *Journal of Computer Assisted Learning, 23*(1), 1–13. doi:10.1111/j.1365-2729.2007.00191.x

Gagne, R. M., & Merrill, M. D. (1990). Integrative goals for instructional design. *Educational Technology Research and Development, 38*(1), 23–30. doi:10.1007/BF02298245

Guribye, F. (2005). *Infrastructures for learning: Ethnographic inquiries into the social and technical conditions of education and training*. Doctoral dissertation, University of Bergen, Bergen, Norway. Retrieved July 5, 2009, from http://hdl.handle.net/1956/859

Häkkinen, P. (2002). Challenges for design of computer-based learning environments. *British Journal of Educational Technology, 33*(4), 461–469. doi:10.1111/1467-8535.00282

Hannafin, M. J., Hill, J., & McCarthy, J. (2002). Designing resource-based learning and performance support systems. In Wiley, D. (Ed.), *The instructional use of learning objects* (pp. 99–129). Bloomington, IN: Association for Educational Communications & Technology.

Ilomäki, L., Lakkala, M., & Paavola, S. (2006). Case studies of learning objects used in school settings. *Learning, Media and Technology, 31*(3), 249–267. doi:10.1080/17439880600893291

Ilomäki, L., & Paavola, S. (2008). Developing and applying design principles for knowledge creation practices. In G. Kanselaar, J. van Merriënboer, P. Kirschner, & T. de Jong (Eds.), *International Perspectives in the Learning Sciences: Cre8ing a Learning World, Proceedings of the Eighth International Conference for the Learning Sciences (ICLS 2008)* (Vol. 3, pp. 258-259). Utrecht, The Netherlands: International Society of the Learning Sciences (ISLS).

Jonassen, D. H., & Land, S. M. (2000). *Theoretical foundations of learning environments*. Mahwah, NJ: Erlbaum.

Jones, C., Dirckinck-Holmfeld, L., & Lindström, B. (2006). A relational, indirect, meso-level approach to CSCL design in the next decade. *International Journal of Computer-Supported Collaborative Learning, 1*(1), 35–56. doi:10.1007/s11412-006-6841-7

Kali, Y. (2006). Collaborative knowledge building using a design principles database. *International Journal of Computer-Supported Collaborative Learning, 1*(2), 187–201. doi:10.1007/s11412-006-8993-x

Kollar, I., Fischer, F., & Hesse, F. W. (2006). Collaboration scripts – A conceptual analysis. *Educational Psychology Review, 18*(2), 159–185. doi:10.1007/s10648-006-9007-2

Kosonen, K., Ilomäki, L., & Lakkala, M. (2008). Conceptual mapping as a form of trialogical learning intervention. In G. Kanselaar, J. van Merriënboer, P. Kirschner, & T. de Jong (Eds.), *International Perspectives in the Learning Sciences: Cre8ing a Learning World, Proceedings of the Eighth International Conference for the Learning Sciences (ICLS 2008)* (Vol. 3, pp. 260-262). Utrecht, The Netherlands: ICLS.

Kozma, R. B. (2003). Technology and classroom practices: An international study. *Journal of Research on Technology in Education, 36*, 1–14.

Kreijns, K., Kirschner, P. A., & Jochems, W. (2003). Identifying the pitfalls of social interaction in computer-supported collaborative learning environments: A review of the research. *Computers in Human Behavior, 19*(3), 335–353. doi:10.1016/S0747-5632(02)00057-2

Lakkala, M., Ilomäki, L., & Palonen, T. (2007). Implementing virtual, collaborative inquiry practices in a middle school context. *Behaviour & Information Technology, 26*(1), 37–53. doi:10.1080/01449290600811529

Lakkala, M., Lallimo, J., & Hakkarainen, K. (2005). Teachers' pedagogical designs for technology-supported collective inquiry: A national case study. *Computers & Education, 45*(3), 337–356. doi:10.1016/j.compedu.2005.04.010

Lakkala, M., Muukkonen, H., Paavola, S., & Hakkarainen, K. (2008). Designing pedagogical infrastructures in university courses for technology-enhanced collaborative inquiry. *Research and Practice in Technology Enhanced Learning, 3*(1), 33–64. doi:10.1142/S1793206808000446

Lakkala, S., Kosonen, K., Bauters, M., & Rämö, E. (2008). *Cross-fertilization of collaborative design practices between an educational institution and workplaces.* Poster presented at the 4th EARLI SIG 14 Learning and Professional Development Conference. University of Jyväskylä, Jyväskylä, Finland. Retrieved July 5, 2009, from http://www.kp-lab.org/project-overview/dissemination-material/kp-lab-posters/Lakkala_EARLI-Sig-14_2008.pdf

Lee, E. Y. C., Chan, C. K. K., & van Aalst, J. (2006). Students assessing their own collaborative knowledge building. *International Journal of Computer-Supported Collaborative Learning, 1*(2), 277–307. doi:10.1007/s11412-006-8997-6

Lipponen, L., & Lallimo, J. (2004). From collaborative technology to collaborative use of technology: Designing learning oriented infrastructures. *Educational Media International, 41*(2), 111–116. doi:10.1080/09523980410001678566

Lowyck, J., & Pöysä, J. (2001). Design of collaborative learning environments. *Computers in Human Behavior, 17*(5-6), 507–516. doi:10.1016/S0747-5632(01)00017-6

Mäkitalo, K., Weinberger, A., Häkkinen, P., Järvelä, S., & Fischer, F. (2005). Epistemic Cooperation Scripts in Online Learning Environments: Fostering Learning by Reducing Uncertainty in Discourse? *Computers in Human Behavior, 21*(4), 603–622. doi:10.1016/j.chb.2004.10.033

Merriënboer, J. J. G., Kirschner, P. A., & Kester, L. (2003). Taking the load off a learner's mind: Instructional design for complex learning. *Educational Psychologist, 38*(1), 5–13. doi:10.1207/S15326985EP3801_2

Muukkonen, H., & Lakkala, M. (2009). Exploring metaskills of knowledge-creating inquiry in higher education. *International Journal of Computer-Supported Collaborative Learning, 4*(2), 187–211. doi:10.1007/s11412-009-9063-y

Muukkonen, H., Lakkala, M., & Hakkarainen, K. (2005). Technology-mediation and tutoring: How do they shape progressive inquiry discourse? *Journal of the Learning Sciences, 14*(4), 527–565. doi:10.1207/s15327809jls1404_3

Muukkonen, H., Lakkala, M., & Paavola, S. (in press). Promoting knowledge creation and object-oriented inquiry in university courses. In S. Ludvigsen, A. Lund, & R. Säljö (Eds.), Learning in social practices. ICT and new artifacts - transformation of social and cultural practices. Routledge.

Paavola, S., & Hakkarainen, K. (2005). The knowledge creation metaphor – An emergent epistemological approach to learning. *Science & Education, 14*, 535–557. doi:10.1007/s11191-004-5157-0

Paavola, S., & Hakkarainen, K. (2009). From meaning making to joint construction of knowledge practices and artifacts – A trialogical approach to CSCL. In C. O'Malley, D. Suthers, P. Reimann, & A. Dimitracopoulou (Eds.), *Computer Supported Collaborative Learning Practices: CSCL2009 Conference Proceedings*. (pp. 83-92). Rhodes, Greece: International Society of the Learning Sciences (ISLS).

Paavola, S., Lipponen, L., & Hakkarainen, K. (2002). Epistemological foundations for CSCL: A comparison of three models of innovative knowledge communities. In Stahl, G. (Ed.), *Computer support for collaborative learning: Foundations for a CSCL community* (pp. 24–32). Hillsdale, NY: Erlbaum.

Palincsar, A. S., & Herrenkohl, L. R. (2002). Designing collaborative learning contexts. *Theory into Practice, 41*(1), 26–32. doi:10.1207/s15430421tip4101_5

Pea, R. (2004). The social and technological dimensions of scaffolding and related theoretical concepts for learning, education and human activity. *Journal of the Learning Sciences, 13*(3), 423–451. doi:10.1207/s15327809jls1303_6

Puntambekar, S., & Kolodner, J. L. (2005). Toward implementing distributed scaffolding: Helping students learn science from design. *Journal of Research in Science Teaching, 42*(2), 185–217. doi:10.1002/tea.20048

Salomon, G. (1992). What does the design of effective CSCL require and how do we study its effects? *ACM SIGCUE Outlook, 21*(3), 62–68. doi:10.1145/130893.130909

Scardamalia, M. (2002). Collective cognitive responsibility for the advancement of knowledge. In Smith, B. (Ed.), *Liberal education in the knowledge society* (pp. 67–98). Chicago, IL: Open Court.

Sfard, A. (1998). On two metaphors for learning and the dangers of choosing just one. *Educational Researcher, 27*, 4–13. doi:10.2307/1176193

Star, S. L. (1999). The ethnography of infrastructure. *The American Behavioral Scientist, 43*(3), 377–391. doi:10.1177/00027649921955326

Vygotsky, L. S. (1978). *Mind in society: The development of higher psychological processes*. Cambridge, MA: Harvard University Press.

Weinberger, A., Ertl, B., Fischer, F., & Mandl, H. (2005). Epistemic and social scripts in computer-supported collaborative learning. *Instructional Science, 33*(1), 1–30. doi:10.1007/s11251-004-2322-4

White, B., & Fredriksen, J. (2005). A theoretical framework and approach for fostering metacognitive development. *Educational Psychologist, 40*, 211–223. doi:10.1207/s15326985ep4004_3

Winn, W. (2002). Current trends in educational technology research: The study of learning environments. *Educational Psychology Review, 14*(3), 331–351. doi:10.1023/A:1016068530070

Wood, D., Bruner, J. S., & Ross, G. (1976). The role of tutoring in problem solving. *Journal of Child Psychology and Psychiatry, and Allied Disciplines, 17*, 89–100. doi:10.1111/j.1469-7610.1976.tb00381.x

Chapter 9
Challenges with Knowledge Construction in an E-learning Environment

Bolanle A. Olaniran
Texas Tech University, USA

Oladayo Olaniran
Federal University of Technology, Nigeria

David Edgell
Texas Tech University, USA

ABSTRACT

Knowledge construction, or new knowledge creation, is believed to be a way to allow learners to gain an in-depth knowledge and a greater control over the materials they are learning. E-learning technology platforms, that facilitate e-collaboration among learners, represent a way to foster knowledge construction. This chapter however, explores challenges facing knowledge construction especially when looking at "Culture" and how it affects two different learning philosophies or paradigms. This chapter elucidates some of the challenges and offers a new direction for accommodating different learners' needs.

INTRODUCTION

E-learning, which addresses the use of electronic media in learning/knowledge dissemination, is rapidly becoming the norm in education and global corporate training. Universities and organizations are continuously supplementing traditional learning with new technologies. The role of technologies in education and especially in e-learning has resulted in customized corporate training and online univer-

sities such as: American InterContinental University Online, Capella University, Devry University, Kaplan University, University of Phoenix, Walden University, and Westwood College Online (Olaniran, 2007a). Furthermore, various courseware; such as IBM Lotus' Learningspace, Blackboard, WebCT, Netware, and others; are employed to support teaching and learning (Horton & Horton, 2002; Sun, Williams, & Liu 2004). E-learning is attractive to corporate travelers, expatriates, traditional and non-traditional students. However, as corporate e-learning solutions continue to explode and gain

DOI: 10.4018/978-1-61520-937-8.ch009

popularity in the sphere of global e-learning, there are concerns about the quality of learning taking place along with its cultural appropriateness. Cost savings is one of the major advantages to e-learning, but a question remains whether it is producing concrete results.

BACKGROUND

It has been argued that the central concern in a technology-mediated environment is how to leverage technology in a way that provides the most effective stimuli to improve knowledge acquisition (i.e., Benbunan-Fitch & Arbaugh, 2006; Olaniran, 2007a). This begs the question of how technologies help foster knowledge and knowledge construction, especially in an e-learning environment. After all, technologies do not inherently possess knowledge. However, technologies can be used to transmit and develop knowledge and learning in an individual self-paced or collaborative/group-based asynchronous and synchronous environments. Furthermore, as e-learning discussion continues, the issue of culture awareness of technologies that facilitate e-learning is gaining traction (e.g., Kawachi, 1999; Olaniran, 2007a, 2007b, 2008; Van Dam & Rogers, 2002). The idea of culture aware technology signifies the importance of culture, which represents the ways of knowing, and different values and beliefs that drive behaviors (Gudykunst & Kim, 2003).

MAIN FOCUS OF THE CHAPTER

The goal in this paper is to explain how knowledge construction (KC) occurs within the context of e-learning and to present some cultural challenges facing KC in e-learning. To achieve this goal, the chapter will discuss the learning paradigms (i.e., objectivist and constructivist) guiding KC in an e-learning environment. The chapter will then explore the role of culture in knowledge construc-

tion and e-learning and especially the challenges it poses to KC and collaboration in e-learning. The *blog* will be used as an example.

Issues, Controversies, and Problems in Knowledge Construction and E-Learning

Information systems and technology scholars have been looking at how information technologies influence the learning process. The investigation of technologies on learning is two-fold; to understand various technologies and to understand the role technology plays on learners' cognitive processes in both self and group collaboration. Specific studies have focused on the role that courseware and other computer-mediated learning platforms play in improving or replacing traditional classrooms and how technology affects knowledge acquisition (Alavi, 1994; Leidner & Fuller, 1997; Benbunan-Fich, & Arbaugh, 2006). A number of scholars however, have questioned the delivery or knowledge transmission function and the use of collaborative learning methods (Benunan & Arbaugh, 2006; Olaniran, 2007a; Sun et al, 2004). Contributing to the issue of knowledge acquisition and knowledge construction is the dichotomy in two learning paradigms (i.e., objectivist vs. constructivist) and their appropriateness to e-learning.

Objectivism is based on knowledge transmission or information delivery to students. On the other hand, constructivism is based on knowledge construction or the individuals' perceived reality (Sun et al., 2004). Benbunan-Fich and Arbaugh (2006) addressed the distinction between objectivism and constructivism paradigms when suggesting that the best way to distinguish between the two is to look at objectivism as a mechanism for delivering information concepts; whereas, constructivism focused on the varieties of information sources and interactions that learners use in the process of knowledge construction. In other words, constructivism focuses on knowledge creation, while objectivism focuses on knowledge delivery and assimilation (Benbunan-Fich & Arbaugh, 2006; Sun et al., 2004). Either of the two paradigms holds different implications for e-learning and knowledge construction; some of which will be addressed in the next section.

The distinction between learning paradigms is crucial to e-learning. However, implications from both perspectives are not readily apparent, especially when addressing culture and the accompanying learning styles (Olaniran, 2007a). The objectivist model implies the transfer of knowledge from a specific source, usually from an instructor to students. According to Benbunan-Fich and Arbaugh (2006), the objectivist model assumes that, "there is a unique and objective knowledge representing the world [truth] that can be articulated or communicated to the students" (p. 780). Consequently, the instructor controls the knowledge with regard to learning pace and materials (Jonassen, 1993). Further inference concerns the suitability of objectivism's approach to factual, technical, or procedural knowledge subject matters (Leidner & Javenpaa, 1995).

Constructivism suggests that knowledge is created or co-created with other learners instead of being transferred by an external person or source (i.e., instructor). There are two different approaches within the constructivists, namely individual and social (Hung & Chen, 1999; Knowlton, 2001). The individual system subscribes to the belief that knowledge creation only occurs within the individual's head. The social system argues that knowledge is co-constructed especially with the aid of other learners via communication interactions. Notwithstanding, the common element in both approaches is the construction of knowledge or meaning. Consequently, the issue of deep learning is considered central to the constructivist approach given the belief that knowledge co-constructed allows students to achieve higher order learning than knowledge transferred or memorized. Furthermore, Knowlton (2001) claimed that knowledge construction is best accomplished through collaboration with others

(e.g., learners and information sources). The next section addresses knowledge construction.

Knowledge construction focuses on the idea that learners construct their own knowledge by connecting and extending new information combined with their past knowledge and interests (Panitz, 1997). It is based on the principle that individual learners are different and thus will come away from the same lesson with different constructions of the presented ideas. Therefore, collaborative interaction in groups offers learners opportunities to build and develop new knowledge. Ertl (2008) alluded to four different processes that are beneficial to knowledge construction:

1. Learners' externalization – which suggests that learners are to present knowledge comprehensibly to others (i.e., active use of what is learned).
2. Elicitation – involves the request for new knowledge from others (i.e., learning partners' externalizing).
3. Conflict oriented negotiation – focuses on the discussion of different views about a subject.
4. Consensus-oriented integration – addresses the effort to find common arguments from different views.

However, Ertl (2008) argued that both externalization and elicitation only facilitate knowledge acquisition and application, where negotiation and integration focus more on new knowledge, hence knowledge construction.

One of the major arguments regarding knowledge construction for e-learning is that it offers greater potential for deeper knowledge than traditional classrooms. One must be careful however, because not all e-learning or e-collaboration leads to new knowledge creation (Kirschner, Sweller, & Clarks, 2006). Depending on the instructional design guiding the e-learning processes, e-learning and e-collaboration can be no better than information exchange or knowledge delivery. By implication, the nature of the communication interaction determines if new knowledge occurs or if it is constructed (Kirschner, et al., 2006; Olaniran, 2006; Olaniran, 2007a). Therefore, e-collaboration partners require structured facilitation to improve their collaboration outcomes (Ertl, 2008). Similarly, under constructivism, learning involves a process of social disclosure enhanced by teachers (Koohang & Harman, 2005). Unfortunately, with constructivism's ideals and learning processes, there is no guarantee about predictability or uniformity in terms of learning outcomes (Koohang & Harman, 2005). Sun & Ousmanou (2006) indicated that there is a significant deficiency in e-learning systems preventing a learner's personal needs to be taken into consideration and as a result this deficiency hinders effective knowledge construction.

This section presents the idea of conflict management as a challenge facing e-learners in knowledge collaboration because a lack of competence in conflict management skills would affect learners' interactions, which will in turn influence knowledge creation or construction. Also, the impact of culture in knowledge creation and meaning sharing is presented. The individual component of e-collaboration is identified as an area that is underdeveloped in the literature and an essential challenge for knowledge construction in e-learning.

Furthermore, it has been noted that the quality of information provision considerably influences knowledge construction driven by the individual users' needs (Sun & Ousmanou, 2002). For knowledge construction to take place in e-learning, the individual and group characteristics of learners and their motivations, along with conflict management patterns, would need to be addressed; especially, when one considers the four processes involved in knowledge construction identified above by Ertl (2008). In particular, learners' externalization, conflict resolution, and consensus integration require some level of conflict management skills. Also, there are different conflict resolution and

communication methods, including positional bargaining, where an individual tries to convince others to accept his or her point of view. There are also accommodating patterns in which participants in collaborative e-learning may try to go along with others' views in an attempt to preserve relationships, regardless of whether that view is the best or not. One strategy is compromising, indicating the splitting of differences between participants, which Karacapilidis (2005) contends is satisfying but not optimizing. Another strategy is collaboration, where parties work together to optimize their joint decision outcomes, for example, group problem solving. Another strategy is avoiding, which involves fear of conflict and postponement of decision. Each of these communication strategies has significant ramifications on the nature and quality of knowledge constructed in e-learning. Individuals are not automatically adept at these conflict resolution techniques, nor are they able to determine their situational appropriateness. In the design of information systems for e-learning, Sun and Ousmanou (2002) concur and also argue that personal information needs should be incorporated to determine a selection of suitable learning content, instruction sequence for learning content, and effective presentation of learning content. However, current research reveals the lack of means by which individual users' information requirements can be effectively incorporated to support personal knowledge construction.

Kock (2004) points to the importance of individual knowledge in group collaboration and mental schemas for knowledge construction. Individual knowledge is important in e-learning and e-collaboration tools because schemas can be socially constructed in a manner that influences groups to interpret information in certain ways and thus affect perception and interaction (Cyr, 2008). The degree to which group members share similar schemas reduces the level of cognitive effort necessary to accomplish the task. Therefore, members of the same cultural group are more likely to share similar mental schemas than those with different cultural groups (Cyr, 2008; Olaniran, 2007a, 2007b). For example, Lee found that Asians and North Americans had different online strategies in their use of e-mail (2002). Also, cultural differences were found in instant messaging between Asian and North American users; where North Americans engage less in multiparty chat and rated emoticons lower in importance than Asians (Cyr, 2008; Kayan, Fusesell, & Setlock, 2006). Trust is another cultural issue that affects virtual interactions or e-collaboration (Olaniran, 2004) such that trust with other users develops over-time if at all rather than instantaneously in e-collaboration. Specifically, Cyr, Bonanni, Bowes, & Ilsever (2005) found culture and trust differences among U.S., Canadians, Germans, and Japanese.

Above, there is an emphasis on the importance of collaborative activities in e-learning and knowledge construction; however, there is also a need to explore individual knowledge construction (Tynjala & Harkinen, 2005). For instance, Hakkarainen, Jarvela, Lehtinen, and Lipponen (1998) have shown that students at school may prefer to think about problems by themselves before collaborating with others. Therefore, it is important that a learning environment also allows space for individuals to reflect before and after collaborative activities. Dillenbourg (2002) called for ways to structure collaborative learning situations on the basis that free collaboration does not systematically produce learning. Interaction in e-learning situations can be structured by means of collaboration scripts embedded in e-learning environments. These scripts are sets of instructions or scaffolding for learners on how they should form groups, how they should collaborate, and how they should tackle the problem. Scripts can be seen as complementary to the online support provided by mentors or tutors during the learning process.

At the same time, the principle of integrating theoretical knowledge needs to allow individuals to incorporate their experiential knowledge.

For example, Tynjala and Hakkinen (2005) suggested that the learners' own experiences and interpretations of theoretical material are helpful in knowledge construction when incorporated in course materials and design. For one, it allows for individual learners to reflect on and identify useful questions that can be addressed or presented during discussion. Consequently, learners are able to make *implicit* knowledge *explicit*.

Group work is another challenge with learning in online or virtual environments because certain aspects of problem-solving and decision making are too complex and may not be amenable to productive sharing and the elaboration needed for knowledge construction through electronic tools (Hansen, Dirckinck-Holmfeld, Lewis, & Rugelj 1999; Olaniran, 1994). Hansen, et al., (1999) found computer conferencing was not adequate in enabling interactivity in an initial problem setting phase. Another critical aspect is the conclusion phase. Olaniran (1994) argues that there is a need for face-to-face interactions in the decision evaluation phase of problem-solving (see also Hansen et al., 1999). Many other studies of e-learning support this conclusion; the best results have been gained by integrated solutions that combined face-to-face and e-learning (Dillenbourg, 2002; Olaniran, 2008). The interaction is critical for KC regardless of whether it is in an integrated or sole technology environment. However, e-learning environments have also been used for learning materials delivery. According to Tynjala and Hakkinen (2005) the delivery approach is a waste of time and resources, especially when the goal is to transform and construct knowledge.

TROUBLING RESEARCH FINDINGS

In a direct test of KC in an e-learning course, Benbunan-Fich and Arbaugh (2006) found that students actually achieve a higher perception of learning in courses where knowledge is transmitted as opposed to where learning is constructed by students, which is contrary to expectation or constructivist arguments. However, the study's saving grace is the direct support for the need for collaboration in KC. This aspect of the finding, on the other hand, is in line with claims from other scholars (e.g., Hiltz & Turoff, 2002; Knowlton, 2001; Leidner & Jarvenpaar, 1995). In essence, students' learning or KC occurs through the give and take among co-learners. Knowlton (2001) noted that as learners offer their contribution to discussions in collaborative environments, they learn what it is that they are trying to say through reflection. At the same time, the respective responses and feedback received from classmates also increase learning (Lindemann, 1995; Knowlton, Knowlton, & Davis, 2000).

Blogging Example

Blogs are a record or reflection of the creators' (individuals) thoughts about particular subjects or topics. Blogging, for example, provides an e-collaboration forum. Blogging can contribute to knowledge construction because of its interactive nature. Nagasundaraman (2008) claimed that blogs can be turned into an interactive space or a community forum because they have the properties of web sites and Usenet-style discussions. As a result, users assume varieties of roles even when used in an e-collaborative network. Myers (2006) identified three main roles that are important as one examines the role of blogs in knowledge construction. They include: producers, reviewers, and pointers. Producers create the content and are considered the source of much of the original content. Reviewers take topics from other sources and add their own material. They can either expand on the topic or take it in a totally different direction. Pointers attempt to connect readers of a given blog to other contents but with very few commentaries of their own. Looking at the three roles, blogging best serves the purpose of information presentation and transmission and not the deep knowledge required by knowledge

construction. Accordingly, Dennen and Pashnyak (2008) argued that blogs may serve as information sharing outlets, while interaction needs to occur in other mediums or forums. They argued however, when blogs are transformed into a community where individuals are able to exchange ideas, ask, and answer each others' questions to establish new knowledge individually, then knowledge construction can occur. The problem with blogging as an e-learning tool that fosters KC is the realization that e-learning communities do not occur by chance, they are intentionally created. Lowe and Williams (2004) found that blogging allows for formatting and uploading of material, freeing students' attention for the actual task at hand. We argue that blogging in these roles avoids meaningful interactivity other than information dissemination. Consequently, this would not fulfill the constructivist objective that argues for interactivity. Furthermore, it has been presented that learning communities are not created by assembling individuals together in the same room or by transferring information, rather, e-learning communities require more than a mere linkage of weblogs; they necessitate active interaction among learners and e-collaborators to establish knowledge while building lasting relationships (Dennen & Pasnyak, 2008). At the same time, there is the fact that intentionally designed blogging communities differ from those that develop organically (Schwen & Hara, 2003). When blogs are lacking in new approaches to problems or learning, knowledge construction cannot occur.

Dennen & Pashnyak (2008) concur with the above assertion when presenting White (2006)'s three blog formats, which consist of the following:

1. A community of posters and commenters whose interactions center on a single blog. The emphasis in this community is that authors maintain total control and can develop rules or censor comments.

2. A common interest or topic blog that unites individuals with a common interest. However, as the communities grow, newer mini communities develop to explore other interests.

3. A platform based community, such as myspace.com and facebook.com, where access to non- registered users is restricted.

It seems that the second blog format community offers the best way to foster KC without limiting freedom and creativity. The common interest can be the course objective for learners. Even at that, it is important that members actively pursue new knowledge while taking into account co-learners diverse backgrounds and preferences. Individual bloggers need to desire and make a conscious effort to reach out to others with similar interests while reaching out to others with diverse backgrounds as well. In a nutshell, blogs may have the potential to promote interactivity or provide opportunity for active learning, but opportunities need not be confused with reality. For instance, Holden (2001) indicated that as knowledge travels, it loses its "contextual embeddedness." The next section discusses the idea of contextual realities more by looking at cultural challenges.

CULTURAL CHALLENGES

More specific to the issue of e-learning is the need to explore how culture influences knowledge construction and learning. After all, mere access, which has a challenge of its own as far as e-learning is concerned, is not the sole determinant of content and knowledge construction. For instance, Olaniran (2007a) illustrates the effect of culture on e-learning using Hofstede's (1980) dimensions of cultural variability (see also Van Dam & Rogers (2002)). Hofstede (1980) identified dimensions of cultural variability, which include Individualism-Collectivism, Uncertainty Avoidance, Power Distance, and Masculinity-

Femininity and later added long versus short time orientation (See also Hofstede, 2001). Power Distance is defined as "the extent to which the less powerful members of institutions and organizations accept that power is distributed unequally" (Hofstede & Bond, 1984, p. 418). Uncertainty Avoidance is "the extent to which people feel threatened by ambiguous situations and have created beliefs and institutions that try to avoid these" (Hofstede & Bond, 1984, p. 419). Individualism-Collectivism plays on the fact that in individualistic cultures, "people are supposed to look after themselves and their family only," while in collectivistic cultures, "people belong to in-groups or collectivities which are supposed to look after them in exchange for loyalty" (Hofstede & Bond, 1984, p. 419). Masculinity-Femininity refers to countries "in which dominant values in society are success, money and things," while femininity refers to countries "in which dominant values are caring for others and quality of life" (Hofstede & Bond, 1984, p. 419-420).

Hofstede's dimension has faced some criticism recently, regarding whether his claim generalizes to national culture given that he collected his data from the IBM organization with representatives from fifty countries (Ess, 2002; McSweeney, 2002). As a matter of fact, a special issue of the Journal of Computer-Mediated Communication was devoted to the dimension of cultural variability (Ess & Sudweeks, 2005). In spite of the criticism, it was found that certain aspects of the dimensions hold. For example, Hermeking (2005) finds a strong correlation between individualism dimension and technology use and a strong negative correlation between high uncertainty avoidance and systems usage. Another study finds consistency with Hermeking's support of Hofstede's dimension of individualism and uncertainty avoidance when looking at Internet usage (Barnett & Sung, 2005).

Arguments have been made that with increased immigration and globalization, a new identity or "third" identities representing shifting hybridization of pre-existing national or historic cultural patterns is developing (Ess & Sudweeks, 2005; McSweeney, 2002). On the contrary, a change in cultural patterns has been found to be restricted to economic changes at best, whereas cultural norms relating to relational patterns have been practically non-existent or remain unaltered (Smith, 2002). Others have agued that just because globalization increased the influx of people through immigration from different cultures does not imply that all cultures are steering toward universal ideals (Olaniran, 2001, 2004; Smith, 2002). Gimenez (2002) concurs and specifies, "while some corporate differences are disappearing with globalization, local cultures and local meanings are still diverse. Matsumoto (2007) also argues the role of context as a mediating variable in culture effects. His argument primarily explores emotions as a universal variable. However, in this paper, the issue is knowledge construction in an e-learning environment where the emphasis is on individual behaviors and relational patterns, not necessarily predicated on emotions, but rather on norms that govern learners' expectations and consequently the ensuing communication interaction.

The uncertainty avoidance dimension and e-learning identify security and risk as primary concerns in some cultures. While e-learning is expected to be seen in a high-risk or innovative culture (i.e., low uncertainty avoidance) as something intriguing and potentially fun, motivational, and interesting; in a low risk cultural environment (i.e., high uncertainty avoidance), the same technology can be perceived as counter-cultural (Olaniran, 2007a; Van Dam & Rogers, 2002). From another standpoint, certain cultures view authority or power distance differently (Hall, 1976; Hofstede, 1980). In a power distance culture (i.e., a measure of inequality in a culture), contrary to a low power distance culture, knowledge is never shared equally, nor is it expected to be shared equally across the society and its people. A high power distance culture recognizes the uneven distribution of power in the society, and

thus, influences how information is viewed and consequently disseminated among people across professions and organizations (Olaniran, 2008).

The effort to realize KC's vision with e-learning across contexts is fruitless without significant effort on the part of the developers and users to attend to and understand the human factors at the center of any knowledge construction activity. After all, it is humans that discern and decide what counts, as well as what does not count, as knowledge (Singh, Iyer, & Salam, 2005).

In essence, the different approaches to power, knowledge, and learning become contradictory to the aim of KC and the e-learning technologies that power it. For instance, different learning styles surface within different cultures. In particular, technology architecture is seen as a convenient way to accomplish the aim of the constructivist idea (e.g., Weigel, 2003) of making learning fun, easy, and for giving greater control to users about learning and knowledge management processes. However, in a power distance culture, such an approach is counter to cultural demands, at times confusing, and often frowned upon. Thus, a learning style that emphasizes the hierarchical transfer of skills (i.e., telling) from authoritative power to students and technology users is the norm (Olaniran, 2007a; Richards & Nair, 2007).

Furthermore, it has been suggested that it might be difficult to get people to use certain technology in power distant cultures where status dictates every aspect of interpersonal communication (e.g., Devereaux & Johansen, 1994; Olaniran, 2007b; Risku & Pircher, 2005). For instance, Japanese technology designers realize the challenge with culture and technology use by acknowledging that not all types of communication can be supported by communication technology systems (e.g., Internet or semantic web). Furthermore, the use of technology for supporting collaborative projects in Japan demands that groups must first meet physically to establish a trust environment before interacting via technology medium (see also Barron, 2000; Olaniran, 2007a). Furthermore, Lee

(2002) acknowledged the importance of culture in the selection of a technology medium. South East Asian cultures show cultural differences in the suppression of e-mail, especially when interacting with people with higher status (i.e., power distance).

The effect of culture on e-learning and KC can be drawn from an explanation provided by Paul Kawachi. Kawachi (1999) argues that the Japanese do not embrace e-learning as a result of their language structure. Specifically, he indicates that the Japanese language, developed early in life, is more susceptible to visual and memorization skills when compared to analytic and argumentation skills. As a result, Japanese use the web to primarily search and print out information for reading or translating and secondarily for entertainment and games (Kawachi, 1999).

However, when there is no fit between technology and culture, the diffusion and eventual acceptance of the technology will be seriously handicapped (e.g., Green and Ruhledder, 1995, Mesdag, 2000; Olaniran, 2007a, 2007b; Risku & Pircher, 2005). To consider knowledge construction from an e-learning standpoint, significant emphasis must be put on overcoming the challenges of e-learning in a cross cultural encounter. First of all, technology systems should conform to the needs of users and cultural preferences (Mesdag, 2000). Thus, the key to resolving cultural problems is to recognize cultural differences and adapt technology for use with the prevailing cultural values, structures, and activities within these different environments. As is, the vision of e-learning within constructivist ideology does not currently address or align with objectivist and arguably power distance perspectives. Therefore, it is important to figure out how to co-create knowledge in an environment where teachers are considered the sole authority for learning. Perhaps, one way of handling the cultural challenges is to first change the philosophy governing the objectivist approach to learning. However, this process would require a core change in cultural norms and beliefs that is bound to face significant resistance because of the change at the belief cultural levels (Olaniran & Agnello, 2008). A more subtle approach might be to explore how to enhance knowledge construction when using e-learning to maintain the objectivists' ideals, but at the same time using it to adapt knowledge learned to new environments and problem settings. The application of knowledge to different environments and problems can result in new knowledge and hence KC. The adaptive use of e-learning technologies appears to be the best way to avoid culture cannibalization that is doomed to meet resistance and subsequent failure. Notwithstanding, consideration for technology media, selection, and task type must remain a priority and should be carefully undertaken. Otherwise, resentment and frustration awaits KC in cross-cultural uses of e-learning and designs. Some scholars discussed a similar idea; when technology is used in coordination with e-learning offering a universal ideology, students fail to be precise and avoid domain specific vocabularies (cultural factors) that render them useless (Cayzer, 2004; Tennis & Sutton, 2008).

Solutions and Recommendations

E-learning does not specify or make assumptions about specific media that learners will use or the sequence in which they will be used. Hence, no single technology medium is ideal or can be prescribed for e-learning as far as KC is concerned. However, open source, based on its adaptability to different technologies and platforms, is recommended as a way to resolve some technical challenges facing e-learning usage and might be a way for encouraging learners to adopt and adapt them to their respective learning preferences. However, there is scarce research or evidence illustrating the validity of this suggestion.

Looking at knowledge construction, most of the available literature, including the ones presented here, does little to explain and incorporate how individual users' information requirements can be effectively supported in personal knowledge construction (Sun & Ousmanou, 2006). Many e-learning platforms, such as knowledge management systems, actually claim that the systems can allow individuals to adapt or tailor learning materials to fit their needs (Alavi & Leidner, 1999; Junnarkar & Brown, 1997; Avegeriou, Papasalouros, Retalis, & Skordalakis, 2003) but the method is never articulated. Sun and Ousmanou (2006) suggest the need for e-learning technologies that not only allow for users' profiling, but also focus on understanding of the user's needs for knowledge construction. They argue that such technologies must allow for the articulation of information requirements for individual and personalized knowledge construction. This approach necessitates that scholars and researchers understand that learning is subjective and thus knowledge construction must involve a process of personal interpretation and negotiation of meaning (Bruner, 1966). Therefore, to simply admit that constructivist ideals are the only way by which knowledge can be created or constructed may be erroneous. After all, constructivists also advocate no cause-and-effect relationship between the world and learners. Thus, learning is negotiated from multiple perspectives. As the debates continue on knowledge construction, learning styles, and e-learning; one must factor individual preference as it relates to information needs. Sun and Ousmanou (2006) argue that the reason for embedding users' information needs is to customize the information in a way that fits users' specific situations. Therefore, as the context changes, users' needs or information requirements would change as well (Cook, Harrison, Millea, & Sun, 2003). The users' information preferences and profiles can also add to knowledge construction by tracking the users' learning activities and patterns, by generating useful feedback for improvements, and by discovering information requirement patterns for information provision and design (Sun, Ousmanou, & Williams, 2004). Sun and Ousmanou (2006) contend that learning objects provide the building blocks for tailoring information to individual users for

their preferences and needs. Learning objects are based on a collection of both static and dynamic instructional content and activities (Cisco, 2003). The pedagogical strength of the learning object is its support of different learning theories that, in return, allow individuals or users to have meaningfully tailored, flexible, and personalized learning experiences (Sun & Ousmanou, 2006). The learning object, however, must take into consideration the different rules and constraints as directed by a given theory or learning perspectives.

FUTURE RESEARCH DIRECTIONS

As knowledge construction discussion moves forward, especially in the context of e-learning and e-collaborative environment, it becomes imperative that e-learning platforms and knowledge designers take into consideration the interoperability of the technology systems to effectively address the students' cultural needs. Therefore, in the selection of a medium, pedagogical concerns must be paramount in how to best convey learning over that medium. It is not sufficient to assume that technology systems will be effective in knowledge construction regardless of the users' needs. Effective accomplishment of learning, regardless of learning paradigm is going depend on the instructor's or trainer's understanding of the technology media and a learner's applications or preference for how they obtain knowledge. Culture, however, plays a central role in how students prefer to acquire information and eventually learn in e-learning environment. Karacapilidis (2005) stresses this factor when suggesting the need to develop customized solutions that adapt to users' or learners' profiles based on their preferences, abilities, and experiences along with technical specifications and know how. Also, more research is welcome in the cross-cultural analysis of e-learning or e-collaborative knowledge construction to evaluate other issues that may be hindering knowledge construction in e-learning situations.

CONCLUSION

This chapter alludes to the key challenges in knowledge construction. This chapter explains how knowledge construction occurs within the context of e-learning and to presents some challenges facing knowledge construction in e-learning. The chapter alluded to two theoretical approaches in learning, namely constructivist and objectivist. It is important to identify the students' roles and beliefs regarding knowledge construction. The two learning paradigms are used to explore the how new knowledge occurs in an e-learning environment and discusses the impacts of culture. Implications for each theoretical approach were identified. The *blog* was used as an example of e-learning technology to illustrate the arguments and discussion provided in this chapter. Finally, the chapter addresses implications regarding future trends in knowledge construction.

REFERENCES

Alavi, M. (1994). Computer-mediated collaborative learning: An empirical evaluation. *MIS Quaterly*, *18*, 159–174. doi:10.2307/249763

Alavi, M., & Leidner, D. E. (1999). Knowledge management systems: issues, challenges, and benefits. *Communication of AIS*, *1*(7), 35–57.

Avegeriou, P., Papasalouros, A., & Retalis, S., & Skordalakis, M. (2003). Towards a pattern of language for learning management systems. *IEEE Education Technology society Journal*, *6*(2), 11-24.

Barnett, G. A., & Sung, E. (2005). Culture and the structure of the international hyperlink network. *Journal of Computer-Mediated Communication*, *11*(1). Retrieved July 15, 2006, from http://jcmc.indiana.edu/vol11/issue1/barnett.html

Barron, T. (2000, September). *E-learning's global migration.* Retrieved on August 26, 2005, from http://www.learningcircuits.org/2000/Sep2000/barron.html

Benbunan-Fich, R., & Arbaugh, J. B. (2006). Separating the effects of knowledge construction and group collaboration in learning outcomes of web-based courses. *Information & Management*, *43*(6), 778–793. doi:10.1016/j.im.2005.09.001

Bruner, J. (1966). *Toward a theory of instruction.* Cambridge, MA: Harvard University Press.

Cayzer, S. (2004). Semantic Blogging and decentralized knowledge management. *Communications of the ACM*, *47*(12), 47–52. doi:10.1145/1035134.1035164

Cisco. (2003). *Cisco reusable learning object strategy: Designing and developing learning objects for multiple learning approaches.* Retrieved from http://www.business.cisco.com/

Cook, S., Harrison, R., Millea, T., & Sun, L. (2003). Challenges of highly adaptable information systems. In *Proceedings of the International workshop on ELISA*, Amsterdam, Netherlands (pp. 128-133).

Cyr, D. (2008). Enhancing e-collaboration through culturally appropriate user interfaces. In Kock, N. (Ed.), *Encyclopedia of E-Collaboration* (pp. 240–245). Hershey, PA: IGI Global.

Cyr, D., Bonanni, C., Bowes, J., & Ilsever, J. (2005). Beyond trust: Website design preferences across cultures. *Journal of Global Information Management*, *13*(4), 24–52.

Dennen, P., & Pashnyak, T. G. (2008). Finding community in the comments: the role of reader and blogger responses in a weblog community of practice. *International Journal of Web Based Communities*, *4*(3), 272–283. doi:10.1504/IJWBC.2008.019189

Devereaux, M. O., & Johansen, R. (1994). *Global work: Bridging distance, culture, & time*. San Francisco, CA: Jossey-Bass.

Dillenbourg, P. (2002). Over-scripting CSCL: the risks of blending collaborative learning with instructional design. In Kirschner, P. (Ed.), *Three Worlds of CSCL. Can We Support CSCL* (pp. 61–91). Heerlen, The Netherlands: Open Universiteit Nederland.

Ertl, B. (2008). E-collaborative knowledge construction. In Kock, N. (Ed.), *Encyclopedia of E-Collaboration* (pp. 233–239). Hershey, PA: IGI Global.

Ess, C. (2002). Cultures in collision philosophical lessons from computer-mediated communication. *Metaphilosophy*, *33*(1-2), 229–253. doi:10.1111/1467-9973.00226

Ess, C., & Sudweeks, F. (2005). Culture and computer-mediated communication: Toward new understandings. *Journal of Computer-Mediated Communication*, 11(1). Retrieved July 17, 2006, from http://jcmc.indiana.edu/vol11/issue1/ess.html

Gimenez, J. (2002). New media and conflicting realities in multinational corporate communication: A case study. *IRAL*, *40*, 323–343. doi:10.1515/iral.2002.016

Green, C., & Ruhleder, K. (1995). Globalization, borderless worlds, and the tower of Babel: Metaphors gone awry. *Journal of Organizational Change Management*, *8*(4), 55–68. doi:10.1108/09534819510090213

Gudykunst, W. B., & Kim, Y. Y. (2003). *Communication with strangers: An approach to intercultural communication* (4th ed.). Boston, MA: McGraw Hill.

Hakkarainen, K., Jarvela, S., Lehtinen, E., & Lipponen, L. (1998). Culture of collaboration in computer-supported learning: a Finnish perspective. *Journal of Interactive Learning Research*, *9*(3/4), 271–288.

Hall, E. T. (1976). *Beyond culture*. New York: Doubleday.

Hansen, T., Dirckinck-Holmfeld, L., Lewis, R., & Rugelj, J. (1999). Using telematics for collaborative knowledge construction. In Dillenbourg, P. (Ed.), *Collaborative Learning. Cognitive and Computational Approaches* (pp. 169–196). Amsterdam: Pergamon, Elsevier Science.

Hiltz, R., & Turoff, M. (2002). What makes learning networks effective? *Communications of the ACM*, *45*(4), 56–59. doi:10.1145/505248.505273

Hofstede, G. (1980). *Culture's consequences*. Beverly Hills, CA: Sage.

Hofstede, G., & Bond, M. (1984). Hofstede's culture dimensions: An independent validation using Rokeach's value survey. *Journal of Cross-Cultural Psychology*, *15*, 417–433. doi:10.1177/0022002184015004003

Hofstede, G. H. (2001). *Culture's consequences: Comparing values, behaviors, institutions, and organizations across nations*. Thousand Oaks, CA: Sage.

Holden, N. (2001). Knowledge management: Raising the spectre of the cross cultural dimension. *Knowledge and Process Management*, *8*(3), 155–163. doi:10.1002/kpm.117

Jonassen, D. (1993). Thinking technology. *Instructional Technology*, 35-37.

Junnarkar, B., & Brown, C. (1997). Re-assessing the enabling role of information technology in KM. *Journal of Knowledge Management*, *1*(2), 142–148. doi:10.1108/EUM0000000004589

Karacapilidis, N. (2005). e-Collaboration Support Systems: Issues to be addressed. In M. Khosrow-Pour (Ed.), Encyclopedia of Information Science and Technology (pp. 939-945). Hershey, PA: Idea Group Reference.

Kawachi, P. (1999). *When the sun doesn't rise: Empirical findings that explain the exclusion of Japanese from online global education.* Retrieved on January 12, 2008, from http://www.ignou.ac.in/Theme-3/Paul%20%20KAWACHI.html

Kayan, S., Fussell, S. R., & Setlock, L. D. (2006, November 4-8). Cultural differences in the use of instant messaging in Asia and North America. In *Proceedings of the ACM Computer Supported Collaborative Work,* Banff.

Kirschner, P. A., Sweller, J., & Clark, R. E. (in press). Why minimal guidance during instruction does not work: an analysis of the failure of constructivist, discovery, problem-based, experiential, and inquiry-based teaching. *Educational Psychologist, 41*(2), 75-86.

Knowlton, D. (2001). Promoting Durable Knowledge Construction Through Online Discussion. *Eric Document, 463*, 724.

Knowlton, D. S., Knowlton, H. M., & Davis, C. (2000). The whys and hows of online discussion. *Syllabus: New Directions in Educational Technology, 13*(10), 54–58.

Kock, N. (2004). The Psychobiological model: Toward a new theory of computer-mediated communication based on Darwinian evolution. *Organization Science, 15*(3), 327–348. doi:10.1287/orsc.1040.0071

Koohang, A., & Harman, K. (2005). Open source: A metaphor for e-learning. *Informing Science: The Inter-national Journal of an Emerging Transdiscipline, 8*, 75–86.

Lee, O. (2002). Cultural differences in email use of virtual teams a critical social theory perspective. *Cyberpsychology & Behavior, 5*(3), 227–232. doi:10.1089/109493102760147222

Leidner, D. E., & Fuller, M. (1997). Improving student learning of conceptual information: GSS-supported collaborative learning vs. individual constructive learning. *Decision Support Systems, 20*, 149–163. doi:10.1016/S0167-9236(97)00004-3

Leidner, D. E., & Jarvenpaa, S. (1995). The use of information technology to enhance management school education: a theoretical view. *Management Information Systems Quarterly, 19*(3), 265–291. doi:10.2307/249596

Lindemann, E. (1995). *A Rhetoric for Writing Teachers.* New York: Oxford University Press.

Lowe, C., & Williams, T. (2004). *Moving to the Public: Weblogs in the Writing Classroom.* Retrieved June 11, 2009, from http://blog.lib.umn.edu/blogosphere/moving_to_the_public.htm

Matsumoto, D. (2007, December). Culture, Context, and Behavior. *Journal of Personality, 75*(6), 1285–1320. doi:10.1111/j.1467-6494.2007.00476.x

McSweeney, B. (2002). Hofstede's model of national cultural difference and their consequences: A triumph of faith – a failure of analysis. *Human Relations, 55*(1), 89–117.

Mesdag, M. V. (2000). Culture-sensitive adaptation or global standardization - the duration of usage hypothesis. *International Marketing Review, 17*, 74–84. doi:10.1108/02651330010314722

Myers, E. (2006). The three types of blogs: Producers, reviewers and pointers. *ICE: Improving customer experience.* Retrieved May 21, 2006, from http://www.egmstrategy.com/ice/direct_link.cfm?bid=F1C806E8-A81C-4D15-58A7EB5FA7EFF8C6

Nagasundaram, M. (2007). E-Collaboration through blogging. In Kock, N. (Ed.), *Encyclopedia of E-Collaboration* (pp. 198–203). Hershey, PA: IGI Global.

Olaniran, B. (2007a). Challenges to implementing e-learning and lesser developed countries. In Edmundson, A. L. (Ed.), *Globalized e-learning cultural challenges* (pp. 18–34). Hershey, PA: Idea Group, Inc.

Olaniran, B. A. (1994). Group performance and computer-mediated communication. *Management Communication Quarterly*, 7, 256–281. doi:10.1177/0893318994007003002

Olaniran, B. A. (2001). The effects of computer-mediated communication on transculturalism. In Milhouse, V., Asante, M., & Nwosu, P. (Eds.), *Transcultural Realities* (pp. 83–105). Thousand Oaks, CA: Sage.

Olaniran, B. A. (2004). Computer-Mediated Communication in Cross-Cultural Virtual Groups. In Chen, G. M., & Starosta, W. J. (Eds.), *Dialogue among Diversities* (pp. 142–166). Washington, DC: National Communication Association.

Olaniran, B. A. (2006). Applying synchronous computer-mediated communication into course design: Some considerations and practical guides. *Campus-Wide Information Systems. The International Journal of Information & Learning Technology*, 23(3), 210–220.

Olaniran, B. A. (2007b). Culture and communication challenges in virtual workspaces. In St-Amant, K. (Ed.), *Linguistic and cultural online communication issues in the global age* (pp. 79–92). Hershey, PA: Information Science Reference.

Olaniran, B. A. (2008). Human Computer Interaction & Best Mix of E-interactions and Face-to-Face in Educational Settings. In Kelsey, S., & St-Amant, K. (Eds.), *Handbook of Research on Computer Mediated Communication*. Hershey, PA: IGI Global.

Olaniran, B. A., & Agnello, M. F. (2008). Globalization, Educational Hegemony, and Higher Education. *Journal of Multicultural Educational Technology*, 2(2), 68–86. doi:10.1108/17504970810883351

Panitz, T. (1997). *Collaborative Versus Cooperative Learning-A Comparison of the Two Concepts Which Will Help Us Understand the Underlying Nature of Interactive Learning.* Retrieved January 29, 2009, from http://capecod.net/tpanitz/tedsarticles/coopdefinition.htm

Richards, C., & Nair, G. (2007). 21st century knowledge-building in the Asia Pacific: Towards a multidisciplinary framework for linking ICT-based social and personal contexts of education and development. *The Electronic Journal on Information Systems in Developing Countries*, 32(7), 1–11.

Risku, H., & Pircher, R. (2005). Facilitating knowledge construction by ICT: Beyond things that make us dumb. In *Proceedings of the 20th International Symposium on Human Factors in Telecommunication*, Sophia-Antipolis, France.

Singh, R., Iyer, L., & Salam, A. F. (2005). The semantic e-business vision. *Communications of the ACM*, 48(12), 38–41. doi:10.1145/1101779.1101806

Smith, P. B. (2002). Culture's consequences: Something old and something new. *Human Relations*, 55(1), 119–135.

Sun, L., & Ousmanou, K. (2006). Articulation of information requirements for personalised knowledge construction. *Requirements Engineering*, 11(4), 279–293. doi:10.1007/s00766-006-0031-z

Sun, L., Ousmanou, K., & Williams, S. (2004). Articulation of learners requirements for personalized instructional design in e-learning services. In Liu, W. (Eds.), *Lecture Notes in Computer Science: Advances in Web-based learning*. New York: Springer.

Sun, L., Williams, S., & Liu, K. (2004). Knowledge Construction in E-learning: Designing an E-learning Environment. In Camp, O., Filipe, J., Hammoudi, S., & Piattini, M. (Eds.), *Enterprise Information Systems V* (pp. 308–315). Amsterdam: Springer.

Tennis, J. T., & Sutton, S. A. (2008). Extending the simple knowledge organization system for concept management in vocabulary development applications. *Journal of the American Society for Information Science and Technology, 59*(1), 25–37. doi:10.1002/asi.20702

Tynjala, P., & Hakkinen, P. (2005). E-learning at work: theoretical underpinnings and pedagogical challenges. *Journal of Workplace Learning, 17*(6), 318–336. doi:10.1108/13665620510606742

Van Dam, N., & Rogers, F. (2002, May). E-Learning cultures around the world: Make your globalized strategy transparent. *E-learning*, 28–33. Retrieved from http://www.elearningmag.com.

Weigel, V. (2003). *Deep learning for a digital age*. San Francisco, CA: Jossey-Bass.

ADDITIONAL READING

Alge, B. J., Wiethoff, Klein, H. (2003). When does medium matter: Knowledge-building experiences and opportunities. e*Organizational Behavior and Human Decision Processes* 91, 26–37.

Avgerou, C. (2002). *Information Systems and Global Diversity*. Oxford: Oxford University Press.

Borghoff, U. M., & Pareschi, R. (1998). Information technology for knowledge management. Berlin, Germany: Springer.Bober, M. J., & Dennen, v: P. (2001). Intersubjectivity: Facilitating knowledge construction in online environments. Education Media International, 38(4), 241-250.

Brussee, R., Grootveld, M., & Mulder, I. (2003). Educating Managers, Managing Education: Trends and impacts of Tomorrow's Technologies. In Wankel, C., & DePhillippi, R. (Eds.), *Educating Managers, with Tomorrow's Technologies* (pp. 1–16). Greenwich, Connecticut: Information Age Publishing.

Chi, L., & Holsapple, C. W. (2005). Understanding computer-mediated interorganizational collaboration: A model and framework. *Journal of Knowledge Management, 9*(1), 53–75. doi:10.1108/13673270510582965

Cummings, D., & Buzzard, C. (2002). Technology, students, and faculty: How to make it happen! *Techniques, 77*(8), 30–33.

Davie, L., & Wells, R. (1991). Empowering the learner through computer-mediated communication. *American Journal of Distance Education, 5*, 15–23. doi:10.1080/08923649109526728

Dede, C. (2000). A new century demand new ways of learning. In Gordon, D. T. (Ed.), *The digital classroom* (pp. 171–174). Cambridge, MA: Harvard Education Letter.

Driscoll, M. P. (2000). *Psychology of learning instruction* (2nd ed.). Boston, MA: Allyn and Bacon.

Dunn, P., & Marinetti, A. (2002). *Cultural adaptation: necessity for global e-learning*. Available online at: www.linezine.com.

Ess, C. (2002). Cultures in collision philosophical lessons from computer-mediated communication. *Metaphilosophy, 33*(1-2), 229–253. doi:10.1111/1467-9973.00226

Gallagher, J. (2003). The place and space model of distributed learning: Enriching the corporate-learning model. In Wankel, C., & DePhillippi, R. (Eds.), *Educating Managers, with Tomorrow's Technologies* (pp. 131–148). Greenwich, Connecticut: Information Age Publishing.

Gudykunst, W. B., Chua, E., & Gray, A. J. (1987). Cultural dissimilarities and uncertainty reduction processes. In McLaughlin, M. (Ed.), *Communication Yearbook* (*Vol. 10*, pp. 457–469). Beverly Hills, CA: Sage.

Hall, E. T. (1976). *Beyond culture*. New York: Doubleday.

Hamlin, M. D., Griffy-Brown, C., & Goodrich, J. (2003). From vision to reality: A model for bringing real-world technology to the management education classroom. In Wankel, C., & DePhillippi, R. (Eds.), *Educating Managers, with Tomorrow's Technologies* (pp. 211–238). Greenwich, Connecticut: Information Age Publishing.

Heaton, L. (2001). Preserving Communication Context: Virtual workspace and interpersonal space in Japanese CSCW. In Ess, C. (Ed.), *Culture, Technology, Communication: Towards an Intercultural Global Village* (pp. 213–240). Albany, NY: State University of New York Press.

Lobel, M., Neubauer, M., & Swedburg, R. (2005). Comparing how students collaborate to learn about the self and relationships in a real-time non- turn-taking online and turn-taking face-to-face environment. *Journal of Computer-Mediated Communication*, *10*(4), 18. Available at http:// jcmc.indiana.edu/vol10issue4/lobel.html.

McAlister, S., Ravenscroft, A., & Scanlon, E. (2004). Combining interaction and context design to support collaborative argumentation using a tool for synchronous CMC. *Journal of Computer Assisted Learning*, *20*, 194–204. doi:10.1111/j.1365-2729.2004.00086.x

Mejias, U. (2007). Teaching social software with social software. *Innovate: Journal of Online Education*, *2*(5). Retrieved December 2, 2007 available online Http://www.innovateonline.ifo/ index.php?view=article&id=260.

Morse, K. (2003). Does one size fit all? Exploring asynchronous learning in a multicultural environment. *Journal of Asynchronous Learning Networks*, *7*(1), 37–55.

O'Reilly, T. (2005). Compact definition. O'Reilly Radar. Retrieved November 15, 2007. from Http:// radar.oreilly.com/archives/2005/10/web_20_ compact_definition.html

Olaniran, B. A., Savage, G. T., & Sorenson, R. L. (1996). Experiential and experimental approaches to face-to-face and computer mediated communication in group discussion. *Communication Education*, *45*, 244–259. doi:10.1080/03634529609379053

Picciano, A. G. (2001). Distance learning: making connections across virtual space and time. Upper Saddle, NJ: Merrill Prentice Hall. Richardson, W. (2007). Teaching in a web 2.0 world. *Kappa Delta Pi Record*, *43*(4), 150–151.

Selinger, M. (2004). Cultural and pedagogical implications of a global e-learning programme. *Cambridge Journal of Education*, *34*(2), 223–239. doi:10.1080/03057640410001700589

Wankel, C., & DePhillippi, R. (2003). Introduction: Emerging technological contexts of management learning. In Wankel, C., & DePhillippi, R. (Eds.), *Educating Managers, with Tomorrow's Technologies* (pp. vii–ix). Greenwich, Connecticut: Information Age Publishing.

Waterhouse, S. (2005). *The power of elearning: The essential guide for teaching in the digital age*. Boston: Pearson.

Wheeler, D. (2001). New Technologies, Old Culture: A look at Women, Gender, and Internet in Kuwait. In Ess, C. (Ed.), *Culture, Technology, Communication: Towards an Intercultural Global Village* (pp. 187–212). Albany, NY: State University of New York Press.

Chapter 10
E-Learning as a Socio-Cultural System

Vaiva Zuzeviciute
Vytautas Magnus University, Lithuania

Edita Butrime
Vytautas Magnus University, Lithuania

ABSTRACT

The chapter analyses issues concerning the nature of virtual communities and learning in the following communities. Firstly, the discussion will focus on the question whether the very existence of technology and its ever increasing influence is an object of culture. Next, the relation between different elements of the culture (including technology) from the perspective of fostering interaction and learning will be discussed. Lastly, the specificity of the socio-cultural system of information and communication technologies (further - ICT) assisted learning together with recommendations for fostering further ICT assisted learning, e-learning and computer supported collaborative learning (CSCL) will be analysed.

INTRODUCTION

Here we provide several excerpts from a series of interviews, carried out in Lithuania, in 2008. A number (12) of therapists were approached in order to clarify their objectives and motives to engage in virtual communities (both for learning/teaching purposes, and in order to organize their work better). A semi-structured format of interviews was chosen in order to have guidelines for conversation, and also to ensure a certain degree of freedom for interviewees. Conversations were recorded, after the transcriptions had been completed, a content analysis was applied in order to identify main ideas, shared by interviewees. The length of interviews varied from 30 minutes to an 1 hour and 45 minutes.

Interviewer: What was the reason for you to start the virtual community? (emergency therapists' virtual community in Lithuania; the community was started by therapists in the beginning of the XXI c. in order to monitor, what Lithuanian hospital lacks an emergency-therapists and also to identify who could assume the responsibility for a day or night shift, in case of a colleague's sudden or planned absence. The community is totally volunteer based, and its purpose is to provide each other with op-

DOI: 10.4018/978-1-61520-937-8.ch010

portunities regarding lifelong learning, and still to make sure that patients in any hospital in Lithuania are provided with the best medical service. Note by VZ and EB, authors of the chapter).

Interviewee (a man, 47 years old, 23 years of experience, MD. The respondent leads a team of er-therapists that applies Web 2.0 technologies, e.g.: Google Groups, Google calendar, shared documents, Skype, e-mail, etc.) What I think – I am still surprised how the thing is actually working...I think... well, this virtual community relies solely on the basis that... well, it provides an opportunity for people's responsibility to manifest itself....it is responsibility that runs it. Just recently I have read a book on organization by ... <...>. It is about the organization that is operated without any management. It is a kind of anarchy, but members of the organization find the ways for going on....they do not need a manager, a boss to say things, to set some guidelines. In any other hierarchical organization it would seem strange, but such practices do exist... I know it is not something extraordinary that we have created.... Other people do similar things... we risk, and it works....We are far away from each other, geographically, and also, some of us have administrative responsibilities, financial too, we do not 'sit' in one place. Therefore we have chosen Google, as everyone has a g-mail account... we have chosen the easiest way...

The chapter begins with the quotation from the interview, one of the many, taken by authors of this chapter in order to highlight the following questions: What makes communities work? What makes virtual communities work? How does culture influence communities? Will we still have communities with such a rapid and overwhelming advancement of technologies that we are witnessing today?

These and the related questions will be further addressed in this chapter, and guidelines for possible directions of where the answers may (or may not) reside will be discussed.

First of all, the discussion will focus on the question, whether the very existence of technology and its ever increasing influence is an object of culture. Next, the relation between different elements of the culture (including technology) from the perspective of fostering interaction and learning is discussed. Lastly, the specificity of the socio-cultural system of ICT assisted learning together with recommendations for fostering further ICT assisted learning will be analysed.

Here we would like to emphasise that the concept, ICT assisted learning' is used as a synonym to ,e-learning', even if authors are well aware of the fact that the level of immersion into face to face social interactions is much higher in, ICT assisted learning', and sometimes almost non-existent in, e-learning'. The choice to use concepts as synonyms is based on the idea that in any case, it is necessary to overcome certain barriers in deciding to enrich learning experiences by introducing at first an element of ICT, and then to befit to its full, and use many opportunities offered by e-learning.

CONCEPTS OF CULTURE AND ITS RELATION TO LEARNING

The widest definition of culture is that it is something created by human beings, and therefore clearly not a part of nature (Christensen, 2003; Kavolis, 1995); ie culture is artificial.

Culture is a sociological concept with a number of different meanings but it usually refers to the totality of knowledge, beliefs, attitudes, and values of a social group (International Dictionary of Adult and Continuing Education, 1999, p. 65). Other authors note that culture is a set of the beliefs, attitudes and behaviours of people, which enables us to identify the similarities or differences that affect our ability to communicate effectively and to focus on our efforts in the process of development and learning (Ricard, 1993, p.6). Christensen (2003) summarizes definitions of culture and provides the following characteristics: culture is learnt; it is not a biological heritage, and it is handed down from one generation to the next. All human beings are embedded in culture. He states that culture generates a common identity for the members of a society and it consists of whatever one has to know or believe in order to operate in a manner acceptable to the members of a particular society. Culture influences the members of a society, so that they could behave in a uniform or predictable manner, therefore it distinguishes the members of one society from the members of another.

It should be noted that for many theoreticians, culture is intimately related to learning. Roberts (1982, p. 24) suggested that culture is a dynamic value system of learned elements, with assumptions, conventions, beliefs and rules permitting members to relate to each other and to the world as well as to communicate and develop their creative potential. Culture informs ways of dealing with social situations and ways to think about the self and social behavior (Simon, 2004). Context and culture always influence as well as shape learning. Experience does not exist in a social or personal vacuum.

Learners construct their own experience in the context of cultural values, particular social settings and economic and political circumstances (Boud & Miller, 1993). Through experiences of the communication with others and interaction with the physical environment, developmental potential is identified as an independent development achievement (Kolb, 1984). Fenwick (2001) suggests that individuals learn as they participate by interacting with community (cultural values, rules, and history), tools (including languages, images, technology) and a moment activity (purposes and norms).

As Kavolis (1995) suggests, we may understand culture as something that makes us persons or beings rather than biological entities. Culture is something material (books, paintings), and immaterial (ideas, conversations, songs) that has significance for us and that turns us into who we

are, and that we are constantly creating. Culture shapes us, and we contribute to culture almost every minute of our life.

Kennedy (2002) notes that culture is a complex of life patterns that characterizes certain groups and that are reproduced from one generation into another. Culture manifests itself through material objects and behavior.

PERSPECTIVES ON CULTURE

One of the three main perspectives on culture (dominates in French tradition) assumes culture to be related to high quality experiences in arts (Kavolis, 1995). Classical texts, classical music, classical architecture and paintings represent culture within the Arts, and contemporary art too has its place in culture. Second perspective (and it would seem that these two comprise a polarity) is based on Anglo-Saxon tradition mainly, and was introduced in its most transparent format by Dewey in the beginning of XX c. (Dewey, 1966; Kavolis, 1995).

According to this second perspective, culture is everything we humans do and have done. In this perspective, the hits of Robbie Williams or Madonna are as a part of a culture, as are sonatas of Mozart. There is the third perspective on culture too; this perspective that emphasizes what meaning an artifact or an activity has for a person experiencing it or creating it (Kavolis, 1995). The authors of this chapter focus on this latter perspective on culture, as the first appears too elitist and seems to exclude a large proportion of population in our world. The second perspective seems so broad and inclusive that it remains unclear where the conscious and unconscious understanding of oneself and what we do lies. In the third (meaning orientated) perspective common beliefs, values, traditions and every day rituals play the major role (Goodenough, 1969; Hall, 1977).

We (the authors of this chapter) have two reasons to choose the third perspective. First, an educator's worldview is the worldview that emphasizes that making the difference is supporting children's and adults' growing and learning, in order to be able to do more than they were able to do before. This worldview seems to be more related to the meaning of our experiences. Human beings have to be explicit (at least on the level of reflection) regarding what is important to us and what is not important, what we believe in and what we reject (actually, this is also a form of belief), and also, what we want, what we want to achieve and who we want to become.

Second, the meaning orientated perspective enables to include technology, whereas the first (high quality experiences orientated) probably would defy it as too mundane.

MODELS OF CULTURE, TECHNOLOGY AND HUMAN INTERACTIONS

One of the models of culture presented here is the model suggested by Schein almost three decades ago. This model was originally aimed at explaining processes that take place in organizations; however, in discussing relationship between culture and the contemporary information technologies, this model seems to be productive. According to Schein (1992) technology, together with behavior and arts, is an integral and important part of culture, which is based on values (mostly people are aware of those), and basic assumptions (sometimes a guided reflection is needed to become aware of those).

Technology plays an important role in our life, and it certainly has meaning. The issue of technology is also considered by other authors. Gullestrop (Gullestrop (from Christensen, 2003)) emphasizes the fact that it is technology that either separates, or defends from nature or helps us to use it more effectively. According to him, one of the fundamental questions that help us to understand a particular culture is: How is nature worked in that

particular culture? Moreover, it is a technology that performs (or is used to perform) the function. Another fundamental question is, How are knowledge, ideas and attitudes communicated? It seems that technology and communication comprise a core of the entity that we regard as culture. Both the technology and ideas that are communicated are integral parts of the entity that makes us human beings belong to a certain culture.

Undoubtedly for many young people, technology and especially the quality of life we enjoy are taken for granted. However, just a superficial historical retrospective would remind that, e.g., water-closets were installed in many grand palaces in Western Europe as late as in the beginning of the nineteenth century. Automobile became a commodity just 70 – 80 years ago, and in some countries - 60 years ago. It means not much earlier than many of us were born. Internet, the invention that changed the world was launched 40 years ago (as ARPAnet in the beginning), and Web – just 18 years ago. These incredibly fast changes do alter our lives, and of course they do have the meaning for us, especially during those moments that we reflect on that and will inevitably impact on culture and how the norms of culture will evolve.

It seems that our society enjoys a better lifestyle than any in history (Castells, 1996); our prosperity is based on technologies, as they free many human beings from physical work in the fields, from the TOIL of mining or factory production, or in the service sector. One tractor ploughs an area of land where hundreds of horses and people were needed. One pump provides water for hundreds of households and thus people are freed from the need to take and carry water from water wells. We live in a knowledge society, i.e. in a society with characteristics of a rapidly changing economy based on science and technologies (Constructing Knowledge Societies: New Challenges for Tertiary Education, 2002). The majority of people can devote their time to learning, teaching or to the search and further development of technologies, which means that more people are engaged in this current process of advancement. Today, there are machines and equipment that sow, plough and harvest, and we learn to read and to write, and choose from a variety of professions, and have many interests and hobbies. However, progress and prosperity should be assessed with care, as a deeper analysis reveals several contradictions (Castells, 1996; Field, 2002). A relatively easier life is very often an illusion. According to Castells (1996) the increasing amount of society's wealth does not mean that society as a whole is becoming wealthier. In many countries of the world, even in those which we consider being the cradles of equality and equal opportunities, some people become incredibly rich while others either become somewhat richer or their economic situation remains the same, leading to an increasing gap in the wealth of society.

Therefore issues of culture, embracing and inclusive and as a culture of social cohesion remain to be addressed, in addition to the questions of the role of technology. Technology is a mere tool that might be used in both ways: to allow people to relate to each other, or to alienate them in a psychological, social, and even economical way.

There are also other models of culture. Some of the models emphasise interactions and focus on displayed communications at quite an individualistic level. What is more, the cultures are defined by concentrating on the way people communicate among each other, and the way they represent each other, rather than on social institutions (Hall, 1977). In individualist cultures clear messages, initiative taking, assertiveness, self–expression characterize its members, and in collective cultures group harmony, avoiding offending others are important. Therefore, despite the fact that such grouping is over simplistic and straightforward, in individualist cultures we might expect the approach to learning to be more individualistic than in collective ones, and therefore, certain forms of e-learning (completely virtual in individualist) might be more acceptable than the other (blended learning in collective).

Parsons (1998) identified two types of functions that any culture should perform for its members, namely: static and dynamic.

Static function means that a given culture has to establish a normative stability, so that members of society are motivated to know and accept its values, ie the role of socialisation structures: family, education. Dynamic functions comprise several main tasks: to integrate its members by coordinating different units of the system, so that the latter contributes to the smooth running of the whole society (the role of law and justice). Also culture helps pursuing (and even setting) common goals (via political structures) and ensures adaptation of its members to their environment by choosing means its members have to implement in order to reach its goals. The role of economic structure is especially important in Western/modernity civilization. It would seem that, even if technology is not mentioned directly, in this model it can be allocated it to the domain of economy, as otherwise, economy and production could not maintain appropriate production in the 21st century.

As we may see, in this model the emphasis is on human interactions, and the way people project individual choices.

As our interviewee shared:

Interviewer: Do you think you could launch the same (open type, Google based) system of documentation at your university?

Interviewee (a man, 47 years old, 23 years of experience, MD). Of course, it is a necessity, and of course the main issue is fairness and trust among people....

It would, therefore seem (and the same ideas were shared by almost all our respondents) that we cannot proceed with an analysis of ICT - role in education and culture, without a due attention to the way people interact between and among each other.

Here a relation among several definitions: distance education, distance learning, and e-learning (in all cases- ICT assisted) should be discussed.

E-LEARNING AS AN OVERARCHING CONCEPT

If ICT dimension is included, it appears that distance education is an important part of educational services today. Distance education is provided by formal, e.g., school or university, and non-formal education. An example of the latter could be e.g., web-based course on any profession, provided as a continuing professional development course for, e.g., accountants, or designers, therapists, or people who have certain disabilities. If people take part in such course, they are engaged in distance learning. However, an individual learner may also benefit from seemingly un-educative virtual encounters (in-formal learning). And every day we experience hundreds of these episodes. We check weather on the Internet, and what is the currency rate in the country we are planning to go for business trip or holidays, or we consult a colleague in another continent via e-mail on a specific professional question.

Therefore, e-learning seems an overarching phenomenon and also a more general concept that both includes benefiting from explicit educational services (distance education course, provided by formal or non-formal education) and latent educative episodes. These episodes are comprised of an ocean of informal learning encounters, and may be implemented with application of ICT tools.

The concept of an information culture seems to be the result of not only the advent of the new digital technologies, but also a new mindset. We are changing the very basic traditional ways in which human beings communicate with each other, inform others, and become informed themselves. The notion of an information culture is increasingly being applied to a greater number of both personal and collective social activities such as in

the workplace, in the factory, in the office, and in the laboratory, not to mention in the activities of informal social groups (Ramirez, 2002).

According to Ramirez (2002) a new information culture should be understood as a dynamic process enabling improvement of intellectual faculties and design and development of the many and diverse mediums and communication forms and formats that are optimally necessary to generate knowledge. Also in information culture the understanding, not just communication, is improved, and also socialization of information and meaning thus expanding and extending its use throughout all spheres of human activity is observable.

Several models of culture have been suggested in above analysis, however, culture is such a complex phenomenon that each model should be considered just a starting point, guidelines, for understanding the way people act.

Culture is so complicated; therefore it is appropriate to identify subcultures. In our case information communication technologies (and, as a consequence, concept 'e-learning' is used here as an overarching concept) are still at the focus.

PERCEPTIONS OF E-LEARNING AND SUBCULTURES

Martin & Siehl (1983) identified at least three types of subcultures, namely Counterculture, Orthogonal subculture and Enhancing subculture.

People, who believe and manifest, and also practise values that are in contradiction with a prevailing culture, comprise counter-subcultures. There are many of subcultures (Kiskina, 2008; Thornton, 1996). These groups are comprised of people of all ages. These groups may demonstrate behaviors and seem to hold beliefs of the kind that the general dominant culture considers delinquent at best and illegal in some cases.

With the technologies, and especially ICT at focus, the example of such counterculture might be extreme ecologists, who protest against atomic power plants, or power plants of any kind for that matter. The early representatives of such counter-culture were workers in Great Britain in the 17th century that damaged and even ruined textile machines. Today, from a historical perspective, we do understand the latter: one machine did, what earlier 6, and later-even 12 workers had done before. That means, 5 (or 11) other people were left unemployed and therefore at danger (absolutely realistic, actually, the age of industrialization was the age of great loss in life) to die of famine (Losee, 1994). However, we do not understand, or at least do not support the former, as, even if their protests seem not without grounds, not knowing how otherwise to provide alternative energy for 6 billion people with recourses, we feel the protests are futile, or unproductive, or both.

Orthogonal subcultures include people, who do not contradict the dominant culture, rather, they emphasise some aspects, or certain values that the culture embraces anyway.

The representatives of the enhancing subculture act as proponents and sometimes even prophets of the values and beliefs that are generally accepted by the dominant culture. They do not contradict, but rather foster and promote the values and also behaviors that manifest the certain values. The example could be teachers in formal and non-formal education, and also in other organisations (e.g., any business company which has a department or at least the certain strategy in Human Recourses Development) who have introduced or are planning to introduce distance education courses, consultations, forums, or any other forms of an educational opportunity. On the one hand, it is known that distance education is promoted at many levels: technological, political, economical, also educational and sometimes institutional. On the other hand, it is also known that the technology changes at a faster speed than pedagogical (child education) and andragogical (adult education) models. Besides, there are other obstacles: sometimes at the political level the sup-

port and even pressure is evident, and financial investment in infrastructure, needed for distance education may not be provided either by a state, or regional authorities, nor management of an organisation. Therefore people, who believe that distance education has certain advantages that make it worth promoting (it helps people with a range of commitments to benefit from educational services), put their time and efforts in fund raising in order to secure investments in infrastructure (computer labs, software) and teacher training, curriculum design, etc.). These people are not outside of the norms of educational demand. They share the idea of the importance of education for social cohesion, equality and fraternity, and also that ICT should be employed to a greater extent for education. However, they do much more than merely agree and passively participate in the process; rather they accelerate the process by emphasising and promoting existing practices. They push an idea and practices for implementation so that they start changing the landscape of education and society at large (Castells, 1996).

E-LEARNING AND CHANGE OF CULTURE

From the analysis above it is clear that for the sake of further analysis, a following working definition (which, for the time being, should only be applicable within this discussion) of culture can be presented:

Culture is an integral entity of interdependent elements, namely: basic assumptions about the nature of human being, nature, activity, time, also of values and beliefs, and of practices, including behaviors, and technology. As broad as it might seem, the working definition emphasizes interdependence, and therefore we can go further into the analysis and state that in such case, development of each element inevitably changes the entity itself.

Here we argue that it is quite difficult to identify which elements of culture are of the independent, causal nature, and which are of the dependant, consequential nature. Some of the models analysed above try to establish this order of causality, and some merely enumerate elements, and the number of elements is quite different. Therefore, it would seem that for further analysis it is sufficient to state that the interdependence exists, and therefore an additional input to one of the elements (in our case- ICT assisted learning; e-learning) inevitably changes the whole system; namely – culture.

In that case at least two issues should be mentioned.

First of all, we have such a rapid change of technologies that the development of this element inevitably will change the culture as we know it. This is particularly true with active enhancing subcultures of educators, business people and even politicians. Virtuality of learning increases with each day, even if not all (or some may argue – just a small part) of learning takes place due to the reflectively constructed educational activities. That is, still just a small part of population (and empirical studies, carried out nationally and internationally (Volungeviciene, Zuzeviciute, Butrime 2008) substantiate this statement) engage in distance education courses. However, a lot of learning happens during other activities that became possible only with the development of ICT: people in different time zones, different hemispheres consult each other, they watch news, and they vote. Many interactions that take place via ICT after a careful reflection turn out to be learning episodes (Butrimiene, Stankeviciene, 2008). An e-learning culture is a learning culture where learners at all levels are enthusiastically communicating through available technologies to learn and prosper in an increasingly turbulent world (Conner, 2006).

Another issue to be mentioned here is the concern that this growth of one of the elements - namely – technologies might intervene with natural status quo of the certain culture. Here we should also be careful to mention that, at least in the model of culture that Parsons (1998) suggested,

culture performs dynamic functions, and therefore is a dynamic system in itself. Therefore, any culture changes, and this is natural, and even necessary. The concern is rather related to the possibility of an unbalanced change, or the change that is too rapid even if we do expect culture to change.

LEARNING IN VIRTUAL COMMUNITIES: ADVANTAGES AND OBSTACLES

Interviewer: How do you come across the information that you fill (upload) on the simulator? (the computer simulator for extreme, e.g., poli-trauma department medical practices; software that the interviewee participated in purchasing and continues to elaborate on, as it is important to have a learning aid for students' use in order to help them to practice before a real case is treated)

Interviewee *(a man, 47 years old, 23 years of experience, MD)*. Well, we hold many fronts… like one of the basic things is still to meet people… one thing is to have a simulator, and another is to meet and work with people who have to feed tasks into a simulator, to talk about something we have experienced, why this task is important and another is even more… if we only afford, we always finance colleagues' travels to meet colleagues abroad, to conferences… how else you will know what to feed into the software…. Software is not that expensive anymore… several years ago its cost equaled to a house's, not now… but the experience of those that know what and how to simulate and design tasks – this is still the most expensive asset… and it is expensive to build up the competence….

In the beginning of this chapter it was planned to discuss how virtual communities work in the context of the technologised reality (also - educational technologised reality). It seems that at the level of groups, in formal and non-formal education, ICT proves to be a powerful tool of communication, and enables seeking for educational goals at both individual and team level. By now we have had a lot of empiric studies substantiating the statement. Jarvenpaa & Shaw (2004) defined virtual communities as a collection of a number (most often –relatively small) of interdependent, geographically dispersed, individuals that have a common goal and depend on electronic linking in order to collaborate and achieve goals. The communities are often temporary and self managed. Learning in virtual communities most often takes a form of e-learning (via some form of computer supported collaborative learning).

According to Batesel (1994), the group learning (in a computer supported collaborative learning) is a form of problem solution in a small group, while ensuring the application of different groups, individual responsibility and encouraging mutual positive dependence. During the application of a group learning there are distinguished a few technical work conditions: it is possible to join into groups, to change them while taking into consideration student's wishes and interests: to allow the student to work independently.

While implementing ICT into a conventional teaching environment, the process of teaching changes into the process of learning. Students have to be prepared for the adaptation to a new style of learning, to become independent, in charge of themselves, learning and capable of adapting to a new interaction with peers and lecturers as well as be able to overcome the fear and stress of new information technologies (Beresneviciene, 2001; Vasiliauskas, 2007).

Switzer & Hartman (2007) note that there are several problems that can be arisen in tradition face-to-face meetings. Issues not related to the relevant task can sidetrack the group. The free flow of a creative thought may be discouraged by ideas being attached or the fear of retribution. There can be a premature closure of the meeting to avoid a conflict. The record of the meeting can be subjective, incomplete or lost. Triguerous, Rivera, Pavesio & Torres (2005) while talking about the discussion as an active learning in a traditional

lecture notice that interaction in class is easier to monitor and foster. The authors prove that it is going on due to the fact that the lecturer or the students interested in the subject can monopolize the managerial role. The rest parts of the audience do not participate in the discussion.

"In knowledge society competence and expertise can no longer be described as the skills of one individual only, but are instead relying on the collaborative expertise of teams and networks, a socially shared cognition and capability." (Rubens, Dean, Leinonen & others, 2003, p. 12). Computer supported collaborative learning (CSCL) – collaboration through ICT, where group members use the computer to structure and define their collaborative endeavors and objectives.

In summary it can be stated that the environment while learning through collaboration will be enriched with ICT or CSCL (i.e. after having supposed the students to communicate in virtual environment), the lecturers 'get far way', and students those in the conventional audience who did not dare or were not ready to collaborate, behave more courageously or they are "forced" to put their contribution into a common project.

E-LEARNING AS A SOCIO-CULTURAL SYSTEM

However, whatever seems to be working among individuals in small groups should not necessarily work at a larger scale, rather, ICT may have an alienating effect.

Juceviciene (2008) analyses the factors, mind models of knowledge management in a contemporary world, and states that our knowledge on how knowledge is generated (focus is on learning processes) is quite superficial. The author states that in any learning episode, even if superficially it seems to be individual based, in reality it always includes social interaction at some point or another. Here the ideas of Vygotskyj (1986) provide useful insights. He emphasizes that even if learning is an individual's responsibility, it is always embedded into a socio-cultural context, and therefore cannot be alienated from the context. Vygotskyj's ideas are classical, however today we have possibilities to implement them for organizing group learning with and application on Web 2.0 technologies. Hung & Der-Thang (2001) compare the principles of the situated cognition and Vygotskian thought and design considerations for e-learning. They identify the following dimensions: situatedness, commonality, interdependency and infrastructure. Hung & Der-Thang (2001) note that "not only would learning principles that work for face-to-face communities apply to e-learning communities, we now have to consider how infrastructures are to be radically transformed in online communities." (p.11)

Here it seems that the analysis has led us to one of the central ideas of this chapter, namely the statement that culture changes with the adoption of ICT (and therefore the growth of e-learning). The adoption of ICT starts to shape new cultural and educational realities. However, the new realities remain a socio-cultural system, even if the proportional importance of the elements has changed.

Analyzing e-learning as a concept of the socio-cultural system, the concepts of ICT, the e-learning and socio-cultural system have to be defined too.

The title of the socio-cultural system (Shchedrovitskij, 1995; Mamardasvili, 1958) consists of two words – society and culture. Society (mankind and people) involves different constituents that make a system. An exclusive unitary element of a society (an indivisible system) is a person (Kvedaravicius, 2006). Culture is an exclusive phenomenon, i.e. an artificially designed system that later is naturalized (Kvedaravicius, 2006). Natural systems can evolve, and artificial ones can develop. On the one hand, a socio-cultural system belongs to a social group. On the other hand; it exists in the culture. Such systems shape culture, and at the same time, they are restricted by culture. Culture establishes parameters and criteria, permissible norms, tendencies and taboo

zones for their functioning. In other words, culture conditions "behaviour, efficiency and effectiveness" of a socio-cultural system (Kvedaravicius, 2006).

In summary, it can be claimed that the socio-cultural system of e-learning is a system where for the increase of efficiency of learning ICT are applied. These technologies have been artificially designed by a human being and they influence the development and structure of this system.

PREREQUISITES OF E-LEARNING AS A SOCIO-CULTURAL SYSTEM

Under structuralism (that is a branch of rationalism theory) (Bitinas, 2005; Levi-Strauss (from Glazer, 1994)) or structural approach towards reality, the investigation of social objects as systems is a significant tool. It is related to the worldview that for the purpose of investigation of complex objects, they can be divided into elements, parts/units, and functions. After the analysis, the integral object can be explained while joining the investigated parts and considering them as a whole. Such a tool aids at revelation of the essentiality of investigated systems.

Castells (1996) distinguishes the essential characteristics of the new paradigm of ICT. Information is the basic asset and ICT affect information. The influence of new ICT is penetrative. Information is a constituent of all human activities; consequently, a new technological environment directly designs all operations of individual and collective activities. A network, the basis of which is ICT, can already be implemented into diverse operations and structures. According to Kelly (1995) 'the only type of an organization that is able to expand without a prejudice as well as to store knowledge apart from outside help, is Network'. Flexibility of ICT enables modification of structures and institutions as well as their substantial change, while reorganizing their constituents. New social forms and operations that have been conditioned by new ICT appear. Gradually, technologies join into a very integrated system, where the old and separate technologies become inseparable/integral ones.

According to Bitinas (2006), such components make complex self-controlled systems: goals which are sought by subjects; tools to achieve these goals; feedback (information) that reveals precise state of implementation; tools for taking solutions. According to Kirkman (2000) and Verhoest & Cammaerts (2001), Alampay (2006) the universal access of ICT has three levels: infrastructure; service; contents (information, knowledge, communication opportunities). Such an explanation can also be comprehended as a system. The basic factor of such a system is a human being, as in this case human's possibilities to access and systematize information and communication are of utmost importance.

Castells (1996) highlights that only a special analysis and empiric observations will enable the identification of possible outcomes of interactions related to ICT. We witness emergence of new social forms. ICT-based educational environments, in regard to ICT applied in learning, differ one from another from the aspect of place and time (Glazer, 1994; Osguthorpe & Graham, 2003, Rentroia-Bonito & Pires Jorge, 2004). That is conditioned by a variety of ICT, applied in learning. Such educational environments can also be considered being a socio-cultural system. The more technological tools are applied, the greater requirements for the developed structure of educational environment are, the more complicated relationship between an instructor (and lecturer) and a student is. To conclude analysis it can be stated that ICT-based ICT assisted learning (or e-learning) can be explained as a social-cultural system (Figure 1). The surrounding system is knowledge society.

According to Castells (1996) the development of information establishes a particularly close relationship between culture and production power. Consequently, we may soon have new social forms of interaction, management of society and, unfortunately, the new forms of social alienation. According to the systematic logics (Bitinas, 2005, Glazer, 1994) and Castells' (1996) ideas, Figure 2 reflects ICT assisted learning (or e-learning) and how socio-cultural system can be divided into objects: virtual learning and blended learning (Christensen, 2003, Osguthorpe & Graham, 2003).

During the analysis of the parts of e-learning as a socio - cultural system provided in Figure 2, and according to Castells (1996), it can be noticed that all of them are united by technologies (ICT), participants (student and lecturer), processes (educational interaction, all processes that guarantee operation and development of a system) and materials (information). According to Castells (1996) information is the basic asset, i.e. technologies affect information.

The flexibility of information technologies (Castells, 1996) secures the diversity of socio-cultural systems in e-learning and learning. Kvedaravicius (2006) points out that the development almost always expands the variety. The socio-cultural system of e-learning and learning can develop, because culture itself has an inclination to develop and change. The development involves changes of socio-cultural systems through the expansion of objectives and possibilities.

The creation of e-learning system can be considered as the newest achievements of learning. Students obtain abilities to work in a modern society. The implication is that the results of e-learning system are promoting knowledge society (see Figure 1). Processes of functioning, reproduction, organization, management, control, creativity, termination and development are all necessary and complement each other and therefore, the continuation is guaranteed.

Through the analysis of Figure 2 and according to the studies (Castells, 1996; Heeks 1999; Kvedaravicius, 2006; Osguthorpe & Graham, 2003; Wentling et al 2000) it can be claimed that achievements of ICT enable to have a rather diverse and multifaceted e-learning, because various

Figure 1. E-learning as a socio-cultural system

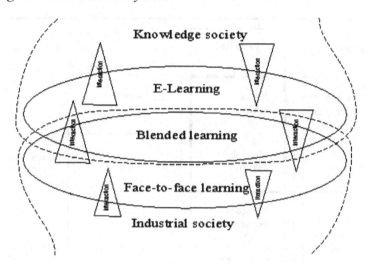

constituents may be included. Modern Web 2.0 - based courses, online learning, and even short face-to-face learning, audio, video, hypertext, synchronic and asynchronous communication, chat rooms, thematic chat rooms and virtual forums may be used. E-learning as a socio-cultural system has many elements, and however the main are: participants, technologies (ICT), processes, relationship/connections; material (information).

The surrounding system is knowledge society. Students want to acquire competencies that enable them to work in a knowledge society (1 Figure). According to Hamilton, Dahlgren, Hult, Roos & Soderstrom (2004), from a socio-cultural perspective, technology has always been a part of the problem and part of the solution.

Human relationships, education, interactions and culture may be hugely alternated due to e-learning, and therefore educationalists, politicians and researchers have to discuss and study a system carefully in order to maintain the balance of change. Even a dynamic system might suffer from un-reflected changes, and it is the role and responsibilities of academia to both perform the task, and organize discussions within their cultures.

Our analysis has revealed that there is no doubt that technology, including ICT, comprises one of the elements of culture. Therefore, e-learning is also a socio-cultural system. However, it is quite difficult to draw conclusions at this stage, concerning the meaning these developments may have on human learning, and on the way we relate to each other and what we learn. As the actions of textile workers in the XVII c. in Great Britain receive other interpretations today than they received 300 years ago. Cultural changes with the adoption of ICT we are witnessing no doubt will be also analyzed from an unexpected perspective; however, that does not acquit us from a duty to reflect on them.

It seems that the analysis above enables the formulation of the following statements (Vitkute-Adzgauskiene, Butrime & Zuzeviciute, 2008):

- ICT assisted learning - is an artifact based learning, combining knowledge and skills of many people (collaboration of users and IT professionals) for the design of virtual environments (conceptual models of real world), influencing information culture of different socio-cultural systems.

Figure 2. Objects of e-learning as a socio-cultural system

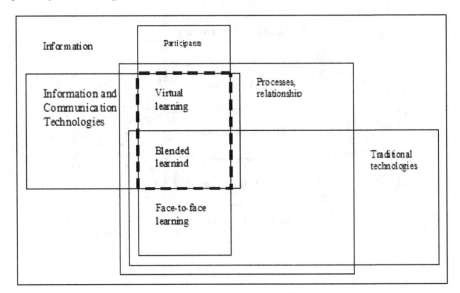

- Members of e-learning socio-cultural system are developing their competence in ICT for better communication, collaboration and knowledge production.
- Competent ICT users (and, therefore, people more intensively engaged in e-learning) stimulate a need for continuous development of ICT, which is intended for teaching/learning. It further fosters the development of culture of information with e-learning as an entity.

Participants in e-learning socio-cultural system represent at least two groups: ICT users (learners), and ICT professionals (who also always develop professional competencies in programming). These two groups sometimes represent different subcultures (Kiskina, 2008). Therefore, it is important to state here that one of the important factors for development e-learning socio-cultural system is the ability of those two groups (subcultures) to communicate effectively.

In relation to the discussion at the beginning of the chapter, it seems that Web 2.0 – based virtual communities (including CSCL) have all the potential to function, as any other community in the world. It is not a channel (ICT, or any other) that prevents people from relating to each other and authentic learning, rather than the channel is one of the important elements that comprise human life. So even if we have to acknowledge certain dangers of the extreme engagement in ICT powered world, we also have to acknowledge that there are other dangers in the society, and it is not the channel that has to be blamed for the certain alienations, but the meaning that is attributed to the channel of communication. E-learning has a great potential for enriching learning, human interaction, and increasing the quality level of professional activities, and to decrease rather than increase social alienation.

CONCLUSION

At the moment it seems that we have enough empiric data to substantiate several claims. First of all, fears that cultural changes will be devastating to culture as we know it are groundless as culture is of a changing nature anyway. We should only be careful to maintain the balance among elements of culture, and work on new designs of pedagogical (child education) and andragogical (adult education) models, making the best use of ever developing ICT in order to support meaningful and rewarding learning. E-learning will remain a socio-cultural system, if we reflect and work towards productive models. Another conclusion seems to stem from the idea that culture is a system of interrelated elements.

Our analysis seems to suggest that what works at individual level, also works at a larger scale, and therefore both local and global virtual communities seem to be viable and effective.

As beliefs and values together with behavior patterns comprise the core of culture, as empiric studies reveal (e-learning) may have a positive impact on learning, and on learner's learning to be a responsible, and a self-sufficient learner, help then to gain impetus in their careers, and, therefore, foster social inclusion.

It would also seem that if cultural changes are inevitable, the reflection on these changes is a cultural act itself. Therefore academia, researchers, educationalists and technology developers should further be encouraged to reflect on what immediate and long term consequences technological developments may have, in order to prevent implementation of models that might foster alienation.

REFERENCES

Alampay, E. A. (2006). Beyond access to ICTs: Measuring Capabilities in the information society. *International Journal of Education and Development using Information and Communication Technology,* 2(3), 4-23. Retrieved January 4, 2007, from: http://proquest.umi.com/

Batesel, P. (1994). Grupinio mokymo esme ir prasme: pedagogines patirties kabinetas [The meaning of learning in groups: class of best practices]. Lietuvos mokytoju kvalifikacijos institutas, Vilnius, Lithuania.

Beresneviciene, D. (2001). Permanent Studies for Quality and Social Justice as Mission of University Education. *ACTA PAEDAGOGICA VILNENSIA,* 8, 175-188. Retrieved March 4, 2008, from http://www.leidykla.vu.lt/inetleid/acta_pae/8/straipsniai/str20.pdf

Bitinas, B. (2005). Edukologijos mokslas ugdymo paradigmu sankirtoje [Education at the intersection of educational paradigms]. *Pedagogika: mokslo darbai,* 79, 5-10. Retrieved March 20, 2007, from http://www.ceeol.com/aspx/publicationlist.aspx

Bitinas, B. (2006). *Edukologinis tyrimas: sistema ir procesas* [Research in education: system and process]. Vilnius, Lithuania: Kronta.

Boud, D., & Miller, N. (1996). *Working with Experience, Animating learning.* London: Routledge.

Butrimiene, E., & Stankeviciene, N. (2008). Enrichment of the Educational Environment with Information and Communication Technologies: State of Art at the Faculty of Pharmacy of Kaunas University of Medicine. *Medicina,* 44(2), 156–166.

Castells, M. (1996). The Network Society: The Information Age: Economy, Society and Culture.: *Vol. I. The Rise of the Network Society.* Cambridge, UK: Blackwell Publishers.

Christensen, S. H. (2003). Profession Culture and Communication. In S.H. Christensen, & B. Delahouse (Ed.), Towards a theory of Occupational Culture (pp. 1-99). Herning: Institute of Business Administration and Technology Press.

Christensen, T. K. (2003). CASE1 Finding the Balance: Constructivist Pedagogy in a Blanded Course. *The Quartely Review of Distance Education.,* 4(3), 235–243.

Conner, M. L. (2006). Introduction to e-Learning Culture. *Ageless Learner,* 1997-2006. Retrieved January 30, 2009, from http://agelesslearner.com/intros/elc.html

Dewey, J. (1966). The Dewey School. In Garforth, F. W. (Ed.), *Dewey's Educational Writings*. London: Heinemann.

Fenwick, T. J. (2001). *Experiential learning: A Theoretical Critique from Five Perspectives. Information Series No. 385*. Columbus: Eric Clearinghouse on Adult, Career and Vocational Education, Center on Education and Training for Employment, College of Education, The Ohio State University.

Field, J. (2002). *Lifelong Learning and the New Educational order*. London: Kogan Page Ltd.

Glazer, M. (1994). *Structuralism*. Retrieved February 15, 2007, from http://www.panam.edu/faculty/mglazer/Theory/structuralism.htm

Goodenough, W. H. (1969). Cultural Anthropology and Linguistics. In P. L. Garvin (Ed.), *Report of the Seventh Annual Round Table Meeting on Linguistics and Language Study* (pp. 167-173). New York: Kraus Reprint Co.

Hall, E. T. (1977). *Beyond Culture*. New York: Anchor Books.

Hamilton, D., Dahlgren, E., Hult, A., Roos, B. & Soderstrom, T. (2004). When performance is the product: problems in the analysis of online distance education. *British Educational Research Journal, 30*(6). Macclesfield, UK: Carfax Publishing.

Heeks, R. (1999). *Information and communication technologies, poverty and development*. Institute for Development Policy and Management, University of Manchester. Retrieved April 15, 2004, from: http://idpm.man.ac.uk/wp/di/di_wp05.pdf

Hung, D. W. L., & Der-Thang, C. (2001). Situated Cognition, Vygotskian thought and Learning from the Communities of Practice Perspective: Implications for the Design of Web-Based E-Learning. *Educational Media International, 38*(1), 2–12. doi:10.1080/09523980110037525

Jarvenpaa, S. L., & Shaw, T. R. (1998). Global virtual teams: Integrating models of trust. In P. Sieber & J. Griese (Eds.), *Organizational virtualness proceedings of the VONet Workshop* (pp. 35-51). Bern: Simowa Verlag. Retrieved December 7, 2003, from http://www.virtual-organization.net/cgi/journal/

Juceviciene, P. (2008). Edukacines ir mokymosi aplinkos - inovacijos socioedukacinio igalinimo veiksnys [Educational and Learning environment – a factor for socioeducational innovation]. *Socialiniai mokslai, 59*(1). Kaunas, Lithuania: KTU.

Kavolis, V. (1995). *Civilization analysis as a sociology of culture*. Lewiston, ME: Mellen Press.

Kelly, K. (1995). *Out of Control: the Rise of Neo-biological Civilization*. Menlo Park, CA: Addison-Wesley.

Kiskina, E. (2008). Subkulturiniu grupiu studijos. Socialiniu grupiu identitetu tyrimu bei studiju pletra [Studies of Subcultures. Development of studies of identity of social groups]. Project Rep. Modulis. ESF/2004/2.5.0-0.3-141/BPD-184/7-306. Kaunas, Lithuania: Vytautas Magnus University.

Kvedaravicius, J. (2006). Organizaciju vystymosi vadyba [Management of organisational development]. Kaunas, Lithuania: Vytauto Didziojo universiteto leidykla.

Losee, J. (1993). *A Historical Introduction of the Philosophy of Science*. Oxford, UK: OUP.

Mamardashvili, M. K. (1958). Procesy analiza i sinteza [Processes of analysis and synthesis]. *Voprosy Filosofii, 2*.

Martin, J., & Siehl, C. (1983, August). Organizational culture and counterculture: an uneasy symbiosis. *Organizational Dynamics*, 52–64. doi:10.1016/0090-2616(83)90033-5

Osguthorpe, R. T., & Graham, C. R. (2003). Blended Learning Environments: Definitions and Directions. *Quarterly Review of Distance Education*, 4(3), 227-33. Retrieved May 18, 2005, from http://web2.epnet.com

Parsons, T. (1998). *Sistema sovremennyh obshesv* [System of contemporary societies]. (L.A. Sedova & A. D. Kovaliova, Trans.). Moskow, Rossyia: Аспект Пресс.

Ramirez, E. (2002). *Reading, Information Literacy, and Information Culture* [White Paper]. Prague, The Czech Republic. Retrieved August 18, 2008, from http://www.nclis.gov/libinter/infolitconf&meet/papers/rarnirez-fullpaper.pdf

Rentroia-Bonito, M. A., & Pires, J. A. (2004). Toward Predictive Models for E-Learning: What Have We Learned So Far? In C. Ghaoui (Ed.), *E-Education Applications: Human Factors and Innovative Approaches* (pp. 441-450). Hershey, PA: Idea Group Publishing. Retrieved May 13, 2005, from http://proquestcombo.safaribookson-line.com/JVXSL

Ricard, V. B. (1993). *Developing Intercultural Communication skills*. Malabar, FL: Krieger Publishing Company.

Rubens, W., Dean, P., & Leinonen, T. (2003). *Innovative Technologies for Collaborative Learning*. Helsinki, Finland: Media Lab.

Schein, E. H. (1992). *Organisational Culture and Leadership*. London: Jossey-Bass Publishers.

Shchedrovitskij, G.P. (1995). *Izbrannye trudy [Selected studies]*. Moskva, Rossiya: Shkola kulturnoj politiki.

Switzer, J. S., & Hartman, J. L. (2007). E-Collaboration Using Group Decision Support Systems in Virtual Meetings. In Kock, N. F. (Ed.), *Encyclopedia of E-collaboration* (pp. 204-209). New York: Idea Group Publishing.

Thornton, S. (1996). *Club culture: Music, media and subcultural capital*. Cambridge, UK: Polity Press.

Trigueros, C., Rivera, E., Pavesio, M., & Torres, J. (2005). Analysis of student participation in university classes: an interdisciplinary experience. *Quality in Higher Education*, 2, 108-121.

Vasiliauskas, R. (2007). The Role of Student Activity in the Context of B. Blooms Taxonomy of Learning Domains. *Pedagogika*, 85, 81-85.

Vitkute-Adzgauskiene, D., Butrime, E., & Zuzeviciute, V. (2008, December). *Impact of ICT on E-learning as a Socio-cultural System*. Paper presented at the conference Adult Learning and e-Learning Quality. Kaunas, Lithuania, Vytautas Magnus University.

Volungeviciene, A., Zuzeviciute, V., & Butrime, E. (2008). E-Learning Course Quality Factors: Learner's Needs Perspective. In *The 6th International Conference on Education and Information Systems, Technologies and Applications: EISTA 2008*, Orlando, Florida, USA (pp.78 – 84).

Wentling, T., Waight, C., Gallager, J., La Fleur, J., Wang, C., & Kanfer, A. (2000). *E-learning: A review of literature*. Retrieved January 15 2007 http://learning.ncsa.uiuc.edu/papers/elearnlit.pdf

KEY TERMS AND DEFINITIONS

Culture: is an integral entity of interdependent elements, namely: basic assumptions about the nature of human being, nature, activity, time, also values and beliefs, and practices, including behaviors, and technology.

Information and Communication Technology (ICT) Assisted Learning: is artifact based learning, combining knowledge and skills of many people for the design of virtual environments (conceptual models of the real world), influencing information culture.

Socio-Cultural System of E-Learning: is a system where for the increase of efficiency of learning information and communication technologies are applied. These technologies are artificially designed by a human being and they influence the development and structure of this system of e-learning.

Virtual Community: is a collection of a number (most often – quite small) of interdependent, geographically dispersed, individuals that have a common goal and depend on electronic linking in order to collaborate and achieve goals; learning in a virtual community most often takes a form of e-learning (via some form of computer supported collaborative learning).

Compilation of References

Adler, A., Nash, J. C., & Noël, S. (2006). Evaluating and implementing a collaborative office document system. *Interacting with Computers, 18*(4), 665–682. doi:10.1016/j.intcom.2005.10.001

Alampay, E. A. (2006). Beyond access to ICTs: Measuring Capabilities in the information society. *International Journal of Education and Development using Information and Communication Technology, 2*(3), 4-23. Retrieved January 4, 2007, from: http://proquest.umi.com/

Alavi, M. (1994). Computer-mediated collaborative learning: An empirical evaluation. *MIS Quaterly, 18,* 159–174. doi:10.2307/249763

Alavi, M., & Leidner, D. E. (1999). Knowledge management systems: issues, challenges, and benefits. *Communication of AIS, 1*(7), 35–57.

Anderson, J. R., Boyle, C. F., & Reiser, B. J. (1985). Intelligent tutoring systems. *Science, 228,* 456–468. doi:10.1126/science.228.4698.456

Anderson, J. R., Corbett, A. T., Koedinger, K. R., & Pelletier, R. (1995). Cognitive tutors: Lessons learned. *Journal of the Learning Sciences, 4*(2), 167–207. doi:10.1207/s15327809jls0402_2

Andrews, D., Preece, J., & Turoff, M. (2001). *A conceptual framework for demographic groups resistant to online community interaction.* Paper presented at the 34th Hawaii International Conference on System Sciences.

Anzai, Y., & Simon, H. A. (1979). The theory of Learning by doing. *Psychological Review, 86*(2), 124–140. doi:10.1037/0033-295X.86.2.124

Armsby, P., Costley, C., & Garnett, J. (2006). The legitimisation of knowledge: a work-based learning perspective of APEL. *Lifelong Learning and Education, 25*(4), 369–383. doi:10.1080/02601370600772368

Arter, J. A., & Spandel, V. (1992). Using portfolios of student work in instruction and assessment. *Educational Measurement: Issues and Practice, 11*(1), 36–44. doi:10.1111/j.1745-3992.1992.tb00230.x

Artz, A. F., & Newman, C. M. (1990). Cooperative learning. *Mathematics Teacher, 83,* 448–449.

Assay T. P., & Lambert, M. J. (1999 February) The empirical case for the common factors in therapy: qualitative findings. *Training Magazine.*

Attwell, G. (2005). *Recognising Learning: Educational and pedagogic issues in e-Portfolios.* Retrieved February 9, 2008, from http://www.knownet.com/writing/weblogs/Graham_Attwell/entries/ 5565143946/7575578504/attach/graham_cambridge.pdf.

Au, K. Y., Ng, A. L., & Ho, F. K. (1999). Using newsgroups to prepare students for the virtual business community: A technological, pedagogical, and motivational analysis. In James, J. (Ed.), *Quality in Teaching and Learning in Higher Education: A collection of refereed papers from the first conference on Quality in Teaching and Learning in Higher Education* (pp. 192–199). Hong Kong: The Hong Kong Polytechnic University, Educational Development Centre.

Avegeriou, P., Papasalouros, A., & Retalis, S., & Skordalakis, M. (2003). Towards a pattern of language for learning management systems. *IEEE Education Technology society Journal, 6*(2), 11-24.

Azmitia, M. (1996). Peer interactive minds: developmental, theoretical, and methodological issues. In Baltes, P. B., & Staudinger, U. M. (Eds.), *Interactive Minds: Life-span perspectives on the social foundation of cognition* (pp. 133–162). Cambridge, UK: Cambridge University Press.

Bailenson, J. N., & Blascovich, J. (2004). Avatars. In W.S. Bainbridge's (Eds.) Encyclopedia of Human-Computer Interaction (pp. 64-68). Great Barrington, MA: Berkshire Publishing Group

Bailenson, J. N., Iyengar, S., Yee, N., & Collins, N. (2008). Facial similarity between voters and candidates causes influence. *Public Opinion Quarterly, 72*(5), 935–961. doi:10.1093/poq/nfn064

Bailenson, J. N., Patel, K., Nielsen, A., Bajscy, R., Jung, S., & Kurillo, G. (2008b). The Effect of Interactivity on Learning Physical Actions in Virtual Reality. *Media Psychology, 11*, 354–376. doi:10.1080/15213260802285214

Bailenson, J. N., Yee, N., Blascovich, J., Beall, A. C., Lundblad, N., & Jin, M. (2008a). The Use of Immersive Virtual Reality in the Learning Sciences: Digital Transformations of Teachers, Students, and Social Context. *Journal of the Learning Sciences, 17*, 102–141. doi:10.1080/10508400701793141

Bailenson, J. N., Yee, N., Patel, K., & Beall, A. C. (2008). Detecting digital chameleons. *Computers in Human Behavior, 24*(1), 66–87. doi:10.1016/j.chb.2007.01.015

Baker, M. J., & Lund, K. (1996). Flexibly Structuring the Interaction in a CSCL environment. In P. Brna, A. Paiva & J. Self (Eds.), *Proceedings of the EuroAIED Conference* (pp. 401-407). Lisbon, Portugal: Edições Colibri.

Balasubramanian, S., & Mahajan, V. (2001). The Economic Leverage of the Virtual Community. *International Journal of Electronic Commerce, 5*, 103–138.

Bandura, A. (1977). *Social learning theory*. Englewood Cliffs, NJ: Prentice-Hall.

Bandura, A. (1995). Social learning. In Manstead, A. S. R., & Hewstone, M. (Eds.), *Blackwell Encyclopedia of Social Psychology* (pp. 600–606). Oxford, UK: Blackwell.

Barab, S. (2006). Design-Based Research, A Methodological Toolkit for the Learning Scientist. In *The Cambridge Handbook of The Learning Sciences* (pp. 153–169). New York: Cambridge University Press.

Bar-Cohen, Y., & Breazeal, C. L. (2003). *Biologically Inspired Intelligent Robots*. Washington: SPIE Press.

Bargh, J. A., & Schul, Y. (1980). On Cognitive Benefits of Teaching. *Journal of Educational Psychology, 72*(5), 593–604. doi:10.1037/0022-0663.72.5.593

Barnathan, M., Columbus, C., & Katz, G. (Producer) & Columbus, C. (Director). (1999). *Bicentennial Man* [Motion picture]. United States: Touchstone Pictures

Barnett, G. A., & Sung, E. (2005). Culture and the structure of the international hyperlink network. *Journal of Computer-Mediated Communication, 11*(1). Retrieved July 15, 2006, from http://jcmc.indiana.edu/vol11/issue1/barnett.html

Barron, T. (2000, September). *E-learning's global migration*. Retrieved on August 26, 2005, from http://www.learningcircuits.org/2000/Sep2000/barron.html

Barrows, H. S. (2000). *Problem-based learning applied to medical education*. Springfield, IL: Southern Illinois University Press.

Bartneck, C., Kanda, T., Ishiguro, H., & Hagita, N. (2007). Is the Uncanny Valley an Uncanny Cliff? In *Proceedings of 16th IEEE International Conference on Robot & Human Interactive Communication*. New York: IEEE Press

Barton, M. (2004, May 21). *Embrace the wiki way!* [Electronic version]. Retrieved February 11, 2007, from http://www.mattbarton.net/tikiwiki/tiki-print_article.php?articleId=4

Basiel, A. (2008). *Offline Project*. Retrieved June 5, 2009, from http://www.mhmvr.co.uk/iwblcoursecd/iwblcoursecd/video/tips4802.html

Basiel, A. (2008). The media literacy spectrum: shifting pedagogic design. In *Proceedings of World Conference on Educational Multimedia, Hypermedia and Telecommunications 2008* (pp. 3614-3630). Chesapeake, VA:

AACE. Retrieved June 5, 2009, from http://www.editlib.org/p/28887

Baskerville, R. L. (1999). Investigating information systems with action research. *Communications of the Association for Information Systems, 2*(19), 1–32.

Baskerville, R. L., & Wood-Harper, A. T. (1996). A critical perspective on action research as a method for information systems research. *Journal of Information Technology, 11*(3), 235–246. doi:10.1080/026839696345289

Batesel, P. (1994). Grupinio mokymo esme ir prasme: pedagogines patirties kabinetas [The meaning of learning in groups: class of best practices]. Lietuvos mokytoju kvalifikacijos institutas, Vilnius, Lithuania.

Bateson, G. (1976). Some Components of Socialization for Trance. In Schwartz, T. (Ed.), *Socialization as Cultural Communication* (pp. 51–63). Berkeley, CA: University of California Press.

Baume, D. (2001). A Briefing on Assessment of Portfolios. *LTSN Generic Centre.* Retrieved May 2009, from http://www.palatine.ac.uk/files/973.pdf

Beall, A. C., Bailenson, J. N., Loomis, J., Blascovich, J., & Rex, C. (2003). Non-zero-sum mutual gaze in immersive virtual environments. In *Proceedings of HCI International* (pp.1108-1112). New York: ACM Press.

Bell, B. L., Bareiss, R., & Beckwith, R. (1994). Sickle cell counselor: a prototype goal-based scenario for instruction in a museum environment. *Journal of the Learning Sciences, 3*, 347–386. doi:10.1207/s15327809jls0304_3

Bell, P., Hoadley, C. M., & Linn, M. C. (2004). Design-based research in education. In Linn, M. C., Davis, E. A., & Bell, P. (Eds.), *Internet environments for science education* (pp. 73–85). Mahwah, NJ: Erlbaum.

Bellman, K. L. (2002). Emotions: Meaningful Mappings Between the Individual and Its World. In Trappl, R., Pettta, P., & Payr, S. (Eds.), *Emotions in Humans and Artifacts* (pp. 149–188). Cambridge, MA: The MIT Press.

Benbunan-Fich, R., & Arbaugh, J. B. (2006). Separating the effects of knowledge construction and group collaboration in learning outcomes of web-based courses. *Information & Management, 43*(6), 778–793. doi:10.1016/j.im.2005.09.001

Bereiter, C. (2002). *Education and mind in the knowledge age.* Hillsdale, NY: Erlbaum.

Bereiter, C., & Scardamalia, M. (2003). Learning to Work Creatively With Knowledge. In De Corte, E., Verschaffel, L., Entwistle, N., & Van Merriënboer, J. (Eds.), *Unravelling basic components and dimensions of powerful learning environments.* EARLI Advances in Learning and Instruction Series.

Bereiter, C., Scardamalia, M., Cassells, C., & Hewitt, J. (1997). Postmodernism, knowledge building, and elementary science. *The Elementary School Journal, 97*, 329–340. doi:10.1086/461869

Beresneviciene, D. (2001). Permanent Studies for Quality and Social Justice as Mission of University Education. *ACTA PAEDAGOGICA VILNENSIA, 8*, 175-188. Retrieved March 4, 2008, from http://www.leidykla.vu.lt/inetleid/acta_pae/8/straipsniai/str20.pdf

Bettencourt, B. A., Brewer, M. B., Croak, M. R., & Miller, N. (1992). Cooperation and reduction of intergroup bias: The role of reward structure and social orientation. *Journal of Experimental Social Psychology, 28*, 301–319. doi:10.1016/0022-1031(92)90048-O

Bickhard, M. H. (1992). How Does the Environment Affect the Person? In Winegar, L. T., & Valsiner, J. (Eds.), *Children's Development in Social Context.* Hillsdale, NJ: Lawrence Erlbaum Assoc.

Bielaczyc, K. (2006). Designing social infrastructure: Critical issues in creating learning environments with technology. *Journal of the Learning Sciences, 15*(3), 301–329. doi:10.1207/s15327809jls1503_1

Biner, P., Bink, M., Huffman, M., & Dean, R. (1995). Personality characteristics differentiating and predicting the achievement of televised-course students and traditional-course students. *American Journal of Distance Education, 9*(2), 46–60. doi:10.1080/08923649509526887

Biocca, F., & Harms, C. (2002). Defining and measuring social presence: Contribution to the networked minds theory and measure. In. *Proceedings of PRESENCE, 2002*, 7–36.

Biocca, F., Burgoon, J., Harms, C., & Stoner, M. (2001). *Criteria and scope conditions for a theory and measure of social presence.* Paper presented at PRESENCE 2001, Philadelphia, PA.

Biocca, F., Harms, C., & Burgoon, J. K. (2003). Toward a more robust theory and measure of social presence: Review and suggested criteria. *Presence (Cambridge, Mass.), 12*(5), 456–480. doi:10.1162/105474603322761270

Biswas, G., Schwartz, D. L., & Bransford, J. (2001). Technology Support for Complex Problem Solving. In Forbus, K. D., & Feltovich, P. J. (Eds.), *Smart Machines in Education: The coming revolution in educational technology* (pp. 71–97). Menlo Park, CA: AAAI Press.

Bitinas, B. (2005). Edukologijos mokslas ugdymo paradigmu sankirtoje [Education at the intersection of educational paradigms]. *Pedagogika: mokslo darbai, 79,* 5-10. Retrieved March 20, 2007, from http://www.ceeol.com/aspx/publicationlist.aspx

Bitinas, B. (2006). *Edukologinis tyrimas: sistema ir procesas* [Research in education: system and process]. Vilnius, Lithuania: Kronta.

Bjørnåvold, J. (2002). Identification, assessment and recognition of non-formal learning: European tendencies. In European Centre for the Development of Vocational Training (CEDEFOP) (Ed.), AGORA V. Identification, evaluation and recognition of non-formal learning (pp. 9-32). Luxembourg: Office for Official Publications of the European Communities. Bromme, R., Hesse, F. W. & Spada, H. (Eds.), Barriers and Biases in Computer-Mediated Knowledge Communication. New York: Springer.

Blascovich, J., Loomis, J., Beall, A. C., Swinth, K. R., Hoyt, C. L., & Bailenson, J. N. (2002). Immersive virtual environment technology as a methodological tool for social psychology. *Psychological Inquiry, 13*, 103–124. doi:10.1207/S15327965PLI1302_01

Bock, G., Zmud, R. W., & Kim, Y. (2005). Behavioral intention formation in knowledge sharing: Examining the roles of extrinsic motivators, social-psychological forces, and organizational climate. *Management Information Systems Quarterly, 29*(1), 87–111.

Bolhuis, S., & Voeten, M. J. M. (2001). Toward self-directed learning in secondary schools: What do teachers do? *Teaching and Teacher Education, 17*, 837–855. doi:10.1016/S0742-051X(01)00034-8

Boud, D. (2001). Creating a work-based curriculum. In Boud, D., & Solomon, N. (Eds.), *Work-based Learning: a new higher education.* Buckingham, UK: Society for Research into Higher Education / Open University Press.

Boud, D., & Miller, N. (1996). *Working with Experience, Animating learning.* London: Routledge.

Bourgeois, D. T., & Horan, T. A. (2007). A design theory approach to community informatics: Community-centered development and action research testing of online social networking prototype. *The Journal of Community Informatics, 3*(1).

Bourne, J. R. (1998). Net-Learning: Strategies for On-Campus and Off-Campus Network-enabled Learning. *Journal of Asynchronous Learning Networks, 2*(2), 70–88.

Bowker, G. C., & Star, S. L. (1999). *Sorting Things Out. Classification and Its Consequences.* Cambridge, MA: The MIT Press.

Brandsford, J. D., Brown, A. L., & Cocking, R. R. (1999). *How People Learn: Brain, mind, experience, and school. Committee on Developments in the Science of Learning Commission on Behavioral and Social Sciences and Education. National Research Council.* Washington, DC: National Academy Press.

Brenner, J. (1997). An analysis of student's cognitive styles in asynchronous distance education courses at a community college. In *Third International Conference on Asynchronous Learning Networks.*

Brewer, M. B. (1979). In-group bias in the minimal intergroup situation: A cognitive-motivational analysis. *Psychological Bulletin, 86*, 307–324. doi:10.1037/0033-2909.86.2.307

Brewer, M. B., & Miller, N. (1984). Beyond the contact hypothesis: Theoretical perspectives on desegregation. In Miller, N., & Brewer, M. (Eds.), *Groups in contact: The psychology of desegregation* (pp. 281–302). New York: Academic Press.

Brown, A. (1987). Metacognition, executive control, self-regulation and other more mysterious mechanisms. In Weinert, F. E., & Kluwq, R. H. (Eds.), *Metacognition, Motivation and Understanding*. New Jersey: Lawrence Erlbaum Associates.

Brown, A. L., & Campione, J. C. (1990). Communities of learning and thinking, or a context by any other name. In D. Kuhn (Ed.), Contributions to Human Development, 21, 108-125.

Brown, J. S., Collins, A., & Duguid, P. (1989). Situated cognition and the culture of learning. *Educational Researcher, 18*(1), 32–42.

Brown, S. (2004). *Interactive Whiteboards in Education*. San Bruno, CA: TechLearn.

Bruner, J. (1964). *The process of education*. Cambridge, MA: Harvard University Press.

Bruner, J. (1966). *Toward a theory of instruction*. Cambridge, MA: Harvard University Press.

Butrimiene, E., & Stankeviciene, N. (2008). Enrichment of the Educational Environment with Information and Communication Technologies: State of Art at the Faculty of Pharmacy of Kaunas University of Medicine. *Medicina, 44*(2), 156–166.

Callison, C. (2001). Do PR practitioners have a PR problem?: The effect of associating a source with public relations and client-negative news on audience perception of credibility. *Journal of Public Relations Research, 13*, 219–234. doi:10.1207/S1532754XJPRR1303_2

Cameron, D., & Anderson, T. (2006). *Comparing weblogs to threaded discussion tools in online educational contexts*. Instructional Technology & Distance Learning.

Campione, J. C., Brown, A. L., Ferrara, R. A., & Bryant, N. A. (1984). The zone of proximal development: Implications for individual differences and learning. In

Rogoff, B., & Wertsch, J. V. (Eds.), *Children's Learning in the "Zone of Proximal Development"*. San Francisco: Jossey-Bass.

Cañas, A. J., & Novak, J. D. (2006). Re-examining the foundations for effective use of concept maps. In A. J. Cañas & J. D. Novak (Eds.), *Proceedings of the Second International Conference on Concept Mapping* (pp. 247-255). San Jose, Costa Rica: Universidad de Costa Rica.

Cannon-Bowers, J. A., Salas, E., & Converse, S. A. (1993). Shared mental models in expert team decision making. In Castellan, N. J. Jr., (Ed.), *Current issues in individual and group decision making* (pp. 221–246). Hillsdale, NJ: Erlbaum.

Carey, S. (1985). *Conceptual Change in Childhood*. Cambridge, MA: MIT Press.

Castells, M. (1996). The Network Society: The Information Age: Economy, Society and Culture.: *Vol. I. The Rise of the Network Society*. Cambridge, UK: Blackwell Publishers.

Cayzer, S. (2004). Semantic Blogging and decentralized knowledge management. *Communications of the ACM, 47*(12), 47–52. doi:10.1145/1035134.1035164

Chang, C. (2001). A study on the evaluation and effectiveness analysis of web-based learning portfolio. *British Journal of Educational Technology, 32*(4), 435–458. doi:10.1111/1467-8535.00212

Chase, C., Chin, D. B., Oppezzo, M., & Schwartz, D. L. (in press). Teachable agents and the protégé effect: Increasing the effort towards learning. *Journal of Science Education and Technology*.

Chavis, D. M., & Newbrough, J. R. (1986). The meaning of "community" in community psychology. *Journal of Community Psychology, 14*(4), 335–340. doi:10.1002/1520-6629(198610)14:4<335::AID-JCOP2290140402>3.0.CO;2-T

Chi, M. T. H., Roy, M., & Hausmann, R. G. M. (2008). Observing tutorial dialogues collaboratively: Insights about human tutoring effectiveness from vicarious learning. *Cognitive Science, 32*, 301–341. doi:10.1080/03640210701863396

Chipuer, H. M., & Pretty, G. M. H. (1999). A review of the sense of community index: Current uses, factor structure, reliability, and further development. *Journal of Community Psychology, 27*(6), 643–658. doi:10.1002/(SICI)1520-6629(199911)27:6<643::AID-JCOP2>3.0.CO;2-B

Choi, I., Land, S. M., & Turgeon, A. J. (2005). Scaffolding peer-questioning strategies to facilitate metacognition during online small group discussion. *Instructional Science, 33*(5-6), 483–511. doi:10.1007/s11251-005-1277-4

Christensen, S. H. (2003). Profession Culture and Communication. In S.H. Christensen, & B. Delahouse (Ed.), Towards a theory of Occupational Culture (pp. 1-99). Herning: Institute of Business Administration and Technology Press.

Christensen, T. K. (2003). CASE1 Finding the Balance: Constructivist Pedagogy in a Blanded Course. *The Quartely Review of Distance Education., 4*(3), 235–243.

Cisco. (2003). *Cisco reusable learning object strategy: Designing and developing learning objects for multiple learning approaches.* Retrieved from http://www.business.cisco.com/

Clark, E. V. (1995). Later Lexical Development and Word Formation. In Fletcher, P., & MacWhinney, B. (Eds.), *The Handbook of Child Language* (pp. 393–412). Cambridge: Basil Blackwell.

cognitive theory and classroom practice (pp. 201-228). Cambridge, MA: MIT Press.

Cohen, T., & Clemens, B. (2005). *Social networks for creative collaboration.* Paper presented at the Proceedings of the 5th conference on Creativity & Cognition.

Cole, J., & Foster, H. (2007). Using Moodle (2nd Ed.). Sebastopol, CA: O'Reilley.

Cole, R., Purao, S., Rossi, M., & Sein, M. K. (2005). Being proactive: Where action research meets design research. In *Proceedings of the 26th International Conference on Information Systems* (pp. 325-336).

Collins, A., & Brown, J. (1988). The computer as a tool for learning through reflection. In Mandl, H., & Lesgold, A. (Eds.), *Learning issues for intelligent tutoring systems.* New York: Springer Verlag.

Collins, A., Brown, J. S., & Duguid, P. (1989). Situated Learning and the Culture of Learning. *Education Researcher, 18*(1), 32–42.

Collins, A., Brown, J. S., & Newman, S. E. (1989). Cognitive Apprenticeship: Teaching the crafts of reading, writing and mathematics. In Resnick, L. (Ed.), *Knowing, Learning and Instruction.* Hillsdale, NJ: Erlbaum.

Collins, E., & Green, J. L. (1992). Learning in classroom settings: making or breaking a culture. In Marshall, H. H. (Ed.), *Redefining student learning: roots of educational change.* Norwood, NJ: Ablex.

Conati, C., & Zhao, X. (2004). Building and Evaluating an Intelligent Pedagogical Agent to Improve the Effectiveness of an Educational Game. In *Proceedings of International Conference on Intelligent User Interfaces 2004.*

Conceição, C., Desnoyers, M., & Baldor, J. (2008). Individual construction of knowledge in an online community through concept maps. In A. J. Cañas, P. Reiska, M. Åhlberg, & J. D. Novak (Eds.), *Proceedings of the Third International Conference on Concept Mapping* (Vol. 2, pp. 445-452). Retrieved February 7, 2009, from http://cmc.ihmc.us/cmc2008/cmc2008Program.html

Cong, V., & Panya, K. (2003). Issues of knowledge management in the public sector. *Electronic Journal of Knowledge Management, 1*(2).

Conner, M. L. (2006). Introduction to e-Learning Culture. *Ageless Learner,* 1997-2006. Retrieved January 30, 2009, from http://agelesslearner.com/intros/elc.html

Cook, S., Harrison, R., Millea, T., & Sun, L. (2003). Challenges of highly adaptable information systems. In *Proceedings of the International workshop on ELISA,* Amsterdam, Netherlands (pp. 128-133).

Corey, S. (1953). *Action research to improve school practice.* New York: Teachers College, Columbia University.

Coventry, L. (1995). *Video Conferencing in Higher Education.* Retrieved from www.man.ac.uk/MVC//SIMA/video3/two1.html

Cress, U., Barquero, B., Schwan, S., & Hesse, F. W. (2007). Improving quality and quantity of contributions: Two models for promoting knowledge exchange with shared databases. *Computers & Education*, *49*(2), 423–440. doi:10.1016/j.compedu.2005.10.003

Cunningham, W. (2006). *Design principles of Wiki: How can so little do so much?* Retrieved February 20, 2008, from http://c2.com/doc/wikisym/WikiSym2006.pdf

Cyr, D. (2008). Enhancing e-collaboration through culturally appropriate user interfaces. In Kock, N. (Ed.), *Encyclopedia of E-Collaboration* (pp. 240–245). Hershey, PA: IGI Global.

Cyr, D., Bonanni, C., Bowes, J., & Ilsever, J. (2005). Beyond trust: Website design preferences across cultures. *Journal of Global Information Management*, *13*(4), 24–52.

Daft, R., & Lengel, R. (1986). Organizational information requirements, media richness, and structure design. *Management Science*, *32*(5). doi:10.1287/mnsc.32.5.554

Davies, A., & Le Mahieu, P. (2003). Assessment for learning: reconsidering portfolios and research evidence. In Segers, M., Dochy, F., & Cascallar, E. (Eds.), *Innovation and Change in Professional Education: Optimising New Modes of Assessment: In Search of Qualities and Standards* (pp. 141–169). Dordrecht: Kluwer Academic Publishers. doi:10.1007/0-306-48125-1_7

Davis, J., Dow, T., Godfrey, W., & Mark, L. (Producer) & Proyas, A. (Director). (2004). *I, Robot* [Motion picture]. United States: Twentieth Century Fox.

Deeley, M. (Producer) & Scott, R. (Director). (1982). *Blade Runner* [Motion Picture], United States: The Ladd Company.

Dennen, P., & Pashnyak, T. G. (2008). Finding community in the comments: the role of reader and blogger responses in a weblog community of practice. *International Journal of Web Based Communities*, *4*(3), 272–283. doi:10.1504/IJWBC.2008.019189

Derry, S. J., Hmelo-Silver, C. E., Nagarajan, A., Chernobilsky, E., & Beitzel, B. (2006). Cognitive transfer revisited: Can we exploit new media to solve old problems on a large scale? *Journal of Educational Computing Research*, *35*, 145–162. doi:10.2190/0576-R724-T149-5432

Desilets, A., Paquet, S., & Vinson, N. (2005). Are wikis usable? In *WikiSym 2005 Conference*, October 16-18, San Diego, CA, USA.

Destatis (2008). Statistik der Studenten. *GENESIS-Online*, Wiesbaden: Statistisches Bundesamt Deutschland. Retrieved Feb. 2008, from http://www-genesis.destatis.de/

Devereaux, M. O., & Johansen, R. (1994). *Global work: Bridging distance, culture, & time*. San Francisco, CA: Jossey-Bass.

Dewey, J. (1916). *Democracy and Education*. New York: MacMillan.

Dewey, J. (1966). The Dewey School. In Garforth, F. W. (Ed.), *Dewey's Educational Writings*. London: Heinemann.

Dewey, J., & Bentley, A. (1949). *Knowing and the Known*. Boston, MA: Beacon Press.

Diaz, P. D. (2002). Online Drop Rates Revisited. *The Technology Source, May/June 2002*. Retrieved June 4, 2009, from http://technologysource.org/article/online_drop_rates_revisited/

Diehl, M., & Stroebe, W. (1987). Productivity loss in brainstorming groups: Toward the solution of a riddle. *Journal of Personality and Social Psychology*, *53*, 497–509. doi:10.1037/0022-3514.53.3.497

Dillenbourg, P. (2002). Over-scripting CSCL: the risks of blending collaborative learning with instructional design. In Kirschner, P. (Ed.), *Three Worlds of CSCL. Can We Support CSCL* (pp. 61–91). Heerlen, The Netherlands: Open Universiteit Nederland.

Dillenbourg, P. (2005). Designing biases that augment socio-cognitive interactions. In Bromme, R., Hesse, F. W., & Spada, H. (Eds.), *Barriers and Biases in Computer-Mediated Knowledge Communication-and How They May Be Overcome*. Dordrecht, The Netherlands: Kluwer. doi:10.1007/0-387-24319-4_11

Dillenbourg, P., & Tchounikine, P. (2007). Flexibility in macro-scripts for computer-supported collaborative learning. *Journal of Computer Assisted Learning*, *23*(1), 1–13. doi:10.1111/j.1365-2729.2007.00191.x diSessa, A. A. (1988). Knowledge in pieces. In Forman, G., & Pufall, P. (Eds.), *Constructivism in the Computer Age* (pp. 49–70). Hillsdale, NJ: Lawrence Erbaum Associates.

Dobson, W. D. (1998). *Authoring tools for investigate and decide learning environments.* Unpublished doctoral dissertation, Northwestern University, Evanston.

Dochy, F., Segers, M., Van den Bossche, P., & Gijbels, D. (2003). Effects of problem-based learning: A meta-analysis. *Learning and Instruction, 13*, 533–568. doi:10.1016/S0959-4752(02)00025-7

Dourish, P., & Bellotti, V. (1992). *Awareness and coordination in shared workspaces.* Paper presented at the ACM Conference on Computer Supported Cooperative Work, Toronto, Ontario.

Drucker, P. (1993, March). According to Peter Drucker (Interview). *Forbes*, 90–95.

Drucker, P. F. (1973). *Management: Tasks, Responsibilities, Practices.* New York: Harper & Row.

Dulaney, K. (2003). Wireless E-Mail Is Driving the Real-Time Enterprise. *Gartner Research Note, Technology, T-19-5799.* Retrieved March 02, 2009, from http://www.bus.umich.edu/ KresgePublic/Journals/Gartner/research/114000/114015/114015.pdf

Ebersbach, A., Glaser, M., & Heigl, R. (2005). *Wiki: Web Collaboration.* Berlin, Germany: Springer.

Ebner, M., & Holzinger, A. (2005). Lurking: An underestimated human-computer phenomenon. *IEEE MultiMedia, 12*(4), 70–75. doi:10.1109/MMUL.2005.74

Edelson, D. C., Pea, R. D., & Gomez, L. (1995). Constructivism in the collaboratory. In Wilson, B. G. (Ed.), *Constructivist learning environments: Case studies in instructional design* (pp. 151–164). Englewood Cliffs, NJ: Educational Technology Publications.

Ellemers, N., Spears, R., & Doosje, B. (2002). Self and social identity. *Annual Review of Psychology, 53*, 161–186. doi:10.1146/annurev.psych.53.100901.135228

Ellemers, N., Spears, R., & Doosje, B. (Eds.). (1999). *Social identity: Context, commitment, content.* Oxford, UK: Blackwell.

Emigh, W., & Herring, S. C. (2005). Collaborative Authoring on the Web: A Genre Analysis of Online Encyclopedias. In *Proceedings of the 38th Hawaii International Conference on System Sciences.*

Erickson, F., & Schultz, J. (1982). *The Counselor as Gatekeeper: Social Interaction in Interviews.* New York: Academic Press.

Erickson, T., & Herring, S. C. (2005). Persistent Conversation: A Dialog Between Research and Design. In *Proceedings of the 38th Annual Hawaii International Conference on System Sciences (HICSS'05) - Track 4,* Big Island, Hawaii (pp. 106).

Ertl, B. (2008). E-collaborative knowledge construction. In Kock, N. (Ed.), *Encyclopedia of E-Collaboration* (pp. 233–239). Hershey, PA: IGI Global.

Ertl, B., Fischer, F., & Mandl, H. (2006). Conceptual and socio-cognitive support for collaborative learning in videoconferencing environments. *Computers & Education. Communication Information, 47*(3), 298–315.

Ertl, B., Reiserer, M., & Mandl, H. (2005). Fostering collaborative learning in videoconferencing: the influence of content schemes and collaboration scripts on collaboration outcomes and individual learning outcomes. *Education Communication and Information, 5*(2), 147–166.

Ess, C. (2002). Cultures in collision philosophical lessons from computer-mediated communication. *Metaphilosophy, 33*(1-2), 229–253. doi:10.1111/1467-9973.00226

Ess, C., & Sudweeks, F. (2005). Culture and computer-mediated communication: Toward new understandings. *Journal of Computer-Mediated Communication, 11*(1). Retrieved July 17, 2006, from http://jcmc.indiana.edu/vol11/issue1/ess.html

Etzioni, A., & Etzioni, O. (1999). Face-to-face and computer-mediated communities; a comparative analysis. *The Information Society, 15*(4), 241–248. doi:10.1080/019722499128402

Fenwick, T. J. (2001). *Experiential learning: A Theoretical Critique from Five Perspectives. Information Series No. 385.* Columbus: Eric Clearinghouse on Adult, Career and Vocational Education, Center on Education and Training for Employment, College of Education, The Ohio State University.

Ferdig, R., & Trammell, K. (2004, February). *Content delivery in 'Blogosphere.' Technological Horizons in Education Journal*. Retrieved from http://www.thejournal.com/articles/16626

Festinger, L. (1954). A theory of social comparison processes. *Human Relations, 7*, 117–140. doi:10.1177/001872675400700202

Field, J. (2002). *Lifelong Learning and the New Educational order*. London: Kogan Page Ltd.

Fillery-Travis, A., & Lane, D. (2006). Does Coaching Work or are we asking the wrong question? *International Coaching Psychology Review, 1*(1).

Fischer, F. (2001). *Gemeinsame Wissenskonstruktion – Theoretische und methodologische Aspekte. Forschungsbericht, 142*. München: LMU, Lehrstuhl für Empirische Pädagogik und Pädagogische Psychologie.

Fishbein, M., & Ajzen, I. (1975). *Beliefs, attitude, intention and behavior: An introduction to theory and research*. Reading, MA: Addison-Wesley Publishing Company.

Flavell, J. H. (1976). Metacognitive aspects of problem solving. In Resnick, L. B. (Ed.), *The nature of intelligence*. NJ: L. Erlbaum.

Fleming, S. (2004). *Virtual Learning Communities – Supporting Learning through Interaction*. Technical Report OUCS-2004-13.

Flood, J. (2002). Read all about it: online learning facing 80% attrition rates. *Turkish Online Jounral of Distance Education, 2*(2). Retrieved June 4, 2009, from http://tojde.anadolu.edu.tr/tojde6/articles/ jim2.htm

Fogg, B. J. (2003). *Persuasive technology: Using computers to change what we yhink and do*. San Fransisco: Morgan Kaufmann Publishers.

Fogg, B. J., Soohoo, C., Danielson, D., & Marable, L. (2002). *How do people evaluate a web site's: Results from a large study (A consumer reports WebWatch research report)*. Standford, CA: Standford University, Stanford Persuasive Technology Lab.

Foltz, P. W. (1996). Latent semantic analysis for text-based research. *Behavior Research Methods, Instruments, & Computers, 28*(2), 197–202.

Fortunato, I., Hecht, D., Tittle, C. K., & Alvarez, L. (1991). Metacognition and problem solving. *The Arithmetic Teacher, 7*, 38–40.

Fox, R., & McDaniel, C. (1982). The perception of biological motion by human infants. *Science, 218*, 486–487. doi:10.1126/science.7123249

French, R. M. (2000). The Turing Test: The First Fifty Years. *Trends in Cognitive Sciences, 4*(3), 115–121. doi:10.1016/S1364-6613(00)01453-4

Frey, B., & Overfield, K. (2002). Audio Professional Development Workshops Less Glamorous More Cost Effective. In *New Horizons. Adult Education, 16*(2).

Gaertner, S. L., Dovidio, J. F., Anastasio, P., Bachman, B. A., & Rust, M. (1993). The Common Ingroup Identity Model: Recategorization and the reduction of intergroup bias. In Stroebe, W., & Hewstone, M. (Eds.), *European review of social psychology (Vol. 4*, p. 1-26). Chichester, UK: Wiley.

Gaertner, S. L., Mann, J., Dovidio, J. F., Murrel, A., & Pomare, M. (1990). How does cooperation reduce intergroup bias? *Journal of Personality and Social Psychology, 59*, 692–704. doi:10.1037/0022-3514.59.4.692

Gaertner, S. L., Mann, J., Murrel, A., & Dovidio, J. F. (1989). Reducing intergroup bias: The benefits of recategorization. *Journal of Personality and Social Psychology, 57*, 239–249. doi:10.1037/0022-3514.57.2.239

Gagne, R. M., & Merrill, M. D. (1990). Integrative goals for instructional design. *Educational Technology Research and Development, 38*(1), 23–30. doi:10.1007/BF02298245

Gallupe, R. B., Bastianutti, L. M., & Cooper, W. H. (1991). Unblocking brainstorms. *The Journal of Applied Psychology, 76*(1), 137–142. doi:10.1037/0021-9010.76.1.137

Ganzha, M. (2008). E-learning with Intelligent Agents. *IEEE Distributed Systems Online, 9*(2), 4. doi:10.1109/MDSO.2008.6

Garau, M., Slater, M., Vinayagamoorhty, V., Brogni, A., Steed, A., & Sasse, M. A. (2003). The impact of avatar realism and eye gaze control on perceived quality of communication in a shared immersive virtual environment. In *Proceedings of the SIGCHI Conference on Human Factors in Computing Systems* (pp. 529-536). New York: ACM Press.

Garner, R. (1987). *Metacognition and reading comprehension*. Norwood, NJ: Ablex Publishing Corporation.

Gelman, R., & Meck, E. (1983). Preschoolers' counting: Principles before skill. *Cognition, 13*, 343–359. doi:10.1016/0010-0277(83)90014-8

Gelman, S. A., & Gottfried, G. M. (1996). Children's causal explanations of animate and inanimate motion. *Child Development, 67*, 1970–1987. doi:10.2307/1131604

Geoghegan, M., & Klass, D. (2007). *Podcast solutions: The complete guide to audio and video podcasting*. Berkeley, CA: Friends of ED.

Gibson, J. J. (1977). The Theory of Affordances. In Shaw, R., & Bransford, J. (Eds.), *Perceiving, Acting and Knowing*. Hillsdale, NJ: Erlbaum.

Gibson, J. J. (1979). *The Ecological Approach to Visual Perception*. Boston: Houghton-Mifflin.

Gimenez, J. (2002). New media and conflicting realities in multinational corporate communication: A case study. *IRAL, 40*, 323–343. doi:10.1515/iral.2002.016

Glazer, M. (1994). *Structuralism*. Retrieved February 15, 2007, from http://www.panam.edu/faculty/mglazer/Theory/structuralism.htm

Goldman, A. (2005). Imitation, Mind Reading, and Simulation. In Hurley, S., & Chater, N. (Eds.), *Perspectives on Imitation: From Neuroscience to Social Science*. Cambridge, MA: The MIT Press.

Gollin, K., & Hu, B. (2008). *Organisationsform und Betreuungsaspekte bei der Durchführung von gruppen-basierten Fallstudien in berufsbegleitenden Studiengängen. 1. Wissenschaftliche Tagung Hochschulpolitik und Hochschulmanagement*. Essen: FOM.

Goodenough, W. H. (1969). Cultural Anthropology and Linguistics. In P. L. Garvin (Ed.), *Report of the Seventh Annual Round Table Meeting on Linguistics and Language Study* (pp. 167-173). New York: Kraus Reprint Co.

Gopnik, A., & Meltzoff, A. N. (1997). *Words, Thoughts, and Theories. Cambridge, MA*. Bradford: MIT Press.

Gordon, A., & Hall, L. (1997). *Collaboration with Agents in a Virtual World. Technical Report, NPC-TRS-97-3*. Department of Computing, University of Northumbria.

Graesser, A. C., Person, N. K., & Magliano, J. P. (1995). Collaborative dialogue patterns in naturalistic one-on-one tutoring. *Applied Cognitive Psychology, 9*, 495–522. doi:10.1002/acp.2350090604

Graesser, A. C., Wiemer-Hastings, P., Wiemer-Hastings, K., Harter, D., & Person, N.TRG. (2000). Using Latent Semantic Analysis to Evaluate the Contributions of Students in AutoTutor. *Interactive Learning Environments, 8*, 128–148. doi:10.1076/1049-4820(200008)8:2;1-B;FT129

Green, C., & Ruhleder, K. (1995). Globalization, borderless worlds, and the tower of Babel: Metaphors gone awry. *Journal of Organizational Change Management, 8*(4), 55–68. doi:10.1108/09534819510090213

Greenberg, A. (2004). *Navigating the sea of research on video conferencing-based distance education: A platform for understanding research into the technology's effectiveness and value*. Retrieved June 5, 2009 from http://wainhouse.com/files/papers/wr-navseadistedu.pdf.

Gresh, L. H., & Weinberg, R. (1999). Data. In Gresh, L. H., & Weinberg, R. (Eds.), *The Computers of Star Trek* (pp. 105–125). New York: Basic Books.

Gross, T., & Koch, M. (2007). Computer-Supported Cooperative Work. In Herczeg, M. (Ed.), *Interactive Medien*. München, Germany: Oldenbourg Wissenschaftsverlag.

Gudykunst, W. B., & Kim, Y. Y. (2003). *Communication with strangers: An approach to intercultural communication* (4th ed.). Boston, MA: McGraw Hill.

Gunawardena, C. (1995). Social presence theory and implications for interaction and collaborative learning in computer conferencing. *International Journal of Educational Telecommunications, 1*(2-3), 147–166.

Gunawardena, C., & Zittle, F. (1997). Social presence as a predictor of satisfaction within a computer mediated conferencing environment. *American Journal of Distance Education, 11*(3), 8–26. doi:10.1080/08923649709526970

Guribye, F. (2005). *Infrastructures for learning: Ethnographic inquiries into the social and technical conditions of education and training.* Doctoral dissertation, University of Bergen, Bergen, Norway. Retrieved July 5, 2009, from http://hdl.handle.net/1956/859

Guzdial, M., & Hmelo, C. (1997). Integrating and guiding collaboration: Lessons learned in computer-supported collaborative learning research at Georgia Tech. In Proceedings of Computer Supported Collaborative Learning '97, Toronto, Ontario (pp. 91-100).

Hakkarainen, K., Jarvela, S., Lehtinen, E., & Lipponen, L. (1998). Culture of collaboration in computer-supported learning: a Finnish perspective. *Journal of Interactive Learning Research, 9*(3/4), 271–288.

Häkkinen, P. (2002). Challenges for design of computer-based learning environments. *British Journal of Educational Technology, 33*(4), 461–469. doi:10.1111/1467-8535.00282

Hall, E. T. (1976). *Beyond culture.* New York: Doubleday.

Hall, E. T. (1977). *Beyond Culture.* New York: Anchor Books.

Hamilton, D., Dahlgren, E., Hult, A., Roos, B. & Soderstrom, T. (2004). When performance is the product: problems in the analysis of online distance education. *British Educational Research Journal, 30*(6). Macclesfield, UK: Carfax Publishing.

Hannafin, M. J., Hill, J., & McCarthy, J. (2002). Designing resource-based learning and performance support systems. In Wiley, D. (Ed.), *The instructional use of learning objects* (pp. 99–129). Bloomington, IN: Association for Educational Communications & Technology.

Hansen, T., Dirckinck-Holmfeld, L., Lewis, R., & Rugelj, J. (1999). Using telematics for collaborative knowledge construction. In Dillenbourg, P. (Ed.), *Collaborative Learning. Cognitive and Computational Approaches* (pp. 169–196). Amsterdam: Pergamon, Elsevier Science.

Harman, K., & Koohang, A. (2005). Discussion Board: A Learning Object. *Interdisciplinary Journal of Knowledge and Learning Objects.*

Harris, P., & Want, S. (2005). On learning what not to do: The emergence of selective imitation in young children's tool use. In Hurley, S., & Chater, N. (Eds.), *Perspectives on Imitation: From Neuroscience to Social Science.* Cambridge, MA: The MIT Press.

Hashimoto, T., Hiramatsu, S., & Kobayashi, H. (2006). Development of face robot for emotional communication between human and robot. In *Proceedings of IEEE International Conference on Mechatronics & Automation.* New York: IEEE Press.

Hattie, J., & Timperley, H. (2007). The power of feedback. *Review of Educational Research, 77*(1), 81-112. Retrieved May 24, 2009 from http://rer.sagepub.com/cgi/content/abstract/77/1/81

Hatzipanagos, S., Commins, R., & Basiel, A. (2007). Web-based video conferencing in transnational higher education: pedagogies and good practice. In Hug, T. (Ed.), *Didactics of Microlearning: Concepts, Discourses and Examples.* New York: Waxmann Publishing Co.

Hawkes, M., & Romiszowski, A. (2001). Examining the reflective outcomes of asynchronous computer-mediated communication on in service teacher development. *Journal of Technology and Teacher Education, 9*(2), 285–308.

Hawkins, J., Sheingold, K., Gearhart, M., & Berger, C. (1982). Microcomputers in schools: Impact on the social life of elementary classrooms. *Journal of Applied Developmental Psychology, 3*, 361–373. doi:10.1016/0193-3973(82)90008-9

Hayes, P., & Ford, K. (1995). Turing Test considered harmful. In *Proceedings of the Fourteenth International Joint Conference on Artificial Intelligence, 1*, 972-977.

Heeks, R. (1999). *Information and communication technologies, poverty and development.* Institute for Development Policy and Management, University of Manchester. Retrieved April 15, 2004, from: http://idpm. man.ac.uk/wp/di/di_wp05.pdf

Hevner, A. R., March, S. T., Park, J., & Ram, S. (2004). Design research in information systems research. *Management Information Systems Quarterly, 28*(1), 75–105.

Hewitt, J. (2001). Beyond Threaded Discourse. *International Journal of Educational Telecommunications, 7*(3), 207–221.

Hewitt, J. (2002). From a focus on tasks to a focus on understanding: The cultural transformation of a Toronto classroom. In T. Koschmann, R. Hall, & N. Miyake (Eds.) Computer Supported Cooperative Learning Volume 2: Carrying forward the conversation, (pp. 11-41). Mahwah, New Jersey: Lawrence Erlbaum Associates.

Hewitt, J. (2003). How habitual online practices affect the development of asynchronous discussion threads. *Journal of Educational Computing Research, 28*(1), 31–45. doi:10.2190/PMG8-A05J-CUH1-DK14

Hicks, D. (1996). Contextual inquiries: A discourse-oriented study of classroom learning. In Hicks, D. (Ed.), *Discourse, learning and schooling* (pp. 104–141). New York: Cambridge University Press.

Higgins, E. T. (1992). Achieving "shared reality" in the communication game: A social action that creates meaning. *Journal of Language and Social Psychology, 11*, 107–131. doi:10.1177/0261927X92113001

Higgison, C., & Harris, R. (2002). *Online tutoring: the OTiS experience.* Retrieved from http://otis.scotcit.ac.uk

Hiltz, R., & Turoff, M. (2002). What makes learning networks effective? *Communications of the ACM, 45*(4), 56–59. doi:10.1145/505248.505273

Hiltz, S. R., & Wellman, B. (1997). Asynchronous learning networks as a virtual classroom. *Communications of the ACM, 40*, 44–47. doi:10.1145/260750.260764

Hinsz, V. B., Tindale, R. S., & Vollrath, D. A. (1997). The emerging conceptualization of groups as informa-tion processors. *Psychological Bulletin, 121*, 43–64. doi:10.1037/0033-2909.121.1.43

Hmelo, C. E., & Evensen, D. H. (2000). Introduction. In Evensen, D. H., & Hmelo, C. E. (Eds.), *Problem-Based Learning, A Research Perspective on Learning Interactions* (pp. 185–195). Mahwah, NJ: Lawrence Erlbaum Associates.

Hmelo, C., Narayanan, N. H., Newstetter, W. C., & Kolodner, J. L. (1995). *A multiple-case-based approach to generative environments for learning.* Paper presented at the Second Annual Symposium on Cognition and Education.

Hmelo-Silver, C. E., & Barrows, H. S. (2006). Goals and strategies of a problem-based learning facilitator. *Interdisciplinary Journal of Problem-based Learning, 1*, 21–39.

Hmelo-Silver, C. E., Duncan, R. G., & Chinn, C. A. (2007). Scaffolding and achievement in problem-based and inquiry learning: A response to Kirschner, Sweller, and Clark (2006). *Educational Psychologist, 42*, 99–107.

Höbarth, U. (2007). Konstruktivistisches Lernen mit Moodle. Praktische Einsatzmöglichkeiten in Bildungsinstitutionen. [Constructivist Learning with Moodle. Practical application possibilities in educational institutions]. Boizenburg, Germany: vwh Verlag.

Hodges, L. F., Anderson, P., Burdea, G. C., & Hoffmann, B. O. (2001). Treating Psychological and Physical Disorders with VR. *IEEE Computer Graphics and Applications, 21*(6), 25–33. doi:10.1109/38.963458

Hofstede, G. (1980). *Culture's consequences.* Beverly Hills, CA: Sage.

Hofstede, G. H. (2001). *Culture's consequences: Comparing values, behaviors, institutions, and organizations across nations.* Thousand Oaks, CA: Sage.

Hofstede, G., & Bond, M. (1984). Hofstede's culture dimensions: An independent validation using Rokeach's value survey. *Journal of Cross-Cultural Psychology, 15*, 417–433. doi:10.1177/0022002184015004003

Holbrook, J., & Kolodner, J. L. (2000). Scaffolding the development of an inquiry-based (science) classroom. In B. Fishman & S. O'Connor-Divelbiss (Eds.), *Fourth International Conference of the Learning Sciences* (pp. 221-227). Mahwah, NJ: Lawrence Erlbaum Associates.

Holden, N. (2001). Knowledge management: Raising the spectre of the cross cultural dimension. *Knowledge and Process Management, 8*(3), 155–163. doi:10.1002/kpm.117

Howard, C. (2007). *Collaborative E-Learning Systems - Increasing the Pace of E-Learning Development at Norfolk Southern.* Case Study, Bersin & Associates. Retrieved April 20, 2007, from http://www.bersinassociates.com/free_research/ns_case_study_1.8.pdf

HRK. (1998). Zum Umgang mit wissenschaftlichem Fehlverhalten in den Hochschulen. *Empfehlung des 185. Plenums,* Hochschulrektorkonferenz. Retrieved Feburary 29, 2008, from http://www.hrk.de/de/beschluesse/109_422.php

Hu, B. (2006). Correction Marks and Comments on Web Pages. In *Proceedings Intelligent Tutoring Systems: 8th International Conference, ITS 2006, Springer Lecture Notes in Computer Science* (pp. 784 - 786). Berlin: Springer.

Hu, B., & Lauck, F. (2004). Prototype of a Web and XML Based Collaborative Authoring System. In *International Conference on Computing, Communications and Control Technologies (CCCT'04), Proceedings,* Austin, USA (Vol. 4, pp. 79-84).

Hu, B., Lauck, F., & Scheffczyk, J. (2005). How Recent is a Web Document? *Electronic Notes in Theoretical Computer Science, 157*(2), 147–166. doi:10.1016/j.entcs.2005.12.052

Huhn, M., & Stephens, L. (1999). Multiagent systems and societies of agents. In *Multiagent Systems: A Modern Introduction to Distributed Artificial Intelligence* (pp. 79–120). Cambridge, MA, USA: MIT Press.

Hung, D. W. L., & Der-Thang, C. (2001). Situated Cognition, Vygotskian thought and Learning from the Communities of Practice Perspective: Implications for the Design of Web-Based E-Learning. *Educational Media International, 38*(1), 2–12. doi:10.1080/09523980110037525

IACM/FORTH. (2008). *ICT4T Final Evaluation Report* [Internal Project Document]. Retrieved February 14, 2009, from http://www.ict4t.net/?q=system/files/Final+Evaluation+Report.pdf

Ihamäki. H. & Vilpola, I. (2004). Usability of a Virtual Learning Environment concerning safety at work. *Electronic Journal on e-Learning, 2*(1), 103-112.

Ijsselsteijn, W., Baren, J. V., & Lanen, F. V. (2003). *Staying in touch: Social presence and connectedness through synchronous and asynchronous communication media.* Paper presented at the 10th International Conference on Human-Computer Interaction. Lawrence Erlbaum.

Ilomäki, L., & Paavola, S. (2008). Developing and applying design principles for knowledge creation practices. In G. Kanselaar, J. van Merriënboer, P. Kirschner, & T. de Jong (Eds.), *International Perspectives in the Learning Sciences: Cre8ing a Learning World, Proceedings of the Eighth International Conference for the Learning Sciences (ICLS 2008)* (Vol. 3, pp. 258-259). Utrecht, The Netherlands: International Society of the Learning Sciences (ISLS).

Ilomäki, L., Lakkala, M., & Paavola, S. (2006). Case studies of learning objects used in school settings. *Learning, Media and Technology, 31*(3), 249–267. doi:10.1080/17439880600893291

Inagaki, K., & Hatano, G. (2002). *Young Children's Naive Thinking about the Biological World.* New York: Psychology Press.

Irele, M. (1999). *Relative Effectiveness of Distance Learning Systems.* Lucent Technologies and the World Campus, Pennsylvania State University Press.

Irons, A. D. (2004). Using portfolios in assessment to reduce plagiarism. In *Proceedings of the Plagiarism: Prevention, Practice and Policy Conference,* Northumbria University.

Ishiguro, H. (2007). Scientific Issues Concerning Androids. *The International Journal of Robotics Research, 26*(1), 105–117. doi:10.1177/0278364907074474

ISO 9241-11:1998. (2008). *Ergonomic requirements for office work with visual display terminals (VDTs) - Part 11: Guidance on usability* [ISO Standard]. Retrieved January 7, 2009, from http://www.iso.org/iso/iso_catalogue/catalogue_tc/catalogue_detail.htm?csnumber=16883

ISO/IEC 26300:2006. (2006). *Information technology -- Open Document Format for Office Applications (Open-Document) v1.0. Abstract.* International Organization for Standardization.

Itakura, S., Kanaya, N., Shimada, M., Minato, T., & Ishiguro, H. (2004). *Communicative behavior to the android robot in human infants.* Poster paper in International Conference on Developmental Learning.

Jarvenpaa, S. L., & Shaw, T. R. (1998). Global virtual teams: Integrating models of trust. In P. Sieber & J. Griese (Eds.), *Organizational virtualness proceedings of the VONet Workshop* (pp. 35-51). Bern: Simowa Verlag. Retrieved December 7, 2003, from http://www.virtual-organization.net/cgi/journal/

Jarvis, J., Lane, D., & Fillery-Travis, A. (2006). *The Case for Coaching - Making Evidence -based decision on coaching.* CIPD London.

Jia, Y. (2005). Building a Web-Based Collaborative Learning Environment. In *ITHET 6th Annual International Conference, Session F2D (7-9).* Juan Dolio, Dominican Republic: IEEE.

Jöbring, O. (2002). *Online Learning Community Research website (English).* Retrieved from http://www.learnloop.org/olc

Johnson, D. W., & Johnson, R. T. (1989). *Cooperation and competition: Theory and research.* Edina, MN: Interaction Book Company.

Johnson, D. W., & Johnson, R. T. (1995). *Teaching students to be peacemakers* (3rd ed.). Edina, MN: Interaction Book Company.

Johnson, D. W., Johnson, R. T., & Holubec, E. J. (1993). *Cooperation in the Classroom* (6th ed.). Edina, MN: Interaction Book Company.

Johnson-Laird, P. (1983). *Mental models.* Cambridge, MA: Harvard University Press.

Jonassen, D. (1993). Thinking technology. *Instructional Technology*, 35-37.

Jonassen, D. (1998). *Technology as cognitive tools: Learners as designers.* IT FORUM Paper 1. Retrieved from http://itech1.coe.uga.edu/itforum/paper1/paper1.html

Jonassen, D. H. (Ed., 2. Edition), Handbook of Research on Educational Communications and Technology. Mahwah, NJ: Lawrence Erlbaum.

Jonassen, D. H., & Land, S. M. (2000). *Theoretical foundations of learning environments.* Mahwah, NJ: Erlbaum.

Jones, C., Dirckinck-Holmfeld, L., & Lindström, B. (2006). A relational, indirect, meso-level approach to CSCL design in the next decade. *International Journal of Computer-Supported Collaborative Learning, 1*(1), 35–56. doi:10.1007/s11412-006-6841-7

Jones, M. (2006). Plagiarism Proceedings in Higher Education – Quality Assured? In *Proceedings of 2nd International Plagiarism Conference.*

Jones, Q., Ravid, G., & Rafaeli, S. (2002). An Empirical Exploration of Mass Interaction System Dynamics: Individual Information Overload and Usenet Discourse. In *35th Annual Hawaii International Conference on System Sciences (HICSS'02)*, Big Island, Hawaii.

Juan, M. C., Alcaniz, M., Monserrat, C., Botella, C., Banos, R. M., & Guerrero, B. (2005). Using augmented reality to treat phobias. *IEEE Computer Graphics and Applications, 25*(6), 31–37. doi:10.1109/MCG.2005.143

Juceviciene, P. (2008). Edukacines ir mokymosi aplinkos - inovacijos socioedukacinio igalinimo veiksnys [Educational and Learning environment – a factor for socioeducational innovation]. *Socialiniai mokslai, 59*(1). Kaunas, Lithuania: KTU.

Junnarkar, B., & Brown, C. (1997). Re-assessing the enabling role of information technology in KM. *Journal of Knowledge Management, 1*(2), 142–148. doi:10.1108/EUM0000000004589

Kali, Y. (2006). Collaborative knowledge building using a design principles database. *International Journal of Computer-Supported Collaborative Learning, 1*(2), 187–201. doi:10.1007/s11412-006-8993-x

Karacapilidis, N. (2005). e-Collaboration Support Systems: Issues to be addressed. In M. Khosrow-Pour (Ed.), Encyclopedia of Information Science and Technology (pp. 939-945). Hershey, PA: Idea Group Reference.

Karmiloff-Smith, A. (1979). Micro- and macro- developmental changes in language acquisition and other representational systems. *Cognitive Science, 3*, 91–118. doi:10.1207/s15516709cog0302_1

Kavolis, V. (1995). *Civilization analysis as a sociology of culture*. Lewiston, ME: Mellen Press.

Kawachi, P. (1999). *When the sun doesn't rise: Empirical findings that explain the exclusion of Japanese from online global education*. Retrieved on January 12, 2008, from http://www.ignou.ac.in/Theme-3/Paul%20%20KAWACHI.html

Kayan, S., Fussell, S. R., & Setlock, L. D. (2006, November 4-8). Cultural differences in the use of instant messaging in Asia and North America. In *Proceedings of the ACM Computer Supported Collaborative Work*, Banff.

Kearney, N. (2007). *Pedagogical Model for the ICT4T course including a draft course structure* [Internal Project Document]. Retrieved February 7, 2009, from http://www.ict4t.net/?q=system/ files/ICT4T_WP4_Pedagogical_Model.doc

Keil, F. C. (1989). *Concepts, Kinds, and Cognitive Development*. Cambridge, MA: MIT Press.

Kelly, K. (1995). *Out of Control: the Rise of Neo-biological Civilization*. Menlo Park, CA: Addison-Wesley.

Kim, H.-C. (Ed.). (2002). From Comments to Dialogues: A Study of Asynchronous Dialogue Processes as Part of Collaborative Reviewing on the Web. In *Proceedings of the 35th Hawaii International Conference on System Sciences (HICSS-35'02)*.

Kimmerle, J., & Cress, U. (2008). Group awareness and self-presentation in computersupported information ex-change. *International Journal of Computer-Supported Collaborative Learning, 3*(1), 85–97. doi:10.1007/s11412-007-9027-z

Kimmerle, J., Wodzicki, K., & Cress, U. (2008). The social psychology of knowledge management. *Team Performance Management, 14*(7/8), 381–401. doi:10.1108/13527590810912340

Kirschner, P. A., Sweller, J., & Clark, R. E. (2006). Why Minimal Guidance During Instruction Does Not Work: An Analysis of the Failure of Constructivist, Discovery, Problem-Based, Experiential, and Inquiry-Based Teaching. *Educational Psychologist, 41*(2), 75–86. doi:10.1207/s15326985ep4102_1

Kiskina, E. (2008). Subkulturiniu grupiu studijos. Socialiniu grupiu identitetu tyrimu bei studiju pletra [Studies of Subcultures. Development of studies of identity of social groups]. Project Rep. Modulis. ESF/2004/2.5.0-0.3-141/BPD-184/7-306. Kaunas, Lithuania: Vytautas Magnus University.

Klenowski, V. (2002). *Developing Portfolios for Learning and Assessment. Processes and Principles*. London: Routledge.

Klimoski, R., & Mohammed, S. (1994). Team mental model: Construct or metaphor? *Journal of Management, 20*, 403–437. doi:10.1016/0149-2063(94)90021-3

Knabben, F. C. (2009). *FCKeditor - The text editor for Internet*. Retrieved February 1, 2009, from http://www.fckeditor.net/

Knowlton, D. (2001). Promoting Durable Knowledge Construction Through Online Discussion. *Eric Document, 463*, 724.

Knowlton, D. S., Knowlton, H. M., & Davis, C. (2000). The whys and hows of online discussion. *Syllabus: New Directions in Educational Technology, 13*(10), 54–58.

Kock, N. (2004). The Psychobiological model: Toward a new theory of computer-mediated communication based on Darwinian evolution. *Organization Science, 15*(3), 327–348. doi:10.1287/orsc.1040.0071

Koedinger, K. R., & Corbett, A. (2006). Cognitive Tutors, Technology Bringing Learning Science to the Classroom. In Sawyer, R. K. (Ed.), *The Cambridge Handbook of The Learning Sciences* (pp. 61–75). New York: Cambridge University Press.

Koh, G. C., Khoo, H. E., Wong, M. L., & Koh, D. (2008). The Effects of Problem-based Learning During Medical School on Physician Competency: A Systematic Review. [CMAJ]. *Canadian Medical Association Journal, 178*(1). doi:10.1503/cmaj.070565

Kohli, R., & Kettinger, W. J. (2004). Informating the Clan: Controlling Physicians' Costs and Outcomes. *Management Information Systems Quarterly, 28*(3), 363–394.

Kollar, I., Fischer, F., & Hesse, F. W. (2006). Collaboration scripts – A conceptual analysis. *Educational Psychology Review, 18*(2), 159–185. doi:10.1007/s10648-006-9007-2

Koohang, A., & Harman, K. (2005). Open source: A metaphor for e-learning. *Informing Science: The International Journal of an Emerging Transdiscipline, 8,* 75–86.

Kosonen, K., Ilomäki, L., & Lakkala, M. (2008). Conceptual mapping as a form of trialogical learning intervention. In G. Kanselaar, J. van Merriënboer, P. Kirschner, & T. de Jong (Eds.), *International Perspectives in the Learning Sciences: Cre8ing a Learning World, Proceedings of the Eighth International Conference for the Learning Sciences (ICLS 2008)* (Vol. 3, pp. 260-262). Utrecht, The Netherlands: ICLS.

Kozma, R. B. (2003). Technology and classroom practices: An international study. *Journal of Research on Technology in Education, 36,* 1–14.

Kraut, R. E., Fish, R. S., Root, R. W., & Chalfonte, B. L. (Eds.). (1990). *Informal communication in organizations: Form, function, and technology.* Beverly Hills, CA: Sage Publications.

Kreijns, K., Kirschner, P. A., & Jochems, W. (2003). Identifying the pitfalls of social interaction in computer-supported collaborative learning environments: A review of the research. *Computers in Human Behavior, 19*(3), 335–353. doi:10.1016/S0747-5632(02)00057-2

Krowne, A., & Bazaz, A. (2004). Authority Models for Collaborative Authoring. In *Proceedings of the 37th Hawaii International Conference on System Sciences.*

Kuhrt, N. (2002). *Korrekturzeichen nach DIN 16511.* Grundlagen und Anwendung. Retrieved February 29, 2008, from http://www.ewrite.de/mg/downloads/data/pdf/ewrite/ korrekturzeichen.pdf

Kurabayashi, N., Yamazaki, T., Yuasa, T., & Hasuike, K. (2002). Proactive Information Supply for Activating Conversational Interaction in Virtual Communities. In *the IEEE International Workshop on Knowledge Media Networking (KMN'02)* (pp.167-170).

Kurbel, K. (2001). Virtuality on the Students and on the Teachers Sides: A Multimedia and Internet Based International Master Program (ICEF). In *Proc. on the 7th International Conference on Technology Supported Learning and Training* (pp. 133-136).

Kuwabara, K., Watanabe, T., Ohguro, T., Itoh, Y., & Maeda, Y. (2002). Connectedness oriented communication: Fostering a sense of connectedness to augment social relationships. *Information Processing Society of Japan Journal, 43*(11), 3270–3279.

Kvedaravicius, J. (2006). Organizaciju vystymosi vadyba [Management of organisational development]. Kaunas, Lithuania: Vytauto Didziojo universiteto leidykla.

Lajoie, S. P., Lavigne, N. C., Guerrera, C., & Munsie, S. (2001). Constructing Knowledge in the Context of BioWorld. *Instructional Science, 29*(2), 155–186. doi:10.1023/A:1003996000775

Lakkala, M., Ilomäki, L., & Palonen, T. (2007). Implementing virtual, collaborative inquiry practices in a middle school context. *Behaviour & Information Technology, 26*(1), 37–53. doi:10.1080/01449290600811529

Lakkala, M., Lallimo, J., & Hakkarainen, K. (2005). Teachers' pedagogical designs for technology-supported collective inquiry: A national case study. *Computers & Education, 45*(3), 337–356. doi:10.1016/j.compedu.2005.04.010

Lakkala, M., Muukkonen, H., Paavola, S., & Hakkarainen, K. (2008). Designing pedagogical infrastructures in university courses for technology-enhanced collaborative inquiry. *Research and Practice in Technology Enhanced Learning, 3*(1), 33–64. doi:10.1142/S1793206808000446

Lakkala, S., Kosonen, K., Bauters, M., & Rämö, E. (2008). *Cross-fertilization of collaborative design practices between an educational institution and workplaces.* Poster presented at the 4th EARLI SIG 14 Learning and Professional Development Conference. University of Jyväskylä, Jyväskylä, Finland. Retrieved July 5, 2009, from http://www.kp-lab.org/project-overview/dissemination-material/kp-lab-posters/Lakkala_EARLI-Sig-14_2008.pdf

Lamb, B. (2004, September/October). Wide open spaces: Wikis, ready or not. *EDUCASE Review, 39*(5), 36-48. Retrieved November 2006, from http://www.educase.edu/pub/er/erm04/erm0452.asp?BHEP=1

Landauer, C., & Bellman, K. L. (1999). Computational Embodiment: Agents as Constructed Complex Systems. In Dautenhahn, K. (Ed.), *Human Cognition and Social Agent Technology.* New York: Benjamins.

Landauer, T. K., & Dumais, S. T. (1997). A Solution to Plato's Problem: The Latent Semantic Analysis Theory of Acquisition, Induction, and Representation of Knowledge. *Psychological Review, 104*(2), 211–240. doi:10.1037/0033-295X.104.2.211

Landauer, T. K., Foltz, P. W., & Laham, D. (1998). An Introduction to Latent Semantic Analysis. *Discourse Processes, 25,* 259–284. doi:10.1080/01638539809545028

Larson, J. R. Jr, & Harmon, V. M. (2007). Recalling shared vs. unshared information mentioned during group discussion: Toward understanding differential repetition rates. *Group Processes & Intergroup Relations, 10,* 311–322. doi:10.1177/1368430207078692

Larson, J. R. Jr, Christensen, C., Franz, T. M., & Abbott, A. S. (1998). Diagnosing groups: The pooling, management, and impact of shared and unshared case information in team-based medical decision making. *Journal of Personality and Social Psychology, 75,* 93–108. doi:10.1037/0022-3514.75.1.93

Larson, J. R. Jr. (1997). Modeling the entry of shared and unshared information into group discussion: A review and BASIC language computer program. *Small Group Research, 28,* 454–479. doi:10.1177/1046496497283007

Larson, J. R. Jr. (2007). Deep diversity and strong synergy: Modeling the impact of variability in members' problem-solving strategies on group problem-solving performance. *Small Group Research, 38,* 413–436. doi:10.1177/1046496407301972

Laurillard, D. (2002, January/February). Rethinking Teaching for the Knowledge Society. *EDUCAUSE Review, 37*(1), 16–25.

Lave, J. (1988). *Cognition in Practice.* Cambridge, UK: Cambridge University Press. doi:10.1017/CBO9780511609268

Lave, J., & Wenger, E. (1991). *Situated Learning: Legitimate Peripheral Participation.* Cambridge, UK: Cambridge University Press.

Lavooy, M., & Newlin, M. (2003). Computer mediated communication: online instruction and interactivity. *Journal of Interactive Learning Research, 14*(9), 157.

Lazar, J. R., Tsao, R., & Preece, J. (1999). One foot in cyberspace and the other on the ground: A case study of analysis and design issues in a hybrid virtual and physical community. *Web Net Journal: Internet Technologies. Applications and Issues, 1*(3), 49–57.

Lazar, J., & Preece, J. (1999). *Implementing service learning in an online communities course.* Paper presented at the 1999 Conference of the International Association for Information Management.

Lee, E. Y. C., Chan, C. K. K., & van Aalst, J. (2006). Students assessing their own collaborative knowledge building. *International Journal of Computer-Supported Collaborative Learning, 1*(2), 277–307. doi:10.1007/s11412-006-8997-6

Lee, O. (2002). Cultural differences in email use of virtual teams a critical social theory perspective. *Cyberpsychology & Behavior, 5*(3), 227–232. doi:10.1089/109493102760147222

Lee, Y., & Chong, Q. (2003, January). Multi-agent systems support for Community-Based Learning Interacting with Computers. *Interacting with Computers*, *15*(1), 33–55. doi:10.1016/S0953-5438(02)00057-7

Leidner, D. E., & Fuller, M. (1997). Improving student learning of conceptual information: GSS-supported collaborative learning vs. individual constructive learning. *Decision Support Systems*, *20*, 149–163. doi:10.1016/S0167-9236(97)00004-3

Leidner, D. E., & Jarvenpaa, S. (1995). The use of information technology to enhance management school education: a theoretical view. *Management Information Systems Quarterly*, *19*(3), 265–291. doi:10.2307/249596

Lensegrav, P., & Pearce, K. (2002). *The responsiveness of elementary students to the use of video conferencing*. Retrieved from http://www.bhsu.edu/education/edfaculty/lq>earce/Responsiveness%20ofl'ib20Elementarv%20Students%20 to%20Video%20Conferencing.htm

Lester, S., & Costley, C. (2009). *Work-based learning at higher education level: value, practice and critique*. Retrieved June 2, 2009 from http://www.sld.demon.co.uk

Leuf, B., & Cunningham, W. (2001). *The Wiki way: Quick collaboration of the Web*. Reading, MA: Addison-Wesley Professional.

Levin, J. A., & Kareev, Y. (1980). *Personal computers and education: The challenge to schools. Technical report no. CHIP 98*. La Jolla, CA: Center for Human Information Processing, University of California at San Diego.

Levine, J. M., Resnick, L. B., & Higgins, E. T. (1993). Social foundations of cognition. *Annual Review of Psychology*, *44*, 585–612. doi:10.1146/annurev.ps.44.020193.003101

Lewis, C. C., & Abdul-Hamid, H. (2006). Implementing Effective Online Teaching Practices: Voices of Exemplary Faculty. *Innovative Higher Education*, *31*(2), 83–98. doi:10.1007/s10755-006-9010-z

Lieberman, H. (1997). Autonomous Interface Agents. CHI 97 Papers (pp. 22-27).

Lim, C. P., & Tan, S. C. (2001). Online discussion boards for focus group interviews: An exploratory study. *Journal of Educational Enquiry*, *2*(1), 50–60.

Lin, F., & Poon, L. (2004). *Integrating Web Services and Agent Technology for E-learning Course Content Maintenance* (pp. 848–856). IEA/AIE.

Linde, G. d. (2005). The Perception of Business Students At PUCMM Of The Use Of Collaborative Learning Using The BSCW As A Tool. In *ITHET 6th Annual International Conference, Session F2D* (pp. 10-15). Juan Dolio, Dominican Republic: IEEE.

Lindemann, E. (1995). *A Rhetoric for Writing Teachers*. New York: Oxford University Press.

Lindgren, R., Henfridsson, O., & Schultze, U. (2004). Design principles for competence management systems: A synthesis of an action research study. *Management Information Systems Quarterly*, *28*(3), 435–472.

Lipponen, L., & Lallimo, J. (2004). From collaborative technology to collaborative use of technology: Designing learning oriented infrastructures. *Educational Media International*, *41*(2), 111–116. doi:10.1080/09523980410001678566

Liu, M., Williams, D., & Pedersen, S. (2002). Alien Rescue: A Problem-Based Hypermedia Learning Environment for Middle School Science. *Journal of Educational Technology Systems*, *30*(3). doi:10.2190/X531-D6KE-NXVY-N6RE

Long, D. A., & Perkins, D. D. (2003). Confirmatory factor analysis of the sense of community index and development of a brief SCI. *Journal of Community Psychology*, *31*, 279–296. doi:10.1002/jcop.10046

Losee, J. (1993). *A Historical Introduction of the Philosophy of Science*. Oxford, UK: OUP.

Low, S. M. (2005). Reduction of Teacher Workload in a Formative Assessment Environment through use of Online Technology. *ITHET 6th Annual International Conference, Proceedings, F4A (18-21)*. Juan Dolio, Dominican Republic: IEEE

Lowe, C., & Williams, T. (2004). *Moving to the Public: Weblogs in the Writing Classroom.* Retrieved June 11, 2009, from http://blog.lib.umn.edu/blogosphere/moving_to_the_public.htm

Lowyck, J., & Pöysä, J. (2001). Design of collaborative learning environments. *Computers in Human Behavior, 17*(5-6), 507–516. doi:10.1016/S0747-5632(01)00017-6

Lucas, G. (Producer & Director). (1977). *Star Wars* [Motion picture]. United States: Twentieth Century Fox.

Luppicini, R. (2003). Categories of virtual learning communities for educational design. *The Quarterly Review of Distance Education, 4*(4), 409–416.

Luzi, D., Ricci, F. L., Fazi, P., & Vignetti, M. (2003). The Clinical Trial Collaborative Writing: A New Functionality of the WITH System. *IADIS International Conference e-Society 2003, (799-803).* IADIS.

MacDorman, K. F. (2005). Androids as an experimental apparatus: Why is there an uncanny valley and can we exploit it? In Cognitive Science 2005 Workshop: Toward Social Mechanisms of Android Science, (pp.106-118).

Mackey, T. P., & Ho, J. (2008). Exploring the relationships between Web usability and students' perceived learning in Web-based multimedia (WBMM) tutorials. *Computers & Education, 50*(1), 386–409. doi:10.1016/j.compedu.2006.08.006

Mader, S. (2006). *Using Wiki in education, the book.* Retrieved November 2006, from http://www.wikiineducation.com.

Madjidi, F., Hughes, H., Johnson, R. & Cary, K. (1999). *Virtual learning environments.*

Maehr, M. L., & Braskamp, L. A. (1986). The motivation factor: A theory of personal investment. Lexington, MA: Lexington.

Maes, P. (1987). *Computational Reflection. MIT Technical Reports, 87-2.* Cambridge, MA: MIT AI Laboratory.

Maier, T. (2003). Unis wollen Internet-Abschreibern an den Kragen. *Heise Online News.* Retrieved February 29, 2008, from http://www.heise.de/newsticker/meldung/34467

Mäkitalo, K., Weinberger, A., Häkkinen, P., Järvelä, S., & Fischer, F. (2005). Epistemic Cooperation Scripts in Online Learning Environments: Fostering Learning by Reducing Uncertainty in Discourse? *Computers in Human Behavior, 21*(4), 603–622. doi:10.1016/j.chb.2004.10.033

Malone, T., & Lepper, M. (1987). Making learning fun: A taxonomy of intrinsic motivation for learning. In Snow, R. E., & Farr, M. J. (Eds.), *Aptitude, learning, and instruction.* Hillsdale, NJ: Lawrence Earlbaum.

Mamardashvili, M. K. (1958). Procesy analiza i sinteza [Processes of analysis and synthesis]. *Voprosy Filosofii, 2.*

Mamdani, A., Pitt, J., & Stathis, K. (1999). Connected Communities from the Standpoint of Multi-agent Systems. *New Generation Computing, 17*(4), 381–393. doi:10.1007/BF03037244

Mandl, H., & Krause, U.-M. (2001). *Lernkompetenz für die Wissensgesellschaft. Forschungsbericht, 145.* München: Ludwig-Maximilians-Universität, Lehrstuhl für Empirische Pädagogik und Pädagogische Psychologie.

Mandl, H., Gruber, H., & Renkl, A. (2002). Situiertes Lernen in multimedialen Lernumgebungen. [Situated Learning in multi-media learning environments] In Issing, L. J., & Klimsa, P. (Eds.), *Information und Lernen mit Multimedia und Internet. Lehrbuch für Studium und Praxis* (pp. 139–148). Weinheim, Germany: Beltz, Psychologische Verlagsunion. [Information and learning with multi-media and internet. Teaching book for studies and practice]

Maret, P., & Calmet, J. (2009). Agent-based knowledge communities. *International Journal of Computer Science and Applications, 6*(2), 1–18.

Markel, S. (2001). Technology and education online discussion forum: it's in the response. *Online Journal of Distance Learning Administration, 4*(2). Retrieved November 17, 2008, from http://www.westga.edu.ezproxy1.lib.asu.edu/%26sim;distance/ojdla/summer42/marke142.html

Markman, E. (1977). Realizing that you don't understand: Elementary school children's awareness of inconsistencies. *Child Development, 48,* 986–992. doi:10.1111/j.1467-8624.1977.tb01257.x

Markus, M. L., Majchrzak, A., & Gasser, L. (2002). A design theory for systems that support emergent knowledge processes. *Management Information Systems Quarterly, 26*(3), 179–212.

Martin, J., & Siehl, C. (1983, August). Organizational culture and counterculture: an uneasy symbiosis. *Organizational Dynamics,* 52–64. doi:10.1016/0090-2616(83)90033-5

Marx, R. W., Blumenfeld, P. C., Krajcik, J. S., & Soloway, E. (1997). Enacting project-based science. *The Elementary School Journal, 97,* 341–358. doi:10.1086/461870

Masoodian, M., Bouamrane, M.-M., Luz, S., & King, K. (2005). Recoled: A Group-Aware Collaborative Text Editor for Capturing Document History. In *IADIS International Conference on WWW/Internet 2005* (pp. 323-330).

Massey, C. M., & Gelman, R. (1988). Preschooler's ability to decide whether a photographed unfamiliar object can move itself. *Developmental Psychology, 24,* 307–317. doi:10.1037/0012-1649.24.3.307

Mathieu, J., Goodwin, G. F., Heffner, T. S., Salas, E., & Cannon-Bowers, J. A. (2000). The influence of shared mental models on team process and performance. *The Journal of Applied Psychology, 85*(2), 273–283. doi:10.1037/0021-9010.85.2.273

Matsumoto, D. (2007, December). Culture, Context, and Behavior. *Journal of Personality, 75*(6), 1285–1320. doi:10.1111/j.1467-6494.2007.00476.x

Mayer, R. E., & Anderson, A. B. (1992). The instructive animation: Helping students build connections between words and pictures in multimedia learning. *Journal of Educational Psychology, 84,* 444–452. doi:10.1037/0022-0663.84.4.444

Mazzolini, M., & Maddison, S. (2007). When to jump in: the role of the instructor in online discussion forums. *Computers & Education, 49*(2), 193–213. doi:10.1016/j.compedu.2005.06.011

McCloud, S. (1993). *Understanding Comics.* Amherst, MA: Kitchen Sink Press.

McGrath, J. E., & Hollingshead, A. B. (1994). *Groups interacting with technology.* Thousand Oaks: Sage Publications.

Mcintyre, R. M., & Salas, E. (1995). Measuring and managing for team performance: Emerging principles from complex environments. In Guzzo, R., & Salas, E. (Eds.), *Team effectiveness and decision making in organizations* (pp. 149–203). San Francisco: Jossey-Bass.

McMillan, D. W. (1996). Sense of community. *Journal of Community Psychology, 24*(4), 315–325. doi:10.1002/(SICI)1520-6629(199610)24:4<315::AID-JCOP2>3.0.CO;2-T

McMillan, D. W., & Chavis, D. M. (1986). Sense of community: A definition and theory. *Journal of Community Psychology, 14*(1), 6–23. doi:10.1002/1520-6629(198601)14:1<6::AID-JCOP2290140103>3.0.CO;2-I

McNaught, A. (2006). Is Moodle accessible? *Joint Information System Committee, TechDis.* Retrieved July 12, 2008, from http://www.techdis.ac.uk/index.php?p=3_10_6_2

McSweeney, B. (2002). Hofstede's model of national cultural difference and their consequences: A triumph of faith – a failure of analysis. *Human Relations, 55*(1), 89–117.

Mehrabian, A., & Ferris, S. R. (1967). Inference of Attitude from Nonverbal Communication in Two Channels. *Journal of Counseling Psychology, 31,* 248–252.

Meislewitz, G., & Sandera, W. A. (2008). Investigating the Connection between Usability and Learning Outcomes in Online Learning Environments. *Journal of Online Learning and Teaching, 4*(2), 234–242.

Meltzoff, A., & Gopnik, A. (1993). The role of imitation in understanding persons and developing a theory of mind. In Baron-Cohen, S., Tager-Flusberg, H., & Cohen, D. (Eds.), *Understanding other minds, perspectives from autism* (pp. 335–366). Oxford, UK: Oxford University Press.

Menzie, K. A. (2006). *Building online relationships: Relationship marketing and social presence as foundations for a university library blog.* Lawrence, KS: The University of Kansas.

Mergendoller, J. R., Maxwell, N. L., & Bellisimo, Y. (2006). The effectiveness of problem-based instruction: a comparative Study of instructional method and student characteristics. *Interdisciplinary Journal of Problem-based Learning, 1*, 49–69.

Merriënboer, J. J. G., Kirschner, P. A., & Kester, L. (2003). Taking the load off a learner's mind: Instructional design for complex learning. *Educational Psychologist, 38*(1), 5–13. doi:10.1207/S15326985EP3801_2

Mesdag, M. V. (2000). Culture-sensitive adaptation or global standardization - the duration of usage hypothesis. *International Marketing Review, 17*, 74–84. doi:10.1108/02651330010314722

Miller, N., Brewer, M. B., & Edwards, K. (1985). Cooperative interaction in desegregated settings: A laboratory analogue. *The Journal of Social Issues, 41*, 63–79.

Milne, S., Shiu, E., & Cook, J. (1996). Development of a model of user attributes and its implementation within an adaptive tutoring system. *User Modeling and User-Adapted Interaction, 6*(4), 303–335. doi:10.1007/BF00213186

Mitchell, R. W. (2002). Imaginative animals, pretending children. In Mitchell, R. W. (Ed.), *Pretending and Imagination in Animals and Children* (pp. 3–22). Cambridge, UK: Cambridge University Press. doi:10.1017/CBO9780511542282.003

Moodle Accessibility Specifications. (2007, June 18). *Development: Moodle Accessibility Specifiations.* Retrieved May 18, 2009, from http://docs.moodle.org/en/ Development:Moodle_Accessibility_Specification

Moreland, R. L., & Levine, J. M. (2008). Building bridges to improve theory and research on small groups. In Salas, E., Burke, C. S., & Goodwin, G. F. (Eds.), *Team effectiveness in complex organizations and systems: Cross-disciplinary perspectives and approaches* (pp. 17–38). San Francisco: Jossey-Bass.

Morey, C., Maybury, M., & Thuraisingham, B. (Eds.). (2002). *Knowledge Management: Classic and Contemporary Works.* Cambridge, MA: MIT Press.

Morgan, B. B., Jr., Glickman, A. S., Woodard, E. A., Blaiwes, A. S., & Salas, E. (1986). *Measurement of team behaviors in a Navy environment* (NTSC Tech. Rep. No. 86-014). Orlando, FL: Naval Training Systems Center.

Mori, M. (1970). Bukimi no tani [The Uncanny Valley]. (K. F. MacDorman & T. Minato, Trans.). *Energy, 7*(4), 33–35.

Mory, E. H. (1995, February). *A new perspective on instructional feedback: From objectivism to constructivism.* Paper presented at the annual meeting of the Association for Educational Communications and Technology, Anaheim, CA.

Mory, E. H. (2004). Feedback Research Revisited. In Jonassen, D. H. (Ed.), *Handbook of Research on Educational Communications and Technology* (pp. 745–783). Mahwah, NJ: Lawrence Erlbaum.

Muir, H. (2009). Emotional robots: Will we love them or hate them? *New Scientist, 2715.* Retrieved July 1, 2009, from http://www.newscientist.com/article/mg20327151.400-emotional-robots-will-we-love-them-or-hate-them.html

Mullen, B., Brown, R., & Smith, C. (1992). Ingroup bias as a function of salience, relevance, and status: An integration. *European Journal of Social Psychology, 22*, 103–122. doi:10.1002/ejsp.2420220202

Mumford, E. (2001). Advice for an Action Researcher. *Information Technology & People, 14*(1), 12–27. doi:10.1108/09593840110384753

Munkes, J., & Diehl, M. (2003). Matching or Competition? Performance Comparison Processes in an Idea Generation Task. *Group Processes & Intergroup Relations, 6*(3), 305–320. doi:10.1177/13684302030063006

Muukkonen, H., & Lakkala, M. (2009). Exploring metaskills of knowledge-creating inquiry in higher education. *International Journal of Computer-Supported Collaborative Learning, 4*(2), 187–211. doi:10.1007/s11412-009-9063-y

Muukkonen, H., Lakkala, M., & Hakkarainen, K. (2005). Technology-mediation and tutoring: How do they shape progressive inquiry discourse? *Journal of the Learning Sciences, 14*(4), 527–565. doi:10.1207/s15327809jls1404_3

Muukkonen, H., Lakkala, M., & Paavola, S. (in press). Promoting knowledge creation and object-oriented inquiry in university courses. In S. Ludvigsen, A. Lund, & R. Säljö (Eds.), Learning in social practices. ICT and new artifacts - transformation of social and cultural practices. Routledge.

Myers, E. (2006). The three types of blogs: Producers, reviewers and pointers. *ICE: Improving customer experience.* Retrieved May 21, 2006, from http://www.egmstrategy.com/ice/direct_link.cfm?bid=F1C806E8-A81C-4D15-58A7EB5FA7EFF8C6

Nagasundaram, M. (2007). E-Collaboration through blogging. In Kock, N. (Ed.), *Encyclopedia of E-Collaboration* (pp. 198–203). Hershey, PA: IGI Global.

National College for School Leadership. (2006). *Learning Conversations in Learning Networks.* Cranfield, UK: NCSL.

Newell, A., & Simon, H. A. (1972). *Human problem solving.* Englewood Cliffs, NJ: Prentice Hall.

Ng-Thow-Hing, V., Thórisson, K. R., Sarvadevabhatla, R. K., & Wormer, J. (2009). Cognitive Map Architecture: Facilitation of Human-Robot Interaction in Humanoid Robots. *IEEE Robotics & Automation Magazine, 1*(16), 55–66. doi:10.1109/MRA.2008.931634

Nielsen, J. (2003). Usability 101: Introduction to usability. *Jakob Nielsen's Alertbox.* Retrieved January 20, 2009, from http://www.useit.com/alertbox/20030825.html

Nielson, J. (2000). *Designing Web Usability: The Practice of Simplicity.* Indianapolis: New Riders Publishing.

Nonnecke, B., & Preece, J. (2000). Lurker demographics: Counting the silent. In *Proceedings of Special Interest Group on Computer-Human Interactions (SIGCHI) Conference* (pp. 73-80). New York: ACM Press.

Norman, D. A. (1988). *The psychology of everyday things.* New York: Basic Books.

Norman, D. A. (1999). Affordance, Conventions, and Design. *Interactions (New York, N.Y.), 6*, 38–42. doi:10.1145/301153.301168

Nowak, K. L., & Biocca, F. (2003). The Effect of the agency and anthropomorphism on users' sense of telepresence, copresence, and social presence in virtual environments. *Presence (Cambridge, Mass.), 12*(5), 481–494. doi:10.1162/105474603322761289

Nye, J. L., & Brower, A. M. (Eds.). (1996). *What's social about social cognition? Research on Socially Shared Cognition in Small Groups.* Thousand Oaks, CA: Sage.

O'Donnell, A. M. (1999). Structuring dyadic interaction through scripted cooperation. In O'Donnell, A. M., & King, A. (Eds.), *Cognitive Perspectives on Peer Learning* (pp. 179–196). Mahwah, NJ: Erlbaum.

O'Donnell, A. M., & Dansereau, D. F. (1992). Scripted cooperation in student dyads: A method for analyzing and enhancing academic learning and performance. In Hertz-Lazarowitz, R., & Miller, N. (Eds.), *Interactions in cooperative groups: Theoretical anatomy of group learning* (pp. 120–141). Cambridge, MA: Cambridge University Press.

Ojala, M. (2004). *Weaving weblogs into knowledge sharing and dissemination.* Nord I&D, Knowledge and Change. Retrieved October 13, 2006, from http://www2.db.dk/NIOD/ojala.pdf

Okita, S. Y., & Schwartz, D. L. (2006). When Observation Beats Doing: Learning by Teaching. In S. Barab, K. Hay & D. Hickey (Eds.), *Seventh International Conference of the Learning Sciences* (Vol. 1, pp. 509-516). Mahwah, NJ: Erlbaum.

Okita, S. Y., & Schwartz, D. L. (2006). Young Children's Understanding of Animacy and Entertainment Robots. [IJHR]. *International Journal of Humanoid Robotics, 3*(3), 393–412. doi:10.1142/S0219843606000795

Okita, S. Y., Bailenson, J., & Schwartz, D. L. (2008). Mere Belief of Social Action Improves Complex Learning. In S. Barab, K. Hay, & D. Hickey (Eds.), *Proceedings of the 8th International Conference for the Learning Sciences,* Utrecht, The Netherlands. New Jersey: Lawrence Erlbaum Associates.

Okita, S. Y., Ng-Thow-Hing, V., & Sarvadevabhatla, R. K. (2009). Learning Together: ASIMO Developing an Interactive Learning Partnership with Children. In *Proceedings of the 18th IEEE International Symposium on Robot and Human Interactive Communication* (RO-MAN), Toyama, Japan.

Olaniran, B. (2007a). Challenges to implementing e-learning and lesser developed countries. In Edmundson, A. L. (Ed.), *Globalized e-learning cultural challenges* (pp. 18–34). Hershey, PA: Idea Group, Inc.

Olaniran, B. A. (1994). Group performance and computer-mediated communication. *Management Communication Quarterly, 7,* 256–281. doi:10.1177/0893318994007003002

Olaniran, B. A. (2001). The effects of computer-mediated communication on transculturalism. In Milhouse, V., Asante, M., & Nwosu, P. (Eds.), *Transcultural Realities* (pp. 83–105). Thousand Oaks, CA: Sage.

Olaniran, B. A. (2004). Computer-Mediated Communication in Cross-Cultural Virtual Groups. In Chen, G. M., & Starosta, W. J. (Eds.), *Dialogue among Diversities* (pp. 142–166). Washington, DC: National Communication Association.

Olaniran, B. A. (2006). Applying synchronous computer-mediated communication into course design: Some considerations and practical guides. *Campus-Wide Information Systems. The International Journal of Information & Learning Technology, 23*(3), 210–220.

Olaniran, B. A. (2007b). Culture and communication challenges in virtual workspaces. In St-Amant, K. (Ed.), *Linguistic and cultural online communication issues in the global age* (pp. 79–92). Hershey, PA: Information Science Reference.

Olaniran, B. A. (2008). Human Computer Interaction & Best Mix of E-interactions and Face-to-Face in Educational Settings. In Kelsey, S., & St-Amant, K. (Eds.), *Handbook of Research on Computer Mediated Communication*. Hershey, PA: IGI Global.

Olaniran, B. A., & Agnello, M. F. (2008). Globalization, Educational Hegemony, and Higher Education. *Journal of Multicultural Educational Technology, 2*(2), 68–86. doi:10.1108/17504970810883351

Olsen, D. R. (1998). *Developing User Interfaces* (1st ed.). San Francisco: Morgan Kaufmann.

Oravec, J. (2002). Bookmarking the world: Weblog applications in education. *Journal of Adolescent & Adult Literacy, 45*(7), 616–621.

Osguthorpe, R. T., & Graham, C. R. (2003). Blended Learning Environments: Definitions and Directions. *Quarterly Review of Distance Education, 4*(3), 227-33. Retrieved May 18, 2005, from http://web2.epnet.com

Oshima, J. (1997). Students' construction of scientific explanations in a collaborative hyper-media learning environment. In Hall, N. M. R., & Enyedy, N. (Eds.), *Computer Support for Collaborative Learning '97*. Toronto.

Paavola, S., & Hakkarainen, K. (2005). The knowledge creation metaphor – An emergent epistemological approach to learning. *Science & Education, 14,* 535–557. doi:10.1007/s11191-004-5157-0

Paavola, S., & Hakkarainen, K. (2009). From meaning making to joint construction of knowledge practices and artifacts – A trialogical approach to CSCL. In C. O'Malley, D. Suthers, P. Reimann, & A. Dimitracopoulou (Eds.), *Computer Supported Collaborative Learning Practices: CSCL2009 Conference Proceedings.* (pp. 83-92). Rhodes, Greece: International Society of the Learning Sciences (ISLS).

Paavola, S., Lipponen, L., & Hakkarainen, K. (2002). Epistemological foundations for CSCL: A comparison of three models of innovative knowledge communities. In Stahl, G. (Ed.), *Computer support for collaborative learning: Foundations for a CSCL community* (pp. 24–32). Hillsdale, NY: Erlbaum.

Palincsar, A. S., & Brown, A. L. (1984). Reciprocal teaching of comprehension-fostering and comprehension-monitoring activities. *Cognition and Instruction, 2,* 117–175.

Palincsar, A. S., & Herrenkohl, L. R. (2002). Designing collaborative learning contexts. *Theory into Practice, 41*(1), 26–32. doi:10.1207/s15430421tip4101_5

Panitz, T. (1997). *Collaborative Versus Cooperative Learning-A Comparison of the Two Concepts Which Will*

Help Us Understand the Underlying Nature of Interactive Learning. Retrieved January 29, 2009, from http://capecod.net/tpanitz/tedsarticles/coopdefinition.htm

Parsons, T. (1998). *Sistema sovremennyh obshesv* [System of contemporary societies]. (L.A. Sedova & A. D. Kovaliova, Trans.). Moskow, Rossyia: Аспект Пресс.

Pea, R. (2002). Learning Science Through Collaborative Visualization over the Internet. *Nobel Symposium (NS 120), Virtual Museums and Public Understanding of Science and Culture,* May 26-29, 2002, Stockholm, Sweden.

Pea, R. (2004). The social and technological dimensions of scaffolding and related theoretical concepts for learning, education and human activity. *Journal of the Learning Sciences, 13*(3), 423–451. doi:10.1207/s15327809jls1303_6

Perkins, A. (1986). *Knowledge as design.* Hillsdale, NJ: Erlbaum.

Perschbach, W. J. (2006). *Blogging: An inquiry into the efficacy of a web-based technology for student reflection in community college computer science programs.* Dissertation, Dissertation Abstracts International. (3206012)

Petter, C., & Helling, K. (2008). Designing ICT-based learning scenarios for special target groups. Meeting senior learners needs. In A. Lingau, A. Martens, & A. Harrer (Eds.), *Proceedings of the Workshop on Inclusive E-Learning: Special Needs and Special Solutions (IEL-2008),* Maastricht, The Netherlands. Retrieved, June 4, 2009, from http://sunsite.informatik.rwth-aachen.de/Publications/CEUR-WS/Vol-387/

Piaget, J. (1954). *The construction of reality in the child.* New York: Basic books. doi:10.1037/11168-000

Polanyi, M. (1966). *The Tacit Dimension.* New York: Doubleday.

Preece, J. (2000). *Online communities: Designing usability, supporting sociability.* New York: John Wiley & Sons.

Preece, J., Nonnecke, B., & Andrews, D. (2004). The top 5 reasons for lurking: Improving community experiences for everyone. *Special Issue of Computers in Human Behavior: An Interdisciplinary Perspective, 20*(2).

Pressey, S. L. (1932). A Third and Fourth Contribution Toward the Coming Industrial Revolution in Education. *School and Society, 36,* 934.

Puntambekar, S. (1996) *Investigating the effect of a computer tool on students' metacognitive processes.* Unpublished doctoral dissertation, School of Cognitive and computing sciences, University of Sussex, UK.

Puntambekar, S., & Kolodner, J. L. (2005). Toward implementing distributed scaffolding: Helping students learn science from design. *Journal of Research in Science Teaching, 42*(2), 185–217. doi:10.1002/tea.20048

Putnam, R. D. (2000). *Bowling Alone. The collapse and revival of American community.* New York: Simon and Schuster.

Qiu, L. (2005). *A web-based architecture and incremental authoring model for interactive learning environments for diagnostic reasoning.* Unpublished doctoral dissertation, Northwestern University, Evanston.

Qiu, L., & Riesbeck, C. K. (2008). Human-in-the-loop: A Feedback-driven Model for Authoring Knowledge-based Interactive Learning Environments. *Journal of Educational Computing Research, 38*(4), 469–509. doi:10.2190/EC.38.4.e

Radjou, N., Schadler, T., Ciardelli, A. J., & Smith, S. (1999). Collaboration Beyond Email. *The Forrester Report.*

Raikundalia, G. K., & Zhang, H. L. (2005). Newly-discovered Group Awareness Mechanisms for Supporting Real-time Collaborative Authoring. In M. Billinghurst & A. Cockburn (Hrsg.), *6th Australasian User Interface Conference (AUIC2005)* (Vol. 40, pp. 127-136). Newcastle: Australian Computer Society, Inc.

Ramirez, E. (2002). *Reading, Information Literacy, and Information Culture* [White Paper]. Prague, The Czech Republic. Retrieved August 18, 2008, from http://www.nclis.gov/libinter/infolitconf&meet/papers/rarnirez-fullpaper.pdf

Reeve, F., & Gallacher, J. (2000). *Researching the implementation of work-based learning within higher education: questioning collusion and resistance.* Paper presented at the AERC, Vancouver, Canada.

Reeves, B., & Nass, C. (1996). *The media equation: How people treat computers, television, and new media like real people and places.* Cambridge, UK: Cambridge University Press.

Reid, E. M. (1991). Electropolis: Communication and Community on Internet Relay Chat. *Intertek, 3*(3), 7–15.

Reinmann, G. (2005). *Blended Learning in der Lehrerbildung. Grundlagen für die Konzeption innovativer Lernumgebungen* [Blended Learning in Teacher Education. Basics for the Conception of Innovative Larning Environments]. Lengerich, Germany: Pabst.

Reiserer, M., & Mandl, H. (2001). *Individuelle Bedingungen lebensbegleitenden Lernens. (Forschungsbericht Nr. 136)* [Individual Requierements for Lifelong Learning (Research Report No. 136)]. München, Germany: Ludwig-Maximilians-Universität, Lehrstuhl für Empirische Pädagogik und Pädagogische Psychologie.

Rentroia-Bonito, M. A., & Pires, J. A. (2004). Toward Predictive Models for E-Learning: What Have We Learned So Far? In C. Ghaoui (Ed.), *E-Education Applications: Human Factors and Innovative Approaches* (pp. 441-450). Hershey, PA: Idea Group Publishing. Retrieved May 13, 2005, from http://proquestcombo. safaribooksonline.com/JVXSL

Resnick, L. B. (1987). *Education and learning to think.* Washington, DC: National Academy Press.

Resnick, L., Levine, J., & Teasley, S. (Eds.). (1991). *Perspectives on socially shared cognition.* Washington, DC: American Psychological Association. doi:10.1037/10096-000

Rettie, R. M. (2003a). *A comparison of four new communication technologies.* Paper presented at the HCI International Conference on Human-Computer Interaction, New Jersey.

Rettie, R. M. (2003b). *Connectedness, awareness and social presence.* Paper presented at the 6th International Presence Workshop, Aalborg, Denmark.

Ricard, V. B. (1993). *Developing Intercultural Communication skills.* Malabar, FL: Krieger Publishing Company.

Rice, F. (2006). Introducing the Office (2007). Open XML File Formats. *MSDN, Microsoft Corporation.* Retrieved February 29, 2008, from http://msdn2.microsoft.com/en-us/library/aa338205.aspx

Rice, R. (1993). Media Appropriateness; using social presence theory to compare traditional and new organizational media. *Human Communication Research, 19*(4), 451–484. doi:10.1111/j.1468-2958.1993.tb00309.x

Richards, C., & Nair, G. (2007). 21st century knowledge-building in the Asia Pacific: Towards a multidisciplinary framework for linking ICT-based social and personal contexts of education and development. *The Electronic Journal on Information Systems in Developing Countries, 32*(7), 1–11.

Ridings, C. M., Gefen, D., & Arinze, B. (2002). Some antecedents and effects of trust in virtual communities. *The Journal of Strategic Information Systems,* (11): 271–295. doi:10.1016/S0963-8687(02)00021-5

Risku, H., & Pircher, R. (2005). Facilitating knowledge construction by ICT: Beyond things that make us dumb. In *Proceedings of the 20th International Symposium on Human Factors in Telecommunication,* Sophia-Antipolis, France.

Riva, G., Bacchetta, M., Baruffi, M., Rinaldi, S., & Molinari, E. (1999). Virtual reality based experiential cognitive treatment of anorexia nervosa. *Journal of Behavior Therapy and Experimental Psychiatry, 30*(3), 221–230. doi:10.1016/S0005-7916(99)00018-X

Rizzo, A. A., Difede, J., Rothbaum, B. O., Johnston, S., McLay, R. N., & Reger, G. (2009). VR PTSD Exposure Therapy Results with Active Duty OIF/OEF Combatants. In Westwood, J. D., Westwood, S. W., Haluck, R. S., Hoffman, H. M., Mogel, G. T., & Phillips, R. (Eds.), *Medicine Meets Virtual Reality, 17- Next Med: Design for the Well Being.* Amsterdam: IOS Press.

Roberts, T. (1998). Are newsgroups virtual communities? In The SIGCHI conference on Human factors in computing systems (pp.360–367).

Roese, N. J., & Amir, E. (2009). Human-Android Interaction in the Near and Distant Future. *Perspectives on Psychological Science, 4*(4), 429–434. doi:10.1111/j.1745-6924.2009.01150.x

Roger, R. (2006). *Creating community and gaining readers through newspaper blogs*. Chapel Hill, NC: The University of North Carolina at Chapel Hill.

Romm, C., Pliskin, N., & Clarke, R. (1997). Virtual communities and society: Toward an integrative three phase model. *International Journal of Information Management, 17*(4), 261–270. doi:10.1016/S0268-4012(97)00004-2

Roschelle, J., & Teasley, S. (1995). The construction of shared knowledge in collaborative problem solving. In O'Malley, C. (Ed.), *Computer-supported collaborative learning* (pp. 69–197). Berlin, Germany: Springer Verlag.

Rouse, W. B., & Morris, N. M. (1986). On looking into the black box: Prospects and limits in the search for mental models. *Psychological Bulletin, 100*, 349–363. doi:10.1037/0033-2909.100.3.349

Rubens, W., Dean, P., & Leinonen, T. (2003). *Innovative Technologies for Collaborative Learning*. Helsinki, Finland: Media Lab.

Ryokai, K., Vaucelle, C., & Cassell, J. (2002). *Literacy Learning by Storytelling with a Virtual Peer*. Paper presented at the meeting of Computer Support for Collaborative Learning.

Ryu, H., & Parsons, D. (2009). Designing Learning Activities with Mobile Technologies. In *Handbook Innovative Mobile Learning*. Techniques and Technologies.

Sagotsky, G., Patterson, C. J., & Lepper, M. R. (1978). Training Children's Self-Control: A Field Experiment in Self-Monitoring and Goal-Setting in the Classroom. *Journal of Experimental Child Psychology, 25*, 242–253. doi:10.1016/0022-0965(78)90080-2

Sakagami, Y., Watanabe, R., Aoyama, C., Matsunaga, S., Higaki, N., & Fujimura, K. (2002). The intelligent ASIMO: System overview and integration. In *Proceedings of IEEE/RSJ International Conference on Intelligent Robots and Systems* (pp. 2478–2383).

Sallnäs, E. L. (1999). *Presence in multimodal interfaces*. Paper presented at the Second International Workshop on Presence, Colchester, UK.

Salmon, G. (2002). *E-tivities. The key to active online learning*. London: Kogan Page.

Salomon, G. (1992). What does the design of effective CSCL require and how do we study its effects? *ACM SIGCUE Outlook, 21*(3), 62–68. doi:10.1145/130893.130909

Salomon, G., & Globerson, T. (1989). When teams do not function the way they ought to. *International Journal of Educational Research, 13*(1), 89–99. doi:10.1016/0883-0355(89)90018-9

Salomon, G., Perkins, D. N., & Globerson, T. (1991). Partners in Cognition: Extending Human Intelligence with Intelligent Technologies. *Educational Researcher, 20*(3), 2–9.

Sarason, S. B. (1974). *The psychological sense of community: Prospects for a community psychology*. San Francisco: Jossey-Bass.

Sarbaugh-Thompson, M., & Feldman, M. (1998). Electronic mail and organizational communication: Does saying 'Hi' really matter? *Organization Science, 9*(6), 685–698. doi:10.1287/orsc.9.6.685

Scardamalia, M. (2002). Collective cognitive responsibility for the advancement of knowledge. In Smith, B. (Ed.), *Liberal education in the knowledge society* (pp. 67–98). Chicago, IL: Open Court.

Scardamalia, M. (2003). Knowledge building. *Journal of Distance Education, 17*(S3), 10–14.

Scardamalia, M., & Bereiter, C. (1991). Higher Levels of Agency for Children in Knowledge Building: A Challenge for the Design of New Knowledge Media. *Journal of the Learning Sciences, 1*(1), 37–68. doi:10.1207/s15327809jls0101_3

Scardamalia, M., & Bereiter, C. (1994). Computer support for knowledge building communities. *Journal of the Learning Sciences, 3*(3), 265–283. doi:10.1207/s15327809jls0303_3

Scardamalia, M., Bereiter, C., & Lamon, M. (1994). The CSILE project: Trying to bring

Schank, R., & Neaman, A. (2001). Motivation and Failure in Educational Simulation Design. In Forbus, K. D., & Feltovich, P. J. (Eds.), *Smart Machines in Education* (pp. 99–144). Menlo Park, CA: AAAI Press/MIT Press.

Schank, R., Fano, A., Bell, B., & Jona, M. (1993). The design of goal-based scenarios. *Journal of the Learning Sciences, 3*, 305–345. doi:10.1207/s15327809jls0304_2

Schein, E. H. (1992). *Organisational Culture and Leadership*. London: Jossey-Bass Publishers.

Schober, M. F., & Clark, H. H. (1989). Understanding by Addresses and Overhearers. *Cognitive Psychology, 21*, 211–232. doi:10.1016/0010-0285(89)90008-X

Schoenfeld, A. H. (1987). What's all the fuss about metacognition? In Schoenfeld, A. H. (Ed.), *Cognitive science and mathematics education* (pp. 189–215). Hillsdale, NJ: Lawrence Erlbaum Associates.

Schofield, J. W. (1995). *Computers and classroom culture*. New York: Cambridge University Press.

Schon, D. A. (1983). *The Reflective Practitioner: How Professionals Think in Action*. NY: Basic Books.

Schon, D. A. (1987). *Educating the Reflective Practitioner*. San Francisco, CA: Jossey-Bass.

Schopler, J., & Insko, C. A. (1992). The discontinuity effect in interpersonal and intergroup relations: Generality and mediation. In Stroebe, W., & Hewstone, M. (Eds.), *European review of social psychology* (pp. 121–151). Chichester, UK: Wiley.

Schroeder, R. (2002). Social interaction in virtual environments: Key issues, common themes, and a framework for research. In R. Schroeder (Ed.), The Social Life of Avatars; Presence and Interaction in Shared Virtual Environments (1-18). London: Springer-Verlag.

Schrott, G., & Beimborn, D. (2003). *Informal Knowledge Networks: Toward a Community-Engineering Framework*. Presented at International Conference on Information Systems.

Schunk, D. H. (1983). Progress Self-Monitoring: Effects on Children's Self-Efficacy and Achievement. *Journal of Experimental Education, 51*, 89–93.

Schwartz, D. L., Blair, K. P., Biswas, G., Leelawong, K., & Davis, J. (2007). Animations of thought: Interactivity in the teachable agent paradigm. In Lowe, R., & Schnotz, W. (Eds.), *Learning with animation: Research and implications for design*. Cambridge, UK: Cambridge University Press.

Schwier, R. A. (2001). Catalysts, Emphases, and Elements of Virtual Learning Communities. Implication for Research. *The Quarterly Review of Distance Education, 2*(1), 5–18.

Schwier, R. A. (2002). *Shaping the Metaphor of Community in Online Learning Environments*. Unpublished Manuscript, University of Saskatchewan.

Schwier, R. A. (2004). Virtual learning communities. In Anglin, G. (Ed.), *Critical issues in instructional technology*. Portsmouth, NH: Teacher Ideas Press.

Seifert, C. M., & Hutchins, E. L. (1992). Error as Opportunity: Learning in a cooperative task. *Human-Computer Interaction, 7*, 409–435. doi:10.1207/s15327051hci0704_3

Selker, T. (1994). Coach: A Teaching Agent that Learns. *Communications of the ACM, 37*(7), 92–99. doi:10.1145/176789.176799

Senge, P. (1990). *The Fifth Discipline: The Art and Practice of the Learning Organization*. New York: Doubleday.

Sergiou, K. (2004). Why do students plagiarise? In *Proceedings of the Plagiarism: Prevention, Practice and Policy Conference*, Northumbria University.

Sesink, W., Geraskov, D., Göller, S., Rüsse, W., & Trebing, T. (2005). Transformation einer Vorlesung durch E-Learning-Elemente. In Sesink, W. (Ed.), *Medien-Pädagogik - Online-Zeitschrift für Theorie und Praxis der Medienbildung, 10 Medien in der Erziehungswissenschaft II (2005)*.

Sfard, A. (1998). On two metaphors for learning and the dangers of choosing just one. *Educational Researcher, 27*, 4–13. doi:10.2307/1176193

Shchedrovitskij, G.P. (1995). *Izbrannye trudy [Selected studies]*. Moskva, Rossiya: Shkola kulturnoj politiki.

Shen, H., & Sun, C. (2004). Improving real-time collaboration with highlighting. [Amsterdam: Elsevier Science Publishers B. V.]. *Future Generation Computer Systems, 20*(4), 605–625. doi:10.1016/S0167-739X(03)00176-6

Sheridan, T. B. (2002). *Humans and Automation: System Design and Research Issues*. New York: John Wiley & Sons, Inc.

Shih, L., & Swan, K. (2005). Fostering social presence in asynchronous online class discussions. *Paper presented at the 2005 Conference on Computer Support for Collaborative Learning.*

Short, J., Williams, E., & Christie, B. (1976). *The social psychology telecommunications*. London: John Wiley and Sons.

Simon, H. (1996). *The sciences of the artificial*. Cambridge, MA: MIT Press.

Simon, H. A. (1987). Computers and society. In Kiesler, S. B., & Sproul, L. S. (Eds.), *Computing and change on campus* (pp. 4–15). New York: Cambridge University Press.

Singh, R., Iyer, L., & Salam, A. F. (2005). The semantic e-business vision. *Communications of the ACM, 48*(12), 38–41. doi:10.1145/1101779.1101806

Skinner, B. E. (1986). Programmed Instruction Revisited. *Phi Delta Kappan, 68*(2), 103–110.

Slavin, R. E. (1990). *Cooperative learning: Theory, research, and practice*. Englewood Cliffs, NJ: Prentice Hall.

Slavin, R. E. (1991). *Student team learning: A practical guide to cooperative* (3rd ed.). Washington, DC: National Education Association of the United States.

Slavin, R. E. (1996). *Education for all*. Exton, PA: Swets & Zeitlinger Publishers.

Sleeman, D. H., & Brown, J. S. (1982). Intelligent Tutoring Systems: An Overview. In Sleeman, D. H., & Brown, J. S. (Eds.), *Intelligent Tutoring Systems* (pp. 1–11). London: Academic Press.

Sloman, A. (1997). Synthetic Minds. In W. L. Johnson (Ed.), *Proceedings of the First International Conference on Autonomous Agents, ACM SIGART* (pp. 534-535). New York: Associations for Computing Machinery.

Smith, E., & Mackie, D. (2000). *Social psychology*. New York, USA: Psychology Press.

Smith, G. (2008). *Tagging: People-powered metadata for the social web*. Berkeley, CA: New Riders.

Smith, P. B. (2002). Culture's consequences: Something old and something new. *Human Relations, 55*(1), 119–135.

Smyth, R. (2005). Broadband videoconferencing as a tool for learner-centred distance learning in higher education. *British Journal of Educational Technology, 36*(5), 805–820. doi:10.1111/j.1467-8535.2005.00499.x

Spielberg, S., Kubrick, S., Harlan, J., Kennedy, K., Parkes, W. F., & Curtis, B. (Producer), & Spielberg, S. (Director). (2001). *A. I. Artificial Intelligence* [Motion picture], United States: Amblin Entertainment.

Stacey, E. (2002). Social presence online: Networking learners at a distance. *Education and Information Technologies, 7*(4), 287–294. doi:10.1023/A:1020901202588

Stahl, G., Koschmann, T., & Suthers, D. (2006). Computer-supported collaborative learning. In Sawyer, R. K. (Ed.), *Cambridge handbook of the learning sciences*. Cambridge, UK: Cambridge University Press.

Stankosky, M. (Ed.). (2005). *Creating the Discipline of Knowledge Management*. Oxford, UK: Butterworth-Heinemann.

Star, S. L. (1999). The ethnography of infrastructure. *The American Behavioral Scientist, 43*(3), 377–391. doi:10.1177/00027649921955326

Star, S. L., & Griesemer, J. R. (1989). Institutional Ecology, Translations' and Boundary Objects: Amateurs and Professionals in Berkeley's Museum of Vertebrate Zoology, 1907-39. *Social Studies of Science, 19*(4), 387–420. doi:10.1177/030631289019003001

Stevens, R. J., & Slavin, R. E. (1995). The cooperative elementary school: Effects on students' achievement, attitudes, and social relations. *American Educational Research Journal, 32*, 321–351.

Steves, M. P., & Scholtz, J. (2005). A Framework for Evaluating Collaborative Systems in the Real World. In *Proceedings of the 38th Hawaii International Conference on System Sciences - 2005.*

Strünkelnberg, T. (2008). Studie - Neun von zehn Studenten zu Plagiat bereit. *Mitteldeutsche Zeitung.* Retrieved Feburary 28, 2008, from http://www.mz-web.de/servlet/ContentServer? pagename=ksta/page&atype=ksArtikel&aid=1202045354659&openMenu=1013083806226&calledPageId=1013083806226&listid=1018881578460

Sun, L., & Ousmanou, K. (2006). Articulation of information requirements for personalised knowledge construction. *Requirements Engineering, 11*(4), 279–293. doi:10.1007/s00766-006-0031-z

Sun, L., Ousmanou, K., & Williams, S. (2004). Articulation of learners requirements for personalized instructional design in e-learning services. In Liu, W. (Eds.), *Lecture Notes in Computer Science: Advances in Web-based learning.* New York: Springer.

Sun, L., Williams, S., & Liu, K. (2004). Knowledge Construction in E-learning: Designing an E-learning Environment. In Camp, O., Filipe, J., Hammoudi, S., & Piattini, M. (Eds.), *Enterprise Information Systems V* (pp. 308–315). Amsterdam: Springer.

Suthers, D. D., & Hundhausen, C. (2003). An experimental study of the effects of representational guidance on collaborative learning. *Journal of the Learning Sciences, 12*(2), 183–219. doi:10.1207/S15327809JLS1202_2

Suthers, D. D., Vatrapu, R., Medina, R., Joseph, S., & Dwyer, N. (2007). Conceptual representations enhance knowledge construction in asynchronous collaboration. In C. Chinn, G. Erkens & S. Puntambekar (Eds.), *The Computer Supported Collaborative Learning (CSCL) Conference 2007* (pp. 704-713). New Brunswick: International Society of the Learning Sciences.

Suthers, D. D., Vatrapu, R., Medina, R., Joseph, S., & Dwyer, N. (2008). Beyond Threaded Discussion: Representational Guidance in Asynchronous Collaborative Learning Environments. *Computers & Education, 50*(4), 1103–1127. doi:10.1016/j.compedu.2006.10.007

Suthers, D., Connelly, J., Lesgold, A., Paolucci, M., Toth, E., Toth, J., & Weiner, A. (2001). Representational and Advisory Guidance for Students Learning Scientific Inquiry. In *Forbus, K. D., and Feltovich, P. J. (2001). Smart machines in education: The coming revolution in educational technology* (pp. 7–35). Menlo Park, CA: AAAI/Mit Press.

Switzer, J. S., & Hartman, J. L. (2007). E-Collaboration Using Group Decision Support Systems in Virtual Meetings. In Kock, N. F. (Ed.), *Encyclopedia of E-collaboration* (pp. 204–209). New York: Idea Group Publishing.

Tajfel, H., & Turner, J. C. (1986). The social identity theory of intergroup behavior. In Worchel, S., & Austin, W. (Eds.), *Psychology of intergroup relations* (pp. 7–24). Chicago, IL: Nelson-Hall.

Taylor, M. (1999). *Imaginary Companions and the Children Who Created Them.* New York: Oxford University Press.

Tennis, J. T., & Sutton, S. A. (2008). Extending the simple knowledge organization system for concept management in vocabulary development applications. *Journal of the American Society for Information Science and Technology, 59*(1), 25–37. doi:10.1002/asi.20702

Thach, E. C. (2002). the impact of executive coaching and 360 feedback on leadership effectiveness. *Leadership and Organization Development Journal, 23*(4), 294–306. doi:10.1108/01437730210429070

Thaiupathump, C., Bourne, J., & Campbell, J. (1999). Intelligent agents for online learning. *Journal of Asynchronous Learning Networks, 3*(2). Retrieved May 17, 2004, from http://www.sloan-c.org/publications/jaln/v3n2/pdf/v3n2_choon.pdf

the classroom into World 3. In K. McGilley (Eds.), *Classroom lessons: Integrating*

Thompson, L. (1998). *The mind and heart of the negotiator.* Upper Saddle River, NJ: Prentice Hall.

Thornton, S. (1996). *Club culture: Music, media and subcultural capital*. Cambridge, UK: Polity Press.

Trammell, K. D. (2004). *Celebrity blogs: Investigation in the persuasive nature of two-way communication regarding politics* (Additional Readings). Unpublished doctoral dissertation, University of Florida, Florida.

Tran, M. H., Raikundalia, G. K., & Yang, Y. (2006). Using an experimental study to develop group awareness support for real-time distributed collaborative writing. *Information and Software Technology, 48*(11), 1006–1024. doi:10.1016/j.infsof.2005.12.009

Trigueros, C., Rivera, E., Pavesio, M., & Torres, J. (2005). Analysis of student participation in university classes: an interdisciplinary experience. *Quality in Higher Education, 2*, 108–121.

Tseng, M. C. (2008). The Use of Blogs in English Classes for Medicine-Related Majors. *Journal of Humanities and Social Sciences, 1*(1), 167–187.

Tu, C. H. (2002). The measurement of social presence in an online learning environment. *International Journal on E-Learning, 1*(2), 34–45.

Tu, C., & McIsaac, M. (2002). The relationship of social presence and interaction in online classes. *American Journal of Distance Education, 16*, 131–150. doi:10.1207/S15389286AJDE1603_2

Turing, A. (1950). Computing machinery and intelligence. *Mind*, 433–460. doi:10.1093/mind/LIX.236.433

Turner, J. C., Hogg, M., Oakes, P., Reicher, S., & Wetherell, M. (1987). *Rediscovering the social group: A self-categorization theory*. Oxford, UK: Basil Blackwell.

Tynjala, P., & Hakkinen, P. (2005). E-learning at work: theoretical underpinnings and pedagogical challenges. *Journal of Workplace Learning, 17*(6), 318–336. doi:10.1108/13665620510606742

University of Linz – Institute Integriert Studieren. (2008). *ICT4T Accessibility Evaluation Report*. [Internal Project Document]. Retrieved January 20, 2009, from http://www.ict4t.net/?q=system/ files/ Accessibility+Evaluation+Report-Moodle.pdf

Uppsala University. (2001). *A comprehensive study of using sap in a university environment*. Report, 2001.

Valacich, J. S., Dennis, A. R., & Nunamaker, J. F. (1992). Group size and anonymity effects on computer-mediated idea generation. *Small Group Research, 23*(1), 49–73. doi:10.1177/1046496492231004

Van Dam, N., & Rogers, F. (2002, May). E-Learning cultures around the world: Make your globalized strategy transparent. *E-learning*, 28–33. Retrieved from http://www.elearningmag.com.

Vasiliauskas, R. (2007). The Role of Student Activity in the Context of B. Blooms Taxonomy of Learning Domains. *Pedagogika, 85*, 81–85.

Virvou, M., Katsionis, G., & Konstantinos, M. (2005). Combining software games with education and evaluation of its educational effectiveness. *Educational Technology & Society, 8*(2), 54–65.

Vitkute-Adzgauskiene, D., Butrime, E., & Zuzeviciute, V. (2008, December). *Impact of ICT on E-learning as a Socio-cultural System*. Paper presented at the conference Adult Learning and e-Learning Quality. Kaunas, Lithuania, Vytautas Magnus University.

Volungeviciene, A., Zuzeviciute, V., & Butrime, E. (2008). E-Learning Course Quality Factors: Learner's Needs Perspective. In *The 6th International Conference on Education and Information Systems, Technologies and Applications: EISTA 2008*, Orlando, Florida, USA (pp.78 – 84).

Vygotsky, L. S. (1978). *Mind in society: The development of higher psychological processes*. Cambridge, MA: Harvard University Press.

W3C Web Accessibility Initiative. (2005). *Introduction to Web Accessibility, Version: 2.0*. Retrieved January 7, 2009, from http://www.w3.org/WAI/intro/accessibility.php

W3C. (2009). *Extensible Markup Language (XML)*. Retrieved May 2009, from http://www.w3.org/XML/

W3C. (2009a). *The Extensible Stylesheet Language Family (XSL)*. Retrieved April 2009, from http://www.w3.org/Style/XSL/

Wagner, C., & Bolloju, N. (2005). Supporting knowledge management in organizations with conversational technologies: Discussion forums, weblogs, and wikis. *Journal of Database Management, 16*(2), i–viii.

Walther, J. B. (1996). Computer-mediated communication: Impersonal, interpersonal, and hyperpersonal interaction. *Communication Research, 23*, 3–43. doi:10.1177/009365096023001001

Wang, H., & Chee, Y. S. (2001). *Supporting workspace awareness in distance learning environments: Issues and experiences in the development of a collaborative learning system.* Paper presented at the ICCE/SchoolNet 2001-- Ninth International Conference on Computers in Education. Seoul, South Korea.

Wasko, M. M., & Faraj, S. (2005). Why should I share? Examining social capital and knowledge contribution in electronic networks of practice. *Management Information Systems Quarterly, 29*(1), 35–57.

Webb, N. (1985). Student interaction and learning in small groups: A research summary. In Slavin, R., Sharan, S., Kagan, S., Hertz-Lazarowitz, R., Webb, C., & Schmuck, R. (Eds.), *Learning to cooperate, cooperating to learn* (pp. 148–172). New York: Plenum.

Webb, N. M. (1989). Peer interaction and learning in small groups. *International Journal of Educational Research, 13*, 21–39. doi:10.1016/0883-0355(89)90014-1

Weber, G. (1999). *Adaptive learning systems in the World Wide Web.* In *Proceedings of the Seventh International Conference User Modeling (UM99)* (pp.371-377). Wien, Austria: Springer.

Weber-Wulff, D. (2002). *Aufdeckung von Plagiaten: Suchen im Internet für Lehrkräfte.* Retrieved February 29, 2008, from http://www.f4.fhtw-berlin.de/~weberwu/papers/plagiat.shtml

Weber-Wulff, D., & Wohnsdorf, G. (2006). Strategien der Plagiatsbekämpfung. [Deutsche Gesellschaft für Informationswissenschaft und Informationspraxis e.V.]. *Zeitschrift IWP, 2/06*, 90–98.

Weigel, V. (2003). *Deep learning for a digital age.* San Francisco, CA: Jossey-Bass.

Weinberger, A., & Reiserer, M. B., Ertl, B., Fischer, F., & Mandl, H. (2005). Facilitating Collaborative Knowledge Construction in Computer-Mediated Learning Environments with Cooperation Scripts. In R. Bromme, F. W. Hesse, & H. Spada (Eds.), Barriers and Biases in Computer-Mediated Knowledge Communication (pp. 15-37). New York: Springer.

Weinberger, A., Ertl, B., Fischer, F., & Mandl, H. (2005). Epistemic and social scripts in computer-supported collaborative learning. *Instructional Science, 33*(1), 1–30. doi:10.1007/s11251-004-2322-4

Weizenbaum, J. (1966). ELIZA, A computer program for the study of natural language communications between men and machines. *Communications of the ACM, 9*, 36–45. doi:10.1145/365153.365168

Wellman, B., Salaff, J., Dimitrova, D., Garton, L., Gulia, M., & Haythornthwaite, C. (1996). Computer networks as social networks: Collaborative work, telework, and virtual community. *Annual Review of Sociology, 22*, 213–238. doi:10.1146/annurev.soc.22.1.213

Wellman, H. M. (1990). *The Child's Theory of Mind.* Cambridge, MA: MIT Press.

Wenger, E. (1987). *Artificial Intelligence and Tutoring Systems: Computational and Cognitive Approaches to the Communication of Knowledge.* Los Altos, CA: Morgan Kaufmann Publishers, Inc.

Wenger, E. (1998). *Communities of Practice: Learning, Meaning, and Identity.* Cambridge, UK: Cambridge University Press.

Wenger, E. C., & Snyder, W. M. (2000). Communities of Practice: The Organizational Frontier. *Harvard Business Review, 78*, 139–144.

Wentling, T., Waight, C., Gallager, J., La Fleur, J., Wang, C., & Kanfer, A. (2000). *E-learning: A review of literature.* Retrieved January 15 2007 http://learning.ncsa.uiuc.edu/papers/elearnlit.pdf

Werquin, P. (2008). Recognition of non-formal and informal learning in OECD countries: A very good idea in jeopardy? *Lifelong Learning in Europe, 3*, 142–149.

Wertsch, J. V. (1978). Adult-child interaction and the roots of metacognition. *Quarterly Newsletter of the Institute for Comparative Human Development, 1*, 15–18.

What is Enterprise 2.0? (n.d.). Retrieved October 15, 2008, from http://www.e2conf.com/about/what-is-enterprise2.0.php

White, B., & Fredriksen, J. (2005). A theoretical framework and approach for fostering metacognitive development. *Educational Psychologist, 40*, 211–223. doi:10.1207/s15326985ep4004_3

Wiebrands, C. (2006). Creating community: The blog as a networking device. In *ALIA 2006 Biennial Conference*, Perth. Retrieved July 12, 2007, from http://espace.lis.curtin.edu.au/archive/00001015/03/Click06_Wiebrands_blogging.pdf

Wilcox, D. L., Cameron, G. T., Ault, P. H., & Agee, W. K. (2003). *Public relations: Strategies and tactics*. Boston: Allyn and Bacon.

Williams, J. B., & Jacobs, J. (2004). Exploring the use of blogs as learning spaces in the higher education sector. *Australasian Journal of Educational Technology, 20*(2), 232–247.

Williamson. B. (2003). *Skype-ing work*. Retrieved from http://www.guardian.co.uk.

Wilson, J. R., & Rutherford, A. (1989). Mental models: Theory and application in human factors. *Human Factors, 31*, 617–634.

Winn, W. (2002). Current trends in educational technology research: The study of learning environments. *Educational Psychology Review, 14*(3), 331–351. doi:10.1023/A:1016068530070

Wittenbaum, G. M., & Park, E. S. (2001). The collective preference for shared information. *Current Directions in Psychological Science, 10*, 70–73. doi:10.1111/1467-8721.00118

Wood, D., Bruner, J. S., & Ross, G. (1976). The role of tutoring in problem solving. *Journal of Child Psychology and Psychiatry, and Allied Disciplines, 17*, 89–100. doi:10.1111/j.1469-7610.1976.tb00381.x

Wooldridge, M., & Jennings, N.v. (1995). Intelligent agents: Theory and practice. *The Knowledge Engineering Review, 10*(2), 115–152. doi:10.1017/S0269888900008122

Woolf, B. P., & Cunningham, P. A. (1987). Multiple knowledge sources in intelligent teaching systems. *IEEE Expert, 2*, 41–54. doi:10.1109/MEX.1987.4307063

Wright, S. P. (2004). *Exploring psychological sense of community in living learning programs and in the university as a whole*. Dissertation, Digital Repository at the University of Maryland, Maryland.

Zhang, Y., & Tanniru, M. (2005). A*n Agent-based Approach to Study Virtual Learning Communities*. HICSS-2005 (best paper award in collaboration track).

About the Contributors

Bernhard Ertl is senior researcher at the Universität der Bundeswehr München. He has realized several research projects in the context of video-mediated learning, Internet collaboration and online-courses with a particular focus on the support of collaborative knowledge construction by the methods of scripts and structured communication interfaces. A further focus of research is the issue of gender in computer and science teaching which includes projects with national and EU funding. Bernhard Ertl earned his Diploma in computer science from the Ludwig Maximilian University Munich in 1998 and his Doctorate in education 2003. From 1999 to 2006, he was researcher at the Department Psychology of Ludwig Maximilian University of Munich and worked with Professor Heinz Mandl in DFG-funded research projects focusing on collaborative learning, e.g. "Collaborative Learning in Graphics-enhanced Tele-learning Environments" and "Collaborative Knowledge Construction in Desktop Videoconferencing".

* * *

Anthony 'Skip' Basiel is a Senior Learning Development Tutor for the Institute for Work Based Learning at Middlesex University, London –UK. He is a founding member of the Adobe International Education Leaders programme for Great Britain. In 2004 he won the eTutor of the year award by the Higher Education Academy for an eLearning project with the British Council and in 2005 he received a Special Mention in the e-Learning Network's eTutor Awards. His research interests focus on 'ePedagogy' with a special focus on web video conferencing and professional social networks.

Edita Butrime graduated from Kaunas University of Technology with master degree of computer sciences (1985) and master degree of education technologies (2004). PhD student at the Department of Education, Faculty of Social Sciences. Edita Butrime works at Kaunas University of Medicine as director of the Teachers' Educational Competence Center. Areas of scientific interests: e-learning as a sociocultural system, computer supported collaborative learning. Teaches undergraduates and also delivers (and organises) professional development courses for higher education teachers. Leads courses: Introduction to Education, Methodology of Development of E-learning Courses and other. Participates in a number of international activities and projects: (6th Framework, INCLUD-ED; „Strategies for Inclusion and Social Cohesion in Europe from Education", No. FP6-028603-2; Socrates, E-learning, FeCONE, No. 2005-3872/001-001ELE-ELEB14, Socrates Minerva, AITMES; No. 225398-CP-1-2005-1-ES-MINERVA-M and other). Membership: member of National (Lithuanian) Association of Distance Education, IADIS (International Association for Development of the Information Society) and other associations.

Maria Chiara Caschera She received her degree in Computer Science Engineering at the University of Rome 'La Sapienza', and the PhD in Computer Science at the 'Roma Tre' University sponsored by the MultiMedia & Modal Laboratory (M3L) of the National Research Council of Italy. She is now researcher at CNR-IRPPS (National Research Council, Institute Of Research On Population And Social Policies). She is mainly interested in Human-Computer Interaction, Multimodal Interaction, Visual Languages, Visual Interfaces and Sketch-based Interfaces and Social Network Visualization.

Alessia D'Andrea She received her degree in Communication Science at the University of Rome 'La Sapienza'. She is being a PhD student in Multimedia Communication at the University of Udine sponsored by the IRPPS of the National Research Council of Italy. She is mainly interested in Communication Science, Social Science, Risk Management, Virtual Communities, Mobile Technologies and Health Studies.

David Edgell is a graduate student in the English Department at Texas Tech University. Lubbock Texas USA. David Edgell has over fifteen years experience as a technical communication practitioner in the healthcare and information technology professions in New Mexico and Wisconsin. He graduated with a B.S. degree from the University of Wisconsin, completed his Masters degree in Technical Communication at Texas Tech University, and is currently working towards his Doctorate in the Technical Communication and Rhetoric program at Texas Tech. His research interests include communication structures surrounding medically informed consent and patient education. He is also concerned with fully utilizing new technologies to improve knowledge creation in technical communication and medicine.

Fernando Ferri He received the degrees in Electronics Engineering and the PhD in Medical Informatics. He is actually senior researcher at the National Research Council of Italy. From 1993 to 2000 he was professor of "Sistemi di Elaborazione" at the University of Macerata. He is the author of more than 100 papers in international journals, books and conferences. His main methodological areas of interest are: Human-Computer Interaction Visual Languages, Visual Interfaces, Sketch-based Interfaces, Multimodal Interfaces, Data and knowledge bases, Geographic Information Systems and Virtual Communities. He has been responsible of several national and international research projects.

Annette Fillery-Travis is part-time Principal lecturer at the Institute for Work Based Learning at Middlesex University, UK and Director at the Professional Development Foundation She is part of the International Coach Research Forum and the Global Coaching Convention Research Working Group. She has over 60 publications in a variety of disciplines from physical sciences through to her most recent book on the Case for Coaching with CIPD. Her research interests currently include knowledge management and coaching as part of the learning organisation.

Daniel Firpo is a PhD student and a research assistant at Claremont Graduate University (CGU) in the Social Learning Software Lab [SL]2 at the School of Information Systems and Technology (SISAT). He received a Master of Software Engineering from the University of Southern California in 2005, and a Bachelor's Degree in Computer Science from Cal State University of Los Angeles in 2003. His research interests are online collaboration and intellectual community in higher education, the use of social software to facilitate learning and academic networking in educational environments, and motivation to participate in online communities. He is currently working with CGU's Knowledge Management Study Group on their Knowledge Management Virtual Acculturation Space Project.

Klaus Gollin was born in 1967 in Germany near Munich. After a vocational training for mechanics in the metalworking industry he studied Informatics and Business Informatics. Since 1992 he works as self employed Software Engineer and IT consultant in different lines of business with a main focus on requirements engineering. Since 2006 he is working as a tutor for the Fachhochschule für Oekonomie und Management (FOM) study center Munich. Since this he is working on and with the collaborative authoring system. He accomplishes case based studies where he supports student whilst they are writing their theses.

Patrizia Grifoni She received the degrees in Electronics Engineering and is actually researcher at the National Research Council of Italy. From 1994 to 2000 she was professor of "Elaborazione digitale delle immagini" at the University of Macerata. She is the author of more than 80 papers in international journals, books and conferences. Her scientific interests have evolved from Query Languages for statistical and Geographic Databases to the focal topics related to Human-Computer Interaction, Multimodal Interaction, Visual Languages, Visual Interfaces, Sketch-based Interfaces, Accessing Web Information and Virtual Communities. She was responsible of several research projects.

Stylianos Hatzipanagos is an academic at King's Learning Institute (King's College London). He is the head of e-learning at the Institute. He teaches in the Institute's undergraduate and postgraduate programmes. He has been the recipient of two Teaching and Research Awards from the Centre for Distance Education (University of London) to investigate assessment processes & practices in distance learning environments. His research interests are in innovation in learning and teaching, assessment in higher education, computer mediated communication, computer supported collaborative work and usability of educational interfaces.

Kathrin Helling M.A. works as a research associate at the Universtity of the Bundeswehr München, Department of Education, and at the Institute for Future Studies Austria, Innsbruck. She studied educational sciences, psychology and sociology at the Ludwig-Maximilians-University (LMU), Munich; she was engaged in scientific work in a DFG-project about cooperative learning in videoconferences at LMU. Current work field: development of computer-based learning scenarios and curricula (for specific target groups, e.g. age group 50+, people with low educational achievement); project evaluation activities in the field of educational technology; implementation of lifelong learning strategies and adult learning in Europe, gender sensibility in the context of mathematics, science and informatics at school. She has also work experience in project management, human resource development, and as trainer in adult education.

Bo Hu is Professor of Business Systems at the Universität der Bundeswehr München since 2002. He also teaches at the Fachhochschule für Oekonomie und Management (FOM) since 2004. His research focuses on e-collaboration systems as well as on business process modeling and simulation. He received Diplom degree from the Technische Universität München in 1987 and Ph. D. in Physics from the Universität Erlangen-Nürnberg in 1993. He worked as senior software engineer (1993-1995) and as manager at the E-Business Unit of KPMG Consulting (1999-2001). He was a scientific staff member at the Fraunhofer Gesellschaft (1987-1993) and served as Professor of Computer Science at the Fachhochschule Magdeburg (1996-1999).

Liisa Ilomäki is a leader and a researcher in the Technology for Education Research Group, Department of Psychology, University of Helsinki. Her research interest is focussed on issues related to ICT and the consequences of its implementation in education; especially on school level. Currently she co-ordinates a large EU-supported project Knowledge Practises Laboratory (KP-Lab, years 2006-2011). She has been responsible of two large local level evaluation studies about ICT in schools in Finland, and she has participated in several European research projects as the responsible researcher in the University of Helsinki (OECD study about Innovative schools, EU-supported projects CELEBRATE, Ernist, P2P).

Sumonta Kasemvilas is a PhD student and a research assistant in the Social Learning Software Lab [SL]2 at Claremont Graduate University's School of Information Systems and Technology (SISAT). She and her lab members developed an online social networking site for her school in spring 2006. Her research interests are Web and Internet technologies, online collaboration, intellectual community, and knowledge management. Her current research is developing plug-ins for Wiki to support group collaboration and knowledge sharing in a classroom setting. She is working with another [SL]2 member on anchored discussion tool and social network analysis. She is also a member of the Knowledge Management Study Group at Claremont Graduate University and is currently working on the Knowledge Management Virtual Acculturation Space project.

Kari Kosonen has a background in the developmental psychology. He is currently working as a researcher in an international project developing pedagogical and technological solutions for supporting collaborative knowledge creation processes. Prior to this work Kosonen served as a certified developmental psychologist in a family councelling center providing diagnostic and rehabitational services for learners with specific pedagogical needs. In his current work and doctoral studies he designs and tests conceptual scaffolding tools for addressing specific learning challenges stemming from the complexity of a target domain or a learner's own individual needs. Kosonen applies and explores a theoretical framework based on the Activity theory and particularly the writings of Vygotsky, Leontiev and Galperin that he was familiarized with in their original language during his psychologist training at the Moscow State University.

Minna Lakkala has a background in general psychology and computer science. She has an extensive experience of in-service teacher training in the educational use of information and communication technology. She has participated in large national follow-up studies concerning school development through ICT (Educational technology projects of Helsinki and Espoo cities), and several international research projects (Netd@ys 1999 Evaluation, ITCOLE, P2P, Celebrate, Ernist, KP-Lab) concerning the pedagogical use of technology at schools and higher education settings. Currently she is a researcher at the Technology in Education Research Group in the Department of Psychology at the University of Helsinki. Her main research interests relate to the issues of pedagogical design of and students' scaffolding for technology-mediated collaborative inquiry and innovative knowledge practices.

Sandra Y. Okita is Assistant Professor of Technology and Education at Teachers College, Columbia University. She is the director of the Sociable Technology and Learning Lab (STL). Her work uses innovative technologies (robots, mixed reality devices, virtual reality environments) as a threshold to learning, instruction, and assessment. Her interests include how sociable technology can facilitate learning, and develop learning partnerships between people and technology. Her interdisciplinary work finds publication in both educational (Learning Science, Educational Technology) and engineering (International Journal of Humanoid Robotics) fields. Theoretical research interest areas include self-other monitoring, learning by teaching, learning by observation, and its influence on behavior in the domain of biology, math, and agency.

Bolanle A. Olaniran is a professor in the Department of Communication Studies at Texas Tech University. His research includes: Communication technologies and Computer-Mediated Communication, Organization communication, Cross-cultural communication, and Crisis Management and Communication. He has authored several articles in discipline focus and interdisciplinary focus Journals (i.e., Regional, National, and International) and edited book chapters in each of these areas. He has served as consultant to organizations at local, national and government level. His works have gained recognition such as the American Communication Association's Outstanding Scholarship in Communication field. He has conducted several workshops in e-learning, communication and technology both nationally and internationally. He is well sought after as speakers at International seminars and workshops.

Oladayo Olaniran is a doctoral student and a lecturer in the metallurgical Engineering Department at the Federal University of Technology Akure (FUTA) Nigeria. Oladayo Olaniran received both his Bachelor and Master's degrees in Metallurgical Engineering at Federal University of Technology Akure in Ondo State Nigeria. He has several year of experiences as High School Science and Technology Teacher in Nigeria. His research interest is in the design and use of technologies in applied settings. He has authored several papers in the use of technologies and design for engineering discipline. He has won many awards for his innovative thinking and research. He also serves as invited guest lecturer at other Nigerian Universities.

Christian Petter works as a research associate and project officer for the Institute for Future Studies Austria, a non-profit institution of applied research. He is also a freelance trainer in adult education specifically focusing on web 2.0 and e-didactics. His current work field comprises -among other aspects of ICT-based learning -e-learning course development and research on ICT-based learning measures specifically targeting groups prone to be excluded from the information society like people 50+ or people with low educational achievement.

Lin Qiu is an assistant professor in the Division of Psychology at Nanyang Technological University. He received his PhD in Computer Science with a graduate specialization in Cognitive Science from Northwestern University. His research interests lie in the area of human-computer interaction. He is broadly interested in educational technology, the impact of technology on social behaviors, user-centered design, and cognitive science. He has received research grants from US National Science Foundation, Microsoft Research, and Hewlett-Packard to study the design and impact of educational technology, and has over twenty peer-reviewed publications.

Peter Ractham is a faculty member at the School of Commerce and Accountancy, Thammasat University, Bangkok, Thailand. He received his doctoral degree in Information Systems and Technology from Claremont Graduate University, USA in 2008. His research interests are educational multimedia, knowledge management, mobile Learning and virtual communities for higher education.

Xuesong Zhang received her PhD in Information Systems and Technology from Claremont Graduate University in 2008, a Master of Science in Applied Computer Science and a Master of Business Administration from Illinois State University in 2002 and 2000. She has been working full-time as a software engineer since 2002. Her research interests focus on software and web development, including campus portal and ERP for higher education, social networking and learning environment, knowledge management systems, Electronic Medical Records (EMR) and Personal Health Record (PHR) systems, open source software, and Internet marketing technologies.

Vaiva Zuzevičiūtė Assoc. prof. of the Department of Education, Faculty of Social Science. Has a master's degree in education (1995), and also a master's degree in public management (1995), defended doctoral thesis in 2005 in the field of higher education didactics, and in 2008 completed a habilitation procedure in the field of lifelong learning culture. Areas of scientific interests: tendencies and theory of adult education, didactics of higher education. Teaches undergraduates, graduates and doctorate candidates. Leads courses: Development and Implementation of Projects, Researching Adults' Learning Needs, Lifelong Learning strategies and other. Also, develops and implements distance education courses and consults on curriculum development methodology. Membership: member of National Association of Distance Education, ASEM- Hub (Asia Europe Meeting, Adult Education HUB), ESREA (European Society for Research on the Education of Adults) and a number of other associations.

Index